Charles Evans Hughes

Politics and Reform in New York
1905–1910

Governor Charles Evans Hughes at his desk in the executive chamber at Albany. (From *McClure's*, XXX [1907–1908], 525; courtesy of the Cornell University Library.)

Charles Evans Hughes

Politics and Reform in New York

1905–1910

By ROBERT F. WESSER

State University of New York at Albany

Cornell University Press

ITHACA, NEW YORK

First published 1967

Library of Congress Catalog Card Number: 67-19029

PRINTED IN THE UNITED STATES OF AMERICA
BY VAIL-BALLOU PRESS, INC.

To my parents

Preface

ON June 18, 1907, Lord James Bryce, noted British critic of American institutions, wrote cordially to Charles Evans Hughes that he would revise his classic *American Commonwealth* "in order to show what may be accomplished by the firmness, tact and courage of a State Governor." [1] Obviously referring to Hughes himself and his achievements in New York, Bryce's tribute capped off a host of congratulatory letters that flooded the Albany executive offices about this time. Though a public servant for only six months, Hughes had already captured the imagination of critics and observers everywhere.

Undoubtedly, these felicitations were fully justified by the events of 1907. As a reformer without the firm support of the leaders of his own state party and without the benefit of personal political experience, Hughes employed new and unusual tactics to implement his ambitious New York program. His four years in Albany, and his remarkable success there, climaxed a period of popular unrest and agitation that had only recently been felt at the state capital.

The story of the origins of progressive government in the Empire State and of the transformation of the main tenets of reform into an effective political program is tied inextricably to the name of Charles Evans Hughes. This study attempts an analysis of Hughes's early political career against the background

[1] Charles Evans Hughes Papers (Manuscript Division, Library of Congress).

vii

of New York politics and reform—from his work as counsel for the gas and insurance investigations through his two terms as governor; as such, it treats of the reform movement itself. After a brief survey of the old Platt system and the tangled web of New York Republican politics down to 1905, the study considers the investigations that impelled both political parties in the state to adapt themselves to changing circumstances and conditions. It then concentrates upon Charles Evans Hughes as a reformer and a political leader, emphasizing his progressive program and his efforts to implement it. Finally, an attempt is made to evaluate the Hughes administration from the stand-point of its actual contributions to progressive government and party reform.

In the preparation of this study, I received encouragement and assistance from a number of people. I am pleased, indeed, to express my gratitude to them while accepting the responsibility for any errors in fact and interpretation that may remain. Professor Glyndon G. Van Deusen of the University of Rochester guided this study as a doctoral dissertation and gave me the benefit of his excellent advice and criticism. Professor Richard C. Wade, now of the University of Chicago, took time from his busy schedule to read and criticize the manuscript in its early stages. My good friend, Dr. Charles W. Stein, a keen student of American history, carefully worked over each draft, questioning facts and interpretations and suggesting numerous stylistic improvements. My wife, Janet Newman Wesser, typed the original draft from an almost illegible handwritten copy and later served as a patient proofreader.

During the course of the research for this study, I received invaluable assistance from the staffs of several libraries, particularly those of the Reference and History Departments of the Buffalo and Erie County Public Library; the Lockwood Memorial Library of the State University of New York at Buffalo; the Manuscript Division of the Library of Congress; the Collection of Regional History of the Cornell University Library; the Rundel Memorial Library of Rochester; the Syracuse University Library; the Manuscript Division of the New York Public Library; the Taminent Institute Library in New York City; the New York State Library at Albany; the Department of Special Collections of the Columbia University Library; the New-York Historical Society Library; the Catholic University Library; the Houghton Library at Harvard University; and the Sterling Library at Yale University. Mr. Reverdy Wadsworth graciously permitted me to peruse the papers of the late Senator James W. Wadsworth, Jr., while they were still housed in Geneseo, New York. I owe a special debt to Mr. John Parsons for granting me permission to quote freely from the papers of his father, Herbert Parsons.

A number of agencies and societies have offered encouragement in a variety of ways. The Research Foundation of the State University of New York awarded me fellowships and a grant-in-aid for the summers of 1964 and 1965 that made possible additional research on this study, as well as on the beginning investigation for a sequel volume covering reform in New York through 1915. A grant-in-aid for travel was awarded me in 1964 by the American Association for State and Local History. The Graduate School of the State University of New York at Buffalo provided me with liberal financial aid in the final preparation of the manuscript. Substantial portions of several chapters of this study originally appeared in the *New-York Historical Society Quarterly*, L (1966), 365–399; much of Chapter III appeared in *New York History*, XLVI (1965), 230–252. I am indebted to the New-York Historical Society and the New York State Historical Association for granting me permission to use this material.

Robert F. Wesser

Albany, New York
December 1966

Contents

Illustrations

PLATES

FIGURES

Abbreviations and
Abbreviated Titles

BECPL	Buffalo and Erie County Public Library.
NYPL	New York Public Library.
RML	Rundel Memorial Library, Rochester.
Fuller Collection	Robert H. Fuller Newspaper Collection (190 vols.; NYPL).
"Allds Investigation Report"	"Report of the Joint Committee of the Senate and Assembly of the State of New York, Appointed to Investigate Corrupt Practices in Connection with Insurance Companies, Other Than Those Doing Life Insurance Business," Feb. 1, 1911, *Assembly Document No. 30, Part I,* 134th session (Albany: J. B. Lyon, 1911).
"Armstrong Committee Report"	"Report of the Joint Committee of the Senate and Assembly of the State of New York Appointed to Investigate the Affairs of Life Insurance Companies," *Assembly Document No. 41,* 129th session (Albany: J. B. Lyon, 1906).
"Laidlaw Committee Report"	"The Anti-Race-Track Gambling Campaign of 1908 for the Agnew-Hart

Measures," in "Thirteenth Annual Report, Federation of Churches and Christian Organizations of New York City" (n.d.), Hughes Collection (NYPL).

"Lincoln Day Conference Report"

"Account of Meeting of February 12, 1910," recorded by Robert H. Fuller, Hughes Collection (NYPL).

Armstrong Committee Hearings

Testimony Taken before the Joint Committee of the Senate and Assembly of the State of New York to Investigate and Examine into the Business and Affairs of Life Insurance Companies Doing Business in the State of New York (10 vols.; Albany: Brandow Printing Co., 1905–1906).

Gas and Electricity Report

Report of the Joint Committee of the Senate and Assembly to Investigate Gas and Electric Lighting Companies (New York: Martin B. Brown, 1905).

Hughes Public Papers

Public Papers of Charles E. Hughes, Governor (4 vols.; Albany: J. B. Lyon, 1908–1911).

LTR

Elting Morison *et al.*, eds., *The Letters of Theodore Roosevelt* (8 vols.; Cambridge: Harvard University Press, 1951–1954).

Charles Evans Hughes

Politics and Reform in New York

1905–1910

CHAPTER I

Introduction

Bossism and Factionalism in New York Republican Politics, 1881-1904

DURING the last quarter of the nineteenth century political organizations in America reflected much the same drive toward concentration and centralization as did the nation's economy. Just as the "captains of industry" strove to weld together highly organized and efficient business units, so political managers, particularly in the populous states of the northeast and midwest, sought to control and direct large blocs of voters. Often discovering a common interest, politicians and businessmen joined forces to raid the public coffers. This union, as much as any other condition, impelled the urban phase of the early twentieth-century reform movement.

The Republican party organization in New York State at that time provides a good illustration of the pattern of politics. For fifteen years, from 1881 to 1896, Thomas C. Platt, Roscoe Conkling's trusted lieutenant, labored indefatigably to forge a political machine that, like a military unit, would function on principles of strict discipline and obedience. At a time when most local and county leaders were indifferent toward the old Conkling system, which had been torn asunder in 1881, Tom Platt rounded up several able and dependable politicians whose services he could employ to achieve his goal. One of these men later remarked nostalgically: "Mr. Platt had the motive, the interest, the ambition, and the personal force to draw to himself . . .

a little band of trained, able and adventurous politicians."[1]

Platt ingeniously gathered together individuals who complemented his own talents. Not the master of the spoken word, he could easily call upon the mellifluent Chauncey M. Depew. He lacked great physical stamina, but he had enlisted a vigorous supporter in Benjamin B. Odell, Jr. Platt was not particularly adept at molding public opinion, but his New York City underling, Lemuel E. Quigg, was well equipped to manage publicity campaigns. Unable to visit upstate areas frequently enough to be acquainted fully with their political affairs, he came to rely upon George W. Aldridge of Monroe County, Francis Hendricks of Onondaga, and William E. Barnes, Jr., of Albany, among others. In the legislature, too, Platt had his coterie of followers, led by John Raines in the senate and Jotham P. Allds and S. Fred Nixon in the assembly.[2]

To coordinate the efforts of the leaders, Boss Platt often held his famous Sunday-school classes in Greenwich Village's old Fifth Avenue Hotel. Doubtless, only his organizational genius held together this contentious and motley group. Violent arguments often spawned personal conflicts during the protracted political sessions. There were bitter encounters between Lou Payn and Quigg or between Barnes and Quigg. There were sectional conflicts on the liquor question, with Canandaigua legislator John Raines advocating high taxation and rigorous state regulation of the liquor traffic. Then there were frequent disagreements over Barge Canal appropriations: members who hailed from sections that made little use of the canal objected strenuously to expenditures for improvement.[3]

Platt learned that he could keep his crew reasonably contented by careful distribution of the patronage at his disposal. He not only doled out minor offices, but generally selected ap-

[1] Lemuel E. Quigg, "Thomas C. Platt," *North American Review*, CXCI (1910), 671.

[2] Harold F. Gosnell, "Thomas C. Platt—Political Manager," *Political Science Quarterly*, XXXVIII (1923), 443–469.

[3] Harold F. Gosnell, *Boss Platt and His New York Machine* (Chicago: University of Chicago, 1924), pp. 69–70.

pointees for the more important and lucrative state offices as well.[4] Thus, for a time George Aldridge enjoyed prestige and comfort as superintendent of public works; Lou Payn thrived on the management of the insurance department; Chauncey Depew aired his political views in the United States Senate; and Benjamin Odell reveled in the New York governorship.

His growing influence with upstate leaders tightened Platt's hold over every facet of New York Republicanism in the late 1880's and the 1890's. After 1894, he found himself in a position to name the speaker of the assembly. Indeed, each year thereafter until he was finally unseated, he personally chose the man who would decide the composition of all committees of the lower house. Even Theodore Roosevelt, noted for his independence as governor, bowed to Platt's nomination of S. Fred Nixon for the speakership in 1899. Nixon's forcefulness and popularity soon won him virtually complete control over that body's legislative record, and he emerged an agent for the state Republican organization's policies and proposals.[5] In the senate, authority was usually divided between the lieutenant-governor and the president *pro tempore*, both of whom, directly or indirectly, were chosen by Platt and his subordinates.

The formal medium for announcing Platt's policies and decisions in the heyday of his leadership was the state Republican committee. Consisting of the boss's most trusted advisors, it had the important task of mapping out plans for the biannual state convention—the preliminaries, the temporary chairmanship, the permanent organization, the party platform, and even the ticket itself.[6] Many a governor, including Frank S. Black, Theodore Roosevelt, and Benjamin Odell, owed his nomination and, to some extent, his election to Platt's iron grip on this committee.

[4] Gosnell, "Thomas C. Platt." As United States senator, beginning in 1897, he also claimed his share of federal patronage.

[5] Ray B. Smith, ed., *History of the State of New York: Political and Governmental* (Syracuse: Syracuse, 1922), IV, 59.

[6] H. E. Deming, "Political Organization in New York, 1882–1904," *New England Conference for Good City Government* (New York: n. pub., 1905), p. 314; Gosnell, *Boss Platt*, p. 73.

With its manifold functions and its complex organizational structure, the Platt machine required large sums of money. For a man of Platt's shrewd practical talents, however, revenue was not difficult to obtain. The firm alliance between business and politics, often considered a basic characteristic of the New York Republican system, actually possessed bipartisan origins in the late 1870's.[7] At this time, the so-called "Black Horse Cavalry," a group of Democratic and Republican self-seeking legislators, sought to take advantage of certain proposed measures designed to regulate public utilities and fiduciary institutions. They extorted money from lobbyists or business representatives who wished to have these "strike" bills scuttled either in committee or on the house floor. Through the years this type of legislation became more and more frequent; it was usually introduced by the very people who received the bribe money. In the early 1890's, when the Democrats controlled the state legislature, the political boss began to assume the functions that lobbyists had hitherto performed. He simply lined up the votes and in return extracted contributions for the party chest. Platt preferred this systematic arrangement, and he perfected it once Republican fortunes improved.[8]

From the early stages of Thomas Platt's determined drive for political power, there were certain factors that modified his leadership and earned him the title "easy boss." Although most of his followers were loyal, he was forced to deal with strong upstate leaders like Barnes and Aldridge whose county organizations were virtually autonomous. He could ill afford to antagonize them lest a substantial defection on election day result in Democratic control of the state. This problem was magnified by the growing Democratic majorities in New York City, a development resulting from significant statewide changes in the last quarter of the nineteenth century. In these years, New Yorkers forged an industrial-manufacturing establishment second to none in the nation.[9] Simultaneous with this tremendous business

[7] Gosnell, *Boss Platt*, p. 262.   [8] *Ibid.*, pp. 262–263.

[9] All indices point to New York's supremacy (New York State De-

expansion was the rapid growth of the city to a position of economic, social, and political pre-eminence. In 1880 New York's seven leading urban centers comprised 44 per cent of the state's total population; by 1900 the figure had risen to 59 per cent. More important, New York City alone contained almost one-half the total state population by the turn of the century, a large percentage of which were immigrants.[10] Crammed into extremely inadequate living quarters, the foreign-born helped supply the rapidly expanding metropolitan labor market and, at the same time, provided a broadening base for New York County's ever-opportunistic Tammany Hall, which for decades had been a haven for Europe's emigrants. The challenge to Platt's upstate Republican machine was obvious.

Events and circumstances in the early 1890's, however, favored the "easy boss" and his drive for total domination of the state's political life. Factionalism within Democratic ranks, revelations of graft and corruption in New York City's Tammany administration, the steady growth of, and agitation by, various metropolitan reform clubs, and the onset of a severe depression in 1893 paved the way for Republican success.[11] In that year, both the senate and assembly fell to the GOP; in itself unrevealing (for the Platt organization usually controlled the legislature during the "gilded age"), this victory nonetheless set the stage for the next election. The year 1894 witnessed a resounding Republican triumph as the Platt machine captured the governorship for the first time in nearly fifteen years, strengthened its

---

partment of Labor, *Report on the Growth of Industry in New York* [Albany: Argus, 1904], ch. 1).

[10] *Manual for the Use of the Legislature of the State of New York, 1889* (Albany, 1889), p. 112; *New York Legislative Manual, 1904* (1904), p. 195; Everett S. Lee *et al., Population Redistribution and Economic Growth: United States, 1870–1950* (3 vols.; Philadelphia: American Philosophical Library, 1957), III, 208.

[11] Charles Garrett, *The La Guardia Years: Machine and Reform Politics in New York City* (New Brunswick: Rutgers, 1961), ch. 2; David M. Ellis *et al., A Short History of New York State* (Ithaca: Cornell, 1957), p. 372.

control over the state legislature, and won a lopsided majority of the state's congressional delegation. Tammany's defeat was rendered complete with William Strong's mayoral victory in New York City on a fusion ticket. Most significant was the fact that the GOP gubernatorial nominee, Levi Morton, while holding the upstate counties in line, almost ran up a plurality in the City, thus accounting for a 12 per cent shift in voting behavior from the previous statewide election. Two years later, New Yorkers' distrust of the Democrats was confirmed by their overwhelming repudiation of William Jennings Bryan and his gubernatorial running mate, Wilbur Porter. Perhaps McKinley's "full dinner pail," amidst a depression that hit all classes and witnessed widespread unemployment in New York City, appealed as much to voters as Bryan's inflationary program of free silver repulsed them.[12] At any rate, Platt reached the apex of his political power in 1896; the next year "his" legislature elected him to the United States Senate.

In a real sense, these Republican victories in the mid-1890's had a hollow ring, for they were achieved not so much through GOP virtue as through Democratic vice and misfortune. What they did teach the Platt organization was the need to court New York City voters, especially those independents and independent Republicans who had attached themselves to the various reform groups. This awareness of middle-class strength had much to do with Platt's ultimate decision, in 1898, to endorse Theodore Roosevelt for the governorship.[13] To be sure, Governor Frank S. Black, Roosevelt's predecessor in Albany, had remained loyal to the organization in his two-year incumbency. He had faith-

[12] For a general discussion of the Republican plight in the city, see Carl N. Degler, "American Political Parties and the Rise of the City: An Interpretation," *Journal of American History*, LI (1964), 41–59. For a more detailed treatment of the strength of Republicanism in New York City for this entire period, see Marvin G. Weinbaum, "New York County Republican Politics, 1897–1922: The Quarter Century After Municipal Consolidation," *New-York Historical Society Quarterly*, L (1966), 63–94.

[13] G. Wallace Chessman, *Governor Theodore Roosevelt: The Albany Apprenticeship, 1898–1900* (Cambridge: Harvard, 1965), pp. 18–24.

fully cooperated in the distribution of the state patronage, and he had adhered to the party line in legislative matters. Yet Black had become vulnerable. He had permitted Barge Canal expenditures to become enmeshed in local politics, and he had failed to mollify the differences between county leaders. Above all, he had ill-advisedly attempted to Republicanize the civil service lists. Thus, Black had erred in his antagonism of the very groups that were vital to GOP success on the statewide level.

If the New York Republican boss turned somewhat reluctantly to Theodore Roosevelt, his apprehensions were fully justified during the course of the next two years, for the presence of an independently inclined executive in Albany was to herald the decline of Platt's domination over Republican affairs. Roosevelt demonstrated clearly that gubernatorial power could be exercised in an opposite manner from bossism. In previous years, the governor had been only an agent of the state machine, and his legislative program had reflected this subserviency. To some extent Roosevelt succeeded in driving a wedge between his own political will and Platt's ideas concerning the state's administration. He proceeded cautiously, however, for he had neither the training nor the inclination to meet the organization on its own ground.[14] Moreover, an open assault would achieve nothing against the deeply entrenched "easy boss."

Roosevelt took seriously his duties and obligations as New York's chief executive. He strove diligently to remain on excellent terms with the organization and, at the same time, to follow an enlightened course of public action. No better example can be cited than his handling of legislative questions. He would first present his program to the legislature in the annual message, perhaps even in special addresses. He would work persistently to mold public opinion in behalf of key proposals—a technique that would later be perfected by Charles Evans Hughes. If legislative and local leaders did not respond to what he deemed the popular will, he would apply the various kinds of political pres-

[14] Theodore Roosevelt, *An Autobiography* (New York: Macmillan, 1913), p. 304.

sure at the governor's disposal. Often this strategy yielded fruit-ful dividends, and Roosevelt won his case.[15]

As governor, Roosevelt faithfully consulted the organization in the matter of appointments. Yet he refused to allow his imme-diate subordinate officers to be named by Platt. This particular issue first presented itself in 1899, when Lou Payn's term as in-surance superintendent expired, and Platt insisted upon his re-nomination. Convinced that Payn was a tangible link between the organization and the fiduciary interests, Roosevelt flatly refused. The forces behind the superintendent remained ada-mant, and a protracted struggle ensued. It culminated with the publication of evidence pointing to Payn's illicit activities with the State Trust Company, and Roosevelt emerged victorious.[16] He then proceeded to name his own insurance head.

Although the Roosevelt administration accomplished little in the way of specific reforms, its independence and its modest suc-cesses caused Platt considerable anguish. There is ample evidence that Platt was so dismayed over Roosevelt's impulsiveness that in 1900 he welcomed the opportunity to "kick him upstairs." [17] When, therefore, the "easy boss" was invited to join forces with Matt Quay of Pennsylvania in behalf of the Governor's vice-presidential nomination, he accepted with undisguised fervor. What he did not anticipate was that within one year the Colonel would be ensconced in the White House as the major dispenser of federal patronage.

By the time that Platt had decided upon Roosevelt's fate, he had also chosen the next governor of New York, Benjamin B. Odell, Jr.[18] This choice, which ultimately proved as disastrous

[15] *Ibid.*, pp. 305–306. This was certainly true regarding passage of the utility franchise tax bill (William H. Harbaugh, *Power and Responsi-bility: The Life and Times of Theodore Roosevelt* [New York: Farrar, Straus, 1961], pp. 117–118).

[16] Chessman, *Governor Theodore Roosevelt*, ch. 5.

[17] *Ibid.*, p. 282. Platt categorically denied that he wished Roosevelt out of the way and that he therefore sponsored the vice-presidential nomination (Louis J. Lang, ed., *The Autobiography of Thomas Collier Platt* [New York: B. W. Dodge, 1910], pp. 395–396).

[18] Lang, *Autobiography of Platt*, p. 390.

for Platt as the decision to send Roosevelt to Washington, was impelled primarily by a desire to return the chief executive to the organizational fold. It was, in short, a reaction against Roosevelt's independence.

Known as the businessman in politics, Ben Odell had steadily ascended the organizational ladder in the 1880's and 1890's. He had served his political apprenticeship under his father, who for years had been one of Newburgh's most prominent citizens, but his early days were devoted to the achievement of business success by diligent work in the family ice company.[19] Not entirely satisfied with his lot in the small town of his boyhood, he turned to his other love—politics. Although defeated in his bid for minor elective offices in the early 1880's, he soon attracted the attention of Tom Platt, who had always been acutely aware of the advantages resulting from the cultivation of young men of means. Odell must have been particularly appealing to the rising New York political leader, for the Newburgh politician had become friendly with his Hudson neighbor, Edward H. Harriman, the famous railroad tycoon. Platt at this time desperately needed the help of such influential financial leaders in his own quest for power. In 1884 Odell was appointed a member of the state Republican committee, a position very much to his liking. He devoted himself to the organizational aspect of politics until 1894, when he was elected to Congress from his Newburgh district. After serving two terms in Washington, he returned to his first love and was placed on the state Republican executive committee. In these later years, Platt came to rely more and more upon his vigorous, efficient protégé and delegated task after task to him. With Roosevelt out of the way, Ben Odell was Platt's logical gubernatorial candidate.

[19] Edgar L. Murlin, *New York Red Book: An Illustrated Legislative Manual, 1901* (Albany: J. B. Lyon, 1901), pp. 31–35; Charles E. Fitch, *Encyclopedia of Biography of New York* (5 vols.; Boston: American Historical Society, 1916), V, 14–16; Robert H. Beattie, "Governor Odell: A Character Sketch," *Review of Reviews,* XXVI (1902), 676–678.

Odell's first administration witnessed the beginning of a violent intraparty fight in New York. With the Rooseveltian example before him, the new governor almost immediately announced his intention to free himself from the shackles of Platt's leadership. He refused the boss's request for passage of several pet legislative measures. As 1901 wore on, he paid less and less attention to Platt's patronage suggestions; his appointments were made largely to further his personal political ambitions. So far had Odell asserted his own leadership by early 1902 that Platt quickly realized that the Governor was organizing his own machine.[20]

There was little, however, for Boss Platt to do about his wayward disciple. Although no reformer himself, the Governor was able to maintain a grip on the New York electorate. The watchword of his administration had become economy. He cleverly conveyed the impression that by reorganizing several commissions and by weeding out waste and extravagance in office, he was saving the taxpayers substantial sums of money. His relations with the press improved noticeably when he inaugurated his drive to abolish the state's direct tax. He appeared to be following in the footsteps of Theodore Roosevelt, and he was rapidly gaining the favor of independent critics. Roosevelt himself displayed some enthusiasm for Odell's efforts.[21]

From Washington, Vice-President Roosevelt closely followed New York developments during 1901. His interest was greater than he would dare admit publicly. Even before McKinley's assassination, Roosevelt privately expressed his opinions on the state Republican situation. Already entertaining the faint hope that he might win the 1904 presidential nomination, he set about calculating Odell's strength. He feared that the Governor would

[20] Lang, *Autobiography of Platt*, p. 430.

[21] Theodore Roosevelt to Charles J. Bonaparte, March 30, 1901; Roosevelt to Clarence H. Esty, April 3, 1901; Roosevelt to Henry L. Nelson, April 8, 1901; and Roosevelt to Charles E. S. Wood, Aug. 27, 1901, *LTR*, III, 36–39, 43–45, 137–138. See also Smith, *History of New York*, IV, 78–79.

be successful in uniting both the machine and the independents, thereby lessening Roosevelt's own chances for the presidency. Nor could he take pleasure in the growing friction between Platt and Odell, because in the final analysis, he reasoned, they had fundamentally more in common with each other than either had with him.[22]

Once Roosevelt was ensconced in the presidency, his interest in the 1904 election deepened substantially, for the nomination was finally within striking distance. His strategy was to follow a course of action that would ensure victory at the next Republican national convention. He thought it essential for his own welfare that he control the strong New York delegation as a nucleus around which to build general support. No longer was he disturbed by Odell's personal aspirations, except in so far as they interfered with the political stability he sought to maintain. His chief objective was to harmonize Republican factionalism within his home state.

President Roosevelt soon found it exceedingly difficult, however, to assume a middle pose between Platt and Odell, thus to heal seemingly reconcilable differences. In 1902 he was forced to handle conflicting patronage demands and his solution satisfied neither party. He immediately perceived that he would have to work more closely with Odell, whose growing strength was apparent to most political observers. Yet he moved cautiously, fearing that a definite commitment might backfire.

The President recognized the very real danger of factional politics during the summer of 1902 shortly before the state Republican convention met at Saratoga. For much of the year Roosevelt had regarded his 1904 chances as slight, and he welcomed the opportunity to commit the party leaders to his cause.[23] In mid-September, therefore, his agents in New York,

[22] Roosevelt to William Howard Taft, July 15, 1901, and Roosevelt to Henry Cabot Lodge, Aug. 20, 1901, *LTR*, III, 120–123, 128–129.

[23] Henry F. Pringle, *Theodore Roosevelt: A Biography* (New York: Harcourt, Brace, 1931), pp. 339–340.

James S. Clarkson and William Loeb, Jr., met with key state and local leaders for the purpose of discussing a resolution of endorsement they had drafted and wished to submit to the convention. Significantly, Odell and his followers joined the President in his stand against the embittered Platt men, who refused to commit themselves on a nomination two years away.[24] Platt and his friends were able to beat back a compromise endorsement, and the Roosevelt forces seemed at least temporarily blocked.

At the convention, the President's nomination resolution received the enthusiastic approval of a majority of the delegates. Roosevelt was thus accorded the pledge he had long sought to obtain. What he did not realize, apparently, was that by permitting Odell to declare unequivocally for him, he had sown the seeds of further discord so far as Platt was concerned. Since Odell's strength had been necessary to win the endorsement at Saratoga, Roosevelt would be forced to work more closely with him in the near future.

Platt's immediate reaction to the supposed Odell-Roosevelt alliance as manifested in the preconvention meeting was to backtrack as far as possible. He refused to support a move initiated by several of his underlings to dump Odell and to name an acceptable candidate for governor.[25] Instead, he met with his wayward disciple in an effort to agree upon a platform and a common slate of candidates. In condescending fashion, Odell allowed Platt the opportunity to select the candidate for lieutenant-governor, and Platt responded with the name of George R. Sheldon, a New York City banker and an organization faithful. A satisfactory solution had apparently been reached when William Berri, owner of the Brooklyn *Standard Union,* published a story viciously attacking Sheldon's alleged trust connections. Infuriated by Platt's seeming indifference toward public opinion in making such a selection in the first place, Odell worked strenuously to undermine Sheldon. Committed to his

[24] James S. Clarkson to William Loeb, Sept. 23, 1902, *LTR,* III, 328–329.

[25] Lang, *Autobiography of Platt,* pp. 430–431.

New York City friend, Platt held firm, and the showdown he wished to avoid now seemed inescapable. Amidst the confusion of the Saratoga gathering, Odell made an unannounced appearance and, in effect, forced Sheldon to withdraw. The nomination for lieutenant-governor then went to Frank W. Higgins—a choice that to many observers saved Platt's face at the eleventh hour.[26] Yet Platt's political demise was now virtually inevitable.

Governor Odell easily won re-election that fall, and his second administration opened inauspiciously for Platt. The aging warrior had been a United States Senator since 1897, and his term would expire in March, 1903. He was convinced that he could secure vindication in the eyes of New York politicians if he presented himself to the legislature for re-election. A preliminary skirmish during the senate Republican caucus in January over the selection of a majority leader, a Platt man, did not noticeably discourage him.[27] Fearlessly, Platt submitted his name to a body of men he had long controlled. But by this time a substantial group, led by Elon Brown, Edgar T. Brackett, and Nathaniel Elsberg in the senate, had taken an implacable stand against him. While they were unsuccessful in defeating his bid, they did contribute substantially toward deflating his rapidly waning prestige.

As 1903 wore on, Roosevelt became more and more apprehensive over his efforts to obtain the presidency in his own right. Although he appeared to hold New York securely, he was unhappy about his relations with Odell. In the spring the difficult patronage question cropped up again. Seeking to observe the traditional senatorial courtesy, Roosevelt permitted Platt to nominate several federal officials for service in New York. The greedy Odell, complaining bitterly to the White House, demanded closer cooperation between Albany and Washington. Roosevelt was irritated and offended at the Governor's impropriety, but he was saved from replying in kind by Elihu Root, who judiciously recognized the implications of an open

[26] Smith, *History of New York*, IV, 82.   [27] *Ibid.*, p. 89.

break with the strongest Republican in the Empire State.[28] For the time being, Roosevelt continued to follow a middle course.[29]

Republican harmony seemed all the more essential to Roosevelt and his followers in the light of Democratic resurgence in New York. The growing power of Tammany Hall has already been suggested. In 1901 Boss Richard Croker had abdicated. For a short time Tammany was run by Lewis Nixon, whose resignation in April, 1902, brought a triumvirate to power.[30] Gradually, one member of this group, Charles F. Murphy, whipped the diverse district leaders into line and consolidated authority within his own aegis. The election of George B. McClellan, Jr., as mayor in 1903, largely the result of Murphy's efforts, served as an object lesson to the GOP. Now the unquestioned master of the New York City Democracy, Murphy was at last in a position to challenge Republican supremacy on a statewide level.[31]

Fully aware of the implications of Murphy's victory, Theodore Roosevelt summoned a group of New York Republican leaders on November 23, 1903. He remained convinced that only a thoroughly united GOP would achieve victory the following year, and he sought to negotiate a truce between contending factions. Thus, he laid the issue squarely before Senators Platt and Depew, Governor Odell, and State Chairman George W. Dunn. Impressed by the President's appeals, the group agreed that Platt should remain the acknowledged leader of the New York party, but Odell was to manage the organizational details. Odell would have a free hand in all areas wherein Platt was given no designated authority. The Governor would approve the Senator's political appointments and was to sponsor no legislation antagonistic to Platt's interests. Both men pledged their loyalty to Theodore Roosevelt as leader of the Republican

[28] Roosevelt to Benjamin B. Odell, March 23, 1903, *LTR*, III, 452–455; see also editors' note, pp. 453–455.
[29] Roosevelt to Nicholas Murray Butler, April 27, 1903, *ibid.*, p. 471.
[30] Gustavus Myers, *The History of Tammany Hall* (New York: Boni and Liveright, 1917), p. 295; M. R. Werner, *Tammany Hall* (Garden City: Doubleday, Doran, 1928), pp. 482–483.
[31] Myers, *Tammany Hall*, p. 306.

party.[32] Four months later, the pact was confirmed at a second meeting between the protagonists. Summoned by Elihu Root, this conference outlined the details of party organization in New York. Platt remained the titular leader, but Odell was to be named chairman of the state committee, a position he had long coveted.[33]

These key agreements, sponsored by the Roosevelt administration, reflected the changed character of New York Republican politics. Already several of the old Platt lieutenants, notably George Aldridge, William Barnes, Edgar T. Brackett, Lucius Littauer, Edward Lauterbach, and Lou Payn, had transferred their loyalty to the Governor-Chairman. In the face of this setback, Platt himself waxed philosophical about the situation. He would make no attempt, at least in the immediate future, to regain his lost power.

The year 1904 saw Theodore Roosevelt draw much closer to Odell than he had ever been in the past. As the Governor consolidated his hold over the New York organization, Roosevelt moved farther and farther away from Platt. Now that he no longer needed the old warrior, the President made almost no effort to honor his patronage requests. Whatever major political decisions regarding New York were made that year resulted from the alliance between Odell and Roosevelt. Fearful of popular reaction against federal interference, they carefully refrained from using the President's name to sanction their maneuvers. Yet they labored behind the scenes to achieve Roosevelt's all-consuming objective—renomination and re-election with his home state solidly behind him.

Although by June, 1904, Odell had achieved virtually complete victory over Platt, the old leader was made chairman of the New York delegation to the Chicago national convention. He did nothing to upset Roosevelt's well-laid plans for renomina-

[32] Roosevelt to Nicholas Murray Butler, Nov. 28, 1903, *LTR*, III, 660–662.

[33] Roosevelt to Elihu Root, March 21, 1904, *ibid.*, IV, 761–762; Lang, *Autobiography of Platt*, pp. 446–447.

tion; indeed, he cooperated fully, albeit reluctantly.[34] Concerned more with the governorship than with the presidency, Platt encouraged talk of drafting Roosevelt's recently retired secretary of war, Elihu Root. The President and the Governor, intent upon restoring party harmony, took Platt at his word and sought out Root. Interested in party affairs yet ever reluctant to campaign for public office, the former secretary refused the bid.[35] Platt then turned to his old friend Timothy Woodruff, while Odell leaned strongly in the direction of Lieutenant-Governor Frank W. Higgins or Onondaga boss Francis Hendricks.[36]

When the Saratoga convention met in mid-September, Roosevelt evidenced genuine concern over the party's gubernatorial choice. He had already vetoed Platt's candidate, whose fortunes the county leaders were loath to advance.[37] He determined to name a man who would run well with him in New York that November. Working through two confidants, Hendricks and Nevada Stranahan, Roosevelt finally intervened in behalf of his old friend Frank Higgins. Odell was happy to oblige, and he was joined in conference by Frank Black, Lou Payn, John Raines, William Barnes, William Ward, and George Aldridge, men who had in the past comprised the hard core of the Platt machine.

Roosevelt's direct intervention at Saratoga in the fall of 1904 was the culmination of three years of meddling in New York politics. In terms of his immediate concern—the presidential nomination—he met with astounding success. Yet his efforts had helped to substitute one political boss for another as the head of the state Republican organization. Tom Platt, to all intents and purposes, had been shorn of his power; Benjamin Odell now

[34] J. Hampton Moore, *Roosevelt and the Old Guard* (Philadelphia: Macrae Smith, 1925), pp. 37–38. Moore maintains that even Odell and Barnes were none too happy about having to work for Roosevelt. Never a true organization man in their eyes, the fickle Colonel was not to be trusted.

[35] Philip C. Jessup, *Elihu Root* (New York: Dodd, Mead, 1938), I, 419–420.

[36] Smith, *History of New York*, IV, 94–95.   [37] *Ibid.*, pp. 94–95.

reigned as state leader. The full impact of this change and, indeed, of the long party feud, however, could be foreseen by no one in the fall of 1904. The entire Republican machine was intimately associated with a pattern of politics that events would soon prove anachronistic. Once again Theodore Roosevelt, the apostle of national progressivism, would emerge the commanding figure in adapting the New York Republican party to the exigencies of new conditions and circumstances.

CHAPTER II

The People Awaken

Gas and Insurance Investigations of 1905

FOR a number of years prior to 1905, there had been widespread public response to the consequences of rapid industrialization and urbanization. Advance agents of reform, spurred by the muckrakers' shocking exposures, had entrenched themselves in local and state governments throughout America. This furious assault upon the corrupt alliance between politics and business had produced tangible results in many parts of the country before New York State was deeply affected. The manifestations of protest that could be detected in the Empire State by 1904 were diffused and blurred.

Except for certain necessary concessions, the leadership of neither political party in New York appeared concerned with the constituents they presumably served. Whether Democratic or Republican, the machine dominated virtually every aspect of political life in the state. The party organization viewed itself as a private institution that competed for the rewards of office and exploited its opportunities to the full once in power. Whatever else it might accomplish was purely incidental. There was, in fact, a deep gulf between those who enjoyed the public trust and their complacent, often indifferent constituencies. As the Albany leader William Barnes put it, the populace had to be cajoled, educated, flattered, and given candy, "or its judgment will not be so good." [1]

[1] Barnes to Charles Evans Hughes, Nov. 26, 1906, Charles Evans Hughes Papers (Manuscript Division, Library of Congress).

Beneath this veneer of conservatism, however, there were significant undercurrents of political restlessness that reflected the great economic and social changes occurring within the state, especially in New York City, during the 1890's. The mushrooming of the urban center spawned a host of municipal problems —public utility service, housing, sanitation and health care, recreation, education, and transportation—which the ruling clique of Tammany Hall, rendered indolent by the spoils of office and dependent upon the mass support of the politically inarticulate newcomers, had failed to solve. Simultaneously, the sinister issue of graft and corruption in the City administration came to a head, and urban reformers, represented chiefly by lawyers, businessmen, and financiers, launched a sustained anti-Tammany crusade.[2] They were joined by independent Republicans like Henry L. Stimson and Elihu Root, whose disgust with machine rule was bipartisan and who insisted upon separating local from national politics.[3] In the good-government tradition, they fashioned a program calling for a higher type of public servant plus a host of mechanical reforms—tighter voter registration laws, the short ballot, home rule, a stronger city executive, and other measures designed to improve the structure of government. By the latter 1890's this limited formula had expanded to include specific proposals for social betterment fostered and directed by a reformed city administration. In 1897 these two strains were brought together in the Citizens' Union, organized (unlike its predecessor, the City Club) as a political

[2] Municipal reform was not confined to New York City, of course, but New York City later provided most of the leadership for the state movement. For reform organizations in Rochester, Albany, Syracuse, Troy, and Yonkers, see Clifford W. Patton, *The Battle for Municipal Reform: Mobilization and Attack, 1875–1900* (Washington: American Council on Public Affairs, 1940), esp. chs. 3 and 4.

[3] Stimson's position is well represented in his correspondence. Especially illuminating is Stimson to Lemuel Quigg, Dec. 3, 1897, Henry L. Stimson Papers (Yale University Library). See also Elting Morison, *Turmoil and Tradition: A Study of the Life and Times of Henry L. Stimson* (Boston: Houghton, Mifflin, 1960), pp. 76–84. On Root, see Philip C. Jessup, *Elihu Root* (New York: Dodd, Mead, 1938), I, 190–195.

party with a platform calling for enforcement of the tenement house laws, construction of schools, extension of parks and playgrounds, the eight-hour day for city employees, and municipal ownership of the city water supply (and the gas and electric utilities, if necessary, as well). With Republican help and considerable support from social reformers, the Citizens' Union succeeded, in 1901, in electing Seth Low as mayor, and his administration provided honest, efficient government together with the expansion of much-needed social welfare activities.[4]

Little of this reform spirit had broken through the political surface on the state level before 1905. To be sure, there were some noteworthy gains in the area of social reform, but these came chiefly through the determined efforts of a small group of urban progressives who had relentlessly bombarded an indifferent legislature and a partly receptive governor with their program.[5] There was also the modest success of a Theodore Roosevelt, although the Platt-dominated legislature could, through its upstate leadership operating alone or in alliance with Tammany Democrats, beat back virtually any and all progressive measures. As late as 1904, even President Roosevelt himself had made use of New York's Republican party primarily to satisfy his personal ambitions. His tactics had been purely opportunistic, for he responded at each juncture to the immediate exigency, nothing more, and once he had secured the presidency in his own right, his interest in state affairs waned appreciably. Despite the bitterness and uneasiness resulting from violent intraparty warfare, Roosevelt apparently saw no compelling reason to initiate further Republican activities in the Empire State.

[4] Charles Garrett, *The La Guardia Years: Machine and Reform Politics in New York City* (New Brunswick: Rutgers, 1961), ch. 2; Steven C. Swett, "The Test of a Reformer: A Study of Seth Low, New York City Mayor, 1902–1903," *New-York Historical Society Quarterly*, XLIV (1960), 5–41; Edward T. Devine, "Municipal Reform and Social Work in New York," *Charities*, XI (1903), 304–307; Lillian D. Wald to Abbott E. Kittridge, Oct. 29, 1903, Lillian D. Wald Papers (NYPL); Allen F. Davis, "Settlement Workers in Politics, 1890–1914," *Review of Politics*, XXVI (1964), 505–517.

[5] See Chapter XIII.

Understandably preoccupied with national problems, the President may have hoped to shift the burden of GOP reunification to his old friend Frank Higgins, the newly elected governor. With a long and creditable record of legislative service behind him, Higgins knew well the inner workings of machine politics; he, too, had always been independently inclined and Roosevelt thought Higgins would bow to no one.[6] But if the Governor possessed certain redeeming features, he also revealed glaring defects, chiefly a marked indecisiveness, which ultimately made him incapable of dealing effectively with the climactic events of 1905 and 1906—events destined to force Roosevelt to turn elsewhere in his quest for the direction and leadership that Higgins could not provide.

The first weeks of the Higgins administration passed uneventfully. There was, indeed, little reason to suppose that the New York electorate, whose apathy had been largely responsible for the existing political order, would soon become aroused over that order's grave limitations. Yet two significant occurrences, both emanating from New York City conditions and both culminating in specific legislative investigations, unleashed the forces that brought greater responsibility and responsiveness to state politics. They also served to introduce the man—Charles Evans Hughes—who would act as the agent for New York progressivism for the next five years. Hughes's entrance into public life and his subsequent career as a reformer were thus inextricably bound to these investigations.

The first effective survey of business immorality and political irresponsibility in the Empire State was prompted by New York City's gas and electric utility problems together with the partisan ends to which their solution might be put in 1905. For many years, huge utility combines had reaped the benefits of preferred status in each of the City's boroughs. Reflecting the general movement toward centralization in the municipal lighting industry, several Manhattan gas and electric companies had

[6] Theodore Roosevelt to Henry Cabot Lodge, Sept. 20, 1904, *LTR*, IV, 948–950.

merged in 1884 into the Consolidated Gas Company. Specific legal prohibitions, enacted earlier by the state legislature against such combinations, had been ignored as the quest for profits through security inspired utility officials. By 1900, Consolidated Gas had expanded its capital assets from approximately $39,000,000 to $80,000,000 and had absorbed its last competitor in the field.[7]

One difficulty accompanying this consolidation movement was a provision of the 1897 Greater New York Charter requiring public bidding on City lighting contracts. Technically this statutory clause could be fulfilled although each year only one set of rates was announced when contracts were renewed. Under such circumstances, there could be no just determination of fair price. Finally, in 1903, the reform-minded Low administration, comparing New York rates with those charged elsewhere, refused to accept contracts drawn up by Consolidated Gas for public lighting in Manhattan and the Bronx. Low reasoned that since the utility was a quasi-public corporation, its officers should negotiate with the City, not merely dictate their rate policy. In this way, a modicum of public control could be exercised over the industry. Company officials rejected the request on the legal ground that the state legislature had never given the purchaser of gas or electricity a voice in the determination of price. The issue was joined, and for the remainder of his term, Low paid New York City's utility bills on a month-to-month basis.[8] The promise of a settlement favorable to Consolidated Gas came with Tammany's victory in the municipal elections of 1903. However, the new mayor, George B. McClellan, Jr., made no effort to find an immediate solution to the problem.[9]

[7] *Gas and Electricity Report*, pp. 5–7.

[8] Robert G. Monroe, "The Relation of the American Municipalities to the Gas and Electric Light Service," *Annals of the American Academy of Political and Social Science*, XXVII (1906), 200–202; "Gas and Electricity Report," pp. 87–88.

[9] Robert G. Monroe, "The Gas, Electric Light, Water and Street Railway Services in New York City," *Annals of the American Academy of Political and Social Science*, XXVII (1906), 111–119.

If McClellan wished to pursue an independent course in New York City, at least one of his underlings, a thoroughgoing Tammany man, did not. Thus in October, 1904, the impetuous commissioner of water supply, gas, and electricity, John T. Oakley, openly came to terms with Consolidated Gas officials.[10] A wave of protest swept the sensitive metropolitan press and the Mayor and his administration were threatened with considerable embarrassment. In righteous indignation, McClellan divorced himself from Oakley's decision and announced his determination to construct a municipal lighting plant that would supply the City's needs.[11] Meanwhile, William Randolph Hearst, long an advocate of municipal ownership and apparently seeking to embarrass Tammany Hall, obtained a court injunction restraining the comptroller from implementing the controversial contracts.

The Republicans immediately perceived the partisan ends to which the explosive New York City situation might be put. They moved cautiously, however, for much was at stake in November, when the City elections were to be held. Moreover, they would have to ride the crest of public opinion in order to defeat the powerful Charles Murphy and reap the dividends accruing from Democratic embarrassment. There was a second reason for the party's hesitation. Although New York civic groups (including the Merchants' Association and the Muncipal Ownership League) agitated for a legislative investigation and so convinced independent Republicans in Albany, others expressed the feeling that nothing more would be revealed than had already been publicized. In fact, word had it that the state's financiers (and, indeed, Consolidated officials) had pressured Republican spokesmen into supporting rate legislation instead of sponsoring a potentially dangerous inquiry.[12] When GOP legislators, therefore, agreed to allow the City government to examine the utility problem, Odell and William Halpin, chairman of the New York County Republican committee, quickly approved.

The gas utility situation continued to capture newspaper headlines throughout February of 1905; yet the McClellan ad-

[10] *Gas and Electricity Report*, pp. 90–91.
[11] New York *Times*, Jan. 3, 1905.   [12] *Ibid.*, Jan. 19, 1905.

ministration took no action. On February 17 top Republican leaders, including Higgins, Assembly Speaker Nixon, Halpin, and Odell, conferred in the old Fifth Avenue Hotel to map out party strategy.[13] They denounced the Mayor's proposed municipal lighting scheme, the alternative that the utilities hated and feared most. They left the way open for compromise by endorsing an eighty-cent gas bill. But at this point, utility officials stiffened their attitude toward any legislation, for reportedly they were now being supported by Senators Platt and Depew, who were allegedly willing to discharge their obligations to Consolidated Gas, always a heavy contributor to Republican campaign coffers.[14]

Platt's reputed support of the public utilities only added fuel to the fires of public protest. Hitherto indifferent to the larger questions involved, Governor Higgins promptly joined forces with State Chairman Odell in encouraging GOP legislators in Albany to caucus in behalf of a resolution sponsored by New York City's Alfred Page demanding a wholesale legislative investigation of the tangled City gas problem. Neither, it appears, envisioned the kind of inquiry the specially formed Stevens committee would undertake. Odell had seized upon the opportunity to embarrass his rivals, Platt and Depew, and simultaneously to enhance Republican chances in the 1905 New York City mayoralty contest. Higgins hoped to allay public furor and engender confidence in his state administration. Any attempt to rescue New York's exploited consumers seemed to be coincidental.

Since the Republicans held firm control of the legislature, the Page resolution easily passed both houses in mid-March, and the joint committee was established.[15] Its able chairman, Senator Frederick C. Stevens of Attica, immediately undertook the task of finding a suitable counsel. He reviewed the names of some fifteen prominent New York City lawyers that had been submitted to him. Among them was Henry Taft, brother of Roose-

[13] *Ibid.*, Feb. 18, 1905.   [14] *Ibid.*, Feb. 25, 1905.
[15] *Ibid.*, March 15 and 17, 1905.

velt's secretary of war, and Stevens' first choice. When Taft refused, the Senator called on Julian T. Davies, who also declined. Finally, Stevens studied the references of Charles Evans Hughes and was genuinely impressed by the recommendations made by William N. Cohen, former justice of the New York supreme court. Cohen had observed Hughes's rise from obscurity to prominence in the highly competitive New York City bar and, earlier in his career, had tasted the bitter fruits of defeat at the hands of the bewhiskered attorney. Bradford Merrill, financial manager of Pulitzer's New York *World*, added his words of praise in behalf of Hughes, and Stevens knew he had found his counsel.[16]

The man who was selected to investigate New York City's gas problems was a serious, intellectual, but shy lawyer whose world seemingly revolved around his books, his family, and his profession. Born in Glens Falls on April 11, 1862, Charles Evans Hughes divided his youth between rural upstate New York and the bustling environs of New York City, where he later practiced law. His father, David Charles Hughes, was a Welsh Methodist minister, turned Baptist, who emigrated from England a few years before his marriage to Mary Catherine Connelly, the descendent of a modest but old Scotch-Irish American family. The couple were drawn together, Hughes's biographer has noted, "by a common zeal for study, by the depth of religious feeling which they shared, and by their evangelical conceptions of Christian truth." [17] This zeal for education, religion, and the traditional Protestant virtues of integrity, sobriety, and industry they determined to pass on to their only child. Young Hughes responded accordingly. His intellectual development was rapid, and at the age of fourteen he entered Madison College (now Colgate University), where he began his studies in preparation for the ministry. After two years, his horizons substantially

[16] Charles Evans Hughes, "Biographical Notes" (unpublished autobiography), pp. 169–170, Hughes Papers; Don C. Seitz, *Joseph Pulitzer: His Life and Letters* (New York: Simon and Schuster, 1924), p. 268.

[17] Merlo J. Pusey, *Charles Evans Hughes* (New York: Macmillan, 1951), I, 3.

broadened, he transferred to Brown University. It was here that he decided upon a career in the law, and in 1881, already the bearer of a Phi Beta Kappa key, he received his A.B. degree.

For one year the youthful Hughes taught at a small boys academy in Delhi, New York, in order to accumulate enough money to matriculate in the Columbia University law school. With scholarship help, he completed his legal training in 1884 and immediately passed the state bar examination. So excellent was his academic record that he won a three-year teaching fellowship at Columbia and a position in the outstanding law firm of Chamberlain, Carter, and Hornblower. Later accused of having been a corporation attorney, Hughes, in truth, specialized in commercial law, making most of his contacts with leading houses in the dry goods business, importers, jobbers, and commission merchants. Writing shortly before his death about these experiences, he intimated his place in the business-commercial world of the 1880's and 1890's: "The giants of the profession were retained in the more important litigation and dominated the legal scene. Their firms were entrenched financially and socially, having as regular clients the large monied institutions and transportation companies. These highly privileged firms seemed to hold in an enduring grasp the best professional opportunities and to leave little room for young aspirants outside the favored groups." [18] Modest though his legal work may have been, Hughes earned a substantial salary even during the severe depression of the mid-90's. His intensive cultivation of those virtues taught him in the home and in the school paid substantial dividends, and in his chosen profession he soon came to occupy the middle rung of the success ladder.

However, long hours and hard work took their toll on the young attorney, who was never to enjoy robust health. For a time he even considered renouncing the law in favor of an academic career. Intensely intellectual and professorial in demeanor (he would later be regarded as cold and aloof by his political

[18] Hughes, "Biographical Notes," p. 114.

enemies), Hughes accepted an appointment to the Cornell University law school, where he remained from 1891 to 1893. By his own admission, he led an "exhilarating" life at Ithaca—in a sense a pastoral interlude in an otherwise restrictive, demanding existence.[19] Still, the rigors of teaching and the numerous other responsibilities associated with the academic world commanded nearly as much of his time as had his legal career. Moreover, his salary was far below what he had earned in New York, and he found it increasingly difficult to support his family adequately. So, bidding farewell to his friends in Ithaca—President Jacob Gould Schurman among them—he moved his wife and children back to the City, where he again pursued his profession with vigor and success. By 1905 he had amassed a modest fortune and had already attained a prominent place in the legal life of the nation's largest city.

Stevens' choice of Hughes as counsel for the gas committee seems not to have been politically motivated, at least in the sense that the investigation itself had been inspired. Indeed, one would have to search widely for knowledge of the attorney's attitudes on the major public questions of the day. To be sure, Hughes's father had imbued him with the traditional ideals of the Republican party—individualism, nationalism, and progress—and his earliest memory was of Lincoln's assassination. Having experienced both the rural and urban ways of life, he was sufficiently broad in his outlook to have some kinship with those middle-class independents who became active during the 1890's in organizations like the City Club and later the Citizens' Union that sought to clean up New York City's government. There is some evidence that Hughes occasionally attended meetings of John Spargo's Social Reform Club, one of the most progressive organizations in the City, but he was in no sense a political activist, for he was simply too involved in the law. On one occasion, his Republican district leader reportedly asked him if he might not wish to run for the state supreme court. Hughes's reply was

[19] *Ibid.*, p. 130.

characteristic: "I'm too busy, and I don't want a judgeship or any other office." [20]

Hughes's scheme of values had early acquired a fundamental distrust of politics and politicians. As a member of a professional group and, what is equally important, as a confirmed moralist—later to be known by critics as "Charles the Baptist"—he had lived through an era in which public servants had hardly been cloaked with genuine respectability. Unlike Theodore Roosevelt several years earlier, Hughes had no intention in 1905 of pursuing a political career.[21] This attitude, it should be noted, set him apart from Professor George Mowry's concept of the typical progressive.[22] He was not dazzled by power, and he seems not to have suffered from the sense of social and economic insecurity that presumably affected his "class" during these years.[23] That his socioeconomic status and his attitudes were middle-class is quite apparent. But if any single factor explained his entrance into the public arena, it was the profound sense of duty which had always formed a significant part of his heritage.

When Charles Evans Hughes was offered the position of counsel for the gas investigation, his initial impulse was to refuse. He had no faith in legislative investigations, especially where the great financial interests were involved. He would seriously impair his own reputation, he thought, and place himself in a compromising position, if he permitted politicians to use his good name in so controversial a public question. Yet he could not ignore the pleas Stevens made, and he believed the Senator to be personally honest and sincere. With the committee's word that they would search out the truth wherever it led them, Hughes carefully gauged the public service he might render as counsel.

[20] Pusey interview with Hughes, Dec. 3, 1947, quoted in *Charles Evans Hughes*, I, 109.

[21] Henry C. Beerits, "The Gas and Insurance Investigations" (unpublished MS), p. 1, in "Memorandum," Hughes Papers.

[22] See Mowry's progressive profile in *The Era of Theodore Roosevelt, 1900–1912* (New York: Harper, 1958), ch. 5.

[23] Richard Hofstadter, *The Age of Reform: From Bryan to F.D.R.* (New York: Knopf, 1955), ch. 4.

Dutifully, he replied to Stevens' repeated assurances: "That's different. I will serve on those terms." [24] Since Governor Higgins had already approved the appointment, Hughes could immediately plunge himself into a study of the gas industry.

Unfettered by the usual restraints, an investigative counsel may well determine the scope of the inquiry for which he has been retained. Such was the case with Hughes in 1905. He enjoyed the committee's complete confidence, and he had, too, the broad statement of the investigation's purpose as defined in the Page resolution. The joint committee was empowered to examine the "organization and operation of the Gas and Electric Companies"—the rates charged by the City utilities, the quality of service provided, the situation surrounding negotiation of the 1904 lighting contracts and anything else "germane to the purposes of such investigation." [25] It was charged with the responsibility of recommending corrective legislation.

By the time the well-publicized Stevens committee hearings opened on March 30, 1905, in New York City's Aldermanic Chamber, counsel Hughes had steeped himself in the facts and figures of the gas industry—the over-all financial organization of the companies, their practices, and the numerous factors entering into the cost of production. His extensive preparation appeared at first to pay few dividends, for to skeptical observers the initial hearings seemed to follow the course of many another investigation into the complicated workings of the financial world.

Hughes, however, was undaunted by the criticism leveled both at him and the committee, and within a few days he proceeded to meet the challenge hurled at him by arrogant and uncooperative business officials. In the course of three weeks, he elicited testimony that more than justified the press's condemnation of the New York City gas industry. Consolidated officials, including former president Harrison E. Gawtry, as well as

[24] Augustus C. Ragsdale, "New York's New Governor," *Eclectic Magazine*, CXLVIII (1907), 84.

[25] *Gas and Electricity Report*, p. 3.

prominent politicians like Mayor McClellan, Tammany chief Charles Murphy, and former City gas commissioner Robert G. Monroe, paraded to the witness stand and revealed the price the public was forced to pay for consolidation. So skillful was the hitherto obscure Hughes in his probing techniques that business representatives were "dazzled" and "confused" by his embarrassing questions concerning their financial operations and over-capitalization schemes.[26]

Hughes divided his time between the various companies that composed the Consolidated Gas combine. He discovered, for example, that Mutual Gas, by putting aside a reserve for depreciation purposes, had circumvented a provision of its charter calling for public distribution of profits over and above 10 per cent. He showed that the New Amsterdam Company had a capitalization far in excess of the physical properties it held, and that in its 1904 statement to the New York City department of taxes and assessments it had arbitrarily subtracted $15,000,000, labeled as "good will," from the book value of its assets.[27]

Countless other detailed criticisms of these subsidiary concerns were aired in the confines of the Aldermanic Chamber. More important, however, were the revelations affecting the huge holding company at the apex of the utility pyramid. Hughes carefully analyzed the successive stages through which Consolidated Gas had moved in its drive toward monopoly. He thus learned that the company was overcapitalized in the amount of almost $8,000,000. This figure, which helped to serve as a basis for determining New York gas rates, represented money expended by the original corporations for their charters from the state. Hughes could find no justification for what he regarded as a form of extortion. When company officials sought to pass off this $8,000,000 sum as "good will," the state's counsel sardonically replied that in a monopolistic situation there could be no true criteria by which to judge good will.[28]

[26] New York *Times*, April 4, 1905.
[27] *Gas and Electricity Report*, pp. 33, 41–42.
[28] *Ibid.*, pp. 14–15, 18.

Hughes moved, too, into a consideration of Consolidated's *raison d'être*. He discovered that, in actuality, the holding company had never legally received the extensive rights in New York City that it enjoyed. Indeed, it had been granted only corporation status, and whatever other functions it assumed were done so without legal foundation. Moreover, he learned that the charters of the original companies (those that consolidated in 1884) had already expired or were about to expire.[29]

All these abuses, characteristic of unregulated monopoly, had resulted in high gas rates for the victim—the consuming public. Consolidated's inflated assets had been used as a basis for determining its general rate schedule. On the one hand, the company would write off little for depreciation so that its total profits might remain substantial. On the other hand, it would juggle figures and deflate its assets when faced with City taxes.[30]

Just as gas schedules had been established by corporate manipulations, so were the rates charged for the distribution of electric current. Hughes discovered that Consolidated's activities had reached into this related field. It had secured control of the New York Edison Company, which itself, in 1901, had absorbed several smaller operating units. Edison's records indicated that the cost of producing each kilowatt hour of electricity was only 3.664 cents but the average amount paid by the consumer was 12.27 cents. Hughes calculated that the retail rate was lowered to ten cents only if an individual burned all his lights over seven hours each day. The people who might take advantage of Edison's separately maintained schedule, Hughes remarked caustically, were those "who otherwise might install private plants." [31]

As soon as the gas hearings ended, Hughes directed his efforts

[29] *Ibid.*, pp. 18–19.

[30] "Testimony Taken before the Joint Committee of the Senate and Assembly of the State of New York to Investigate the Gas and Electric Situation in the City of New York," *Senate Document No. 30*, 128th session (4 vols.; Albany: J. B. Lyon, 1905), I, 126; *Gas and Electricity Report*, p. 17.

[31] *Gas and Electricity Report*, p. 61.

to writing the committee report summarizing its findings and suggesting specific recommendations. He worked in close co-operation with the majority members, who, at the outset, re-jected proposals for municipal ownership and operation of New York's gas and electric facilities.[32] Republican policy dictated another approach to the perplexing problem, and the final report contained that solution.

The Stevens committee permitted publication of its various recommendations on April 29, 1905. Recognizing that public opinion demanded an immediate reduction of gas rates, the re-port urged the legislature to enact a measure reducing gas prices from one dollar per thousand cubic feet to seventy-five cents. Hughes himself had determined this figure by a careful analysis of the actual cost of gas production.[33] He had also helped the committee draft proposals for standardized gas pressure and for periodic inspection of meters. The most important recommenda-tion, however, concerned the need for a commission to supervise gas and electric companies in all New York State. Shocked by the flagrant effects of what they deemed a ruthless consolidation movement, Hughes and his comrades could not hope to restore a basis for free competition. Rather, they squarely faced the situa-tion as they found it and devised a plan to "prevent a recurrence of the mischiefs revealed in this investigation." Apparently a product of Hughes's own mind, the proposed commission would have investigative authority over the gas and electric utilities throughout the state. It would be empowered "to make sum-mary investigation of complaints, to supervise issues of securities and investments in stocks or bonds of other companies, to regu-late rates and to secure adequate inspection, and otherwise to en-force the provisions of law."[34]

The broad regulatory authority granted the state commission on gas and electricity would have seemingly obviated the need for specific legislation like the maximum rate bill. Both Senator Stevens and Hughes perceived this and were disturbed little, in May, when the so-called eighty-cent measure (the modified Re-

[32] New York *Times*, April 27, 1905.
[33] *Gas and Electricity Report*, pp. 28, 92.   [34] *Ibid.*, p. 94.

publican bill) went down to defeat. With the passage of his primary proposal, however, Hughes enthusiastically endorsed the work accomplished by the legislature.[35]

That the general public could not share Hughes's faith in the efficacy of regulatory commissions is certainly understandable. In the past such bodies had been ineffective in curbing the practices that they were empowered to correct. More important, however, in explaining this indifference was the fact that by May the entire gas question was being overshadowed by another, graver issue. Newspapers and magazines were already concentrating upon the shocking insurance scandals, which had begun several months earlier as a personal struggle for control of the Equitable Life Assurance Society and had gradually assumed national significance. If the gas investigation raised searching questions about the responsibility of private utilities engaged in the public business, the situation in insurance, agitated by an increasingly sensitive press, brought into full public view the ugliness of politico-business maneuverings.

Like the gas industry (and so many other corporate forms of business) the insurance field had undergone rapid consolidation in the late nineteenth century. The Equitable, New York Life, and Mutual companies, together with a host of minor concerns whose order of being was determined largely by the "big three," dominated the field. Centralization, however, had not provided the stability it promised. Sporadic fluctuations in the volume of new policies issued from year to year and intense public suspicion of certain kinds of insurance combined to cast a shadow over the economic outlook. Helping to worsen the situation were the dangers of financial weakness accompanying this consolidation movement—the temptation afforded officials by great accumulations of capital and unwarranted stock and bond issues.[36]

---

[35] New York *Times*, May 6, 1905; Stevens to George B. Agnew, May 12, 1905, George B. Agnew Papers (NYPL).

[36] Shepard B. Clough, *A Century of American Life Insurance: A History of the Mutual Life Insurance Company of New York, 1843-1943*

The genesis of the famous 1905 insurance scandals was a struggle for power between two executives of the Equitable Life Assurance Society. James Hazen Hyde, pampered son of the company's renowned founder, had inherited from his father vast sums of money as well as controlling interest in Equitable. His profligacy, epitomized by the extravagant French Ball held in New York's Sherry's on January 31, 1905, impelled James W. Alexander, the company's president, to demand a change in Equitable's management.[37] He accused Hyde of using insurance funds to finance his personal indulgences, a practice that was not uncommon among insurance executives. But on February 16, when Alexander presented his proposed plan for a mutual company to Equitable's board of directors, he met with stiff opposition, and Hyde was re-elected to the vice-presidency.

At this point, Hyde seemed willing to compromise. He agreed to a modified change in structure in which twenty-eight of the company's fifty-two directors would be chosen directly by the policyholders. On March 31 he submitted this proposal to Insurance Superintendent Francis Hendricks for approval, only to have it vetoed at once by a special policyholders' committee that put in an appearance in the department offices.[38] Believing Alexander to be the dissenters' guiding light, Hyde issued an open declaration of war; six days later, he placed before Equitable's board of directors a series of charges against Alexander.

If the Equitable battle had been limited to the central figures themselves, little would probably have come of it. But it was not. In one way or another, several of New York's leading financiers were implicated. E. H. Harriman, Hyde's close friend, had recently come into possession of enough company stock to put him on the board of directors. In this capacity he pleaded the cause of the youthful vice-president and by so doing drew

---

(New York: Columbia, 1946), pp. 215, 218; Robert Reppenhagen, "New York State Investigation of Life Insurance in 1905" (unpublished M.A. thesis, University of Buffalo, 1956), pp. 11–14.

[37] New York *Times*, Feb. 14, 1905.   [38] *Ibid.*, April 1, 1905.

bitter criticism from the House of Morgan, obviously inclined toward Alexander.[39]

As the Hyde-Alexander rift deepened, it became a favorite subject for newspaper headlines. New York City journals, especially, carried every detail of the unfolding drama, and unlike the gas question it rapidly assumed widespread significance. An eager public, conditioned by the revelations of the Stevens committee, was moved to inquire if the insurance business as a whole was not actually entangled in the confusion and manipulations of high finance itself. Several months before the Equitable issue had developed, the muckraking sensationalist Thomas W. Lawson had suggested this very possibility, promising his anxious readers that he would presently reveal "the actual conditions which surround, influence, and control the life insurance companies." [40] He soon made good with scathing accounts in "Frenzied Finance" of the abuses committed by the so-called money manipulators in using insurance funds for investment purposes.

Exactly how much Lawson influenced public opinion against the insurance complex and in favor of a legislative inquiry is difficult to ascertain.[41] His attacks upon the exploitation of the "small man's" investments tended to be of a general nature and without detailed factual foundation. More important, perhaps, in arousing real anger and hostility toward the insurance companies was Joseph Pulitzer's New York *World*. Early in the Hyde-Alexander feud, this responsible journal recognized the larger issue at stake and condemned the insurance firms as "great agencies in high finance and trust exploitation." [42]

Pulitzer himself was not convinced that his subordinates were prudent in plunging enthusiastically into the insurance question.

[39] Louis Filler, *Crusaders for American Liberalism* (New York: Harcourt, Brace, 1950), pp. 193–194.

[40] "Lawson and His Critics," *Everybody's Magazine*, XI (1904), 72.

[41] His assaults did unleash a barrage of criticism from such muckraking journals as the *Era*, *World's Work*, *Independent*, *North American Review*, *Review of Reviews*, and *Nation* (Reppenhagan, "New York State Investigation," p. 15).

[42] *Literary Digest*, XXX (1905), 268.

He judged their efforts to be somewhat premature, for the gas investigation was then under way and excessive muckraking, he thought, might boomerang. Yet he permitted them to print scorching editorials.[43] In early March, 1905, one of Pulitzer's reporters launched a personal investigation of the insurance field and discovered that the companies had, indeed, frequently been guilty of corrupt practices; worst of all was the alliance between insurance magnates and political leaders, a relationship implicit in the buying and selling of laws in the New York State legislature.[44] With this information at their disposal, Frank Cobb and John Heaton filled the *World*'s editorial pages with column after column of insurance evils.[45]

Harriman's official introduction into the Equitable battle and Hyde's declaration of war upon Alexander in early April provoked intense press criticism throughout the nation. Conservative journals joined muckraking organs in defense of the victims —the small policyholders. Some went so far as to echo the *World*'s demands for a general legislative investigation.[46]

Equitable's board of directors was not unaware of the potential danger of mounting public hostility toward the insurance world. Its officers faced the difficult task of restoring confidence in a company that was daily attacked as economically unsound and financially irresponsible. The board, therefore, appointed a special committee, headed by Henry Clay Frick, to scrutinize the Alexander-Hyde charges and countercharges. The Frick

[43] Mark Sullivan, *Our Times: The United States, 1900–1925* (6 vols.; New York: Scribner, 1926–1935), III, 50–51; Seitz, *Joseph Pulitzer*, p. 273.

[44] Most of this information proved to be accurate in light of the later insurance investigation.

[45] It was not until the end of June that Pulitzer actually ordered his subordinates to "concentrate on Equitable Corruption without exaggeration." Yet the *World* had long demanded a general legislative investigation of the insurance companies (Seitz, *Joseph Pulitzer*, p. 273; John L. Heaton, *The Story of a Page: Thirty Years of Public Service and Public Discussion in the Editorial Columns of the New York World* [New York: Harper and Bros., 1913], pp. 214–215).

[46] *Literary Digest*, XXX (1905), 533–535, 577–578, 619–620.

committee submitted its report on May 31, forcefully condemning both sides and pointing up the need for a reorganization of the company's directorship.[47] Alexander had already resigned the presidency, and when the board rejected what it viewed as an insulting attack upon its own efficacy, Frick, Harriman, and Cornelius Bliss stepped down as company policyholders. Several days later Hyde announced that his father's controlling stock had been sold to Thomas Fortune Ryan and that he, too, would resign.[48]

By early June the public had become so concerned about the Equitable situation that the board's rejection of the Frick report and Ryan's purchase of the Hyde stock only served to incense popular opinion.[49] Ryan himself had been a favorite target for criticism since his and William C. Whitney's manipulation of the New York City traction companies. Whatever plans of reorganization he would launch, his motives would in any case be impugned. Therefore, his efforts to call into service as Equitable trustees such highly esteemed figures as former President Grover Cleveland, former Secretary of the Navy Paul Morton, and George Westinghouse proved of no avail. An angry, belligerent press regarded Ryan with as little confidence as it had Hyde.[50]

Throughout June demands for a legislative investigation multiplied. The Higgins administration, correctly viewing the issue as a powder keg, had remained aloof during the early stages of the Equitable fight. After Hyde's countercharges against Alexander in April, however, the Governor together with Insurance Superintendent Hendricks agreed that a departmental investigation of the company should be undertaken. Already there were signs of restlessness in the state legislature over the general insurance situation. Twice, several Republican senators had broken party ranks and resorted to insurgency. Led by Senator Edgar T. Brackett of Saratoga, this group, on the very day of the

[47] New York *Times*, June 1 and 4, 1905.   [48] *Ibid.*, June 10, 1905.

[49] The conservative *Wall Street Journal*, for example, severely condemned Equitable directors for refusing to censure their own behavior (*Literary Digest*, XXX [1905], 850).

[50] *Ibid.*, pp. 921–923.

Higgins-Hendricks decision, demanded a thorough legislative inquiry into the insurance business.[51] They placed little faith in Hendricks' department, for they had often seen the indifference with which examinations had been conducted in the past.[52]

This distrust of the insurance department together with a growing suspicion of the Higgins administration was much in evidence in the spring of 1905. Once Odell's friend Harriman had become implicated in the Equitable battle, observers questioned the validity of any executive investigation. The Hartford *Times*, for example, was not convinced that Hendricks could conduct an inquiry "as impartial as the circumstances of the case require." [53] The New York *Sun* added a bitter note of pessimism in admitting that Harriman even "controls the legislature . . . and he is a powerful and most baleful figure in the depraved politics of our unhappy State." [54]

Accompanied by these caustic assaults, Superintendent Hendricks undertook his personal investigation of Equitable on May 9. He moved slowly and cautiously, for Higgins apparently wished to ride out the storm without disturbing the routine of administrative or legislative procedure. The Governor soon called the legislature into special session, however, in order to hear impeachment charges against Supreme Court Justice Warren Hooker, and the demands for a complete insurance inquiry reached a crescendo. Yet Higgins remained adamant.

Meanwhile, State Chairman Odell was steadily moving toward support of investigation. He had been extremely sensitive to the inflamed public opinion against Equitable and more so against the Republican party for doing little to help the thousands of small policyholders. Just as he calculated the value of a gas inquiry in terms of political strategy, so he viewed a similar exposure of insurance corruption.[55]

The event that goaded Higgins into action was the unexpected publication, in mid-July, of certain evidence that Hen-

[51] New York *Times*, April 4, 1905.
[52] Reppenhagen, "New York State Investigation," pp. 14-15.
[53] *Literary Digest*, XXX (1905), 533.   [54] *Ibid.*, p. 578.
[55] There was also word that Harriman wished an inquiry in order

dricks had unearthed during his personal investigation. The superintendent had probed deeply into the controversial business affairs of United States Senator Chauncey M. Depew, Platt's confidant, and discovered to his amazement the existence of certain illicit insurance activities. He was at a loss to know what to do with this damaging material, and perhaps the fear of embarrassing Governor Higgins, who had opposed Odell's demands for a general investigation, impelled him to suppress it. Somehow the state chairman learned of the Depew involvement and saw his opportunity to discredit Roosevelt's friends together with Platt's ally.[56] On the evening of July 13 he conferred with New York Attorney-General Julius Mayer, whose own loyalty to the state administration was in question. Next day the damaging revelations blazed forth from newspapers all over New York State.[57] Factionalism again fed the flames of protest.

Higgins now had no choice. He waited several days, then made his retreat. In a special message to the New York legislature, he explained that he had avoided recommending any course of action because of the seriousness of the Hooker impeachment trial, now in its last stage. He too had for some time lacked confidence in the insurance department despite Superintendent Hendricks' insistence that he did not possess the necessary investigative powers to satisfy the growing demands of public opinion. What had actually changed the Governor's mind, he said, was the "intense alarm" registered by policyholders over Equitable's internal battle. Yet the cautious Higgins still warned against generalizing on the basis of one company's experiences, and he called for calmness, deliberation, and intelligence in handling the matter. He proposed the establishment of a joint legislative investigating committee for the purpose of recommending corrective legislation.[58]

---

to embarrass his bitter enemy Thomas Fortune Ryan, now in control of Equitable (New York *Times*, June 21, 1905).

[56] *Ibid.*, July 13, 1905.

[57] Buffalo *Morning Express* and New York *Times*, July 14, 1905.

[58] "Special Message," July 20, 1905, *Public Papers of Frank W. Higgins, Governor* (2 vols.; Albany: J. B. Lyon, 1906–1907), I, 176–180.

The legislature immediately proceeded to comply with Higgins' wishes. For over two months the Brackett group (including Alfred Page, Frederick Stevens, and George Malby) had agitated in the state senate for such an inquiry. When the opportunity finally came, they were prepared and had secured the services of the capable, conscientious Senator William W. Armstrong of Rochester as committee chairman. Indeed, the list of investigators selected suggests that the Governor, who had made his own position clear through his legal advisor, was determined to prevent an insurance "white wash." Once Higgins' decision was made, he welcomed the opportunity to embarrass State Chairman Odell, whose interest in the whole matter he knew to be superficial.[59]

If the newly formed Armstrong committee hoped to investigate the insurance situation completely, it faced the difficult task of selecting an adequate counsel. Edgar T. Brackett himself, considered one of the ablest lawyers in Albany, was approached, but he refused the offer. Theodore Roosevelt, renewing his interest in the explosive New York situation, submitted the name of James Sheffield. To Higgins he emphasized the need for a man who was a "guarantee of probity and courage." [60] Chairman Armstrong and cohort William Tully visited the best law offices in New York City seeking to find just this kind of man. After learning that every "available" leading member of the bar was already occupied, they drifted into the office of Ervin Wardman, editor of the New York *Press*. Wardman directed them to Don Seitz of the *World*, who suggested the name of Charles Evans Hughes. With Joseph Pulitzer's wholehearted approval, Armstrong moved to select the man who only recently had emerged as a successful public investigator.[61]

In many ways Hughes was ideal for the insurance committee

[59] Buffalo *Morning Express*, July 21, 1905; New York *Sun*, Aug. 12 and Oct. 10, 1905; New York *Times*, Dec. 17, 1905.

[60] Roosevelt to Higgins, July 24, 1905, Frank W. Higgins Papers (Syracuse University Library).

[61] Seitz, *Joseph Pulitzer*, pp. 278–279; Sullivan, *Our Times*, III, 52; Beerits, "Gas and Insurance Investigations," p. 12.

appointment, though his attitude toward public service had not changed. Except for having worked briefly for James Alexander in the early stages of the Equitable battle, he had no affiliation with the insurance companies.[62] It is true that shortly before he served the Stevens committee he had been labeled a corporation lawyer by the Hearst press; yet he subsequently proved his worth even to Hearst's satisfaction. Above all, Hughes had never been involved in politics and he possessed no political ambitions. He wished only to further his own career as a distinguished lawyer and, if summoned, to answer the call to public service.[63]

After the trying gas investigation, Hughes had joined his family in Europe for a much-needed vacation. While in the German Alps, he received the telegram from Chairman Armstrong asking that he serve as counsel for the newly formed committee. Hughes immediately grasped the significance of the offer. "My dear," he told his wife, "you don't know what this investigation would mean. It would be the most tremendous job in the United States." [64] He journeyed quickly to Munich, where, after receiving assurances that he would have complete freedom in his conduct of the inquiry, he accepted the assignment.

For the second time in six months, Charles Evans Hughes had been the recipient of more good fortune than most prominent professional men could hope to achieve in a lifetime. To be sure, he had already become an outstanding member of the New York bar and had attained a senior partnership in a well-known firm at the age of twenty-five. Yet neither in March nor in August of 1905 did his name head the list of prominent attorneys available for investigative work. Almost by a stroke of fate did Hughes move from a quiet, satisfying law practice to the center of the public stage.

[62] Beerits, "Gas and Insurance Investigations," p. 3; Daniel T. Pierce, "Charles Evans Hughes, Life Insurance Investigator," *World To-Day*, IX (1905), 1173–1174.

[63] Beerits, "Gas and Insurance Investigations," p. 5; Pusey, *Charles Evans Hughes*, I, 134–135, 142.

[64] Hughes, "Biographical Notes," p. 172.

With the Stevens committee work behind him, Hughes needed no introduction to the people of New York. He had received much favorable publicity for his firm but fair treatment of Consolidated Gas officials. He was not a sensationalist and he therefore inspired confidence among the skeptical, conservative journalists. Shortly after his arrival in New York on August 22, he strengthened this confidence by stating flatly: "The time for rumors and the sensational reporting for conjectures [has] passed, and now evidence must be produced and the actual situation fully ascertained in a responsible manner." [65]

For the next two weeks Hughes was busy preparing for the impending investigation. Almost immediately he learned that the committee had named an associate counsel, James McKeen, who presumably would share equal authority with him. When, however, Chairman Armstrong guaranteed Hughes full responsibility for the examination of witnesses, he selected Matthew Fleming, a colleague in the gas investigation, as his general assistant. Together Hughes and Fleming undertook a systematic survey of corporate books and papers. They flatly rejected the use of newspaper materials for their inquiry, and although they worked feverishly to prepare for the committee hearings, they were compelled to launch the proceedings with a minimum of data at their disposal.[66]

On September 6, amidst the flashes of newspaper cameras and the buzzing of eager spectators, the New York insurance investigation was at last inaugurated. For over three months counsel Hughes called before the committee's scrutiny not only high-ranking business officials and financial tycoons but also several of the state's most prominent politicians. The graft and corruption characteristic of machine politics were thus laid before an electorate that was rapidly becoming more critical of its public servants. Hughes played practically a lone hand in the investigation to the extent that he personally assumed responsibility for most of the examining. The facts he unearthed were as surprising to him as to anyone. He would plan a day's session in ad-

[65] *Ibid.*, p. 173.　　[66] *Ibid.*

vance, but during the course of the hearings he was often diverted to a particular line that had to be further explored. In this way he elicited little-known but significant data concerning life-insurance manipulations.[67] From time to time he antagonized committee members by his inability to carry through a session's planned activities; yet he would never permit his freedom of inquiry to be impaired.

Hughes was, indeed, a brilliant examiner. He conducted the hearings masterfully and, even when confronted with adamant and uncooperative witnesses, restrained himself from resorting to invective or calumny. Since witnesses could not have the benefit of counsel while on the stand, Hughes recognized his responsibility to be absolutely fair. He permitted company officials to make full statements pertinent to their testimony. He even allowed company lawyers, sitting in the front row, to break into a line of questioning with requests that clients be allowed time to explain their acts more fully.[68]

The pressures upon Hughes to extend the inquiry into a careful scrutiny of politicians with damaged reputations were almost overwhelming. As revelation after revelation pointed to a host of corrupt politico-business alliances, the press resounded with demands for a full-scale political investigation. Believing that such a diversion would destroy the inquiry's original purpose, Hughes flatly refused. His aim had been "to disclose such abuses as there were in the insurance business and seek to provide for their correction." He would in no way alter it.[69]

However limited the hearing was viewed by the sensationalist press, the evidence Hughes brought forth was damaging enough. Concentrating on the "big three" of life insurance—Mutual, Equitable, and New York Life—he revealed some of the glaring deficiencies of American high finance. He stressed the wholesale mismanagement and misuse of company funds implicit in unreasonably high salaries (and commissions) and tax

[67] *Ibid.*, p. 174.   [68] *Ibid.*, p. 175.
[69] *Ibid.*, p. 176; "Governor Hughes—Now and Later," *World's Work*, XIV (1907), 8912.

evasion. The youthful Hyde, for example, drew an annual salary
of $100,000 from Equitable. Mutual Life's president was paid
$150,000, while his son received commissions in excess of $300,-
000, even after severing his connections with the company, and
his son-in-law earned almost $150,000. Executives of New York
Life were shown to have removed stocks from company vaults
in order to escape taxes. In 1901 Mutual had falsified profit-and-
loss reports to the amount of almost one million dollars.[70]

Even worse were the countless syndicated transactions in
which policyholders' money, presumably held in trust, was carelessly invested in risky and often unsound enterprises. Hughes
discovered that Equitable officials had blithely converted company funds into bonds of the Chicago, Burlington, and Quincy
Railroad. The generous profits they realized were retained for
themselves. Mutual Life held over eight thousand shares of the
Guaranty Trust Company, and Washington Life invested liberally in several industrial stocks.[71]

The most significant and shocking revelations were those
pointing to political bribery, graft, and corruption. John Mc-
Call, president of New York Life, directed the Armstrong investigators into this area with his sensational testimony early in the
proceedings. Embittered because so much of his company's
money had gone into payoffs, McCall complained to Hughes
that "three-quarters of the insurance bills introduced in the
United States are blackmailing bills."[72] Insurance company
managers, whom he naturally defended, trembled during the
early part of each year as widespread legislative threats were
intimated.

When Hughes probed more deeply into political corruption,
he disclosed an almost incredible pattern. New York Life had
cooperated for years with both Mutual and Equitable in main-

[70] "Armstrong Committee Report," pp. 106, 11–13, 15; *Armstrong
Committee Hearings*, VII, 5734–5736.
[71] *Armstrong Committee Hearings*, II, 1115–1124; I, 195–196; VI, 5466,
5469.
[72] *Ibid.*, II, 1415.

taining a centralized bureau, headed by Andrew Hamilton, to influence matters of legislation and taxation in most states throughout the nation.[73] Each company assumed responsibility for a designated area, and expenses were divided up by a "clearing house." Mutual's bureau chief calmly explained that the primary purpose had been "to create something of a public sentiment against vicious legislation, against strike bills, and in favor of lower taxation for life insurance." [74] In 1904 his company spent perhaps $15,000 to accomplish this result. New Yorkers were even more shocked by testimony that Mutual, since 1895 or 1896, had maintained a so-called "house of mirth" in Albany. Carried on the company's books as a "Supply Department," it was used as a clearing agency for strike legislation pending in the state assembly and senate. Its chief, Andrew C. Fields, worked in conjunction with Equitable officials and, from time to time, entertained members of the legislature. Indeed, Hughes discovered that in 1903 Senators William J. Graney and Charles P. McClelland, both serving on the insurance committee, had resided at the "house of mirth" during the entire session.[75]

New York's political leaders did not escape personal scrutiny by Hughes for whatever insurance dealings they had made. Platt, Depew, and Odell all appeared before the Armstrong committee and verified certain stories that, taken as a whole, served only to discredit the state Republican party and weaken its already precarious hold over the electorate.

With evidence before him that Mutual had made substantial contributions to the 1900 and 1904 national and state political campaigns, counsel Hughes called Thomas Platt himself to the stand. No longer a real force in Republican circles, "Boss" Platt could safely recount his role in these earlier matters. Without compunction, he related how Equitable, Mutual, and New York Life officials "kicked in" their share in return for special legislative considerations:

---

[73] *Ibid.*, VII, 5863–5866, 5868–5873.   [74] *Ibid.*, II, 1543.
[75] "Armstrong Committee Report," pp. 17–23; *Armstrong Committee Hearings*, III, 2062–2074, 2080.

Hughes: Is not that the way it really comes about, Senator, that the use of these contributions in the election of candidates to office puts the candidates under . . . moral obligation not to attack the interests supporting?

Platt: That is what would naturally be involved.

Hughes: That is really what is involved, is it not?

Platt: I should think so.

Hughes: And that is what you meant when you said that they would expect you, through your relations to the State Committee, to defend them?

Platt: Yes.[76]

Platt's trustworthy follower Senator Chauncey Depew was summoned to explain the real-estate transactions that had earlier caused him difficulty with the insurance department. While a director of Equitable several years earlier, he had been induced by a group of speculators to lend his name to a large Buffalo real-estate company engaged in operations in western New York. As a member of Equitable's executive committee, he subsequently voted in favor of a $250,000 loan to this same Depew Improvement Company. In 1901, however, the state insurance department appraised the property that was purchased with the loan at $100,000 less than the price which had been paid. Depew appealed for a reconsideration. When it was refused, Equitable foreclosed on the property and the improvement company failed. Depew could not satisfactorily explain his position to Hughes on the stand, although he sought to deny that he had used his influence to obtain the loan in the first place.[77] Indeed, he handled himself so poorly that the Republicans would soon find him expendable.

If this, the Platt wing of New York's Republican party, was discredited by the insurance hearings, so too was the dominant Odell faction. The state chairman had earlier been accused by James H. Hyde of sponsoring certain "strike" bills in the legislature. Several years earlier Odell had purchased over $184,000 worth of bonds in the Mercantile Trust Company, much of whose stock was held by Equitable officers. When he undertook

[76] *Armstrong Committee Hearings*, IV, 3397.   [77] *Ibid.*, p. 3189.

to unload his interests, he suffered a substantial loss. He then sued Mercantile and before the case was settled legislation had been introduced in Albany repealing the company's charter. Hyde was convinced that Odell had inspired this bill. On the witness stand, the elusive state chairman denied categorically that he had exerted political pressure on Mercantile in behalf of his own interest. Although he admittedly knew of the repeal bill even before it was submitted, he assured Hughes he had not requested its introduction. On the other hand, he conceded that he "saw no objections to it." [78]

Nor was Odell's position strengthened when his good friend Harriman appeared before the Armstrong committee. Questioned carefully about the alleged manner in which he threatened opposition to Ryan's Equitable reorganization, the railroad tycoon was inevitably drawn into a discussion of his political interests. Modesty was not one of his traits and, when asked if he had influence through his relationship with Odell, he replied indiscreetly: "I should think that Mr. Odell had political influence because of his relations with me." [79]

The Higgins administration did not entirely escape criticism by the relentless insurance examiners. Hughes learned that the insurance department had not adequately protected small policyholders against company extravagance and mismanagement. On the stand Hendricks admitted that his officers had made incomplete examinations and that the department had done nothing about irregularities in company reports.[80] Castigating several examiners in particular, Hughes insisted that almost all the "evils which have been disclosed . . . would have been impossible had there been a vigorous performance of the duties already laid upon the department, a vigilant watchfulness in the interest of policyholders, and a courageous exercise of the powers which the statute confers." [81]

When the hearings ended on December 30, Hughes undertook the ambitious task of drawing together the thousands of

[78] *Ibid.,* p. 3144. [79] *Ibid.,* VI, 5154. [80] *Ibid.,* pp. 5676–5690.
[81] "Armstrong Committee Report," p. 360.

pages of testimony into one compact report. He and his associates labored day and night for almost six weeks.[82] Then, in conference with committee members, he drafted the outlines of the massive regulatory legislation that was deemed necessary to rectify the many insurance abuses disclosed in the hearings. For these efforts, the now-famous counsel earned the plaudits of the American press. Even the skeptical Hearst papers commended the committee, and the New York *American* ventured to suggest that adoption of the recommendations would end the "use of policy holders' money to help the political party friendly to the managers of the insurance company." The reformist *World*, chiming in with its unequivocal support, noted the great value in "this exhibition of honesty, ability and integrity." [83]

It was perhaps in this simple display of integrity, amidst the sordidness of New York politics, that the true merit of the 1905 insurance investigation lay. Hughes's report, completed in February, 1906, and his many recommendations in it culminated one full year of antimonopoly agitation in the Empire State. Indeed, the work of the Stevens and Armstrong committees, guided by Hughes, afforded hope to those seeking to establish a new and more responsible political order. Neither major party, faced with a statewide election in 1906, could ignore this growing demand.

[82] Hughes, "Biographical Notes," p. 177.
[83] *Literary Digest*, XXXII (1906), 307–308.

CHAPTER III

Republican Response

The Nomination of Charles Evans Hughes

THE New York Republican party was badly shaken by the revelations of the Armstrong committee. Since it held the reins of power in Albany when the disclosures were made, its leaders —Platt, Odell, and Depew—were themselves implicated in the insurance scandals. By the end of 1905, as one student has put it, "the Republican party contained the ruins of two machines; in the disorganization of its leadership it resembled most that anarchy which is denominated 'feudal.' " [1] Thus, it became imperative for the state GOP to reorganize or face certain defeat at the polls.

Needless to say, public reaction to the Armstrong committee hearings was both strong and bitter. The New York City press sounded its oft-repeated call for political reform. "Not only Bosses," demanded the irate New York *Sun*, "but punk politicians have got to be kicked out." [2] Whatever the nature of the appeal, it was invariably tied to the name of Theodore Roosevelt, alleged overseer of the state Republican party and symbol of national progressivism. The President, of course, had long been aware of the weaknesses of the New York GOP, but the sensational findings of the insurance committee kindled anew his

[1] Frank E. Kilroe, "The Governorship of Charles Evans Hughes: A Study in Reform (1906–1910)" (unpublished M.A. thesis, Columbia University, 1934), p. 6.

[2] Nov. 28, 1905. For similar opinion, see *Literary Digest*, XXXI (1905), 813, 814.

keen sense of political morality. The issue at home, he recorded, now related "to the bedrock principle of popular government —that is, financial honesty and decency in public men." [3] In another letter, Roosevelt singled out Platt's shocking testimony as impugning the good name of New York Republicanism.[4]

If the President was appalled by Platt's performance, he was equally disturbed by Odell's conduct. Although Roosevelt had extended Odell many kindnesses in the past, he had for some time harbored certain reservations with regard to the ambitious Newburgh politician. As governor, he had often been irritated by Odell's opposition to whatever program of reform he advocated in his legislative messages.[5] When Odell became New York's chief executive, Roosevelt welcomed, albeit guardedly, the assault upon Platt, for he mistakenly associated anti-Plattism with antibossism. Soon, however, he interpreted Odell's excessive and unreasonable patronage demands as evidence of a drive toward political tyranny in the Empire State. More than anything else, the 1904 campaign convinced the President of his mistake in permitting the Governor to consolidate power in New York. The so-called Governor-Chairman, condemned by both the press and disgruntled politicians, became the major issue of the state campaign. In an effort to offset Democratic cries against "Odellism," Roosevelt had found it necessary to devote special attention to New York.[6] Although he himself won handily that November, he found Odell to be a political liability.

Shrewd politician that he was, Roosevelt had little recourse but to intervene in a situation he had come to deplore. For most of his New York contacts he had learned to rely upon a small group of loyal federal officeholders, including Nevada Stranahan, William Loeb, and James S. Clarkson. Their efforts were

[3] Roosevelt to Nevada Stranahan, Nov. 17, 1905, *LTR*, V, 78–79.

[4] Roosevelt to Stranahan, Nov. 23, 1905, *ibid.*, pp. 91–92.

[5] Henry F. Pringle, *Theodore Roosevelt: A Biography* (New York: Harcourt, Brace, 1931), pp. 211–212.

[6] Roosevelt's concern for Higgins and himself is shown in his correspondence during the campaign (Roosevelt to George B. Cortelyou, Sept. 29, 1904; to Higgins, Sept. 30, 1904; to Elihu Root, Oct. 3, 1904; to Cortelyou, Oct. 4, 1904, *LTR*, IV, 959–960, 961–962, 968, 970–971).

often coordinated by the President's able confidant, Elihu Root, himself never a champion of machine politics.[7] From time to time Roosevelt could also call upon Governor Higgins, whose own independence was well known.

Swelling the chorus of demands for Republican reorganization, in the fall and winter of 1905, were several of these loyal followers. Joined by George Aldridge, William Barnes, Hamilton Fish, and Timothy Woodruff, they blamed Odell for every Republican reversal in the Empire State. During the insurance investigations there occurred a crucial New York City mayoralty election, where Republican New York County Chairman William Halpin, an Odell agent, met with little success in winning votes for the party nominee, William Ivins. Indeed, Ivins ran a poor third to Democrat George B. McClellan, Jr., and the candidate of the Independence League, William Randolph Hearst. Rumor had it that Odell himself deliberately undermined the municipal ticket in order to get Hearst's support for Republican assembly candidates.[8] Failure in New York City and alleged treachery, together with the shocking insurance revelations, had rendered the state chairman expendable, and the Roosevelt forces sought an opening to launch their assault upon his power. Sensitive to criticisms of federal interference in local politics, the President turned to Governor Higgins for the necessary leadership.

Higgins wasted no time in undertaking the reorganization program. His search for a weak link in Odell's chain of command led him inevitably to Halpin, the state chairman's servant in the alleged 1905 deal with Hearst. Evidently reasoning that

[7] Richard W. Leopold, *Elihu Root and the Conservative Tradition* (Boston: Little, Brown, 1954), pp. 21–22; Charles W. Thompson, *Party Leaders of the Time* (New York: G. W. Dillingham, 1906), p. 401; John M. Blum, *The Republican Roosevelt* (Cambridge: Harvard, 1954), pp. 47–48. Root's special interest in the New York Republican situation in late 1905 is confirmed in Henry L. Stimson, "Diary, 1909," Henry L. Stimson Papers (Yale University Library).

[8] New York *Times*, Nov. 5, 1905. In a letter to Henry Cabot Lodge, dated Nov. 8, 1905, Roosevelt stated that he was not sure whether "Tammanyism" or "Odellism" was more discredited in the election (*LTR*, V, 70–71)

"The Quarrel of the Guides." Under the supervision of Theodore Roosevelt, Herbert Parsons and Governor Frank W. Higgins attempt to remove former Governor Benjamin Odell, chairman of the Republican state committee, from his position as boss of the state party machine. (From *Harper's Weekly*, L [1906], 3; courtesy of the Cornell University Library.)

Halpin's removal would strike a staggering blow to Odell's strength and prestige, Higgins, backed by Roosevelt, worked swiftly and shrewdly. Together they narrowed the list of prospects for the key New York post to two congressmen—J. Van Vechten Olcott and Herbert Parsons. When the relentless City press found reason to associate Olcott's candidacy with a reported Platt comeback, the Governor's forces, at Roosevelt's behest, quickly rallied behind Parsons.[9] On November 29 Parsons was elected as Halpin's successor to the New York County committee chairmanship. He crowned his victory with a well-timed public statement declaring his independence from all "bosses"—an assertion favorably received by President Roosevelt, his New York allies, and the thousands of reformers attached to the City organization.[10]

Flushed by his decisive triumph in New York City, Governor Higgins immediately carried to a successful conclusion a second step designed to clip Odell's wings and pave the way for general party reform. This move had actually been inspired by the sudden death, early in October, of New York Assembly Speaker S. Fred Nixon, long a symbol of the old-guard politician in the Empire State. A member of Platt's inner council in the 1890's, Nixon had risen as a staunch conservative to the powerful speakership position in 1899. Sometime before 1905, he, like so many of his opportunistic colleagues, had shifted his loyalty to Odell, and his name soon became closely linked with that of the state chairman. For two months after his death, speculation was rife concerning Republican efforts to fill the crucial assembly post. Seizing the initiative, Odell declared early for Edwin A. Merritt, Jr., of Potsdam, an able legislator who would later distinguish himself as cosponsor of the Hughes public-utility regulation bill. For obvious reasons, Governor Higgins could not endorse Merritt regardless of his qualifications and, after considerable delay, selected as his own nominee the youthful, energetic James W. Wadsworth, Jr., then only a freshman in the state assembly.[11] With the growing demand for

---

[9] Roosevelt to Nevada Stranahan, Nov. 21, 1905; to William R. Willcox, Nov. 24, 1905; to Thomas C. Platt, Nov. 25, 1905; to Herbert Parsons, Nov. 27, 1905, *LTR*, V, 86–88, 94–95, 97–99.

[10] New York *Sun*, Nov. 30, 1905; Herbert Parsons to Roosevelt, Nov. 28, 1905, and Roosevelt to Parsons, Nov. 29, 1905, Herbert Parsons Papers (Columbia University Library).

[11] Henry F. Holthusen, *James W. Wadsworth, Jr.: A Biographical Sketch* (New York: Putnam, 1926), pp. 44–49. Wadsworth's own account is given in "Autobiography" (unpublished MS), pp. 85–90, James W.

a complete Republican housecleaning, the Governor had little difficulty convincing his colleagues, in mid-December, of the need for naming so young, yet so dedicated, a man as Wadsworth to the task of reforming the notoriously inefficient New York assembly.

Wadsworth's nomination as state assembly speaker fully exemplified the firm leadership Governor Higgins exercised in these early efforts at reorganizing the New York Republican party. So effective was the Governor that President Roosevelt had felt obliged to offer only periodic encouragement. The President confessed that he had not even been informed of the Wadsworth selection until he read it in the newspapers.[12] Yet Roosevelt had had at least one opportunity to make known his views on the all-important speakership question if he had so wished. Shortly before Higgins' announcement of Wadsworth, the President had been approached by New York City Republicans disturbed by rumors that the Governor would endorse a "county candidate" and thus continue to rob the City of its rightful representation in the high councils of the state GOP. Though sympathetic to their pleas (for Roosevelt knew well the political ambitions of the City Republicans), he flatly refused to discuss the matter with Higgins.[13] Still determined to remain in the background of the reorganization movement, he would not interfere in a situation that, on the whole, had been well handled. The New York City group then had no alternative but to acquiesce in the gubernatorial decision and thus to aid in Wadsworth's election to the assembly speakership.

The state administration's impressive victories in the fall of

---

Wadsworth, Jr., Papers (Hartford House, Geneseo, New York; now on deposit in the Library of Congress).

[12] Roosevelt to George W. Dunn, Dec. 19, 1905, and to Herbert Parsons, Dec. 20, 1905, *LTR*, V, 119–121; Alfred W. Cooley to Jonathan M. Wainwright, Dec. 26, 1905, Jonathan M. Wainwright Papers (New-York Historical Society Library).

[13] Herbert Parsons to William S. Bennet, Dec. 17, 1905, and Bennet to Parsons, Dec. 18, 1905, Parsons Papers; "Handwritten Notation of Speakership Conference," Dec. 18, 1905, George B. Agnew Papers (NYPL).

1905 only served to motivate Theodore Roosevelt to undertake the next and most crucial step in the reorganization program—namely, the removal of Benjamin Odell as state chairman.[14] For a time, Higgins seemed to take seriously the President's plea to move swiftly against the tottering Odell and in February, 1906, privately expressed his personal candidate for the position. Then, suddenly, he backtracked, defending his refusal to unseat the state chairman with a curious appeal for party harmony. Although Higgins failed to spell out the reasons for his about-face, they were readily apparent: they stemmed from the general political situation confronting the state administration together with the Governor's own ambitions. Word that Higgins was about to nominate Odell's successor had generated tremendous interest among the party faithful, and several candidates immediately entered the race. To the cautious Governor, this development may have indicated an ugly intraparty battle, which was to be avoided at all costs in a state election year. If Higgins hoped for renomination and re-election, as he apparently did in the spring of 1906, he could ill afford such a struggle, especially since much of it was of his own making.[15]

There was good reason, too, for Governor Higgins to consider himself worthy of renomination. After a slow start, his administration had made a creditable legislative record. The 1905 session saw the passage of several commendatory measures. Although the eighty-cent gas bill was defeated, the state gas commission bill, a truly progressive step in the regulation of New York's private utilities, was enacted. The next year, Higgins had recommended the passage of the entire program of legislation called for by the Armstrong committee. He was able to secure the adoption of several key bills that, in essence, limited insurance company operations strictly to insurance, guaranteed that business be conducted in a thoroughly conservative manner,

[14] New York *Times*, Feb. 17, 1906; Roosevelt to Nevada Stranahan, Feb. 14, 1906, *LTR*, V, 153.

[15] *LTR*, V, 153. Roosevelt himself was aware of the possibility of party strife, but nonetheless drove for party reform. This theme was also editorialized in the New York *Times*, Jan. 12, 1906.

and, generally, instituted a new ethical code for the industry.[16]

The Governor's decision to call a halt to GOP reorganization jolted Theodore Roosevelt, who by this time was looking well beyond the state chairmanship issue—indeed, to the fall election campaign, when a thoroughly-reformed and revitalized Republican party, united behind a progressive gubernatorial candidate, would make its appeal to an enlightened citizenry. Whether the President considered Higgins' action as a breach of trust is problematical. In any case, the Governor was soon incensed over widely circulating rumors that Roosevelt, "as acknowledged leader of New York's Republican organization," was already screening prospective gubernatorial nominees and that, above all, Higgins' name did not head the list.[17] So deep was the gulf between the two leaders that in May they met at the White House in an effort to smooth over their various differences. At this conference, Higgins revealed his distress at the President's "high-handedness" in New York and urged Roosevelt to refrain from further intervention in such delicate state affairs. From the President's point of view, however, the die had already been cast. Although he "gladly" assented to the Governor's request, he added the condition that, should circumstances change, he would reconsider his pledge.[18]

Much as Theodore Roosevelt might have liked to defer to Higgins in New York, circumstances dictated his active participation in the GOP reform program. Republican reorganization became even more essential in 1906 because of the growing strength of the New York Democratic party. After Charles F. Murphy's consolidation of Tammany power in 1903, the state

[16] *Laws of New York, 1906* (2 vols.; Albany: J. B. Lyon, 1906), Vol. I, chs. 228, 231, 236, 238, 239. For good summaries of the new insurance laws, see "Preliminary Text of Annual Report of the Superintendent of Insurance, February 4, 1907," *Assembly Document No. 31, Part I*, 130th session (Albany: J. B. Lyon, 1907), and J. Owen Stalson, *Marketing Life Insurance: Its History in America* (Cambridge: Harvard, 1942), pp. 552–553.

[17] New York *Times*, March 17, 1906.

[18] *Ibid.*, May 6, 1906; Roosevelt to Elihu Root, Aug. 18, 1906, *LTR*, V, 367–369; Roosevelt to Herbert Parsons, July 18, 1906, Parsons Papers.

Democrats had improved slightly at the polls, and they were expected to gain substantially from the recent Armstrong committee's sensational investigation into "Republican" graft and corruption. Moreover, the Democrats had a worthy prospective candidate—newspaper publisher William Randolph Hearst—who could effectively exploit the sordid relationship between business and politics. As Hearst's nomination became imminent during the summer of 1906, the Republican situation in New York failed to improve.

The disastrous results of Higgins' refusal to move directly against Odell became apparent in July when the news broke that State Chairman Odell and former boss Thomas Platt had patched up their differences and had forged a united front against Roosevelt and his allies.[19] Characteristically, the President remained calm, but his New York County confidant, Herbert Parsons, now fully initiated in the ways of Odell and Platt, nearly panicked. Excitedly, Parsons wrote to Roosevelt urging him to repudiate his May pledge to Higgins and become more active in New York Republican affairs. If Roosevelt had decided in favor of the Governor's renomination, the county chairman conjectured, the President's decision ought to be made public. In this case, continued Parsons, the Odell-Platt alliance would disintegrate in the face of presidential intentions. If, on the other hand, Higgins was not to be renominated, Parsons advised that Roosevelt immediately force the selection of another state chairman and thus carry through the reorganization efforts begun nine months before. In any case, the President should act and act soon.[20]

Roosevelt's response to Parsons' plea was typical. He reiterated his commitment to the GOP reform program, but argued that the time had not yet arrived for him to plunge into the uncertain state situation.[21] In the first place, the President had not

[19] Buffalo *Morning Express,* July 12, 1906.
[20] Parsons to Roosevelt, July 17, 1906, Parsons Papers.
[21] Thus he wrote: "There are plenty of things which are right if done at the right time and utterly wrong if done at the wrong time" (Roosevelt to Parsons, July 18, 1906, Parsons Papers).

been able to discern Higgins' intentions. The Governor himself, for reasons of poor health, was beginning to waver on the re-nomination question, and his final decision had to be left to the future. In the second place, Roosevelt could only guess at what course Odell and Platt would pursue. Until he could operate on fact, not conjecture, he would do nothing. To be sure, he was angry at Higgins, but to repudiate the Governor might play into the hands of the "bosses," who undoubtedly were preparing to split the President's forces. In utter isolation, then, Higgins would have no chance for renomination if he decided to seek it, and Roosevelt's own prestige would be damaged for having assumed the role of interloper.

The rapid turn of events in July and August, 1906, justified President Roosevelt's policy of "watchful waiting." That Odell was playing his usual political game soon became apparent. On July 18 the redoubtable state chairman unleashed a blistering verbal attack upon the Governor, insisting that, because of Higgins' overall weakness and the probability of Hearst's nomination by the Democrats, the Republicans should select someone else as their 1906 standard-bearer.[22] His personal choice, declared Odell, was the independent Charles Evans Hughes, whose availability had already been discussed from time to time by GOP politicians and observers. If by this affront State Chairman Odell had deliberately sought to goad Higgins into action, he could not have been more successful. Bewildered by persistent rumors that Roosevelt was preparing to dump him (perhaps even in favor of a Hughes nomination) and more recently by Odell's frontal assault, Governor Higgins determined to meet the challenge. He chose as the place the Republican state committee meeting scheduled for August 15, where in a test of strength his allies—George Aldridge, William Barnes, and Francis Hendricks—would attempt to name their candidate, Lieutenant-Governor M. Linn Bruce, as temporary chairman of the fall state GOP convention in Saratoga. The move itself was un-

[22] New York *Times,* July 19, 1906.

precedented, for the convention's temporary organization usually went undetermined until the very eve of the Republican assemblage. This fact, together with Higgins' long delay in confronting Odell, made an administration victory unlikely from the beginning. So it came as no surprise on August 15 that the combined Odell-Platt forces dealt the inept Governor a staggering blow by beating back the Bruce nomination. Exulting over his triumph, Odell repeated his July pronouncement on Higgins and appealed for Republican harmony under the leadership of Charles Evans Hughes.[23]

Odell's victory in the August state committee meeting confirmed Theodore Roosevelt's judgment that Higgins had ineptly handled Republican affairs in New York. Unfortunately, the President complained to Elihu Root, the Governor had delayed reorganization long enough for the "bosses" to reunite, making Higgins "look like a weak and incompetent creature." Under these circumstances, Roosevelt added, "it may be that it will be found necessary to nominate someone else in his place." Carefully weighing the Odell-Platt agreement on Hughes, the President admitted he was "not at all certain but that it would be well to nominate him." [24]

Actually, Roosevelt need not have been prodded by the "unholy" alliance regarding the virtues and strengths of a Hughes gubernatorial candidacy, for by the summer of 1906 he himself had come to know a good deal about the famed investigator. One year earlier the President had been impressed by Hughes's brilliant examination of insurance-company witnesses. At the same time, Roosevelt learned of the counsel's political independence. In the midst of the Armstrong committee investigation, New York City Republicans, facing the aforementioned municipal election, were compelled to undertake a search for an acceptable mayoralty candidate. They came upon Hughes's name

[23] Rochester *Union and Advertiser*, Aug. 16, 1906; New York *Times*, Aug. 17, 1906.
[24] Roosevelt to Root, Aug. 18, 1906, *LTR*, V, 367–369. The press, too, lambasted Higgins (*Literary Digest*, XXXIII [1906], 229–230).

and placed the nomination at his doorstep.[25] Under the circumstances, Hughes could not help but question the motives of these politicians, for the proposal came at the very time he was unearthing damaging evidence against the GOP state leaders. Yet a small group among them, including State Senator Alfred Page, Assemblyman George B. Agnew, and Congressman Herbert Parsons, sincerely hoped for a progressive nomination and even urged President Roosevelt to convince Hughes of the fine public service he might render as mayor of New York City. Immediately grasping the repercussions of pulling the counsel out of the investigation at hand, Roosevelt refused to interfere.[26] On the same day, Hughes formally rejected his first political offer.

The exact point at which Theodore Roosevelt came to regard seriously a Hughes gubernatorial candidacy is difficult to determine. In mid-March, it was rumored that the President was leaning toward Hughes largely because he wished to have nominated an independent Republican who was in no way involved with the insurance lobby.[27] Shortly thereafter, the two men met for the first time. Roosevelt had thought enough of Hughes's investigative ability to ask his assistance in Attorney-General William H. Moody's special inquiry of the coal industry. During the Easter holidays Hughes journeyed to Washington to confer with Moody and Roosevelt about this appointment. At the conclusion of one such conference in the White House, as he rose to leave the presidential office he was stopped by Roosevelt, who, in the presence of his secretary William Loeb, casually remarked: "In the next Republican Convention you will have two votes for Governor—mine and Loeb's." [28]

Although Hughes may have been momentarily flattered by

---

[25] Henry C. Beerits, "Entry into Politics and Election as Governor," pp. 1–4, in "Memorandum," Charles Evans Hughes Papers (Manuscript Division, Library of Congress); New York *Times*, Oct. 7, 1905.

[26] Hughes, "Biographical Notes," p. 178, Hughes Papers; Roosevelt to Root, Oct. 8, 1905, *LTR*, V, 49–50; Roosevelt to Parsons, Oct. 9, 1905, Parsons Papers.

[27] New York *Times*, March 17, 1906.

[28] Beerits, "Entry into Politics," p. 9.

the presidential tribute, he did not take the remark seriously and, indeed, later confessed that he rejected it as a mere "pleasantry." [29] Despite the publicity and acclaim his investigative activities had received, Hughes still entertained no political ambitions. He was content to return to his thriving law practice in New York City. Moreover, even if he succeeded in developing an interest in politics, he judged himself unavailable for public office. He had already turned down one request to aid his party, and he was convinced that the Republican state leaders would refuse him a second chance. [30]

Hughes's estimate of his own availability for statewide public office reveals his unawareness of the GOP plight in New York in 1906. That he would not be popular with the county and state leaders he fully recognized; that it made any real difference was another matter. In the final analysis it was Theodore Roosevelt, committed as he was to Republican reorganization, who would determine the party's gubernatorial nominee, and Roosevelt was tremendously impressed by Hughes's qualifications. The famed counsel was, of course, entirely free of embarrassing ties with Platt and Odell. More important, as a fearless investigator of graft and corruption Hughes had become a symbol of what was right and honorable in public service. Finally, although inexperienced in elective office, he had built for himself a solid reputation for constructive reform as the author of all the major legislation growing out of both the gas and insurance inquiries. As a "representative of the new conditions in the Republican party," as Roosevelt put it, Hughes provided the best hope for GOP redemption and progressive government in the Empire State. [31]

Few hard-boiled politicians, however, agreed with the President that the party's future in New York depended upon a political tyro. Much as Barnes, Hendricks, and Woodruff were criti-

[29] Hughes, "Biographical Notes," p. 178.

[30] *Ibid.*, p. 178; Henry C. Beerits, "The Gas and Insurance Investigations," pp. 2, 13, in "Memorandum."

[31] Roosevelt to Henry Cabot Lodge, Sept. 27, 1906, *LTR,* V, 427–429; Hughes, "Biographical Notes," pp. 179–180.

cal of Higgins' delay in unseating Odell, they retained a measure of loyalty to the Governor. Apparently tying the completion of GOP reorganization to Higgins' renomination, Barnes and Hendricks continued to work for him. Meanwhile, Timothy Woodruff, ultimately to be Odell's successor, labored indefatigably to quash rumors that Hughes possessed strong support within the party ranks.[32] Parsons also remained loyal to the Governor. To be sure, in July he had urged Roosevelt to repudiate his May pledge to Higgins and become a more active participant in New York Republican affairs. Yet his own personal inclination was to renominate the seasoned Higgins instead of turning to an independent like Hughes who, he argued, would "play into the hands of Odell, Platt and Quigg."[33] Even after the disastrous August 15 state committee meeting, Parsons wrote favorably of the Governor's re-election chances, insisting that only he could forge a united front against the Democrats.[34]

By midsummer of 1906, the GOP situation in New York had thus crystallized. For their part, State Chairman Odell and deposed boss Thomas Platt continued to wave the Hughes banner hoping to split what they regarded as a tight alliance between Roosevelt and Higgins. The county leaders, meanwhile, remained adamant in their determination to tie party reorganization to the safe and sound Governor. Finally, Theodore Roosevelt, now fully apprised of the forces at work, looked more and more to Hughes as the man best equipped to complete the Republican reorganization program. "I am inclined to think that Hughes would be the strongest man we could nominate for Governor," he wrote to Root.[35] So determined was Roosevelt that he asked the counsel's close friend, Cornell president Jacob Gould Schurman, to warn Hughes not to "commit himself about the Governorship until I get a chance to see him."[36]

[32] New York *Times*, Aug. 18, 1906.
[33] Parsons to Roosevelt, July 17, 1906, Parsons Papers.
[34] Parsons to Roosevelt, Aug. 17, 1906, *ibid.*
[35] Sept. 4, 1906, *LTR*, V, 394–396. See also Roosevelt to Alexander Lambert, Aug. 27, 1906, *ibid.*, pp. 388–389.
[36] Roosevelt to Schurman, Sept. 1, 1906, Jacob Gould Schurman Papers (Cornell University Library). Actually, so far as the present writer

While President Roosevelt and the state leaders wrestled with the thorny Republican problems in New York, the principal object of their concern, Charles Evans Hughes, was enjoying his customary summer holiday in Europe. Hughes's attitude toward entering politics remained constant. Shortly before sailing in July, he had told two of Parsons' New York County men that "he did not wish the nomination, that he could not afford it, [and] that he wished simply to practice law."[37] A July letter written from Edinburgh to his parents confirms his distaste of public life:

I was informed yesterday by the Cable Company that a code name had been registered for Communications with Timothy L. Woodruff—and I suppose there will be cables ere long. (Keep this to yourselves of course.) As soon as I have an opportunity I shall put a quietus on the whole business. It's the only thing that worries me. It gives me a cold sweat to think of going through a Campaign with the alternative of defeat or two years at Albany. I don't [know] which would be worse. I can be of more service and far happier in my chosen profession. So "fling away" any political ambition you may have for your son—and take counsel of your philosophy—for of all vanities there is no vanity like that of politics.[38]

Despite Hughes's expressed dislike of politics, never once in the summer or fall of 1906 did he attempt to "put a quietus on the whole business." Doubtless, the reason had nothing to do with a secret ambition he possessed, nor was he playing coy. Rather, it involved a principle regarding public service that Hughes held throughout his entire political career. He deemed it

---

can determine, there was no September meeting between Roosevelt and Hughes. Nor did they apparently exchange correspondence in this period. What might have transpired through a third party like Schurman cannot be determined through the available sources. It is possible that Roosevelt simply interpreted Hughes's silence as a willingness to run.

[37] Parsons to Roosevelt, Aug. 17, 1906, Parsons Papers. Later he said essentially the same thing to Frederick Stevens (Stevens to Roosevelt, Sept. 11, 1906, Theodore Roosevelt Papers [Manuscript Division, Library of Congress]).

[38] Quoted in Merlo J. Pusey, *Charles Evans Hughes* (New York: Macmillan, 1951), I, 170.

presumptuous for an individual actively to seek public office, but if asked to serve his fellow citizens, he believed it his duty to oblige. This principle explains Hughes's silence on his prospective candidacy through the September Republican convention at Saratoga and, after his nomination, his insistence that the governorship would have had little appeal to him if two candidates "representing the best ideas of American citizenship" could have been nominated.[39] Hughes undoubtedly felt constrained to justify his campaign against Hearst, and thus he did.

On September 5, 1906, Charles Evans Hughes returned from his European travels and immediately announced to newspapermen that he was surprised to find a "strong movement to bring about my nomination." [40] Whether absolutely true or not, this statement fell perfectly in line with Theodore Roosevelt's cautious handling of the delicate question up to the Saratoga convention. Respectful of the image Hughes had created in the public mind, the President sought to keep the counsel as remote as possible from the machinations of practical politics. He thus made no attempt to see Hughes personally, in spite of his earlier communication to Jacob Gould Schurman, or even to write directly to him about the GOP gubernatorial nomination. Yet, at the same time, Roosevelt stepped up his private efforts in Hughes's behalf—efforts which were carried on so carefully as not to convey the impression that New York Republican affairs were being directed from Washington.

President Roosevelt's first significant move in New York was the selection of a personal representative to do his bidding at the Saratoga convention. Inevitably, he turned to Herbert Parsons, who, since Higgins' about-face on reorganization, had been his most dependable ally in the Empire State. Although Parsons had been cool to a Hughes candidacy in mid-August, he wavered as the month wore on. Aside from apparent White House pressures, he felt the need more and more for public presidential sup-

[39] Ervin Wardman, "Charles Evans Hughes," *Review of Reviews*, XXXIV (1906), 553.

[40] Hughes, "Biographical Notes," p. 179; New York *Times*, Sept. 6, 1906.

port of his work in New York County. Facing the dreaded challenge of the combined Odell-Platt forces in the September primaries, Parsons hoped especially for a presidential statement endorsing his slate of delegates to Saratoga. Characteristically, Roosevelt seized the opportunity and deftly pronounced his blessings on the county chairman's "purposes and methods." [41] Somewhat of a departure from White House policy, this endorsement reaped the anticipated dividends. On September 18 Parsons scored an impressive victory over Platt and Odell in the primaries. Next day the grateful chairman pledged himself to Roosevelt, averring that he was proud to have led "the forces that wanted the organization known as loyal to you." [42]

Parsons' triumph in New York County, together with Roosevelt's plunge into local politics, generated widespread newspaper speculation concerning the management of the impending Saratoga convention. Some observers interpreted the whole affair as an assurance of Higgins' renomination if he really desired another term in Albany.[43] Others viewed the results quite differently—as public approval of the President's intervention at the expense of the Governor, whose hold over the New York Republican party had become tenuous.[44] In full accord with the latter interpretation, Roosevelt immediately took the necessary second step to bring about Hughes's nomination—the elimination of Higgins as a prospective gubernatorial candidate. This task might have proved difficult had the Governor regained his health. As it was, however, Higgins' continued illness had all but destroyed his hopes for renomination, and the President's request that he formally withdraw from the race only hastened a decision which he would ultimately have made anyway. The Governor further obliged Roosevelt by withholding his retirement announcement until the very eve of the GOP state con-

[41] *Ibid.*, Aug. 31 and Sept. 5, 1906.
[42] Parsons to Roosevelt, Sept. 19, 1906, Roosevelt Papers.
[43] New York *Times*, Sept. 19, 1906; "The Progress of the World," *Review of Reviews*, XXXIV (1906), 395.
[44] New York *Sun*, Sept. 19, 1906.

vention, thus giving Parsons an added advantage in the work yet to be done.[45]

Even with Governor Higgins' withdrawal, Herbert Parsons faced a hard struggle at Saratoga. Outside of New York County, where admittedly Hughes commanded solid support, there was little enthusiasm for his nomination. Moreover, the powerful county leaders, embittered by the allegedly shabby treatment Higgins had received from the President, remained unalterably opposed to a Hughes candidacy. They refused to support a man whose views they felt were unknown and who completely lacked experience in organization politics.[46] Their task was to find an acceptable candidate—one who would launch moderate party reform free from Washington control.

The Saratoga convention opened officially on September 25, but events on the floor during the first session proved of little consequence. By this time the disgruntled county leaders had settled upon Lieutenant-Governor Bruce as their first choice for the gubernatorial nomination, and backstage they frantically searched for support among the delegates.[47] Into the evening they struggled, but to no avail. Finally, in utter desperation, they met with their bitter enemy, Benjamin Odell, who only recently had reversed himself on the question of a Hughes candidacy. However, Odell's insistence that former Governor Frank S. Black be nominated disrupted the conference. The erstwhile Higgins champions were now left with one alternative—to carry the matter to the convention floor the next day. There they could observe the various tendencies among the delegates and then hopefully negotiate the necessary alliances in behalf of an acceptable candidate.[48]

[45] New York *Times*, Sept. 25, 1906. Roosevelt's account of Higgins' withdrawal is given in a letter to Henry Cabot Lodge, Sept. 27, 1906 (*LTR*, V, 427–429).

[46] New York *Sun*, Sept. 21 and 23, 1906; New York *Times*, Sept. 25, 1906; Robert H. Fuller, "Governor Hughes and the Bosses" (unpublished MS), p. 3, Charles Evans Hughes Collection (NYPL); John A. Sleicher to Roosevelt, Sept. 23, 1906, Roosevelt Papers.

[47] New York *Times*, Sept. 26, 1906.

[48] *Ibid.;* New York *Sun*, Sept. 26, 1906.

In the meantime Herbert Parsons, informed of the leaders' tactics, reached the unhappy conclusion that Hughes's chances for the nomination in an open convention were practically nil. Aldridge, Barnes, and Woodruff, he feared, would ultimately join forces with the Odell-Platt faction and thus dash President Roosevelt's fondest hopes. There was but one thing to do—invite the President to issue a public statement endorsing the Hughes candidacy well before the session opened the next day. Roosevelt himself had prepared for this eventuality in dispatching a second personal representative, Congressman William W. Cocks, to Saratoga. The urgent request sent by Parsons to the President on the morning of September 26, therefore, bore Cocks's name. Cautiously, but firmly, Roosevelt answered the appeal for help: "I think that Mr. Hughes is the strongest candidate before the convention. We need just his qualities in the coming campaign." [49] And so the final step toward the nomination was taken.

The presidential statement, as anticipated, settled matters at Saratoga. Governor Higgins quickly made it clear that he personally had never opposed Hughes's nomination. One by one the county leaders grudgingly capitulated as Cocks spread the tidings from Oyster Bay. Bruce graciously accepted the lieutenant-governor nomination. Doubtless as a further concession to the older leaders, Timothy Woodruff was named the new Republican state chairman. When the delegates awoke later that morning, they discovered that their work had already been done for them and they needed only to "rubber stamp" Roosevelt's decision. A final tribute was paid to the President with the convention's adoption, on September 26, of a progressive platform endorsing the national administration's reform program and pledging progressive government in New York State. Specifically, it called for an extension of the state gas commission law to include "the regulation of all public utility corporations," adoption of a unified conservation policy regarding the forest

[49] Burton J. Hendrick, "Governor Hughes," *McClure's*, XXX (1908), 536; Roosevelt to Lodge, Sept. 27, 1906, *LTR*, V, 427–429.

preserves and underdeveloped water resources, and passage of stricter corrupt-practices legislation if the situation warranted it.[50]

Suddenly catapulted to the center of New York State's political life, Charles Evans Hughes responded to the call in the same spirit that characterized President Roosevelt's definition of Hughes's own fitness for the nomination. In thanking Herbert Parsons for his role in the Saratoga proceedings, he noted that the chairman's efforts were expended through a recognition of "the need of the hour." [51] That need he then expressed in a telegram to New York City Republican Alfred Page accepting the convention's nomination. The Republican party, Hughes said, "has been called to defend the honor of the State and to represent the common sense of the people." He, therefore, would pledge himself to a "sane, efficient and honorable administration, free from taint of bossism or of servitude to any private interest." [52]

Hughes's gubernatorial nomination marked a victory for Republican progressivism in New York, the chief architect of which was Theodore Roosevelt, supported largely by the New York County GOP. As such, it represented a turning point in state politics. Long concerned over the often irresponsible, ultraconservative Republican leadership—first under Platt, then under Odell—Roosevelt launched a reorganization program only after GOP corruption and abuse were brought into full public view. Until the Armstrong committee revelations of 1905, Roosevelt himself had pursued an essentially opportunistic policy toward the state organization. His shift and the method he employed to achieve his objective were characteristic of his political leadership. He remained cautious but firm, and when direct intervention was necessary, he responded decisively. This

[50] New York *Times* and New York *Sun*, Sept. 27, 1906.

[51] Hughes to Parsons, Sept. 27, 1906, Parsons Papers. In his autobiography, Hughes states flatly: "I think it was generally assumed that the party faced defeat in the State unless I were nominated" ("Biographical Notes," p. 180).

[52] New York *Times*, Sept. 27, 1906.

move, indeed, brought the President into the open and stamped the national administration's seal of approval on the Hughes cause in New York. Expertly handled, it also left the nominee relatively free of obligations to the older leaders. From this point forward, Charles Evans Hughes, the political newcomer, moved to the center of Republican progressivism in the Empire State.

CHAPTER IV

Democratic Challenge

The Nomination of William Randolph Hearst and the Campaign of 1906

WHILE the Republicans were busily engaged in adjusting their New York State party to the exigencies of changing political conditions, the Democrats, under new leadership, faced their own problems and difficulties. Charles F. Murphy's ascension to Tammany leadership in 1902 held profound meaning for the party not only in New York City, with its growing population, but across the state as well. Since Boss Richard Croker's defeat of former Governor and United States Senator David B. Hill in the 1898 state Democratic convention, Tammany had been the dominant force in New York Democratic politics. Outside of the half-dozen upstate cities where, from 1898 to 1904, the party occasionally matched Republican strength in gubernatorial and presidential years, the Democrats fared poorly from election to election. In many localities, indeed, the Democracy hardly possessed an organization.[1]

[1] Herbert J. Bass, *"I AM A DEMOCRAT": The Political Career of David Bennett Hill* (Syracuse: Syracuse, 1961), pp. 245–246; Alfred B. Rollins, Jr., "The Political Education of Franklin D. Roosevelt: His Career in New York State Politics, 1910–1928" (unpublished Ph.D. diss., Harvard University, 1953), p. 5. For the presidential vote, see Edgar E. Robinson, *The Presidential Vote, 1896–1932* (Stanford: Stanford, 1937), pp. 102–103, and for the gubernatorial vote, see *Manual for the Use of the Legislature of the State of New York, 1900* (Albany, 1900), pp. 839–935, and *1903* (Albany, 1903), pp. 748–749; and Edgar L. Murlin, *New York Red Book: An Illustrated Legislative Manual, 1902* (Albany: J. B. Lyon, 1902), p. 610, and *1906* (Albany: J. B. Lyon, 1906), p. 610.

The man chiefly responsible for reading the political barometer and charting the course of Democratic success in the Empire State in 1906 formed a marked contrast to his well-educated, respectable GOP counterparts, Theodore Roosevelt and Charles Evans Hughes. Born on New York City's East Side of Irish-Catholic, immigrant parents, Charles Murphy had moved through the political ranks in characteristic Tammany fashion. Having little formal education, he labored at odd jobs during his teens and at the age of twenty, in 1878, secured his first political preferment as driver of a cross-town horse car. With modest savings he opened a saloon in his native Gas House District, where through his ubiquitous geniality to dock workers and longshoremen, together with his sponsorship of baseball and rowing teams, he soon gained a political following. His political fortunes reflected his business success, and by 1892, the owner of four taverns, he became district leader. An extremely popular figure on the East Side, Murphy in these years was admired for his reticence and his charity.[2]

Tammany's victory in the New York City mayoralty election of 1897 gave Charles Murphy his first and only official public office. Recognized for his stellar party work on the East Side, he was named dock commissioner, one of the most lucrative jobs at the organization's disposal, by Mayor Robert Van Wyck and Boss Croker. There is some evidence that Murphy exploited his new position to the full: in 1901, the year of Tammany's resounding defeat after a scandal-ridden two years, he organized the New York Contracting and Trucking Company, which leased docks from the City and earned profits estimated at 5,000 per cent. This concern also received a number of rich contracts that reportedly made Murphy a millionaire. Some of this wealth he used to purchase a country estate at Good Ground, Long Island, where as Tammany boss he could hold many an outing for his political disciples. In the City, Murphy established his headquarters in "The Scarlet Room of Mystery" on the second floor

2 This sketch is taken mainly from M. R. Werner, *Tammany Hall* (Garden City: Doubleday, Doran, 1928), pp. 483–487.

of the fashionable Delmonico's Restaurant, representing for the Democrats what the Fifth Avenue Hotel had long symbolized for Platt's GOP.[3]

Murphy's native intelligence, his shrewd practical tactics, and his cultivation of "Big Tim" Sullivan, the most powerful organization man next to Croker, gave him Tammany's leadership in 1902. The machine that he inherited was thoroughly discredited. Almost a decade of continuous assault by the good-government and reform clubs, fusionists, crusading independents, and the City's muckraking press had taken its toll on Tammany, and in 1901 Seth Low won a solid municipal victory. It was this humiliation that retired Croker to his Ireland hermitage.

There was—and had been all along—considerable merit in the charges leveled against Tammany Hall during the Croker years. The machine's abuses and frauds are well known and need not be chronicled here. Nonetheless, the Democratic organization in New York City was hardly different from the state Republican machine under Platt. To the young reformer Samuel Seabury, writing in 1895, the parties were much alike: "Both Platt and Croker are representatives of the spoils system; both are absolutely opposed to nonpartisanship in municipal affairs; both believe that this city is a rich field to be harvested only by party spoilsmen; both represent a gang of plunderers who seek to prey upon the prosperity of the city." [4] In structure, too, Tammany's committee system, with the "boss" at the top demanding obedience, regularity, and loyalty from his followers, paralleled Platt's system. If, indeed, there was a difference, it was one of degree, for by its very nature the Republican organization, with its upstate orientation, was less unified and monolithic than New York County's Democratic committee, whose jurisdiction was geographically concentrated within a small area. In this small area there dwelt the hundreds of thousands of lower-middle- and lower-class elements that formed the backbone of Tam-

[3] *Ibid.,* p. 486.
[4] Herbert Mitgang, *The Man Who Rode the Tiger: The Life and Times of Judge Samuel Seabury* (Philadelphia: Lippincott, 1963), p. 32.

many's support—elements that relied upon the Hall and its solicitous ward heelers for the many services and functions the
welfare state would later provide. Finally, during the Croker
years and even through the early part of Murphy's long tenure,
Tammany depended upon the financial backing of some of New
York City's largest corporations—in certain instances, the same
corporations that supported the Platt machine.[5]

That Tammany's methods were undoubtedly cruder and
more flagrant than those of its opposition was perhaps a tribute
to its relative sense of security in New York City. This confidence, however, was badly shaken by 1903, and Murphy was
precisely the man to reconstruct the tottering organization. Unfortunately, the popular image of this colorful leader—as a
coarse, dishonest Irish opportunist unconcerned over the means
by which he gained and wielded power—was that projected
largely by his political enemies, especially the muckraking press.
Those who really knew Murphy have given a far different picture of his character and his place among political leaders. To
the patrician, well-educated James W. Gerard, who for several
years sat on the state supreme court and later served as American
ambassador to Germany, the "boss" was a "real statesman," one
who "always kept his word" and who "with the hard-boiled
eggs in Tammany Hall . . . just knocked their heads together
as leader." [6] Jeremiah Mahoney, another member of Tammany
and also the law partner of Robert F. Wagner, considered
Murphy "one of the most forward-looking leaders in the whole
country," ever willing to adjust the Democratic party to the
vicissitudes of politics.[7] Speaking of his most redeeming qualities, Mahoney added: "He was picking young men always, two

[5] Werner, *Tammany Hall*, pp. 420–421; Walter Chambers, *Samuel
Seabury: A Challenge* (New York: Century, 1932), pp. 65–66, 94.

[6] "Reminiscences of James W. Gerard" (Oral History Project, Columbia University Library, 1949–1950), pp. 21–22. For an equally laudatory
evaluation, see James W. Gerard, *My First Eighty-three Years in America* (Garden City: Doubleday, 1951), pp. 137–138.

[7] "Reminiscences of Jeremiah T. Mahoney" (Oral History Project,
Columbia University Library, 1957), p. 27.

or three years in advance, so that when the proper time came he slipped them in. These young men that he picked like [Alfred E.] Smith, Wagner and myself—we all received the endorsements of the most rabid reform organizations." [8] The municipal reformer Lawson Purdy, a Tammany critic, has also praised Murphy for this quality, insisting, too, that he was "a man of force and ability and a good deal broader man than Croker." [9] On Murphy's death in 1924, even the New York *World*, one of the organization's harshest critics during the progressive years, saw in the fallen leader an individual who could "grow from unpromising beginnings, as a typical city boss over men strangely varied from the corrupt to the frantically partisan, into a better sense of public responsibility." [10]

To be sure, much of this evaluation was made in later years and reflects the long-run change in Tammany Hall from the days of "Big Tim" Sullivan and Bill Devery to those of the newer leaders like Smith and Wagner, who came into their own after 1910. But that "very subtle change," to which Purdy refers, was in evidence early in Murphy's tenure though often obscured by the cruder methods of the past.[11] Murphy's great strength lay in his ability to read and interpret election returns, and so in 1903 he dealt the fusion group a major setback with his nomination of George B. McClellan, Jr., highly respected by municipal reformers, as the New York City Democratic mayoral candidate.[12] Son of the famous Civil War general, well-groomed and Princeton-educated, McClellan, then a member of

[8] *Ibid.*

[9] "Reminiscences of Lawson Purdy" (Oral History Project, Columbia University Library, 1948), p. 22.

[10] April 26, 1924, in Citizens' Union Collection (Columbia University Library).

[11] "Purdy Reminiscences," p. 59.

[12] "Reminiscences of Edward J. Flynn" (Oral History Project, Columbia University Library, 1950), p. 6; Harold C. Syrett, ed., *The Gentlemen and the Tiger: The Autobiography of George B. McClellan, Jr.* (Philadelphia: Lippincott, 1956), p. 169; Anna Lanahan, "The Attempt of Tammany Hall to Dominate the Brooklyn Democratic Party, 1903–1909" (unpublished M.A. essay, Columbia University, 1955), p. 18.

Congress, was the essence of respectability and for Murphy provided Tammany's answer to the equally respectable, but cold and aloof Seth Low. Murphy even raided the fusion administration to place Comptroller Edward M. Grout and Charles V. Fornes, president of the Board of Aldermen, on the Tammany ticket. Thus, he satisfied most antimachine elements without alienating his own district leaders, with the result that a Democratic majority was restored in New York City.

Almost immediately Murphy declared his intention to root out the worst of Tammany's evils. He implored McClellan to clean up the police department, for, as he remarked, "police scandals and police corruption have been the bane of Tammany Hall as long as I can remember." [13] Yet his own methods, in part a carry-over from the dim past and in part reflecting a facet of his own personality, remained crude and offensive. He sought to control McClellan's department heads, he apparently interfered with the City's court system, and he endeavored to obtain contracts for his family company.[14] Still, notwithstanding, McClellan was able to maintain a working arrangement with Tammany and in 1905 easily won renomination. But for the emergence of William Randolph Hearst as a force in municipal and state politics in 1905 and 1906, Murphy's efforts to balance respectability with organizational needs might have been relatively simple.

For over a decade, William Randolph Hearst had used his metropolitan newspapers to inveigh against the political conservative who allegedly served the "Plunderbund." [15] Since 1896, when he put his New York *Journal* to work for William Jennings Bryan, he had been identified with the "radical" wing of the national Democratic party. Many called him a prophet of

[13] "Reminiscences of John A. Heffernan" (Oral History Project, Columbia University Library, 1950), p. 40.

[14] Syrett, *Autobiography of McClellan*, ch. 9; Mitgang, *Man Who Rode the Tiger*, pp. 68–69.

[15] This term was one of Hearst's favorites. It referred to the political organization that worked hand-in-hand with businessmen to raid the public coffers.

unrest.[16] But Hearst considered himself an urban Jeffersonian, and he not only supported the cause of good government in New York City, but advocated a host of social reforms as well.[17] His vulgar, sensational journalism must have provided a breath of fresh air for the many who found the conventional politician and the middle-class press to be virtually stale.

Hearst's sincerity as a reformer has often been challenged by historians. His latest biographer offers what appears to be a balanced judgment of the man: he was selfish and ruthless, yet possessed of generosity and human compassion, he held deep sympathies for the masses, and he had clear-cut political ambitions that were defined fairly early.[18] Hearst wanted the presidency itself, and much of his peculiar, sometimes erratic behavior in these years can be explained on that basis.[19] As a rank opportunist, he pursued the course of action that would best achieve his goal. In 1902 he accepted a Murphy nomination for a New York City congressional seat in return for newspaper support of the newly chosen organization leader. He was easily elected in his Tammany district, and then re-elected in 1904. The next year Hearst became an independent mayoralty candidate.

The Hearst decision to run against McClellan in 1905 seems not to have been the result of a carefully drawn, elaborate plan. That Hearst had a falling out with Murphy after the 1904 Democratic presidential nomination of Alton B. Parker there can be little doubt. The publisher had counted on Tammany

---

[16] Oliver Carlson and Ernest S. Bates, *Hearst, Lord of San Simeon* (New York: Viking, 1936), p. 133; Charles W. Thompson, *Party Leaders of the Time* (New York: G. W. Dillingham, 1906), p. 234; Louis Filler, *Crusaders for American Liberalism* (New York: Harcourt, Brace, 1950), pp. 132–133; "The Progress of the World," *Review of Reviews*, XXXIV (1906), 516.

[17] James A. Myatt, "William Randolph Hearst and the Progressive Era, 1900–1912" (unpublished Ph.D. diss., University of Florida, 1960), ch. 1.

[18] W. A. Swanberg, *Citizen Hearst: A Biography of William Randolph Hearst* (New York: Scribner, 1961), pp. 173–174.

[19] John Tebbel, *The Life and Good Times of William Randolph Hearst* (New York: Dutton, 1952), p. 202; Carlson and Bates, *Hearst*, pp. 120–121.

backing in the St. Louis convention, but Murphy declared for Grover Cleveland in an effort to strengthen Parker's supporters. The conservative nomination, indeed, disillusioned Hearst (though he remained loyal to the party ticket).[20] Moreover, the restless reformer was unhappy in the Congress, with its conservative leadership and its complex legislative machinery, and he compiled a mediocre record. Most important, however, in Hearst's decision to make the run in New York City was the opportunity provided by a decade of municipal agitation and unrest climaxed by the gas and insurance investigations. His long campaign against the "Plunderbund" finally seemed to materialize as he freely expressed his disillusion with the Democratic machine's response to politico-business immorality.

The organization under whose banner Congressman Hearst ran for mayor was the Municipal Ownership League, which by 1905 boasted a membership of over 100,000, including a host of respectable reformers like Samuel Seabury, John Ford, and J. G. Phelps Stokes.[21] Since the late 1890's Hearst had agitated for city ownership and operation of the gas, electric, and transportation services. His personal efforts to prevent the issuance of lucrative municipal franchises through court action and to cajole the legislature into enacting bills lowering New York City's skyrocketing gas rates were partly redeemed with the establishment of the league in December, 1904, at an Albany conference of reform groups. Hearst's genuine concern over these problems won him the league chairmanship, and through 1905 he and his colleagues, anticipating the fall City elections, sought to bring about fusion with the Republicans. When this proved impossible, he agreed to accept the mayoralty nomination himself.[22]

As a well-organized political unit with vigorous newspaper

---

[20] Myatt, "Hearst and the Progressive Era," p. 53; Swanberg, *Citizen Hearst*, p. 222.

[21] M. F. Ihmsen to J. G. Phelps Stokes, March 31, 1905, J. G. Phelps Stokes Papers (Columbia University Library).

[22] Mrs. Fremont Older, *William Randolph Hearst: American* (New York: D. Appleton-Century, 1936), pp. 205–208; Swanberg, *Citizen Hearst*, pp. 230–232.

support—most of it from Hearst's own journals—the Municipal Ownership League turned the City campaign of 1905 into one of the most hard-fought political battles in New York's history. Its attack was aimed mainly at the Democratic organization—Murphy, the "boss," and McClellan, the candidate—for the Republicans were not really in the running. Hearst effectively used his papers to smear Tammany and to appeal to working-class elements throughout the metropolis. To interpret the campaign merely as the publisher's personal crusade, however, is to err, for it attracted and held the support of respectable good-government champions, social reformers, and socialists, as well as a host of labor leaders.[23] The result was an election so close that a recount became necessary. Indeed, students agree that but for the usual Tammany malpractices, Hearst would have been elected mayor.[24] Whether victor or not, the "prophet of unrest" had proved to be a successful vote-getter, especially in the City's working-class districts, and he could now turn to an even richer political reward—the New York governorship—in his unceasing drive for the presidency.

Publisher Hearst wasted no time in launching his campaign for the state's largest political prize. His followers broadened his municipal organization, renaming it the Independence League, and expanded its antiboss and anticorporation appeals. During the spring and summer of 1906, Hearst toured the length and breadth of New York State concentrating on the twin issues. His attacks upon Murphy and Tammany Hall were just as vituperative as they had been during the violent mayoralty campaign a few months earlier.

Whether in the early phase of these efforts Hearst set as his objective the Democratic gubernatorial nomination or an independent candidacy is not clear. In any case, he must have deeply

[23] Darwin J. Meserole to J. G. Phelps Stokes, Oct. 27, 1905, Stokes Papers; Irwin Yellowitz, *Labor and the Progressive Movement in New York State, 1897–1916* (Ithaca: Cornell, 1965), pp. 191, 193–194.

[24] Myatt, "Hearst and the Progressive Era," pp. 73–74; John K. Winkler, *William Randolph Hearst: A New Appraisal* (New York: Hastings, 1955), p. 143.

impressed Charles Murphy, who, for the first time since his assumption of Tammany leadership, looked favorably upon Democratic chances for a statewide election victory. Factionalism and corruption, often the twin nemeses of a party long in power, had, it appeared, sapped the Republicans of the vital energy necessary for success in the fall of 1906. But who would carry the Democratic banner? Mayor McClellan, perhaps the most prominent young Democrat in the state, might adequately serve the public will, but since his re-election he had so offended Tammany that he could not be entrusted with the nomination.[25] So it was with the able and conscientious New York County district attorney, William Travers Jerome. Nor to Murphy's way of thinking were there any prominent upstate Democrats who could simultaneously serve both the organization and the people. Negative factors, indeed, served to motivate the shrewd Tammany leader in his ultimate capitulation to Hearst. There was simply no one else who could make as strong a showing in New York City, especially in Tammany's lower Manhattan districts, and still possess substantial upstate appeal.[26] Furthermore, if Hearst was not nominated by the Democrats and decided to run as an independent, the party would again face an ignominious defeat. Personalities aside, politics required a *modus vivendi*, and both Hearst and Murphy were practical men.

The first step toward "regularizing" Hearst came in late June, when Murphy met with prominent upstate Democrats concerning the make-up of the state committee and leadership in the fall campaign. Although details of conferences with Erie County leaders Norman Mack and William J. Conners were kept secret, Conners' Buffalo *Daily Courier* reported on June 29 that National Democratic Chairman Mack, an ardent Bryan man, would be recognized as state leader by Murphy. Equally important, the Tammany boss, conditioning himself to Hearst's peculiar appeal,

[25] Syrett, *Autobiography of McClellan*, pp. 284–285.
[26] Hearst's support in Tammany working-class districts is analyzed in Yellowitz, *Labor and the Progressive Movement*, pp. 198–199.

"The Twins of Ooze." In the shadow of his *New York Journal's* anti-
Tammany headlines, William Randolph Hearst seeks the support of Tammany
boss Charles F. Murphy in the 1906 gubernatorial campaign. (From *Harper's
Weekly*, L [1906], 1445; courtesy of the Cornell University Library.)

recognized that "circumstances require the effacement of Tammany influences as well as Wall Street influences from the campaign." [27]

Within one month—and, significantly, less than two weeks
after the Republican Odell-Platt *rapprochement*—Murphy conferred alone with William J. Conners, upstate New York's

[27] Buffalo *Daily Courier*, June 29, 1906.

avowed Hearst supporter. At the conclusion of this meeting, the Tammany leader admitted that Hearst might receive his organization's backing. Conners himself jubilantly strode out of New York's Waldorf-Astoria announcing: "Hearst's nomination is a foregone conclusion." [28] Although he discreetly added that the publisher could win the Democratic nod without Tammany support, it seems fairly clear that an understanding had been reached between Hearst and Murphy through Conners, who, it was assumed, would become chairman of the state committee.[29]

One week later, Murphy attempted to discharge his apparent obligation to Conners, but a stubborn, conservative state committee beat back his efforts.[30] Working together, the Murphy-Conners forces were successful, however, in having Buffalo selected as the site for the fall convention. This triumph, boasted Conners' *Courier*, was a "victory . . . for Buffalo and a victory for the friends of William Randolph Hearst." [31]

Meanwhile, Hearst continued to play the political game that had made him so popular with the electorate and so indispensable to Murphy. He denounced the Democratic machine and vigorously denied having negotiated with Tammany.[32] Yet, at the same time, he sought fervently to persuade his Independence League followers to nominate only a partial state ticket, thus leaving the door open for fusion. Finally, on September 9, two days before the Independence League convention, Hearst publicly confessed his willingness to accept the Democratic nomination if it were offered to him.[33]

Although as a candidate Hearst was obviously flexible in these matters, his followers were not. Consisting mostly of defectors from the traditional parties, they remained unhappy about joining forces with either of them. When, on September 10, William

[28] *Ibid.*, July 25, 1906.
[29] Syrett, *Autobiography of McClellan*, p. 286. It is interesting to note that nothing more was said about Mack's assumption of the state leadership. It appears that he was ignored at the expense of a true enthusiast.
[30] New York *Times*, Aug. 1, 1906.   [31] Aug. 2, 1906.
[32] New York *Times*, Aug. 29, 1906.   [33] *Ibid.*, Sept. 10, 1906.

J. Conners made a personal appearance before the Independence
League convention to plead for fusion, he was received coolly
and without enthusiasm.[34] Two days later a rebellious force of
delegates answered Conners by choosing a complete slate of
candidates and adopting a resolution expressing fear that reform
Democrats might "be unable to overthrow the bosses entrenched in established machines and fortified by the power of
corrupt corporations." [35]

If Hearst could not restrain his organization, Murphy and
Conners had no more success in rallying the Democrats to the
publisher's cause. Indeed, the understanding between Murphy
and Hearst was violently denounced by conservative and independent Democrats alike throughout New York State. As early
as February 1 Thomas Mott Osborne, former reform mayor of
Auburn and avid anti-Tammanyite, sought to find the means not
only to head off the Hearst movement "but to get things into
trim" for the fall campaign.[36] A Cleveland Democrat, Osborne,
since the late 1890's, had attempted sporadically to unite New
York City independents with those from upstate, intent upon reforming and reorganizing the state party. The force and power
of Hearst, whom Osborne had come to know while they were
students together at Harvard, triggered a burst of action on his
part during the spring and summer of 1906. Approximately one
week before the Independence League convention in September,
he sponsored a conference in Albany of some hundred anti-
Hearstites, representing forty-one counties, for the purpose of
consolidating forces against "bossism." [37] This noisy assemblage
enthusiastically proclaimed their opposition "to protectionism,
Socialism and imperialism" and, though refusing to mention the
publisher by name, determined to carry their fight to the Buffalo
convention. Implicit in their resolution was the threat of defec-

---

[34] Buffalo *Daily Courier*, Sept. 11, 1906.   [35] *Ibid.*, Sept. 13, 1906.
[36] Osborne to George F. Peabody, Feb. 1, 1906, Thomas Mott Osborne
Papers (Syracuse University Library).
[37] Rudolph W. Chamberlain, *There Is No Truce: A Life of Thomas
Mott Osborne* (New York: Macmillan, 1935), pp. 148–149.

tion if their warning went unheeded and the Independence League slate was accepted by the Democrats.[38]

Individual Democratic gubernatorial aspirants voiced similar indignation over the so-called corrupt bargain of 1906. In August, William Travers Jerome, New York's fighting district attorney, had dedicated his candidacy "to free the people and parties from the domination of . . . political panhandlers." [39] William Sulzer, New York City congressman, and his loyal followers claimed to be the real spokesman of the working man and could point to support within the Workingmen's Federation to prove it. Such other prominent New York Democrats as George McClellan and Brooklyn leader Patrick McCarren were sympathetic to the anti-Hearst cause.[40]

Throughout the summer of 1906 a substantial segment of the state press abetted the anti-Hearst forces by seizing upon every opportunity, real or imagined, to embarrass Murphy and Hearst. Although the Tammany leader actually consolidated his authority over his organization in the all-important September 18 primaries, his defeat in Kings and Queens enheartened "true" Democrats. What prestige Murphy yet retained was supposedly shattered the next day, when Norman Mack announced his defection to the conservatives.[41] "It looked as if there was nothing to the Hearst movement but W. J. Conners, with Charley Murphy as his unknown quantity," declared the progressive Republican Buffalo *Express* on the very day that the Democrats were scheduled to begin their festivities.[42]

[38] New York *Times*, Sept. 5, 1906; Eleanor M. Piller, "The Hearst-Hughes Gubernatorial Campaign of 1906" (unpublished M.A. thesis, Columbia University, 1937), p. 22.

[39] New York *Times*, Aug. 20 and 22, 1906.

[40] Syrett, *Autobiography of McClellan*, p. 286; Chamberlain, *There Is No Truce*, p. 150; New York *Herald*, Sept. 16, 1906; unidentified newspaper clipping, "William Sulzer Clippings, 1890–1918," William Sulzer Papers (Cornell University Library).

[41] Buffalo *Evening Times*, Sept. 19, 1906; New York *Evening Telegram*, Sept. 19, 1906, "William Sulzer Clippings"; New York *Times*, Sept. 21, 1906.

[42] Buffalo *Morning Express*, Sept. 25, 1906.

Despite indications to the contrary, there was no crack in the Tammany wall. By mid-September the Conners-Murphy forces seemed invincible, and Norman Mack's efforts in preconvention meetings to separate the two leaders were futile. What slight opportunity there was to defeat Hearst on the convention floor was lost when the national chairman failed to organize the conservatives into a solid bloc supporting another candidate.[43]

The Buffalo convention opened on September 25, 1906, the same day on which the Republicans gathered at Saratoga. Its first session was devoted to a brief welcoming speech by Temporary Chairman Lewis Nixon and the appointment of the three important committees—platform, permanent organization, and contested seats. Immediately following the opening ceremonies, the latter group met to begin the task of verifying delegate representations. By midnight the contested anti-Hearst men had been unseated, and Tammany had once again proved its supremacy.[44]

On the evening of September 26 the Democrats assembled in Buffalo's Convention Hall for their second session. Although Hearst's victory was now conceded in most quarters, an imposing array of party stalwarts determined to battle Murphy to the bitter end. Nomination speech after nomination speech, delivered primarily to release pent-up emotions, ripped into the Hearst candidacy and the "corrupt" deal that allegedly imposed it upon the party. The publisher's mediocre record in congress was stressed; his vituperative assaults on Tammany were revealed in order to impugn his sincerity as a Democrat; and his whole brand of politics was labeled "un-American." [45] But when the tumult and shouting were over and the anti-Hearst

[43] *Ibid.*, Sept. 24 and 26, 1906. As late as September 21 Osborne was convinced that Hearst was beaten and still hoped that the anti-Tammany forces would unite on an acceptable candidate (Osborne to Oswald Garrison Villard, Sept. 21, 1906, Oswald Garrison Villard Papers [Harvard University Library]).

[44] New York *Times*, Sept. 26, 1906.

[45] *Ibid.*, Sept. 27, 1906; Buffalo *Morning Express*, Sept. 27, 1906; Chamberlain, *There Is No Truce*, p. 149.

group settled back for the balloting, Hearst scored a sweeping victory. Murphy had been able to put together over three-hundred votes in his favor, obliterating his nearest rival, William Sulzer, by almost two-hundred ballots. Quickly the rest of the ticket was chosen; the Murphy steamroller pushed through two Independence Leaguers, Lewis S. Chanler and John Whalen, for lieutenant-governor and secretary of state respectively. "Regular" Democrats were named for the other offices, and, contrary to earlier threats, Hearst's organization readily assented.[46]

Whatever efforts were made to heal the party wounds inflicted by one of the most bitter conventions in New York's history proved futile as Democrats throughout the state registered their protests against fulfillment of the Hearst-Murphy understanding. Speaking for Sulzer, *Democracy* refused to support the publisher on the ground that he was a maverick.[47] Other anti-Tammanyites like William T. Jerome repudiated his candidacy and joined forces with George McClellan, who sought to establish an organization for Hughes. Still other dissenters, too loyal to party traditions to bolt, satisfied their consciences either by working against Hearst from within the ranks or refusing to work for him at all.[48] During the course of the campaign Thomas Mott Osborne, for example, directed an appeal to independent Democrats everywhere to reject the "organizer of hatred" and restore control of the party to responsible leaders. Only in this way, declared Osborne in his widely publicized open letter, could future travesties of justice be prevented.[49]

The Democratic press, too, showed signs of cracking under the weight of the Hearst candidacy, though less so than muckraking journals had anticipated. A survey conducted in early October by the *Literary Digest* revealed that of eighty-three

---

[46] New York *Times*, Sept. 29, 1906.

[47] Oct. 6, 1906, "William Sulzer Clippings."

[48] New York *Times*, Sept. 27, 28, and 29, 1906; New York *Sun*, Sept. 28, 1906; Syrett, *Autobiography of McClellan*, p. 288.

[49] "An open letter addressed to every Democrat who wishes to act for the best interests of real Democracy," Oct. 27, 1906, Chester C. Platt Papers (Cornell University Library).

Democratic papers canvassed, seventy-one declared for the publisher. Yet a large percentage of the faithful conceded that party commitment and loyalty alone had dictated their position. On the other hand, the dissenters were vehement in their condemnation of both Hearst and the Democrats. "This is a day of political pigmies!" cried the disillusioned Utica *Observer*.[50] "The Democratic party," added the Rochester *Herald*, "delivered by Murphy and his kind as a purchased chattel into the hands of Hearst has . . . no further claim upon [our] support or countenance." [51] Surely, insisted the New York *Sun*, "no party in this State ever nominated for Governor a worse citizen than William R. Hearst." [52]

The earnest hope of conservative Democrats that somehow their candidate would suddenly assume the aura of "dignity" and "respectability" was shattered shortly after the Buffalo convention. On September 28 Hearst met with his Independence League followers in New York City's Madison Square Garden, where he fervently repudiated the main planks of the Democratic platform and reaffirmed his commitment to the September 11 I.L. declarations.[53] Labeling his program "Americanism," he decried extremism, pointed up the distinction between public and private property, and called for governmental ownership of utility systems. Five days later, in a letter to the league, he clarified his stand against the politico-business alliance that had so corrupted New York State and openly accused his opponent of being associated with that system.[54]

Hearst spent virtually his entire campaign endeavoring to convince voters that Charles Evans Hughes was merely a corpo-

[50] *Literary Digest*, XXXIII (1906), 491.

[51] Sept. 27, 1906.   [52] Sept. 29, 1906.

[53] The Buffalo platform, drawn up largely by conservative Democrats under the leadership of Bourke Cockran, declared unequivocally against governmental ownership of public utilities, although it recognized the need for governmental regulation. The Independence League convention, on the other hand, had adopted as its main plank the public ownership principle (James McGurrin, *Bourke Cockran: A Free Lance in American Politics* [New York: Scribner, 1948], p. 268).

[54] New York *Times*, Sept. 29 and Oct. 4, 1906.

ration lawyer who had soft-pedaled his public investigations. His lieutenants, too, exploited this line of attack and employed their journalistic talents against Hughes's "corporationism." Writing for the *Independent*, Arthur Brisbane, editor of the New York *Journal*, conceded the Republican's ability as a lawyer but insisted that his activities had been improperly channelled. This campaign, concluded Brisbane, could be reduced to a choice between a candidate of the "trusts" and a candidate of the people.[55]

Needless to say, Hughes's anger was aroused by the opposition's efforts to impugn the respectability of his candidacy. From the very beginning, the insurance counsel deemed his entry into politics a matter of public duty. During the campaign he thus sought to counter the Hearst charges with the pious importunity that, in Roosevelt's words, he was fighting "the battle of civilization."[56] Hughes labored throughout to translate his efforts into a moral crusade, devoid of demagoguery and obvious political ambition.

Once he thawed the icicles that apparently stiffened his initial speechmaking, candidate Hughes met squarely the issues Hearst presented. He concentrated on the controversial corporation question and forthrightly championed the Roosevelt theory of regulation, a theory basic to his own gas and electric commission bill of 1905.[57] In Brooklyn, on October 6, Hughes offered a defense of the corporation in terms of its contribution to American economic development. The chief difficulty, he insisted, was not that the corporation *per se* was bad, but that in so many enter-

[55] "William Randolph Hearst," *Independent*, LXI (1906), 785–787; Piller, "Hearst-Hughes Gubernatorial Campaign," p. 32.

[56] Roosevelt to Hughes, Oct. 5, 1906, *LTR*, V, 443–444.

[57] Early in the campaign the President reviewed for Hughes their common approach to problems as "moderates." Writing to contrast their methods with Hearst's, he said: "You believe in reforming the relations between the Government and the great corporations as drastically as is necessary to meet the needs of the situation, but you believe in having it done in a spirit of sanity and justice" (Roosevelt to Hughes, Oct. 5, 1906, *ibid.*, pp. 443–444).

prises there was an "evasion of responsibility." [58] In other speeches he made it clear that the institution was basically sound but that the men running it were often corrupt. In Glens Falls, on October 18, he added to this moderate stand the regulatory doctrine: "I believe there should be effective governmental control of all great enterprises in which the public is interested and which depend upon the public for their right to be and to do." Specifically, he proposed necessary changes in governmental machinery "to carry out the intent of the law and to see to it that companies live up to their charter obligations and perform the functions which they are intended to perform." [59] In this way Hughes hoped to make public service corporations more responsible to the citizenry without resort to municipal or state ownership.

Hughes, however, had to do much more than meet Hearst's challenge on public ownership with his own theory of regulation, especially in light of the violent Democratic attacks on special privilege. [60] If, indeed, he wished to wage a successful campaign, he faced the unpleasant task of assailing his opponent's sincerity as a critic of corporate abuses. Hughes's strategy was to show that as a public investigator, he, not Hearst, had gained wide experience in dealing with the intricate corporation problem.

The official opening of the Republican campaign took place on October 5 in New York's Carnegie Hall. Here Charles Evans

[58] New York *Times*, Oct. 7, 1906.

[59] *Ibid.*, Oct. 19, 22, and 23, 1906; "Corporations and Democracy" (editorial), *Outlook*, LXXXIV (1906), 354–356.

[60] So violently did Hearst condemn corporations during the campaign (and by corporations he meant special privilege) that his appeal boiled down to a reversion to a simpler economic order in which ideally there would be no special privilege. Hughes, on the other hand, accepted "bigness" and sought to prescribe rules and regulations by which large business units could be supervised. This difference, some argued, clearly associated Hughes with Roosevelt and Hearst with western radicalism epitomized by William Jennings Bryan ("Corporations and Democracy"; Charles Johnston, "Charles Evans Hughes and the Contest in New York State," *North American Review*, CLXXXIII [1906], 897–905; New York *Times*, Oct. 8 and Nov. 4, 1906).

Hughes addressed himself primarily to general issues. In the course of his remarks, however, he scored irresponsible journalism as "a most dangerous enemy of the state." [61] Obviously referring to Hearst, whose name he never mentioned, Hughes demanded "a serious and determined attempt to ascertain the [corporation] evil and to remedy it." Next day, he shifted to an analysis of the publisher's sincerity in attacking Republican progressivism and laid the groundwork for his first swing through upstate New York. Then in Yonkers, Mount Vernon, Lyons, and Buffalo, Hughes unmercifully attacked Hearst's own corporation activities citing, in particular, his opponent's *Morning Journal* Association.[62]

So effective was this segment of the Republican campaign that Hughes's backers were jubilant. Shortly after the speechmaking began, State Chairman Timothy L. Woodruff enthusiastically reported to Roosevelt that their inexperienced candidate had proved himself to be an excellent campaigner. Much later Herbert Parsons admitted that, although his appeals needed broadening, Hughes had exposed Hearst as a "fakir." Joining the chorus of approval were Charles Sprague Smith, president of New York City's People's Institute, and progressive Republican George B. Agnew.[63] The pro-Hughes press, too, moved along with the momentum that the GOP campaign had quickly gathered. Gotham journals—especially the *Times*, the *Press*, the *Herald*, the *Evening Post*, and the *World*—carried editorial after editorial castigating Hearst and endorsing Hughes's biting attacks.

Although the Republican campaign progressed smoothly, particularly in its early stages, there were perplexing problems that demanded solution. In having President Roosevelt as its overseer,

[61] New York *Times*, Oct. 6, 1906.

[62] New York *World*, Oct. 9 and 10, 1906; Buffalo *Morning Express*, Oct. 11, 1906.

[63] Woodruff to Roosevelt, Oct. 8, 1906; Parsons to Henry L. Stimson, Oct. 20, 1906; and Smith to Roosevelt, Oct. 29, 1906, Theodore Roosevelt Papers (Manuscript Division, Library of Congress). See also note in George B. Agnew Papers (NYPL), Oct. 27, 1906.

however, the New York organization could meet those problems with a minimum of factionalism. The President, as party leader, had dedicated himself to defeating Hearst, and he would permit no pettiness to interfere with the achievement of that objective. Thus he remained available for consultation, and he served as intermediary between Hughes and the state organization. Roosevelt's influence undoubtedly went a long way toward keeping the Republican ship at even keel in the stormy 1906 campaign. This was one great advantage the GOP had over the Democracy.

Just one week after Hughes's nomination, the President's ability as conciliator was put to the test. At this time Herbert Parsons complained bitterly to Roosevelt that the New York City judiciary candidates imposed upon the Republican party were unacceptable to him and his workers. The ticket had been selected on a nonpartisan basis by a group of prominent lawyers, among them Joseph Hodges Choate, Henry W. Taft, and Hughes himself. The chief objections were that of the thirteen nominees only four were actually Republicans and the slate was overloaded with Catholics. Parsons was equally disturbed by a circular letter that the nominating group issued along with the announcement of their decision. In charging that active politicians were not qualified for the bench, it offended his political dignity. Previously, the county chairman had admonished these "independents" not to be provincial but to recognize conditions; now, he suggested to Roosevelt, "we ought to make sufficient changes to teach a lesson for the future." [64]

The President sympathized wholeheartedly with Parsons' objections, labeled the nominators "amateur politicians," and advised the party to follow their prescriptions only in a general way.[65] In the meantime, he had discreetly put the matter to Hughes, one of those "amateur politicians," and urged the candidate to talk with the county chairman. Hughes was not

[64] Parsons to Roosevelt, Oct. 3, 1906, Roosevelt Papers.

[65] Roosevelt to Parsons, Oct. 8, 1906, Herbert Parsons Papers (Columbia University Library)

offended by the President's tactful appeal, and, although his reply was defensive, he suggested that Otto Rosalsky, a prominent Jewish jurist and a regular, be named to the ticket.[66] He took this opportunity, however, to remind Roosevelt that the nomination of a partisan slate was tantamount to inviting defeat, for partisan Republican candidates could not win in New York County. Parsons himself ultimately came around to the Hughes position and, soon after his initial outburst to Roosevelt, wrote soothingly that "we thought it best not to make any [other] changes in the ticket." [67]

A more perplexing problem for the Republicans in the 1906 campaign was that of appealing to the workingman of New York State. From the beginning, Hearst relied on the support of organized labor in his drive for the governorship. Based partly on the success of his long newspaper crusade for the worker's confidence, partly on his political achievements through 1905, and partly on commitments made to him by the Central Federated Union of New York City, he anticipated a campaign which would organize under his banner the working class across the state. Early in the summer the C.F.U. established the Independent Labor Party, one of the many efforts undertaken in these years to mobilize the disparate political tendencies of the trade union movement.[68] The plan was that the I.L.P. would share the major portion of a statewide ticket with Hearst, whose name would appear at the head of it. When, however, the unpredictable publisher made his peace with Tammany Hall, at least long enough to win the Democratic nomination, the labor alliance collapsed, for the C.F.U. had little more use for Tammany than for the GOP. Still, Hearst, it was generally believed, had great appeal for the rank and file of organized labor throughout New York State.

This fact Theodore Roosevelt fully appreciated early in the

[66] Roosevelt to Hughes, Oct. 5, 1906, *LTR*, V, 443–444; Hughes to Roosevelt, Oct. 7, 1906, Charles Evans Hughes Papers (Manuscript Division, Library of Congress).

[67] Parsons to Roosevelt, Oct. 11, 1906, Roosevelt Papers.

[68] Yellowitz, *Labor and the Progressive Movement*, pp. 203–208.

campaign. Acknowledging the Hearst efforts at attracting non-propertied elements to his candidacy, he complained to his friend Henry Cabot Lodge of the growing "radicalism" and "socialism" among workmen.[69] He feared that Hughes might not cut into this vote substantially enough to score a victory in November unless some direct appeals were made to labor leaders. Hughes was immediately apprised of the situation and, through his New York City chiefs, Parsons and Woodruff, determined to solve the problem.[70] Several days later Woodruff reported that a group of key labor spokesmen were engaged in organizing a league for the Republican ticket. On October 16 the Workingmen's Political League of the State of New York, composed of disgruntled officials of the C.F.U., the State Bricklayers' Union, and the New York City Typographical Union, took the field against Hearst, whom they peremptorily dismissed as a "fakir and a demagogue." [71] They were joined later in the campaign by various other New York City unions disillusioned by the vagaries of the Hearst candidacy.[72]

Still not satisfied with Woodruff's promise of some labor support, Hughes determined to devote several of his key speeches to issues which appealed to the rank-and-file workers. In Buffalo, on October 10, he took a sympathetic attitude toward labor's right to organize. He advocated the eight-hour day for public construction work, called for legislation regulating child labor and improving the state employers' liability system, and demanded that the state labor department itself be reorganized. Three days later in Little Falls he reiterated his Buffalo declarations but was careful to point out that he did "not believe in leg-

[69] Oct. 2, 1906, *LTR*, V, 439–440. See also Roosevelt to Lodge, Oct. 1, 1906, *ibid.*, pp. 436–437.

[70] Roosevelt to Hughes, Oct. 2, 1906, *ibid.*, pp. 438–439; Hughes to Roosevelt, Oct. 4, 1906, Hughes Papers.

[71] New York *Times*, Oct. 17, 1906; Woodruff to Roosevelt, Oct. 10, 1906, Roosevelt Papers.

[72] Yet Hearst seems to have maintained his grip on the labor leaders throughout New York State (Yellowitz, *Labor and the Progressive Movement*, p. 209).

islating for classes . . . and in talking about working classes or
any other classes." [73]

Despite these efforts, the labor question plagued the Republican managers throughout the campaign. A constant source of
concern was the fact that in upstate urban areas Hearst's audi-
ences were nearly always larger than Hughes's. National Com-
mitteeman William L. Ward was so worried about this state of
affairs that he suggested that President Roosevelt make a direct
appeal to the workingmen of America so there would be no
question of Washington's enthusiasm for the New York ticket.[74] Even the usually unruffled Hughes was "somewhat disturbed by the newspaper reports of the Hearst meetings" and
feared "the great silent vote of the working-men." [75] Yet
after three weeks of campaigning he could at least say confidently that the great mass of voters who had originally been inclined toward Hearst were wavering. The question was, asked
Hughes: "Can they trust *me?*"

Broadly speaking, Hughes's significant query referred not
only to labor but to that massive, fluid element of the voting
population known as the independents. From the outset, Republican leaders had been aware that victory depended upon
Hughes's success in attracting independents as well as disgruntled Democrats. So, on October 2, when Hughes boldly announced that the campaign would be "fought out on State
issues," he indicated what he considered the necessary course of
action.[76] This strategy would preclude undue reference to the
Roosevelt administration, lest national partisanship determine the

[73] Buffalo *Morning Express*, Oct. 11, 1906; New York *Times*, Oct. 14,
1906.

[74] Ward to Roosevelt, Oct. 19, 1906, Roosevelt Papers; also Gherardi
Davis to Roosevelt, Oct. 27, 1906, Gherardi Davis Papers (NYPL).

[75] Hughes to Roosevelt, Oct. 21, 1906, Roosevelt Papers. Thomas Mott
Osborne, too, was disturbed (Osborne to Oswald Garrison Villard, Oct.
3, 1906, Villard Papers).

[76] New York *Times*, Oct. 3, 1906; Roosevelt to James S. Sherman,
Oct. 3, 1906, and to Timothy L. Woodruff, Oct. 11, 1906, *LTR*, V, 441–
442, 454–455; Roosevelt to Hughes, Oct. 12, 1906, Hughes Papers.

November voting pattern. It required also that no national leaders be brought into the state during the foray.

Approximately one week before the Saratoga convention, President Roosevelt had invited Secretary of State Elihu Root to speak in New York State prior to election day. After Hughes's announcement, Roosevelt naturally backtracked, but, strangely enough, Herbert Parsons renewed the offer and Root prepared for an engagement in New York City later that month.[77] In addition, Speaker Joseph Cannon, the focal point of House conservatism, had been asked by James Sherman to aid those faltering regulars running for local and national offices in the state. Again Roosevelt's steady hand was required to palliate the differences within Republican ranks in New York.

As the time for Cannon's appearance drew near, the President was besieged with letters advising him against permitting the national leaders to carry out their plans. State Chairman Woodruff, in full sympathy with Hughes's strategy, insisted that although it was too late to cancel Cannon's October 19 meeting, Roosevelt should prevent "Uncle Joe" from stressing the delicate labor issue. Hoping to attract Democratic support for the state ticket, Woodruff suggested that Root's engagement be cancelled. It would be dangerous, declared the state chairman, to have Hughes's campaign overshadowed for even a day.[78]

Under the circumstances, Roosevelt's only alternative was to seek out Hughes and the rest of the state leaders and put the issue squarely to them. Although he fully appreciated Woodruff's arguments, he had received appeals from others to the effect that orthodox Republican interest in New York had to be maintained at all costs. Speeches by Cannon and Root could most certainly achieve this objective, they had argued. The President himself would make no decision on the question of interference. Instead, he urged that Sherman, Woodruff, and Parsons join Hughes in reaching a solution. He requested them also to consider the wisdom of making the national administration's

[77] Philip C. Jessup, *Elihu Root* (New York: Dodd, Mead, 1938), II, 113.
[78] Woodruff to Roosevelt, Oct. 13, 1906, Roosevelt Papers.

record an issue in the campaign. He cared not what course they took so long as they kept in mind the primary goal of the state campaign—Hughes's election. "If we carry Hughes," he adjudged, "it is my triumph, because it is the triumph of all of us, and if we lose him, then it is a defeat for all of us." [79]

The New Yorkers complied with Roosevelt's wishes. Immediately, Parsons met with Woodruff, J. Van Vechten Olcott, and William S. Bennet. They conferred with Sherman by telephone and then visited Hughes. Rather disappointingly, wrote Parsons in a letter to the President, Hughes again declared "against any outsiders" and failed to appreciate "that it was not possible to get local speakers who would attract people to a large meeting." [80] Parsons personally adjudged the campaign against Hearst to be ineffective, requiring, he thought, some outside help. He and his cohorts agreed that Cannon should deal with general issues only, perhaps focusing on Hearst's inadequate congressional record. Parsons then joined the others in advising cancellation of Root's New York City engagement, for the secretary's corporate connections might prove embarrassing to Hughes. They cared less about his appearance in Utica, where he could limit himself to Sherman's congressional candidacy, but they feared that even here he might prove a handicap to the state campaign.

Root's plans were altered accordingly, and Cannon followed the course prescribed for him. So unsuccessful was his October 19 address and so dismayed was he at the overall New York picture, however, that Parsons and Woodruff were shaken. They now pleaded with the President to make a personal appeal in behalf of the state ticket. "If Hughes were purely our own candidate," declared Parsons, obviously referring to himself and Roosevelt, "they [Woodruff and Ward] would think differently about it. They consider him, however, *their* candidate, so want anyone who can help him." [81]

[79] Roosevelt to Woodruff, Parsons, and Sherman, Oct. 14, 1906, *LTR*, V, 456–458.

[80] Oct. 15, 1906, Roosevelt Papers.

[81] Parsons to Roosevelt, Oct. 22, 1906, Parsons Papers.

If the state leaders were not aware of their inconsistency, Theodore Roosevelt was. He spurned any direct interference in New York and even ruled out the possibility of a letter expressing his deep commitment to Hughes. The only concession he would make was to have Root change the nature of his November 1 address in Utica in order to emphasize state issues.[82] Writing several years later, Root himself recaptured the desperate plight of the New York leaders: "When the time came, the situation got so bad I decided instead of talking about Jim, I'd talk about the Governorship."[83]

Elihu Root's appearance in Utica, though melodramatic, underscored the moderate tone of Charles Evans Hughes's 1906 campaign. Although Hughes had never encouraged federal intervention, there is little evidence to show that he was irked over Roosevelt's decision to compromise. More likely, some of the organizational gloom wore off on him, and he simply welcomed the outside help. At any rate, he willingly joined the Secretary of State in Utica on November 1.

Before his arrival in Sherman's bailiwick, Root had turned his speech over to the Associated Press so that it would not miss the morning papers. By the time the Republican entourage had crept through the heart of Utica to the public meeting place, Hearst's New York *Journal*, carrying the publisher's answer, was being distributed throughout the city. Appearing on this edition's front page was a cartoon of "Root the Rat" gnawing at the defenses of the people. Irate Republican workers invaded city newsstands, buying up as many copies as they could get hold of, intent on destroying all of them.

At the meeting itself, Hughes and Root were greeted by a wild, tumultuous throng. Planted among Republican faithfuls, however, were paid representatives of Tammany Hall, whose function it was to break up the gathering. They interrupted Root's fighting speech from time to time with shouts and heck-

---

[82] Roosevelt to Parsons, Oct. 24 and 27, 1906, *LTR*, V, 466–467, 483–484.

[83] Root to Philip C. Jessup, Sept. 15, 1930, quoted in Jessup, *Elihu Root*, II, 116.

ling, but their most concerted efforts were drowned out in a wave of Republican enthusiasm. The secretary's own good humor prevented at least one act of physical violence. When he reached a section of his speech denouncing Hearst, a Tammany man ill-advisedly cried out, "It's a lie!" to which a loyal Republican replied, "Throw him out!" Root glanced up from his notes and quietly quipped, "No, let him stay and learn!" [84]

So forcefully did Root combine issue and personality in this brilliant speech that Philip Jessup has judged it "the most effective campaign speech which Root ever delivered." The secretary pulled no punches in pinning the demagogic label on Hearst. He accused the publisher of hypocrisy in posing as a friend of the workingman while accumulating great wealth for himself through corporate juggling, and in viciously condemning Murphy and Tammany Hall, then forming an alliance with "bossism." Root reviewed Hearst's mediocre record in congress and he openly castigated his yellow journalism, quoting freely from the newspapers themselves. The secretary finally moved into Roosevelt's denunciation of the Democratic candidate, presumably in answer to those who assumed the President's silence could be interpreted as evidence of indifference toward Hughes. At the time of McKinley's death, said Root, the new president had accused Hearst of appealing "to the dark and evil spirits of malice and greed, envy and sullen hatred." Now, with Roosevelt's approval, Root added dramatically: "I say . . . that what he thought of Mr. Hearst then he thinks of Mr. Hearst now." [85]

Just as Root echoed Hughes's personal charges against Hearst, so he presented the key campaign issues. "Corporations are not bad in themselves," the secretary declared, "but the managers of some of them and of many of the greatest ones have used them as opportunities for wrongdoing." [86] President Roosevelt, he added, had devised the policy of minimizing evil practices through the agency of the national government, and Governor Hughes would do likewise on the state level. The election of

[84] Elihu Root, Jr., to Jessup, April 11, 1934, and Richard S. Sherman to Jessup, April 10, 1933, quoted in *ibid.*, p. 117.
[85] *Ibid.*, p. 120.   [86] *Ibid.*, p. 118.

Hughes, Root insisted, was akin to an endorsement of the Roosevelt administration and its policies.

Although the Republican campaign was carried to the eve of the election (November 5), events that followed the Utica speech seemed anticlimactic, at least for the national and state leaders. Roosevelt was pleased beyond words with the political bombshell his spokesman had dropped in Hearst's lap. William Howard Taft labeled it a "great speech," and State Chairman Woodruff was so impressed that he immediately had thousands of copies printed on pamphlets, post cards, and posters to be distributed throughout the state before election day.[87]

As the long, hard-fought campaign drew to a close, political observers made the usual predictions ranging from a Hearst victory by several hundred thousand to a Hughes triumph by the same margin. Although Wall Street gave the Republicans five-to-one betting odds, the *Literary Digest*, after canvassing the "experts," could come up with no forecast. They were content to quote Lindsay Denison, who had observed perceptively that the "straws which show the way the wind blows are whirling in a cyclone of gutter-dust, and either side may, in good faith, read victory in them." [88]

On November 6, 1906, one and one-half million New Yorkers went to the polls and elected Charles Evans Hughes governor by a plurality of slightly under 76,000 votes. Significantly, every other candidate on the state Republican ticket was defeated, Hughes ran well ahead of his more "regular" colleagues, and Hearst substantially behind his fellow-candidates.

An analysis of the election returns indicates that Hughes won every upstate county (as expected) but one and cut substantially into heavily Democratic New York City districts.[89] In

[87] *Ibid.*, pp. 121–122; Taft to Roosevelt, Nov. 4, 1906, William Howard Taft Papers (Manuscript Division, Library of Congress); Woodruff to Root, Nov. 1, 1906, Elihu Root Papers (Manuscript Division, Library of Congress).

[88] XXXIII (1906), 623; New York *Times,* Nov. 4, 1906.

[89] Hughes, of course, lost New York City, but by only about 70,000 votes. These figures and calculations are based upon official election re-

Kings County, for example, the Republican standard-bearer ran almost 17,000 votes ahead of his own lieutenant-governor candidate, M. Linn Bruce, and in New York County he received over 14,000 more votes than Bruce. At the same time, Hearst fell behind his running mate, Lewis S. Chanler, by nearly 27,000 votes in these two counties. Since each gubernatorial candidate ran generally as strong (or as weak) as the rest of his ticket in the upstate areas, New York City—and Kings and New York Counties, in particular—accounted for the difference.[90] If Hearst had been as popular in the City as were his colleagues, he would have emerged victorious.

Although it is difficult to single out a specific factor explaining Hughes's success in New York City, one is tempted to suggest that the Republican managers had achieved their objective of appealing to the independent and independent-Democratic voters who undoubtedly had been aroused by the 1905 gas and insurance revelations and who may have followed the lead of Osborne, McClellan, and Jerome. Woodruff and Roosevelt, both schooled in the old Platt organization, had been particularly sensitive to this need, and their decision to "Republicanize" the campaign near its end came only after the gloomy and foreboding reports of "Uncle Joe" Cannon. In writing of the New York experience, the President himself gloated at having "ridden ironshod over Gompers and the labor agitators" and, at the same time, at watching the financiers stand "aloof" or give "furtive aid to the enemy." [91]

Unlike Hearst, whose demagoguery imparted a negative quality to his candidacy, Hughes had geared his entire campaign to

---

turns published in Edgar L. Murlin, *New York Red Book: An Illustrated Legislative Manual, 1907* (Albany: J. B. Lyon, 1907), pp. 615–616.

[90] It is true that Hearst did better in upstate cities like Buffalo, Rochester, Syracuse, and Troy than other Democratic gubernatorial candidates in recent years, but his gain in the working-class vote was evidently made up in his apparent loss of independent and independent Democratic votes. For Hearst's strength in the cities, see Yellowitz, *Labor and the Progressive Movement*, pp. 213–214.

[91] Roosevelt to Alice Roosevelt Longworth, Nov. 7, 1906, *LTR*, V, 488–489.

the "safe" and "sane." At every opportunity, he played down the publisher's appeal to the "have-nots"; his corporation stand was the essence of moderation. Hughes's promise of radical moral reform in the conduct of business and government, combined with assurances of moderation in economic change, concludes one observer, "struck the proper note, and he was elected by an eruption of respectability." [92] He had projected exactly the image he wished to project.

Equally important in accounting for the Republican victory was the fact that not only had Hearst been unsuccessful in holding moderate Democrats like Thomas Mott Osborne in line, but he had also experienced bad relations with New York City leaders. Murphy had apparently never forgiven him for his 1905 apostasy and had dictated the Buffalo nomination only in the face of political exigency. During the campaign, Hearst had indiscreetly continued his attacks upon Tammany and threatened an open break on the issue of City judiciary candidates. Although this matter was ultimately resolved, the wound was not healed. Murphy never warmed to his candidate and near election day conceded publicly that he did not "like Mr. Hearst any more than Mr. Hearst likes me." [93]

Nor were Hearst's relations with Kings County leader Pat McCarren any better. Early in the campaign, McCarren had admonished the Independence League with regard to certain practices it had followed in other counties. Recklessly, Hearst had dismissed the warning with the accusation that its author was simply a "hired agent of the corporations." The result was that, although the Brooklyn Democratic Club did endorse the Hearst candidacy, McCarren later appealed to his own organization to repudiate him. [94]

[92] Frank E. Kilroe, "The Governorship of Charles Evans Hughes: A Study in Reform (1906–1910)" (unpublished M.A. Thesis, Columbia University, 1934), p. 24.

[93] New York *Times*, Nov. 2 and Oct. 11, 1906. From Ireland came severe criticism of the Hearst candidacy by former Tammany boss Richard Croker (*Outlook*, LXXXIV [1906], 590).

[94] New York *Times*, Oct. 5 and 17, 1906; Gherardi Davis to Roosevelt, Oct. 27, 1906, Davis Papers.

The bitterness which New York City Democrats displayed toward their candidate formed a sharp contrast to the cooperative attitude Parsons and Woodruff assumed toward Hughes. Their diligent work in the campaign underscores one advantage the Republicans possessed from the very beginning. When key decisions had to be made, they could rely upon a respected, powerful national leader who, in essence, controlled the state organization. So influential was Roosevelt that he could even pass on to others his spirited dedication to Hughes and make them forget, at least for the time being, that the ticket was headed by a political novice.[95] How deepseated that dedication became only time would tell. At any rate, the ranks had closed long enough to elect a governor, and the Roosevelt-Hughes team had given the GOP in New York a new lease on life.

[95] Woodruff could write enthusiastically to George Agnew: "This is without doubt the most important State election in the history of the Republican Party" (Oct. 25, 1906, Agnew Papers).

CHAPTER V

The First Skirmish

Preparation for the Governorship

ALTHOUGH New York Republicans had elected a governor
and a friendly legislature, they could hardly exult over the November, 1906, election results. The balance of their state ticket
had gone down to a humiliating defeat, giving the Democracy,
under the firm control of Tammany Hall, a substantial portion
of the New York patronage for the next two years. Moreover,
GOP majorities in both the senate and assembly had been reduced. Finally, to most of the Republican state and legislative
leaders, their new chief executive remained an unknown quantity.

Rarely expansive in his feelings, Governor-elect Charles
Evans Hughes regarded his narrow victory rather philosophi-
cally: "My feelings," he said, "are not those of elation, but those
of responsibility." [1] If on the day after the election Hughes had
scanned the New York City newspapers, he would have found
that, on the whole, they expressed disappointment over his negli-
gible plurality.[2] Summarizing this attitude, the friendly *World*
concluded that Hearst's good showing was "morally a Republican defeat, a popular repudiation of the corrupt Republican machine and its alliance with corrupt corporations." [3]

[1] New York *Times*, Nov. 7, 1906.

[2] *Literary Digest*, XXXIII (1906), 661–662; Oswald Garrison Villard,
Fighting Years: Memoirs of a Liberal Editor (New York: Harcourt,
Brace, 1939), p. 185.

[3] New York *World*, Nov. 7, 1906.

Others joined the chorus of appeals for a leadership free from organization control. One writer later even went so far as to insist that the New York electorate expected "Mr. Hughes to do what a Democratic Governor would have done." [4]

If Hughes needed additional encouragement, he received it immediately from President Roosevelt, the man chiefly responsible for converting his 1905 popular image into solid political reality within one year. Roosevelt, of course, had for some time harbored reservations regarding the manner in which the powers of the New York governorship had been exercised. "You will cut out relentlessly and without regard to consequences everything evil, paying no heed whatever to the influence or opposition of any man who may be affected thereby," he exhorted Hughes.[5] Not only must the new governor eliminate all graft, added the President, but "mismanagement and inefficiency shall be treated with but little more leniency." Roosevelt concluded his advice enthusiastically: "I feel that you and I, my dear Mr. Hughes, approach our work in the same spirit."

The independence that, in terms of his background and inclination, typified Hughes's attitude toward politics and political organization was now being encouraged by both press and President. Behind Roosevelt's exhortation lay the basic philosophy of Rooseveltian reform. Somehow the Republican party must adjust to changing times. The moral precepts of American civilization, now clearly audible in the voice of protest, must be reinstated as the sole impulse to political action, thus terminating the evil politico-business alliance especially evident on the state and local levels. It was the function of the enlightened statesman—a Hughes, for example—to educate others in this crusade for clean, honest government, so essential to the success of the democratic experiment. As governor of New York, Roosevelt himself had fully embodied this spirit in his efforts to bring in-

[4] Augustus C. Ragsdale, "New York's New Governor," *Eclectic Magazine*, CXLVIII (1907), 86. Even James Wadsworth, Jr., ascribed Hughes's victory to Democratic votes (Wadsworth to George B. Agnew, Nov. 13, 1906, George B. Agnew Papers [NYPL]).

[5] Roosevelt to Hughes, Nov. 7, 1906, *LTR*, V, 490–491.

tegrity into state politics and to subordinate partisan and local interests to the general welfare. He saw that Hughes had an even greater opportunity, since the old system with which Roosevelt had had to contend was torn asunder in 1905 and 1906 and, what is equally important, since he, as president, would stand behind the new state administration. Inexperienced though he was, Hughes enjoyed advantages Roosevelt had not possessed eight years earlier. If Odell and Higgins had been sorely disappointing as Roosevelt's gubernatorial successors in New York, Charles Evans Hughes offered real promise as a political progressive—at least to the President's way of thinking.

The Governor-elect responded to the challenge. He chose the occasion of a Republican Club dinner, held in New York City's Waldorf-Astoria approximately two weeks after the election, to inform key members of his own party where he stood in regard to the organization and organizational politics: "I shall be my own spokesman," he declared. "Pleasant as have been the intimate relations which I have sustained with many of you, and desirous as I am at all times to have the full benefit of your friendship, it is proper and necessary that I should reserve for myself the privilege and the duty of stating my personal views." [6] Then for the benefit of Odell, Platt, Aldridge, Barnes, Wadsworth, and a host of other party leaders, Hughes reviewed the Republican plight in New York. He was determined to appeal to independents and disgruntled Democrats in converting his campaign promises into legislative actions. His remarks, indeed, revealed the same spirit of nonpartisanship that permeated the New York City good-government clubs in the 1890's. At this incipient stage of his long political career, Hughes regarded the reform impulse as a citizen's movement to restore honesty and decency in public life. "Public service is the best politics," he declared, adding that his appointees must give "satisfactory assurances of complete devotion to the public interest."

From the outset, the new governor made it clear that he would temper his independence with moderation in his overall

[6] New York *Times*, Nov. 24, 1906.

approach to politics and the problems of New York State. He grasped the role he was to play, and he determined to play it according to a new set of rules. He would listen to party advice, but, in the final analysis, he would make executive decisions himself.[7] In this vein, Hughes accepted Timothy Woodruff's invitation, shortly after election day, to vacation in the state chairman's Adirondack retreat. Likewise, he appealed to Herbert Parsons for "intelligent advice and effective support." After all, he assured Parsons, "you will never wait for an invitation from me to tell me what I ought to know and to aid me with your counsel."[8]

Only to the outspoken and tactless William Barnes did Hughes find it necessary to reiterate his November 23 declarations. Brilliant and Harvard-educated, this grandson of Thurlow Weed epitomized upstate conservatism with its narrow, limited outlook and during the reform period remained its most articulate defender. By virtue of hard work, organizational talent, and his own newspaper (the Albany *Evening Journal*), Barnes had built for himself a county machine second to none in efficiency and loyalty. His was a virtual feudal barony amidst the crumbling state structure of 1905 and 1906. He had, of course, joined Roosevelt and his followers in their sustained drive against Odell, not because Odell had failed to convert the anti-Platt movement into reform, but because Odell had become a divisive influence in GOP affairs. And as a practical politician and a rabid partisan, Barnes intensely disliked intraparty squabbling. It was for this reason that he reacted to the new governor's remarks with alacrity and dismay. In reminding Hughes that the state organization had to be put in "fighting trim" for the 1908 elections, Barnes warned against a reform program for New York, lest factionalism split the party. Hughes's reply was crisp

[7] Robert H. Fuller, "Comment on Hughes as Governor" (unpublished MS), Charles Evans Hughes Papers (Manuscript Division, Library of Congress), p. 2.

[8] Hughes to Parsons, Nov. 17, 1906, Herbert Parsons Papers (Columbia University Library); Henry C. Beerits, "Entry into Politics and Election as Governor," pp. 16–17, in "Memorandum," Hughes Papers.

and to the point. He argued that harmony was not the issue of the day. The Republicans, he explained, must be concerned with "harmonious action in an endeavor to interpret and to meet public sentiment in a just manner." Taking the "long view," he asserted that what might at first appear to be of partisan advantage might ultimately prove to be of no value. "The capacity of a party to take a disinterested view," he added, "will itself aid in commanding popular approval." Failure to enact a specific reform program might have no bearing upon the honesty or dishonesty of an administration, Hughes admitted in conclusion, but it would have a pronounced effect upon public opinion.[9] This exchange revealed the basic differences between the independent reformer and the partisan politician, the neophyte and the professional, the "new" leader and the "old" boss.

The Governor-elect's relations with New York Republicans remained cordial well into December, despite the strained correspondence with Barnes and sporadic, ill-advised efforts on the part of the muckraking press to sensationalize a potential clash in the state. Hughes, the amateur, turned first to Herbert Parsons, progressive leader of New York County, for specific advice on a wide array of matters.[10] By the same token, Parsons felt free to pen requests of Hughes when the occasion demanded. On November 20, he inquired in behalf of General Nelson H. Henry, candidate for New York's adjutant-generalship. As inauguration day approached, the two men met and corresponded concerning the Governor's first legislative message. Parsons made various suggestions that had been approved by Theodore Roosevelt, and Hughes seriously considered them, replying warmly: "I was glad to know the President's view and I hope he will have no reluctance in giving me the benefit of his advice at any time."[11]

Yet, as Hughes had intimated earlier, he never once intended to leave the impression that his willingness to cooperate meant

[9] Hughes to Barnes, Dec. 3, 1906, and Barnes to Hughes, Nov. 26, 1906, Hughes Papers.

[10] Hughes to Parsons, Nov. 30 and Dec. 3, 1906, Parsons Papers.

[11] Hughes to Parsons, Dec. 27, 1906, and Parsons to Hughes, Nov. 20 and Dec. 26, 1906, *ibid.*

that he would follow blindly all the advice tendered him. On this matter, he seemed to be hypersensitive. When Parsons suggested on one occasion that he travel to Washington for Roosevelt's advice on the annual message, Hughes replied candidly: "I'll gladly talk with him about the points to be dealt with in the message; but the people of this State elected me to be Governor of New York and not an agent by which they might be governed from Washington." [12]

In December, the President invited the Governor-elect to the White House for a dinner held primarily for the purpose of introducing Hughes to Taft, Lodge, Cannon, Sherman, and other members of the national Republican high command. At the conclusion of the festivities, Roosevelt and his New York colleague adjourned to the President's quarters, where for well over an hour they amiably discussed state politics. Hughes freely outlined his program to the interested Roosevelt, who apparently endorsed the main principles. "Roosevelt was cordiality itself," wrote Henry Beerits years later, "and a close relationship had been established between them." [13] Still, the new governor felt constrained at the time to remain silent about the political significance of the White House gathering. It was of paramount importance for him, in keeping with his stated position, to maintain an air of independence, even aloofness, from the President of the United States as well as from local and state leaders. Feelings ran high about a possible sell-out to the organization, and already Hughes had suffered mild criticism at the hands of the press for his postelection vacation with State Chairman Woodruff. Fearful of alienating the very groups he wished to rally around his program, Hughes insisted to probing reporters upon his return to New York that he had not discussed politics at the White House. [14]

With Theodore Roosevelt's blessing, Hughes worked diligent-

[12] Beerits, "Entry into Politics," p. 17; Hughes to Parsons, Nov. 22 and Dec. 27, 1906, Parsons Papers.
[13] Beerits, "Entry into Politics," p. 18.
[14] *Ibid.*, p. 17; "Governor Hughes—Now and Later," *World's Work,* XIV (1907), 8914.

ly, late in December, on his inaugural message and his first address to the 1907 legislature. Both documents carried greater significance than the usual gubernatorial state papers, for Hughes, the newcomer, was expected to define his general reform program and to transform his various campaign promises into specific legislative proposals. In short, he would have his first real opportunity to earn the acclaim already accorded him by the electorate and the press.

Certainly, the January 1 inauguration proved no disappointment to those New Yorkers who had repudiated the GOP but endorsed its gubernatorial candidate. Curious spectators had jammed into Albany from all over the state to witness what was termed the most colorful ceremony since the days of Theodore Roosevelt.[15] The festivities began on New Year's Eve with a glittering military ball sponsored by New York City's Squadron A in honor of the Governor-elect and Mrs. Hughes. The next day, Albany's streets were packed with enthusiastic people awaiting a glimpse of Hughes as in dignified fashion he made his way to the capitol's assembly doors.

When the new governor finally reached the legislative quarters, he was greeted by an overflowing crowd of admirers. At 1:00 P.M. the ceremonies began. As onlookers scanned the specially constructed inaugural platform, they could not help but detect the sharp contrast between the young, vigorous Hughes and the gaunt, bedraggled retiring executive, Frank Higgins. Rabid partisans of the "new order" might have been tempted to view this difference symbolically. Actually, Higgins' health had worsened since the summer, and he had made the trip from his Olean home to Albany only out of respect for his successor, who had served him so well.[16] So ill was the outgoing governor that when it came time to welcome Hughes he could not even read his prepared manuscript.[17] The new governor, in contrast,

---

[15] New York *Times*, Jan. 2, 1907.

[16] He would live but one month longer.

[17] Frank S. Perley to Roscoe C. E. Brown, n.d., Ray B. Smith, ed., *History of the State of New York: Political and Governmental* (Syracuse: Syracuse, 1922), IV, 134–135.

repeated the oath of office in such crisp and vibrant tones that he could be heard in every corner of the assembly chamber. Although Hughes had already proved himself an excellent extemporaneous speaker, he chose to read his inaugural address—a document that would set the tone for his entire administration and, more immediately, lay the foundations for the legislative message to be delivered the next day.

Hughes began his address in an unorthodox fashion by bluntly stating that he had not sought the position he now held—an implicit admission of Theodore Roosevelt's handling of the New York Republican crisis in 1906. As chief executive, he could, therefore, "undertake the task of administration without illusion." [18] Much of the message was devoted to advising legislators and policymakers; the rest was a brief discourse on his own progressive philosophy of administration.

An abiding goal among legislators, Hughes declared at the outset, must be the "quality of our present and of our proposed enactments." Conventional generalities, he added, could in no way restrict legislative action; rather, the overriding impulse should be "sympathy with every aspiration for the betterment of conditions and a sincere and patient effort to understand every need and to ascertain in the light of experience the means best adapted to meet it." [19] Hard, cold, rational examination, he was convinced, not preoccupation with shibboleths of the past, should guide legislative efforts in the immediate future.

The many evils of his time, the new governor insisted, could be attributed to the law itself, to carelessly granted privileges, and to the Republican failure to safeguard the public by providing satisfactory governmental regulation of those endeavors that were contingent upon public franchises. The authority of the state had to be redirected toward the common good. This "logical" extension of government into areas such as supervision of highways, the forest preserves, public health, and various urban activities carried with it an increased demand for administrative efficiency. Therefore, administration was to be placed in the

---

[18] *Hughes Public Papers*, I, 7.   [19] *Ibid.*

hands of men of "singleminded devotion to the public interests." [20]

Efficiency in administration, impartiality in executing the laws, and intelligence in formulating them, Hughes concluded, would "disarm reckless and selfish agitators and take from the enemies of our peace their vantage ground of attack." Dramatically, the Governor pledged himself to this task, convinced that the people of the state were behind him.[21] His message ended on the same note of moderation he had sounded in the campaign of 1906 and during the period between election and inauguration.

If Governor Hughes's inaugural address outlined the approach his administration would assume toward the state's accumulated problems, his first annual message to the legislature supplied the details. This, too, fully embodied the progressive ideal as Hughes had come to understand it. The message delineated the areas in which work had to be done—election and party nomination procedures, public utility and railway regulation, and extension and improvement of the various police and welfare services of the state. His emphasis clearly rested upon the first two categories, and as such, it reflected the complexion of his program for the Empire State for the next four years. Though the Hughes administration would, indeed, witness considerable advances in the broad field of economic and social reforms, the Governor would wage his most serious battles in behalf of clean, "unbossed" politics and corporation regulation— the twin issues of the 1906 campaign against Hearst.

Having justified New York State's growing expenditures as an indication of the inevitable "extension of governmental activities," Governor Hughes plunged immediately into the political aspects of his reform message: "Our entire system of government," he said, "depends upon honest elections and a fair count." [22] Rising above petty politics, he called for legislative action to bring about an electoral recount of the controversial Hearst-McClellan New York City mayoral contest in 1905. Hughes was aware that Hearst had sought repeatedly to reopen

[20] *Ibid.*, p. 8.   [21] *Ibid.*, p. 9.   [22] *Ibid.*, p. 24.

the ballot boxes, but one obstacle after another had prevented him from succeeding. This failure, stemming largely from loopholes in the election law, asserted the Governor, "has aggravated the sense of injustice." He therefore urged the enactment of new legislation providing clear-cut machinery—lodged preferably in the state supreme court—for recounting ballots in a contested election.

Added to this recount proposal was an elaborate set of recommendations designed specifically to improve party standards and voting behavior. He advocated adopting the Massachusetts ballot, which would group candidates on the election ballot by position instead of party affiliation. As an independent, Hughes was conscious of voting carelessness under the present system, where the uninformed citizen could conveniently mark off his choices by party. Next, the Governor advised passage of a bill limiting political campaign expenditures. Finally, he underscored the need for changes in the state's primary law granting, in particular, that "any general committee of a party may adopt a rule providing for direct nominations." Hopefully, Hughes suggested, this experiment would be tried in several important counties, and its results would "enable us to determine the wisdom of its extension." [23]

The heart of the Governor's program for 1907, however, was the enactment of a law regulating more strictly those public service corporations operating in New York State. Hughes had campaigned vigorously on this issue and now offered a set of recommendations which would soon become the basis for the Page-Merritt public service commissions bill. He began his detailed discussion by outlining the worst railroad abuses—the system of rebates, unjust discrimination in rates, wanton monopolization, and inadequate service—and by showing the inefficiency of the existing board of railroad commissioners. Thinking in terms of administrative efficiency, he would do away with the recently created commission of gas and electricity, a regulatory body he himself had conceived, and in its stead consolidate au-

23 *Ibid.*, p. 28.

thority over all public service corporations within one commission. To this new agency he would grant "all the powers possessed by the present commissions and such additional powers as may be needed to insure proper management and operation." [24] It should have wide authority to act upon its own initiative as well as upon complaint, to approve issuances of securities, to scrutinize properties, books, and accounts, to set reasonable rates, to mandate adequate service, and "generally to direct whatever may be necessary or proper to safeguard the public interests and to secure the fulfillment of the public obligations of the corporations under its supervision."

The remainder of Hughes's message was devoted to a host of other reforms that struck a progressive note in one way or another.[25] He called for reorganization of the labor department and enactment of a more stringent child labor law. He advised continuation of the program "to encourage agriculture and to promote the extension of scientific and gainful methods." He insisted upon codification of the pure food laws so that the public would be safeguarded against "impositions through skillful adulterations." He encouraged the state to expand its forest preserves and to keep out of private hands whatever undeveloped water resources still remained. Finally, the new governor appealed for reforms in administration of the state prisons and Manhattan's overworked municipal court.

So clear and forthright a statement of progressivism as Hughes's first two messages inevitably evoked unusual press comment. Since the election, sympathetic journals had waited impatiently for a statement of the incoming administration's precise methods and objectives. They had seized upon every scrap of information to drive a wedge between Hughes and the prominent leaders of the state GOP. Now, their voices swelled with praise for what the New York *Evening Post* called "an open challenge to the bosses of his own party." Pulitzer's *World* singled out election reform and public utility regulation in the drive to "strike directly at political corruption . . . and corpo-

[24] *Ibid.*, p. 31.   [25] *Ibid.*, pp. 32–41.

ration corruption." The *Herald* added its own analysis of the message arguing that it had been written "in the interest of the people by a man who seems to be their, not the politicians', servant." In a similar vein, the *Times* insisted that public utility reform "would disjoint the old Republican machine," while the *Commercial* emphasized the notion that the Governor had declared "thorough and absolute independence." [26]

Many neutral and unfriendly newspapers endorsed the reform proposals but chided Hughes for naively anticipating success from a legislature dominated by the Republican old guard.[27] As evidence, they could cite the remarks of "Uncle John" Raines, crusty old tryant of the state senate, who categorically refused to commit himself on the entire program but insisted that the Massachusetts ballot would be ill advised in New York. Or they could read between the lines of William Barnes's mild endorsement ending with the jibe that the message "like all of Mr. Hughes's works does not thunder in the index." [28]

Aside from these few stray comments, Republican leaders remained noticeably silent on the ambitious legislative recommendations Hughes urged upon the assembly and the senate. Enamored of tradition, they may simply have discounted the reform proposals as the wishful thoughts of an impractical politician or merely as unimportant in and of themselves. One unidentified state senator offered a clue to this quiescence with the remark that gubernatorial messages "have been forgotten in a week." Another added confidently that "while setting up a cry of reform and all that, he [Hughes] will treat with us quietly and effectively when it comes to patronage, as Roosevelt did when he was Governor." [29]

[26] New York *Evening Post*, Jan. 2, 1907, and New York *Herald*, Jan. 3, 1907, Fuller Collection, Vol. XLIX; New York *World* and New York *Times*, Jan. 3, 1907; *Literary Digest*, XXXIV (1907), 46.

[27] Among them were Hearst's New York *American*, *Literary Digest*, XXXIV (1907), 45–46; Mack's Buffalo *Evening Times* and Conners' Buffalo *Daily Courier*, Jan. 3, 1907.

[28] New York *Times*, Jan. 3, 1907; Albany *Evening Journal*, Jan. 2, 1907, Fuller Collection, Vol. XLIX.

[29] New York *Times*, Jan. 3, 1907.

This problem of patronage—and particularly that of appointments on the upper levels—had naturally concerned Hughes from the very day of his election. What made matters unusually difficult in 1906 was the fact that humiliation at the polls had robbed the GOP of some of the choicest spoils of office.[30] Party leaders were inclined, therefore, to be somewhat more persistent than usual in securing their share of the patronage grab bag. By precedent, they could not really claim the Governor's personal advisors, consisting of a private secretary, a legal counsel, and a military secretary. But they could make demands upon two judgeships, two state tax commissionerships, and the all-important superintendencies of banks, elections, and public works, offices which, as prescribed term positions, became vacant shortly after January 1, 1907.

Especially enticing were the executive offices—the superintendencies—for with them went a great deal of the patronage the state administration had at its disposal. New as he was to the political game, Hughes appreciated their value and the extent to which, in the hands of ambitious politicians or even a clever governor, they could be turned into the machinery for creating powerful organizations. He saw clearly that the success of his administration, in terms of its avowed purpose, depended largely upon the efficient management of these executive departments.[31]

Hughes's ideas concerning appointments had been clearly spelled out in his November 23 address to the Republican Club. Political considerations, he then held, should not be the primary criteria for nomination to public office. Indeed, in practice, the new governor often eliminated prospective appointees because of their political activity. Republican faithful Job Hedges, for example, was denied a lucrative state post for that very reason. "Mr. Hedges," Hughes said shortly after the election, "the fact that you have been so actively campaigning in my behalf precludes the possibility of my appointing you to any office. I can-

[30] In particular, the departments run by the comptroller, the secretary of state, and the attorney-general.

[31] "Governor Hughes—Now and Later," *World's Work*, XIV (1907), 8914–8915.

not have it said that I have distributed offices as a reward for support." [32]

Hughes, of course, was never presumptuous enough to think that working alone he could organize a smooth and efficient administration. Writing years later, he pointed out that he was always glad to receive recommendations and acted favorably upon them whenever the party leaders named "men of such ability and character that I was confident there would be no successful interference with the faithful . . . discharge of official duties." [33] In practice he often sought advice from the organization men, but, in the final analysis, he made appointment decisions himself. Regarding the patronage, the Governor wrote to Parsons on one occasion: "I desire all the responsibility or none of it." [34]

In this vein, Hughes undertook the challenging task of selecting his executive colleagues. He began by considering candidates for the bank superintendency. This department had recently undergone severe criticism for its inefficiency and lack of leadership; indeed, during the campaign Hughes had promised outright investigation and reorganization. He felt obliged, therefore, to name the banking superintendent as soon as possible, although the appointment itself did not have to be announced officially until twenty days after the inauguration. Among the available candidates was a prominent Buffalo businessman, Charles Hallam Keep, who impressed Hughes deeply. Since Keep was then an assistant secretary of the treasury, the Governor-elect turned to Theodore Roosevelt for advice and consultation. The President cooperated fully and arranged a conference between the two men. Once having met Keep, Hughes confessed that he very much wanted the Buffalonian for the post, and he immediately cleared the appointment with the state committee.[35]

[32] Quoted in Arthur W. Dunn, *From Harrison to Harding: A Personal Narrative* (2 vols.; New York: Putnam, 1922), II, 323–324.

[33] Hughes, "Biographical Notes," p. 186, Hughes Papers.

[34] Hughes to Parsons, Dec. 6, 1906, Parsons Papers.

[35] Hughes to Roosevelt, Dec. 6, 7, and 15, 1906, Theodore Roosevelt Papers (Manuscript Division, Library of Congress).

In making this selection, Hughes revealed a high degree of political common sense. He had not only consulted the party leaders but apparently made them feel that he actually depended upon their approval. There was no clash of interest since Hughes's high standards for public office could be met by a capable party regular.

Not always, however, was the new governor so congenial to Republican leaders, especially when he believed that they were seeking to force his hand. On December 4 Herbert Parsons made a request of Hughes concerning an appointee to the position of superintendent of elections for the metropolitan district of New York. Earlier that year, the incumbent, George W. Morgan, had expressed a desire to resign and recommended that the chief deputy, Lewis N. Swasey, be named his successor. At first, Parsons was not kindly disposed toward Swasey, and he prevailed upon Morgan to retain the position through the campaign. In the meantime, Parsons confessed to Hughes, he changed his mind, and Governor Higgins agreed that the chief deputy should be designated superintendent. Therefore, Parsons went to Morgan and guaranteed that Swasey would receive the appointment. To the county chairman's embarrassment, Higgins backtracked, insisting now that Hughes be consulted since, within a month, the new governor would have to name a man to this office.

Parsons apologized profusely to Hughes for imposing his own commitment upon the Governor-elect. "I shall be very greatly embarrassed," he admitted, "if Mr. Swasey is not appointed." [36] He blithely thrust the matter aside by pointing out that Hughes probably did not wish to be bothered about the issue at this time, though he hoped the Governor-elect would treat it "absolutely frankly." Parsons ended his appeal with unconcealed praise for Swasey, arguing that he would "make a fine and efficient head of office." Doubtless, Hughes's response was more candid than Parsons was prepared to hear. He assured the county chairman that Higgins should not hold back in making the appointment

[36] Parsons to Hughes, Dec. 4, 1906, Parsons Papers.

for fear of embarrassing the new administration. He, the Governor, must act as chief executive—according to his own judgment —until his term expired, Hughes informed Parsons bluntly. "All that I desire," he concluded, "is that I shall not be charged with responsibility in part for anything that may be done before January 1." [37]

The truth of the matter was that Hughes did not as yet wish to concentrate on other executive appointments. At this time, early in December, he was busy collating materials for his January messages and meeting the many additional demands made on him.[38] Early consideration of a choice for the banking position had been dictated by the exigency of a dangerous situation. There was no such compelling reason, as he saw it, to choose his elections superintendent until shortly after the new year.

Higgins' decision to make the appointment, announced on December 16, forced the new governor to face the Swasey issue squarely. When, shortly after his inauguration, Hughes did turn to it, he could hardly avoid questioning the superintendent's qualifications if only because of Parsons' own original doubts. A careful investigation served to confirm his reservations, for Hughes discovered that Swasey was an "ordinary sort of district leader in Brooklyn, a mere tool of the machine." [39] Furthermore, Swasey had been involved in bitter factional quarrels and was still being vehemently denounced by one of the contending groups in his district. Hughes considered the superintendency to be nonpartisan. Its main function was the supervision of elections in New York City, and it employed a large force of deputies in discharging that responsibility. The Governor's avowed principles would not permit such a position to remain in the hands of an unproven party hack, who might be tempted to use it for partisan advantage.[40]

[37] Hughes to Parsons, Dec. 6, 1906, *ibid.*
[38] Hughes, "Biographical Notes," p. 181.   [39] *Ibid.*
[40] Beerits, "First Term as Governor," p. 3, in "Memorandum"; Robert H. Fuller, "Governor Hughes and the Bosses," pp. 5–8, Charles Evans Hughes Collection (NYPL).

Hughes immediately informed Parsons and State Chairman Woodruff, who were both in Albany, that under the circumstances Swasey could not be made a member of the new administration. The leaders were momentarily stunned but quickly regained their composure and apparently left the Governor's office determined to have their way. In keeping with his appointment principles, Hughes had assured them that he would "be glad to appoint anyone else whom they would recommend provided he was a fit man for the place." [41] They had committed themselves to Swasey, however, and were obliged to fulfill their pledge.

As chairman of the county organization under whose jurisdiction Swasey's district fell, Woodruff was as determined as Parsons to obtain this appointment. On January 10, therefore, he and several of his Brooklyn legislators strode into Hughes's office and sought to make a case for their friend and colleague. The Governor was courteous but adamant. He thanked them for their interest, but insisted that in the final analysis he had to employ his own judgment, however erroneous it might later prove to be.[42] This conference was followed by a second session, with Parsons and Woodruff again urging Hughes to honor the political commitment they had made. The Governor could not sympathize, he later wrote, for he "had given them every chance to save their faces and they had quite needlessly made an issue and brought their trouble upon themselves." [43] He merely reiterated his well-defined position: he was Governor of New York and he alone was responsible to the electorate. Because he wished not to sacrifice good government for partisan advantage, he would not back down. After several hours of fruitless discussion, Hughes abruptly terminated the session. Still unconvinced that the final word had been said, Herbert Parsons remarked casually as he left the office: "I think we'll find a way." [44]

[41] Hughes, "Biographical Notes," p. 182.
[42] New York *Evening Post*, Jan. 10, 1907; Beerits, "First Term," p. 4.
[43] Hughes, "Biographical Notes," p. 183; Burton J. Hendrick, "Governor Hughes," *McClure's*, XXX (1908), 672.
[44] Beerits, "First Term," p. 4.

Governor Hughes could not appreciate the significance of Parsons' comment for several days. In the meantime, Assembly Speaker Wadsworth journeyed to Washington for a conference with Theodore Roosevelt. Insisting all along that the Swasey matter was a test of strength in New York, the Hughes press caught the meaning of this White House get-together. When it was over, eager reporters besieged the participants with searching questions, but to no avail.[45] The next day, Wadsworth was back in the state capital. He hurried to the executive office, where he cordially met Hughes and delivered a message from Roosevelt. Although the President had expressed profound faith in the Governor's judgment, Wadsworth confided, he thought that under the circumstances it might be best to name Swasey. Surprisingly unruffled, Hughes told the speaker that he regretted the President's message and deemed it impossible to heed his advice. "I wish you would tell the President," Hughes added, "that I have thought over this matter very carefully and that I'm sending in the nomination of William Leary this evening." [46]

However sensational a rebuke the Governor's words conveyed, the Leary nomination was meant to be a salve for the wound. William Leary was himself a party regular and had been recommended by a party regular—Job Hedges. He was a good friend of Roosevelt's and had been manager of Herbert Parsons' last congressional campaign.[47] His selection as elections superintendent pointed up Hughes's willingness to cooperate but not to submit. Though, indeed, Parsons and Woodruff had been disturbed by the Governor's "stubbornness" in handling this situation, they seemed contented with its outcome. And Hughes, on his part, had driven his point home.

Governor Hughes made January 14 the occasion for announcing his other key administrative appointments—Frederick C. Stevens, superintendent of public works, and Charles Hallam Keep, superintendent of banking. The Keep nomination invited

[45] New York *Times*, Buffalo *Daily Courier*, and New York *Evening Post*, Jan. 14, 1907.

[46] Beerits, "First Term," p. 5.   [47] *Ibid.*, p. 6.

no criticism, but the Stevens selection, on top of the Swasey matter, threatened to drive a wedge between the new executive and a key member of the Republican high command, Assembly Speaker Wadsworth.

Fred Stevens, former state senator and gas committee chairman, hailed from Wyoming County in the heart of Wadsworth territory. Until 1905 he and his followers had enjoyed great political power by virtue of a working alliance with the powerful Geneseo family. The understanding was that Stevens would deliver Wyoming and Allegany Counties to the Wadsworths when they were needed and, in return, could depend upon Livingston County for his own political endeavors. In this way, Stevens controlled the forty-sixth state senatorial district and Wadsworth, Sr., the thirty-fourth congressional district.[48] Never a happy relationship, the pact was terminated in 1906, when personal bickering and Stevens' own ambition moved young Wadsworth, as assembly speaker, to redistrict the Senator out of existence.[49] So embittered was Stevens that during the next year he bolted the GOP and supported Democrat Peter Porter's successful efforts to capture the elder Wadsworth's congressional seat.

This whole affair, of course, had left its scars on Stevens. Although the Wadsworths were equally bitter, they had reaped some satisfaction in that their rival no longer wielded any political power—that is, until the earthshaking appointment of January 14, 1907. This announcement descended like a bombshell on the assembly speaker, who had not been informed that Hughes was even considering Fred Stevens for the public works superintendency.[50] Wadsworth could only envisage the use of this de-

[48] New York *Tribune*, Jan. 15, 1907; Smith, *History of New York*, IV, 124–125.

[49] The 1906 Reapportionment Act changed Stevens' senatorial district by lumping Genesee County (which he did not control) with Wyoming and Livingston. In this way, the Wadsworths could control the district.

[50] New York *Times* and Buffalo *Morning Express*, Jan. 15, 1907; Brooklyn *Eagle*, Jan. 15, 1907, Fuller Collection, Vol. VI.

partment's enormous resources against his smooth-running Livingston organization. "Gee!" exclaimed S. Percy Hooker, Wadsworth's own state senator. "This smashes our county machine." [51]

Actually, Governor Hughes had no intention of permitting the public works department to be used for factional purposes and certainly not for inviting trouble with one of the most powerful Republicans in Albany. Although he had known of the rivalry between Stevens and Wadsworth, he was unaware that it had become so intense.[52] Not politically minded himself, Hughes must have assumed that others would view the appointment as he did: Stevens was an exceptionally able man and for that reason alone should, if available, hold a high office in the new administration. However, the eager antiorganization press once more seized upon the incident, and interpreted Hughes's action as a direct assault upon Wadsworth in particular and the state machine in general. The new governor, it was argued, had once more bypassed the leaders in naming a subordinate officer. Parsons' recommendation of McDougall Hawkes, made in at least two letters and in several conferences, had gone unheeded. Aldridge, Barnes, and Woodruff, championing the cause of Deputy Superintendent Winslow Means, had been ignored.[53] What further evidence was needed to show that Hughes was blazing a path of independence?

These hasty conclusions must, indeed, have moved the stubborn Governor into action. Realizing that his whole legislative program would be endangered if Wadsworth were alienated, Hughes issued, on January 15, the following statement:

[51] New York *Herald*, Jan. 15, 1907.

[52] Hughes, "Biographical Notes," p. 183; Frank H. Simonds, "Governor Hughes, A Twentieth Century Roundhead," *Putnam's Monthly*, III (1907), 34.

[53] Utica *Observer* and Utica *Herald-Dispatch*, Jan. 15, 1907, Fuller Collection, Vol. VI; New York *Times*, New York *Herald*, New York *World*, New York *Evening Post*, and Buffalo *Morning Express*, Jan. 15, 1907; Parsons to Hughes, Dec. 26, 1906, and to Robert H. Fuller, Jan. 7, 1907, Parsons Papers.

The appointment of Senator Stevens was not a political appointment. It is not the intention to make the administration a party to
any factional controversy. The appointment was a personal one and
was made simply to secure for the State . . . the services of a loyal
friend and a man of conspicuous business ability. The Governor
particularly desires that the appointment should not be regarded as
showing the slightest antagonism to Speaker Wadsworth, for whom
he has the most unqualified esteem.[54]

On the same afternoon, Hughes held a conference with
Wadsworth and reviewed the entire matter in detail. He repeated the substance of his press statement and the two men
parted amicably. To reporters waiting eagerly outside the executive office, the fair-minded speaker announced that he was convinced Governor Hughes "had no intention of playing politics." [55] He informed them that he contemplated no revenge and
his personal loyalty to the administration was unshaken.

Although these Hughes appointments naturally evoked no
real enthusiasm from the organization leaders, they did not engender the deepseated hatred that critics of the old guard predicted. Woodruff was perhaps more disturbed over the Governor's aloofness than most of his "machine" colleagues and refused to be quoted on the matter. The others fell quickly into
line and endorsed Wadsworth's position. New York County
Chairman Parsons judged the Stevens and Leary selections to be
"good from one point of view," but perceptively added that
Hughes had needlessly stirred up "political antagonisms where
no principle was involved." [56] Cantankerous William Barnes actually praised the appointments, noting that the Governor was
not the kind of man "deliberately to upset the working machinery of the Republican party in the State." [57]

Barnes's judgment on the matter was accurate. Hughes had
never intended to antagonize his own party to the point of

[54] "Statement Issued by the Executive Chamber," Jan. 15, 1907, Hughes
Collection (NYPL)

[55] New York *World* and New York *Times*, Jan. 16, 1907.

[56] Parsons to Richard C. Daniel, Jan. 15, 1907, Parsons Papers.

[57] Albany *Evening Journal*, Jan. 15, 1907, Fuller Collection, Vol. VI.

jeopardizing the all-important reform program he would soon submit to the legislature. He did wish to make it clear, however, to the county and state leaders as well as to President Roosevelt, that he, and only he, would discharge the office of governor. In so doing, Hughes would inevitably stir the political waters, for his concept of executive responsibility together with his reform inclinations conflicted with the ideas and prejudices of many an entrenched Republican leader. Indeed, the course he outlined in both his appointments and his initial messages required the maintenance of a delicate balance between independence and moderation—one which he repeatedly enunciated but which he, as a political newcomer, would find increasingly difficult to achieve.

CHAPTER VI

The Kelsey Fight and Administrative Reform

DESPITE rumblings of criticism, Governor Hughes was gratified by the reception of his initial executive appointments, and with their formal approval by the state senate, he turned his attention to other pressing matters.[1] Before plunging into the fight for his reform program, much of which was not yet ready for presentation to the legislature, he undertook the essential task of investigating the administrative units associated with the executive department. This work proved more taxing than he had anticipated, and although it resulted in significant legislation enhancing gubernatorial authority, it opened a breach between Hughes and his own party.

The executive branch of New York's government, in 1907, was a hodgepodge of bureaus, boards, commissions, and departments whose administrative framework defied classification. There was no uniform scheme for appointment or removal. Terms often extended beyond that of the governor, and the separate units went directly to the appropriating agency for the funds necessary to sustain operations. There was, therefore, no clear line of authority from the lower echelons to the chief executive, and the result was confusion in formulating policy and assigning responsibility. During the 1906 campaign, Hughes had

---

[1] Hughes, "Biographical Notes," p. 184, Charles Evans Hughes Papers (Manuscript Division, Library of Congress).

displayed a remarkable understanding of this situation and correctly observed that loose administrative organization went hand in hand with certain forms of corruption and graft. As a progressive dedicated to restoring government to the citizenry, he determined to render his offices as efficient as possible within the existing framework.[2]

Initiating the new administration's campaign to clean up the state government was a brief, but thorough, investigation of the department of public buildings. This agency had been accused of inefficiency in providing various services and supplies to other governmental units, and the specter of corruption hung over it. Joined by Lieutenant-Governor Lewis S. Chanler and Assembly Speaker James W. Wadsworth, Jr., both departmental trustees, Hughes and his legal counsel, Ernest W. Huffcut, soon exposed a web of petty graft that culminated in the summary dismissal of the deputy superintendent and the chief engineer. The trustees then resolved to prohibit state employees from holding an "interest" in any corporation transacting business with New York.[3]

Although Governor Hughes, in early 1907, intended to follow up the investigation of the department of public buildings with a systematic study of the other agencies associated with the executive office, he soon found himself involved in a prolonged battle to bring efficiency to one of the key departments. So far as the public was concerned, the dramatic Kelsey fight began on February 4 with an executive release announcing that Hughes had recently requested the resignation of Otto Kelsey as superintendent of insurance.[4] For several days thereafter, the eager pro-Hughes press dramatized this story as "another" example of

[2] "A Defeat for Governor Hughes," *Outlook*, LXXVI (1907), 41–43; Jacob Gould Schurman, "Governor Hughes," *Independent*, LXIII (1907), 1533.

[3] New York *Times*, Feb. 5, 1907. As trustees of the department, the lieutenant-governor and the assembly speaker were equally responsible with the governor for the "charge and care" of its organization (*Manual for the Use of the Legislature of the State of New York, 1907* [Albany, 1907], p. 438).

[4] Buffalo *Morning Express*, Feb. 5, 1907.

the open warfare raging between the administration and the Republican organization.[5]

To a certain extent, Otto Kelsey did represent the "old" politics. He was a product of Wadsworth's upstate machine and, like most public servants of his day, had slowly ascended the organization ladder. From 1894 to 1902 he had served in the assembly, where he developed into one of the GOP's leading figures. In 1903, Governor Odell recognized Kelsey's achievements and appointed him comptroller. Two years later, Higgins moved him up to the insurance superintendency, which had been left vacant through Francis Hendricks' resignation. In his fourteen years of public service (up to 1907), Kelsey had won a reputation among the party faithful for "an unimpeachable integrity." [6]

Governor Hughes never once questioned Kelsey's basic honesty; rather, he impugned the superintendent's executive ability. Kelsey had been named insurance head shortly after the Armstrong committee investigation and was expected to restore the tattered department in the public confidence. Indeed, counsel Hughes and Senator William Armstrong spent several hours at this time with the new superintendent outlining the reforms they deemed necessary to prevent "a recurrence of evil practices." [7] When Hughes assumed the governorship, he discovered that none of the most vital changes had been made. He therefore concluded that Kelsey lacked courage, independence, and initiative as an administrator.

Once the decision for removal was made, Hughes determined to handle the matter in his own quiet way. On January 31 he summoned the superintendent to the executive mansion and privately requested his resignation. Kelsey was startled and in his

[5] New York *Herald,* Feb. 6, 1907; New York *Tribune,* Feb. 8, 1907; New York *Evening Post,* Feb. 9, 1907.

[6] James W. Wadsworth, Jr., "Autobiography," p. 103, James W. Wadsworth, Jr., Papers (Hartford House, Geneseo, New York; now on deposit in the Library of Congress); Charles E. Fitch, ed., *Official New York: From Cleveland to Hughes* (4 vols.; New York: Hurd, 1911), III, 307–308.

[7] Hughes, "Biographical Notes," pp. 184–185.

uncertain reply managed to muster up a plea for time to consult with his friends.[8] Hughes had no alternative but to acquiesce, for an outright refusal might have invited recrimination from organization stalwarts already nettled by the Governor's alleged highhandedness. Their cooperation was necessary should Kelsey refuse to yield, since the insurance superintendency carried a fixed tenure and the incumbent's removal hinged upon senate approval. The upper house, at this time, was a haven for old-guard Republicans, who had little appreciation for Hughes's version of administrative reform.

In the meantime, Hughes seized upon the strategy of a personal appeal to the party leaders in which he presented his side of the case. He tactfully put the issue to them, emphasizing that Kelsey was simply not the man for so important a job. "If I can appoint Kelsey to any other position for which I think he is qualified," Hughes said, "I'll do it." After all, he added, "he is honest, and I don't want his removal to reflect on him." [9]

After discussing the matter with Kelsey and his friends, the leaders, including Herbert Parsons and James Wadsworth, reported back to the Governor. They confessed deep concern over the superintendent's persistence in retaining a post Hughes insisted should go to someone else and, more particularly, over the decision of Kelsey's supporters to fight the administration. Though themselves party men, they were, nonetheless, moved by the argument that Hughes would break tradition in dismissing a man whose term still had two years to run. Moreover, Kelsey had been a loyal Republican and an honest public official. If he resigned without fighting, it was alleged, his reputation would certainly be tarnished. Forced into a corner, the superintendent, they realized, had no alternative but to show that he

[8] "Proceedings of Hearing Held before the Senate Judiciary Committee on a Message from the Governor Recommending the Removal from Office of Mr. Otto Kelsey, Superintendent of Insurance," *Senate Document No. 42*, 130th session (Albany: J. B. Lyon, 1907), pp. 446–447.

[9] Henry C. Beerits, "First Term as Governor," p. 9, in "Memorandum," Hughes Papers. Hughes does not tell us who exactly these party leaders were.

was not a quitter when he sincerely believed his case to be strong. The leaders were sympathetic to his position but dreaded the inevitable confrontation.[10]

With Kelsey's flat refusal to resign, it was only a matter of time before the issue dominated the headlines. The superintendent drew first blood when, on February 3, he prematurely released his preliminary annual insurance report hurling defiance at the Hughes-sponsored laws of 1906. This document seriously questioned the advisability of making public the lists of insurance company policyholders, suggested that company contingency reserves be lowered, and advocated other changes designed to loosen restrictions imposed upon the industry.[11] If, up to this point, the Governor had hesitated to take his case to the people, he now had no alternative. His only chance, he thought, was to mold public opinion against what promised to be a stubborn state senate, and so, on February 4, he announced his stand on the Kelsey matter.[12]

This significant executive release, apparently issued as a feeler for press reaction, was followed by two moves made by Kelsey in an attempt to weaken Governor Hughes's position. On February 6 he announced that he was requesting the resignation of several insurance department officials, including Chief Deputy Robert H. Hunter.[13] This man was one of two individuals whom the Armstrong committee had singled out as being responsible for the department's inefficiency. Hunter's release belatedly placed Kelsey in line with some of the Armstrong recommendations. Second, on the twelfth (although not given to the press until the seventeenth), the superintendent dispatched a

[10] *Ibid.;* Herbert Parsons to Charles E. Hughes, Feb. 18, 1907, Herbert Parsons Papers (Columbia University Library); Horace White to Francis Hendricks, Feb. 13, 1907, Horace White Papers (Syracuse University Library).

[11] "Preliminary Text of Annual Report of the Superintendent of Insurance," Feb. 4, 1907, *Assembly Document No. 31, Part I,* 130th session (Albany: J. B. Lyon, 1907), pp. 25-31.

[12] Hughes, "Biographical Notes," p. 185.

[13] New York *Times,* Feb. 7, 1907.

long letter to the Governor seeking to justify his performance as insurance head.[14]

The Kelsey letter of February 12 was significant in presenting the basic defense arguments that were consistently cited throughout the ensuing imbroglio. The superintendent's chief contention was that he had served most of his term under difficult circumstances. In addition to routine demands, special work in fire insurance resulting from the San Francisco earthquake and the adjustment of established procedures to the Armstrong changes had overloaded his department's schedule. Still, Kelsey added, he had submitted a plan to Governor Higgins for reorganization of certain department branches, and it soon would be put into effect. "My official conduct," he insisted, "has never been censured by any responsible person familiar with the facts." He could not understand, therefore, the basis for Hughes's decision to remove him. The new governor, he charged, had not intimated what other changes should be made in the department, and had not given him (the superintendent) the opportunity to show his "promptness or willingness" in adapting his management to "the views of the present Governor." To defend his good name, and his fine record, Kelsey concluded, he was compelled to assume the stand he was now taking.[15]

The next move was up to Hughes, and Kelsey himself had given the Governor the opening he needed to put his best talents to work. Toward the end of the superintendent's impassioned defense had come the statement: "I respectfully remonstrate against the proposed summary disposition of my official life and invite the justice of considering the details of my administration prior to January 1, 1907." The shrewd Governor seized upon this offer, apparently tendered to the state senate, unearthed an old statute authorizing the executive "to take proofs," and on February 18 directed Kelsey to appear before him, that same afternoon, for a public hearing. [16]

[14] *Ibid.*, Feb. 18, 1907; *Hughes Public Papers*, I, 245–247.
[15] *Hughes Public Papers*, I, 246–247.
[16] Hughes to Kelsey, Feb. 18, 1907, *ibid.*, p. 248; Beerits, "First Term," p. 12.

No match for Hughes's keen mind, the insurance superintendent fared badly on the afternoon of February 18. The Governor recounted the facts he had accumulated to justify his resignation request. He forced Kelsey to admit that he had not systematically read the Armstrong committee report or made any
concerted effort to acquaint himself with the irregularities revealed by the public inquiry.[17] Turning to the department's
1903 examination of Mutual, Hughes questioned the superintendent about the two controversial officials, Robert Hunter and
Isaac Vanderpoel. Despite their poor handling of this investigation, and other evidence of incompetence, they had been retained, for Kelsey "felt that under the changed circumstances I
was getting faithful service." Senator Armstrong's explicit advice, repeated by Hughes in January, to rid the department of
its dead wood had thus gone unheeded. Moreover, Kelsey reluctantly admitted that no basic changes had been made since he
assumed the superintendency in May, 1906.[18]

The harassed insurance head must have been aware of his poor
showing before eager newspapermen and anxious politicians, for
on that same evening he drafted a letter summarizing his side of
the case, and the next day he presented it to the Governor as a supplement to the recorded testimony. Like the February 12 defense,
it emphasized the additional burden of work imposed upon the
superintendent. On this ground only could Kelsey justify his re-
tention of the department's "experienced" personnel.[19]

With the well-publicized insurance hearing still fresh in the
minds of New York's citizenry, Governor Hughes quickly
moved in for the kill. He had already consulted with former
members of the Armstrong committee regarding the procedure
involved in presenting the case to the state senate. On February
20 he dispatched to the upper house a scathing indictment of
Kelsey and formally demanded that the superintendent be removed from office. The general issue, he explained, was that
Kelsey "has conspicuously failed to perform obvious duties of

[17] *Hughes Public Papers*, I, 319.   [18] *Ibid.*, pp. 330, 346–347.
[19] Kelsey to Hughes, Feb. 19, 1907, *ibid.*, pp. 359–361.

the first importance, and his neglect has demonstrated his unfitness for the trust confided to him." Careful not to assail the superintendent's personal integrity, Hughes insisted that "the assiduity of a departmental chief in attention to the details of routine cannot compensate for the lack of administrative capacity." [20]

It was difficult, indeed, for organization leaders to accept at face value Hughes's criticism of a man, who in the past had rendered to the party loyal, efficient service and who was not now revealed to be dishonest. Speaker Wadsworth, a moderate, found that the Governor's "demands . . . for removal could not be justified." [21] Herbert Parsons, a Hughes supporter in this matter, understood why, under the circumstances, Kelsey was compelled to put up a fight. The issue was not clear-cut, and to many of the Governor's supporters there was some question concerning the justification of his position. To a few it even appeared that Hughes, the newcomer, sought to sweep out of office everyone associated with past Republican administrations.[22]

If the moderate wing of the New York GOP was disturbed by the Kelsey issue and Hughes's obstinate stand, the old guard seethed with resentment over the attempt to humble a party faithful. Leading this group of small, but willful, standpatters was John Raines, the senate's president *pro tempore*. In many ways Raines epitomized the old-line conservative Republican politician. Like Kelsey, an upstate man, he had risen through the organization ranks, but his greater ability had, over the course of the years, made him the leading Republican spokesman in the upper house. Since 1902 he had served as majority leader. Conservative by nature and background, Raines was flexible enough, or so he boasted, to have been a close advisor of several different governors, including Morton, Roosevelt, Odell, and Higgins. His every effort, however, to play the same role with Hughes had thus far been thwarted as the new governor remained aloof,

[20] *Ibid.*, pp. 249, 255; Buffalo *Morning Express*, Feb. 6, 1907.
[21] Wadsworth, "Autobiography," p. 103.
[22] Parsons to Hughes, Feb. 18, 1907, Parsons Papers.

as much as possible, from the machinations of legislative-
executive politics.[23]

Although sympathetic toward Kelsey from the beginning,
Raines had been willing, on February 17, to have the senate insurance committee, of which he was not a member, consider the
case. "Nominations for superintendent of insurance," he then
said, "have almost invariably gone to the committee on insurance
and it would do likewise with this matter." [24] But Kelsey's insistence that the public hearing presented only one side of the
case impressed Raines. Viewing the Governor's grueling cross-
examination as cruel and unnecessary, he and his coterie determined to give the superintendent "a fair show." [25] This Raines
could personally guarantee by transferring the whole question
to the senate judiciary committee, of which, as majority leader,
he was a member.

Meanwhile, the outspoken pro-Hughes press continued to
polarize the issue as one between the Governor and the "bosses."
From outright ridicule of Kelsey's inept defense to vehement denunciation of the entire Republican organization, New York
City newspapers, in particular, joined the crusade to make state
government more responsible.[26] There was little honest effort
to show that only a small percentage of Republicans in Albany
had even partially committed themselves against the Governor.
Hughes himself may have contributed to giving the press this
one-sided picture of the situation. On February 27, for example,
he took advantage of an Albany County organization dinner to
call for an "honorable party policy." He issued the warning that

[23] Charles F. Milliken, *A History of Ontario County, Genealogical and
Biographical* (2 vols.; New York: Lewis Historical Publishing Co.,
1911), II, 339; Edgar L. Murlin, *New York Red Book; An Illustrated
Legislative Manual, 1907* (Albany: J. B. Lyon, 1907), p. 64; Horace White
to Francis Hendricks, March 14, 1907, White Papers.

[24] Buffalo *Morning Express*, Feb. 18, 1907.

[25] New York *World*, Feb. 21, 1907; Beerits, "First Term," p. 12.

[26] New York *World*, Feb. 15 and 21, 1907, Fuller Collection, Vols.
XLIX, XCIV; New York *Evening Post*, Feb. 18, 1907; New York *Times*
and New York *Sun*, Feb. 19, 1907.

"the people will smash any organization that is devoted to selfish interests" and, referring to Kelsey, insisted that the man "who does not make good" should be denied party support.[27]

It is probable that, at this point, Governor Hughes was looking beyond the Kelsey issue, which to many observers constituted but a part of the larger struggle between progressivism and conservatism. Although the key feature of the administration's reform program, the public service commissions bill, had not yet been introduced in the legislature, several others had been presented. Already, rumors were rife that the Kelsey impasse was only a preview of an intense internecine contest and that Hughes had just begun to define his position.[28] This interpretation seemed to be confirmed when, at the same Albany dinner, William Barnes struck back at the administration for the Governor's ill-advised appeal to public opinion, implying that executive salvation lay in working with the organization, not against it.[29]

Two days later, on March 1, Hughes responded in two speeches. At Ithaca, he sought to combine administrative reform with his legislative program. Before governmental regulation could be instituted on a large scale, he argued, government itself had to be rendered honorable and just. Back in New York City, he added that no power, "financial or political," could stand in the way of state expansion "in the protection of the common welfare."[30] In these addresses, the new governor thus made clear the relationship between two significant aspects of his program for the Empire State.

Whether John Raines had any desire to use the Kelsey issue as a test case, or whether he simply wished to employ it as a weapon with which to bludgeon Hughes, the independent, into "dealing" directly with his party through the accepted channels,

[27] "Albany Republican Organization Address," Feb. 27, 1907, Hughes Collection (NYPL).

[28] New York *World*, n.d., Fuller Collection, Vol. XCV; Buffalo *Morning Express*, Feb. 25, 1907.

[29] New York *Times*, March 1, 1907.   [30] *Ibid.*, March 2, 1907.

he faced the difficult task of gathering together adequate support in the state senate. As matters stood shortly after the Governor's indictment, the majority leader could not count on much help from the moderate wing of the GOP. Parsons had already committed himself to Hughes. Woodruff, vacationing in Europe, was not available for comment, but his three Brooklyn senators had no sympathy for Kelsey. Although Wadsworth could not support the Governor, he remained neutral. Even Barnes, then in violent disagreement with Hughes over the role of the political party in American life, surprisingly declared for the administration. Finally, an early canvass of Republicans showed that approximately fifteen senators were leaning toward Hughes.[31] A party caucus at this time might have settled the issue once and for all, enhancing the Governor's growing prestige and reducing Raines's waning influence.[32]

The real danger for Hughes, for his position among rank-and-file Republicans, and possibly for his reform program was that the majority leader might strike up an alliance with New York City Democrat Thomas F. Grady, Tammany leader in the senate, and Patrick McCarren, Brooklyn boss. Often in the past these opportunists had joined forces with the most conservative wing of the GOP in order to beat back threatening legislation. The Kelsey case presented a tempting opportunity for Grady and McCarren to widen the gap between the Governor and his own party. Such a combination, assuming Raines could muster up ten or twelve moderate Republican votes, would provide the necessary strength to defeat the administration.

Raines's decision to have the judiciary committee consider the Kelsey case was made against this background of public assault upon the machine and a potential Republican alliance with Tammany. There was, indeed, no better place to give the superintendent a "fair show" than a committee of which Raines was a

[31] Parsons to Hughes, Feb. 18, 1907, Parsons Papers; Wadsworth, "Autobiography," p. 104; Albany *Evening Journal*, March 2, 1907, Fuller Collection, Vol. CI; Buffalo *Morning Express*, Feb. 16 and 18, 1907.

[32] Brooklyn *Eagle*, March 10, 1907, Fuller Collection, Vol. CI.

member and on which sat Tom Grady and Pat McCarren. The majority leader's strategy, too, became immediately apparent. He would drag out the hearings as long as possible, allowing sufficient time for Hughes's opposition to mount its attack. Meanwhile, Kelsey was to "clean out" his department and launch the reorganization scheme that had earlier been planned but never implemented. In this way, wavering senators might be attracted to the Raines position, which would, as a result, be strengthened.[33]

The judiciary committee proceedings on the Kelsey question began on March 13 and spanned one whole month. Representing the superintendent was attorney Edward G. Hatch, former justice of the New York supreme court. At the outset, Hatch wisely singled out the two charges made by Hughes—failure to remove incompetent officials and lack of administrative ability and initiative—and addressed himself to refuting them. Then, for three days, he examined Kelsey on detailed administrative procedures, carefully selecting his material to prove that the accused fully grasped the techniques of his department. Finally, on March 29, he turned to the cases of Hunter and Vanderpoel. Kelsey followed the same line he had taken in his earlier defense, emphasizing that the late Governor Higgins had regarded these men as indispensable to the proper adjustment of the thousands of San Francisco claims. He went on to accuse Hughes of being rude and inconsiderate in privately requesting his resignation on January 31. In the last two sessions, held on April 11 and 12, Hatch called before the committee various officials who testified in behalf of Kelsey as an administrator. In his poignant summation, the able counsel attacked the Governor's charges, accusing Hughes of thinking only in terms of the Armstrong legislation. "The Governor considered half a case," he appealed to committee members in conclusion, "you have the whole [case]."[34]

During these judiciary hearings John Raines remained relatively quiet. The strength of his appeal, he realized, was con-

---

[33] New York *Times*, Feb. 21, 1907; *Senate Document No. 42, passim.*
[34] *Senate Document No. 42*, p. 642.

tingent upon his ability to convince others that he had not pre-
judged the issue. But on April 3 he broke this discreet silence and
intimated his stand on the Kelsey question. Only two days before, Hughes had made a strong appeal at Utica for passage of
the public service commissions bill, and the air was filled with
charges that opposition to the superintendent's removal implied
opposition to the legislative reform program. "I think it would
be a great calamity," Raines declared in answer to these assaults,
"if the important measures for which he [Hughes] stands should
fall." [35] Then pledging his support "in every way," the Senator
added that "he and I understand each other." Only in matters of
detail, concluded Raines, was there any disagreement.

One such detail, of course, was the Kelsey removal, and on
April 25 the majority leader finally declared unequivocally
against Hughes. Having heard and read all of the testimony, he
announced authoritatively, "I see nothing . . . which would
lead me to vote for Mr. Kelsey's removal. . . . I shall vote to
retain Mr. Kelsey in office." [36]

Apparently, Raines was now confident of victory. Five days
later, the judiciary committee voted to take the Kelsey case to
the senate floor with no recommendations, a decision that spread
gloom among the Hughes forces, which had sought persistently
to get a report favorable to the administration. Then, as if to add
insult to injury, the committee resolved that Hatch be permitted
to make a final plea for Kelsey before the entire upper house.[37]
The significance of these decisions lay in the fact that the Tammany senators had joined Raines and three of his comrades to
thwart the minority's efforts. The feared bipartisan alliance,
anathema to reformers in the past, had now become a reality.

On May 1 the Kelsey fight entered its final phase as the
judiciary committee report, embodying only the recommendation concerning the Hatch defense, was presented to the senate
for approval. For two hours pro-Hughes senators debated heat-

[35] New York *Herald*, April 4, 1907.
[36] Buffalo *Morning Express*, April 26, 1907.
[37] New York *Times*, May 1, 1907.

edly with Raines and Grady men in a vain effort to convince wavering legislators to vote with the administration. But Kelsey's sympathizers easily won out, and Hatch was permitted to reiterate the main lines of Kelsey's defense.[38]

By this time, Governor Hughes must have been aware that his case was virtually lost. Up to now, he had not resorted to what one would call "traditional politics" in order to whip reluctant legislators into line.[39] He had refused to use patronage and he had rejected outright the advice that he utilize other gubernatorial weapons at his disposal. He had earnestly hoped that the strength of his position and the force of public opinion would bring ultimate victory, despite the well-organized group fighting him and his administrative reform. Desperation, however, often requires new strategy, and on May 1 the Governor seized an issue that threatened to stir up fear among enough Republican legislators to shift the balance of power in the senate.

In early April the New York court of appeals had declared unconstitutional the 1906 Apportionment Act on the ground that two senatorial districts—both in the New York City area —had been improperly delineated. Even then, in many quarters, the potential value of this issue for the administration was readily perceived.[40] With the veto threat, the Governor could force upon the legislature a new act altering not only the districts in question but also those represented by men reluctant to support the administration. During the month of April, Hughes did not push the apportionment question, and Republican senators, under Raines's leadership, drafted a measure to their own liking. They subsequently tabled the matter, however, and it lay dormant until the Kelsey case came to a head.[41] Then, on the day that Hatch carried his defense to the senate floor, Hughes astonished his oppo-

[38] *New York Senate Journal,* 130th session (Albany: J. B. Lyon, 1907), pp. 1331–1332; New York *Times,* May 2, 1907.

[39] Robert H. Fuller, "Governor Hughes and the Bosses," p. 12, Hughes Collection (NYPL); New York *Sun,* March 30, 1907.

[40] New York *Times,* April 3 and 9, 1907; Buffalo *Morning Express,* April 4, 1907.

[41] New York *Times,* April 24 and May 1, 1907.

nents with a sensational legislative message calling for settlement of the apportionment issue before adjournment. Obviously designed to cause confusion within the ranks of his own party, this message not only scored the 1906 Apportionment Act for the two malapportioned districts but also insisted that "the whole apportionment was rendered invalid." It demanded that the legislature pass a new law providing "such equality of representation as can be had under constitutional provisions." [42]

The very factionalism that Republican legislators had hoped to avoid when they tabled the apportionment issue was now being threatened by a desperate chief executive. GOP strongholds in the upstate areas, it was generally conceded, would be endangered if districts were carved out in accordance with the letter and spirit of the 1894 Constitution. So fearful of this possibility were several legislators that, reportedly, telegraph wires to all parts of New York were kept open so that local leaders might be consulted.[43]

On the day after Hughes's threatening message, the final and most bitter debate on the Kelsey question raged in the usually calm and placid state senate. "Raines Republicans" and "Grady Democrats" joined forces in castigating the administration's newfound power. Pat McCarren accused Governor Hughes of assuming an air of infallibility, and S. Percy Hooker, Genesee County Republican, strongly resented Hughes's efforts to place apportionment and the Kelsey issue on the same plane. Disturbed also by the aloofness that allegedly marked the Governor's treatment of the senate, Hooker queried: "Are his opinions like those handed down on Mount Sinai? Does he represent all the honesty, integrity, courage and brains in the state of New York?" [44]

The chief Hughes defenders were Alfred Page of New York City, William Armstrong of Rochester, and Harvey D. Hinman of Binghamton. Administration supporters to the end, these able

[42] *Hughes Public Papers,* I, 46–47.
[43] New York *Times,* May 2, 1907.
[44] Buffalo *Morning Express* and New York *Times,* May 3, 1907.

progressives sought valiantly to explain the purpose of the new politics as expressed by the articulate Governor. "The people are tired of the partnership between rich corporations and politicians," Hinman shouted. He urged Republicans to modernize and, viewing the Kelsey issue in its broadest terms, climaxed his appeal with the warning: "Unless we correct the evils that beset our Government we will have trouble, and very serious trouble, in the near future." [45]

Despite this ringing plea and Hughes's last-minute effort against Raines and his group, the administration, as anticipated, was defeated in a close vote.[46] The majority leader had successfully forged the feared bipartisan alliance, for nine Tammany senators and four McCarren Democrats had joined four upstate Democrats and ten Republicans to compose the majority. Among the GOP legislators voting against Hughes were Wadsworth's S. Percy Hooker, Hendricks' Horace White and, of course, John Raines and his closest legislative friend, Jotham P. Allds. Nonetheless, it is not quite correct to say that the Republican organization had taken its stand against the administration or that, as Merlo Pusey has put it, "Hughes had lost the support of the bosses . . . [and] the legislature." [47] Herbert Parsons' four senators, Woodruff's three legislators, Barnes's William Grattan, Aldridge's Thomas B. Dunn, and John F. O'Brien's H. Wallace Knapp remained loyal to the Hughes cause.

A close analysis of the vote reveals that, aside from the bipartisan alliance, Raines had succeeded, for one reason or another, in attracting moderate Republicans to the superintendent's cause. Probably the nature of the issue itself goes a long way toward explaining that success. It was never as clear-cut as Hughes made it out to be, especially to Republicans steeped in the party tradition and possessed of some loyalty to such an organization man. In several cases, the choice was made between a

[45] New York *Times*, May 3, 1907.
[46] *New York Senate Journal*, 130th session, p. 1370.
[47] Merlo J. Pusey, *Charles Evans Hughes* (New York: Macmillan, 1951), I, 199. Indeed, Pusey sees the entire Kelsey imbroglio as a pitched battle between Hughes and the organization.

personal commitment to a local leader supporting Kelsey and a growing sympathy for Hughes and his reform efforts. Although the Governor might have achieved victory if the case had come to a head on or about March 1, the brilliant Hatch defense weakened his strong position immeasurably. Then, too, Hughes's own constant appeals to the people, often embodied in derogatory attacks upon the organization, had perhaps the opposite effect in some quarters than anticipated. Even the apportionment bombshell fell in line with the administration's constant play to the popular press. Many stalwarts simply resented what was considered the Governor's brandishing of a dictatorial sword whose weightiness was upheld by public opinion. Finally, despite the administration's acceptance and espousal (borne undoubtedly of sincere anguish) of the position assumed by the Hughes press—that opposition to Kelsey's removal meant opposition to the reform program—most Republicans who voted against Hughes disagreed violently and said so.[48]

Although in the immediate sense the Kelsey fiasco resulted in a defeat for the Hughes administration to bring about a higher degree of unity in the state's executive department, other gains, in 1907, more than compensated for the setback. It is ironic, perhaps, that the drama of so protracted a struggle obscured the sponsorship and passage of the very measure that, if successfully enforced, would help to prevent such occurrences in the future.

Early in the Kelsey case, Governor Hughes had suffered the frustration of being unable legally to scrutinize the books, records, and accounts of the insurance department, thereby to verify conclusively his demands for the superintendent's removal.[49] Fortunately for his case, he possessed such a complete

[48] Herbert Parsons to Hughes, Feb. 18, 1907, Parsons Papers; New York *Tribune*, Feb. 22, 1907; New York *Times*, May 4, 1907; Buffalo *Daily Courier*, May 7, 1907; Edgar T. Brackett to Robert H. Fuller, May 5, 1907, Hughes Papers.

[49] J. Ellsworth Missall points out that his correspondence with Hughes shows that the Governor sponsored the Moreland bill as a result of the Kelsey case (*The Moreland Act: Executive Inquiry in the State of New York* [New York: King's Crown Press, 1946], p. 12).

knowledge of this department's activities that he could build up a substantial indictment without gaining access to its files. But what about the countless other agencies over which the Governor held at least partial jurisdiction and which he also wished to examine?

In answer to this question, Hughes worked diligently with assembly floor leader Sherman Moreland, progressive Republican of Chemung, on legislation to help the chief executive learn how the administrative heads were running their departments and whether they possessed the necessary ability. Moreland had begun drafting such a bill as early as February, and through April Hughes suggested various changes, including a key provision lodging investigative responsibility over the separate units with the Governor himself. Introduced in the assembly on April 15, the original Moreland proposal directed the chief executive, at least once every three years or more often if he saw fit, to appoint examiners to investigate all departments, boards, bureaus, and commissions of the state—their budgeting procedures, their methods of requisitioning supplies, their record-keeping systems, their employees, and, in general, "the methods and systems of doing business." [50]

Like the other major features of the reform program, the Moreland bill was held back until after the Kelsey issue had been decided. In the meantime, the opposition crystallized, for, as one student has maintained, the measure "attacked too directly the accepted pattern of thought about separation of powers and home rule for county governments." [51] Although Hughes was quick to give assurances on this score, the danger remained, according to one newspaper, that a "bad" governor could easily abuse this new-found power. [52]

The collapse of opposition to the Governor's reform program, occasioned by his victory in the public utility bill fight, made possible the legislature's speedy enactment of the More-

[50] New York *Times* and New York *Tribune*, April 13, 1907.
[51] Missall, *Moreland Act*, p. 15.
[52] New York *Sun*, May 25, 1907; Missall, *Moreland Act*, p. 18.

land proposal.[53] In final form, this key measure allowed potentially for as much assertion of executive authority as the original draft, though its exercise would depend upon the strength and determination of the governor. Still lodging investigative responsibility in the chief executive, the bill was stripped of the mandatory three-year provision and contained no mention of examination of county governmental units. In all, concludes J. Ellswerth Missall, the legislature was "betting on few of the Hughes type coming to office." [54]

During the three-year period, 1907 to 1910, Governor Hughes turned to the Moreland Act on five separate occasions. His most energetic and dramatic effort involved none other than Otto Kelsey. Visibly disturbed by his May, 1907, setback at the hands of the beleaguered insurance superintendent, Hughes reopened the case three months later. On August 20 he unflinchingly invoked the new law for the first time, announcing that his "crusade" for efficient administration would begin with a thorough examination of the insurance department.[55] At the same time, he named as his chief examiner Matthew Fleming, a cohort in the 1905 Armstrong committee hearings.

Fleming's handling of the Kelsey case reflected the broad scope of investigative power now lodged in the governor's office. In addition to holding several public hearings, he dipped liberally into department records. The upshot was a set of charges, published on January 30, 1908, that supplemented Hughes's earlier complaints regarding the superintendent's failure to reorganize his department. Under the general heading of "failure to enforce the law," these new grievances covered such matters as permitting false bookkeeping by companies, discrimination in dividends against deferred-dividend holders, injustice to small policyholders in connection with loans, false advertis-

[53] Missall adds that Moreland's leadership and Hughes's firm backing greatly facilitated the passage of this bill (*Moreland Act*, p. 16).

[54] *Ibid.*, p. 21; *Laws of New York, 1907* (2 vols.; Albany: J. B. Lyon, 1907), I, ch. 539.

[55] New York *Times*, Aug. 21, 1907; *Hughes Public Papers*, I, 257–258.

Governor Hughes and his daughter Catherine. (From *McClure's*, XXXV [1910], 499; courtesy of the Cornell University Library.)

Charles Evans Hughes campaigning during the 1906 gubernatorial race between Hughes and William Randolph Hearst. (From *Review of Reviews*, XXXIV [1906], 521; courtesy of the Cornell University Library.)

Upper left: John Raines, president *pro tempore* of the state senate and conservative Republican leader of Boss Platt's senate followers. *Upper right:* Patrick H. McCarren, Democratic senator from Brooklyn who led the anti-Tammany revolt of 1908. (Both from *McClure's*, XXX [1907–1908], 677; courtesy of the Cornell University Library.) *Lower left:* James W. Wadsworth, Jr., Republican speaker of the assembly, who opposed Governor Hughes's compromise on the direct primary bill. (From *McClure's*, XXXV [1910], page 503; courtesy of the Cornell University Library.) *Lower right:* Herbert Parsons, a supporter of Theodore Roosevelt and chairman of the New York County Republican committee. (From *Review of Reviews*, XXXIII [1906], 140; courtesy of the Cornell University Library.)

ing, and agreements among companies for establishing interlocking directorates.[56]

On February 11, 1908, when Governor Hughes dispatched his second indictment of Kelsey to the senate, he followed closely the Fleming charges. He reiterated the main line of his own 1907 case and added the Moreland investigation disclosures. To Hughes's way of thinking, the superintendent's position was now more precarious than it had ever been, for Fleming had shown Kelsey to be lax even in routine matters. "The failure to take full advantage of the machinery provided by law for the protection of the rights of policyholders, [and] the lack of proper attention to matters as to which the department is in a position to aid policyholders," he charged, "are without excuse." [57]

If the administration regarded its case more clear-cut in 1908, the senate leadership obviously did not. Despite reported "strong influences" being exerted upon Kelsey and his upper-house champions to abandon the fight, John Raines announced confidently on February 13 that there would be no Republican caucus. The issue, insisted Raines, was essentially one "for the exercise of the individual judicial opinion of the senators." [58] Yet three days later, Hughes summoned "his" majority leader to the executive chamber and appealed for support, warning that the consequences of an administration defeat would be fatal to Republican prestige. Again, however, the Governor threw away his trump card in pledging that he would not intimidate the senate by insisting upon a party vote, and Raines left feeling as unfettered as ever.[59] Thus, on February 26 a remarkably calm, unmoved upper house obstinately voted a second time for Superin-

[56] "Report of Matthew C. Fleming, Appointed by the Governor to Examine and Investigate the Management and Affairs of the Insurance Department of the State of New York," Jan. 30, 1908, *Senate Document No. 45*, 131st session (Albany: J. B. Lyon, 1908), pp. 11–12, 57–336.

[57] *Hughes Public Papers*, II, 183.

[58] Buffalo *Morning Express*, Feb. 14, 1908.

[59] New York *World*, Feb. 20, 1908.

tendent Kelsey. Again, the bipartisan alliance was in evidence, as fifteen Republicans joined fifteen Democrats to comprise the majority.[60]

One of the most significant factors in this 1908 Kelsey fight was the marked indifference with which the administration actually presented its case and then calmly sustained the February 26 defeat.[61] In contrast to the first battle, little fanfare accompanied Hughes's efforts. Perhaps the main reason for this apparent lack of enthusiasm was the Governor's own political education up to this point. The 1907 insurance fiasco had not sounded the death knell to his legislative reform program, as Hughes thought it surely would during the winter and spring of his first year in office. Instead, it contributed to the administration's success, for the force of public opinion permitted no compromise. If, therefore, he had won in 1907 by mobilizing the state's respectable elements behind his leadership, he might do so again in 1908 regardless of the senate's action in the Kelsey matter. Hughes thus learned that his opposition was not monolithic. Moreover, he became increasingly aware of the fact that there were other ways in which he might establish and maintain high administrative standards, and so he dropped, once and for all, the campaign against the insurance department. Kelsey remained in office until March, 1909.

The second Kelsey defeat notwithstanding, the Moreland Act, in the fullness of time, contributed solidly to making the Governor responsible for the management of New York's executive office—a movement destined to reach fruition in the years of Alfred E. Smith.[62] Hughes had always insisted upon the need for centralized authority in Albany as the modern state expanded its functions to meet the growing demands of a complex, interdependent society. The new law was a long first step in that direction. Over the next quarter of a century, nine chief

[60] "Action of the Senate in the Kelsey Matter," *Hughes Public Papers*, II, 185–186.

[61] Buffalo *Morning Express*, Feb. 21 and 27, 1908.

[62] See Oscar Handlin, *Al Smith and His America* (Boston: Little, Brown, 1958), ch. 5.

executives established thirty-three Moreland commissions for a variety of inquiries ranging from routine studies of boards, hospitals, and institutes to full-scale investigations of bureaus, departments, and commissions. Nor was the Moreland Act's influence confined to New York. Indeed, so important a link in the evolution of gubernatorial responsibility did it become that, within two decades, some eighteen states had copied its main features.[63] For Hughes, in the meantime, the new law proved to be a workable formula with which to implement some of the principles of administration that were earlier reflected in his executive appointments and somewhat later in the disappointing Kelsey fight.

[63] Missall, *Moreland Act*, pp. 25, 140.

CHAPTER VII

The 1907 Legislature
and the Reform Program

CHARLES EVANS HUGHES'S independence in naming his own executive officers together with his obstinate stand on the Kelsey issue undoubtedly caused strained relations with some of the Republican leaders. Although the Governor had sought only to make his administration secure, he inevitably stepped on toes in so doing. Even from party moderates like Parsons and Wadsworth, men whom Hughes had certainly wished to placate, his aloofness and unorthodoxy evoked criticism.[1] Yet the new governor clung tenaciously to the thought that he had been chosen primarily to reorganize a rapidly deteriorating party and, at the same time, to reform the state administration. His dedication to these objectives and his instinctive aversion to politicians made him appear all the more unfriendly to his Republican co-workers.

Hughes's approach to public service was clearly defined in his attitude toward the new legislature. As Governor-elect, in December, he had categorically refused to interfere with the organization of the 1907 legislature.[2] Believing firmly in the concept

[1] Herbert Parsons to Charles Evans Hughes, Feb. 18, 1907, and to Robert H. Fuller, April 1, 1907, Herbert Parsons Papers (Columbia University Library); James W. Wadsworth, Jr., "Autobiography," pp. 103–104, James W. Wadsworth, Jr., Papers (Hartford House, Geneseo, New York; now on deposit in the Library of Congress); Brooklyn *Eagle*, March 10, 1907.

[2] New York *Times*, Dec. 29, 1906.

of "divided responsibility" and fully expecting that each house would faithfully discharge its own duties, he subsequently told Speaker Wadsworth that he had "no suggestions to make, nor any wish to impress upon you." [3] Perhaps in return for surrendering a traditional gubernatorial weapon, Hughes threatened to appeal directly to the public if he found himself at odds with the legislature.

Taking the Governor at his word, Wadsworth and senate majority leader Raines, both recently re-elected to their coveted positions, undertook the task of organizing their respective houses. The 1906 elections had witnessed a substantial turn-over among legislators. For one thing, the Republican majority had been reduced in the senate from 36 to 31, the Democrats now having 19 members (with 1 independent), and from 107 to 98 in the assembly, where the Democrats numbered 50. For another, changes in the senate and assembly districts, arising from application of the 1906 Apportionment Act, together with the usual retirements, resulted in the appearance of many new legislative faces.[4]

Significantly, senate changes operated to the advantage of the GOP's dominant conservative wing. When John Raines strictly applied the seniority rule in doling out committee chairmanships, generally more progressive legislators were replaced by stand-patters. Thus, maverick Edgar T. Brackett, judiciary committee chairman, was succeeded in 1907 by Erie's George A. Davis; Frederick Stevens, now superintendent of public works, was supplanted by Francis H. Gates of Madison as head of banks; Nathaniel Elsberg's successor as codes chairman was Henry W. Hill, Erie conservative; and Jotham P. Allds replaced Merton E. Lewis of Monroe in the taxation and retrenchment committee. More significant was the fact that only two firm Hughes supporters held key committee chairmanships. William Armstrong of Rochester was named to head the powerful finance commit-

[3] New York *World*, Jan. 11, 1907.
[4] Buffalo *Morning Express*, Dec. 31, 1906.

tee, and Harvey D. Hinman of Binghamton became chairman of the miscellaneous corporations committee.[5]

There was evidence, too, that on those occasions when Raines deviated from the seniority principle, he did little for the new administration. Hinman, for example, was passed over for the insurance chairmanship in favor of Raines's own man, Albert T. Fancher, and Alfred Page, in line for the penal institutions committee, which presumably would be overworked in 1907, was shunted to public education, H. Wallace Knapp securing the more important assignment. Likewise, the key railroads committee, which moderates hoped would add progressive George B. Agnew and middle-of-the-roaders Otto Foelker and S. Percy Hooker, was packed with standpatters.[6]

These assignments reflected the basically conservative character of the state senate, and especially of its leadership. Since the 1890's, the Republicans had resorted to every device to maintain their hold on the legislative machinery of New York. They had even written a provision into the 1894 Constitution guaranteeing upstate domination over both the senate and assembly.[7] The rapid growth of New York City's population through the first decade of the twentieth century only enhanced the disparity between constitutional requirements and political realities. Repeated Democratic complaints about the "Republican hyenas from the wilds of the State" went unanswered, since a large majority of the GOP members of the upper house still owed their political fortunes to old upstate county organizations harking back to the Platt days.[8] There were, for example, Barnes of Al-

[5] Edgar L. Murlin, *New York Red Book: An Illustrated Legislative Manual, 1906* (Albany: J. B. Lyon, 1906), pp. 576–578; New York *Times* and Buffalo *Morning Express*, Jan. 10, 1907.

[6] Parsons to Hughes, Dec. 3, 1906, Parsons Papers.

[7] Alexander C. Flick, ed., *History of the State of New York* (New York: Columbia, 1935), VII, 216–217.

[8] "Report from the Executive Committee," June 20, 1907, Tammany Society Minutes, 1897–1915 (Columbia University Library); also "Report from the Executive Committee," June 4, 1897, and "Minutes of the General Committee," May 1, 1903, *ibid.*

bany, Hendricks of Onondaga, Aldridge of Monroe, and Fred Greiner of Erie, to name but a few of these local bosses.

No less conservative was the minority party, dominated by the colorful but anachronistic Thomas Grady, Tammany leader, and Patrick McCarren, Kings County boss. These two seasoned parliamentarians controlled fourteen of the senate's nineteen Democrats, a substantial enough majority so that no party caucus could succeed without their blessing. More often than not they played strictly opportunistic politics, usually exploiting Republican factionalism to the full. Sometimes, as in the Kelsey case, they forged the infamous bipartisan alliance with GOP standpatters to defeat advanced legislation. Even into the early years of the twentieth century, contemporaries have testified, Tammany and machine Republicans actively participated in sponsoring "strike" bills.[9] It would be another four years before Charley Murphy's younger Democrats, men like Alfred E. Smith and Robert F. Wagner, would succeed in moving Tammany leadership in another direction.

In 1907, the assembly was far more progressive, on the whole, than the placid state senate. Since January, 1906, the able, conscientious James Wadsworth, Jr., had sought to carry out the task broadly defined for him by Governor Higgins. Chosen, in large part, to reorganize the GOP in the lower house, the Geneseo politician, inheritor of a tradition of public service, radically altered committee assignments by turning aside the older men and placing younger legislators in positions of responsibility. Of the thirty-five standing committee chairmanships, twenty-four actually changed hands in Wadsworth's 1906 shuffle. Given complete freedom to do as he saw fit, the new speaker assigned such progressives as Sherman Moreland to ways and means (and made him floor leader at the same time), Jonathan M. Wainwright of Westchester to banks, George B.

[9] "Reminiscences of Martin Saxe" (Oral History Project, Columbia University Library, 1948–1949), p. 16; "Reminiscences of William S. Bennet" (Oral History Project, Columbia University Library, 1949–1950), pp. 13–14.

Agnew, then in the assembly, to electricity, gas, and water supply, and Robert Lynn Cox of Buffalo to the judiciary committee.[10]

Wadsworth's stellar performance offers a good clue to the mounting pressures on the Republican upstate machine in these years, pointing to an obvious countertrend within the party. His own election as speaker had come only after a serious challenge by the New York County committee and its new, vigorous leader, Herbert Parsons. Representing thousands of independents as well as a group of cosmopolitan, liberally inclined politicians, Parsons had tried to win the position for Wainwright or Moreland, then threw his support to Wadsworth when Governor Higgins' views were made known. Wadsworth's immediate response was to represent, as far as possible, the aspirations of New York County in the assembly's leadership, and, on the whole, his selection of legislative subordinates even satisfied the usually critical Citizens' Union, spokesman of the City's independents.[11]

In other ways, Wadsworth helped to reform the legislature's lower house. First of all, he ended the timeworn abuse of making appointments from the "extra lists." For years, the assembly had had to appropriate supplementary funds to pay a group of employees who actually rendered no public service but whose names appeared on lists compiled by greedy organization members hoping to remunerate faithful supporters. In addition, the speaker curtailed the practice of permitting assembly members to accept Pullman passes for personal junkets. Although state law prohibited this abuse, railroad men, seeking to spread their

[10] Wadsworth, "Autobiography," pp. 91–93; *New York Red Book, 1906*, pp. 578–580; Henry F. Holthusen, *James W. Wadsworth, Jr.: A Biographical Sketch* (New York: Putnam, 1926), pp. 51–52.

[11] "Report of the Committee on Legislation of the Citizens' Union for the Session of 1906," p. 3, in Citizens' Union Collection (NYPL); Alfred Cooley to Theodore Silkman, Dec. 5, 1905, Jonathan M. Wainwright Papers (New-York Historical Society Library); Parsons to William S. Bennet, Dec. 17, 1905, Parsons Papers.

influence, had traditionally written out passes to legislators' wives.[12]

It was the latent power of the assembly speakership itself, however, that tested (and would continue to test) Wadsworth as a leader of the party's better elements. This exalted position, by custom, made him chairman of the most powerful committee of the lower house—the rules committee—whose entire membership he selected. An old assembly rule required the standing committees to report on all items referred to them by April 5. What business remained unfinished—and a large percentage of it was usually unfinished—had to be turned over to the rules committee, which would then complete the necessary work and make recommendations to the assembly as a whole. In reality, this compact group of legislators, firmly controlled by the speaker, determined the course of most legislation. Even if the assembly were to adjourn before the April 5 deadline for committee work, the rules committee would have a hand in practically all pending bills, for by special provision it considered each and every measure during the last ten days of the legislative session.[13]

Perhaps the most significant feature of the 1907 legislature was its political divisions in relation to Governor Hughes's progressivism. The administration, indeed, came to rely upon a small contingent of Republicans, numbering no more than twenty, to carry through its program. A close examination of these men shows that by residence, education, and profession they resembled the Governor more than their GOP colleagues or the Democrats. Almost 60 per cent of them resided in New York City or its immediate environs, and nearly all the rest came from upstate commercial-industrial centers like Utica, Binghamton, Rochester, and Buffalo. The group was youthful, the aver-

[12] Holthusen, *James W. Wadsworth, Jr.*, p. 53; Wadsworth, "Autobiography," pp. 94–96.

[13] Charles E. Fitch, ed., *Official New York: From Cleveland to Hughes* (4 vols.; New York: Hurd, 1911), III, 24–26; "Legislative Procedure" (unpublished MS), Hughes Collection (NYPL).

age age being thirty-six. They were mainly lawyers by profession, and over 70 per cent of them held degrees from Ivy League institutions. The majority of those from New York City had been identified with a variety of reform organizations from the mid-1890's through the turn of the century, and at least two had been active in the Citizens' Union.[14] On the whole, these progressives in the legislature were broad-minded, independent thinkers who, in keeping with Governor Hughes's inaugural request, remained unhampered by clichés and shibboleths of the past. They did not look back nostalgically to an older socioeconomic order; rather, they coupled a dedication to good government and political reform with a determination to regulate corporations engaged in public service and, when necessary, to expand the police and welfare functions of the state. Their outlook, like Hughes's, was pragmatic and flexible, though often they displayed a deepseated intolerance toward the old political organizations. To a large extent, they represented the city, particularly New York City, in a state whose older political leaders had failed to solve the major urban problems of the day.[15]

To a legislature, then, with at least three significant divisions —the dominant upstate Republican machine, the Tammany-controlled Democratic minority, and the small pro-Hughes progressive contingent—the administration submitted its 1907 reform program. Although the protracted Kelsey fight postponed serious consideration of its important features (some said

[14] This information is gleaned from Edgar L. Murlin, *New York Red Book: An Illustrated Legislative Manual, 1907* (Albany: J. B. Lyon, 1907), pp. 64–97, 99–169.

[15] By contrast, 80 per cent of the more conservative Republicans came from the upstate areas with the small towns especially well represented, and only three out of ten were college educated. Almost three-fifths listed themselves chiefly as businessmen, and one in three was a lawyer. The average age of this group was forty-five years old. Among the Democrats, almost 80 per cent resided in New York City, approximately two out of five were college educated, and nearly 40 per cent were businessmen, with one-third being lawyers. The average age of the Democrats was forty years old. Although the largest single group of businessmen in the legislature remained unclassified, the largest classified groups were real estate, newspaper, insurance, mercantile, and banking.

deliberately so), virtually all of the Governor's measures had at least been introduced by mid-April. Sponsorship of the sixteen bills was distributed among ten senators and assemblymen usually considered within the Hughes camp. Alfred Page assumed responsibility for four different proposals and Assemblyman Ezra Prentice, also of New York County, introduced three measures.[16] Senators William Armstrong, Eugene Travis, and George Agnew and Assemblymen Jonathan M. Wainwright, Jesse Phillips, and Edwin A. Merritt, with several others, sponsored the remainder of the program.

The key to the new governor's first annual message was, of course, the appeal for stricter and more comprehensive public utility regulation. Rather early in his career, Hughes relates, he had been introduced "to the close study of administrative agencies, their necessity and appropriate sphere of action." [17] As counsel for the Stevens committee in 1905, he had become acquainted with utility problems and tried to solve some of them by sponsoring the bill establishing the state commission on gas and electricity. Much of his 1906 campaign had been devoted to discussing his theory on the government's responsibility for supervising private companies engaged in public business. When, after the election, Hughes looked more closely into the corporation problem, he discovered that New York State possessed several agencies, none of which, for one reason or another, functioned adequately. There was the impotent board of railroad commissioners, created in 1882, having statewide jurisdiction over the railroads as well as the surface lines and elevated railways in New York City. The board was not only weak in that it had to rely upon the attorney-general's office to enforce its

[16] Page introduced the child and woman labor bill, the pure drug measure, the New York City charter revision measure and the public service commissions bill. Prentice presented another child and woman labor bill, the Hearst-McClellan recount bill and the employment certificate bill (*New York Senate Journal,* 130th session [Albany: J. B. Lyon, 1907], pp. 14, 154, 415, 374; *New York Assembly Journal,* 130th session [Albany: J. B. Lyon, 1907], pp. 35, 30, 650).

[17] Hughes, "Biographical Notes," p. 190, Charles Evans Hughes Papers (Manuscript Division, Library of Congress).

orders, but, in recent years, it had become a refuge for the Republican organization.[18] A second agency was the board of rapid transit commissioners, established in 1891 for the limited purpose of watching over construction of the City's subway system. Finally, the gas and electric commission possessed ample authority, but, by its very nature, was restricted to a particular area of jurisdiction.

Pressure on the state administration to unify utility regulation and extend supervision to all public service corporations in the Empire State came largely from New York City citizens', taxpayers', and trade organizations. Doubtless, this drive was partly in response to the municipal ownership agitation that reached its zenith in the 1905 mayoral campaign. Much of it, however, came also from the City's merchants, represented chiefly by the Board of Trade and Transportation, the same organization that was so instrumental in the development of regulatory ideas culminating in the federal Interstate Commerce Act of 1887.[19] Members of the board were particularly disturbed by the rising shipping rates within the state and became convinced that a more powerful commission would check these increases. Finally, they joined other civic organizations in a drive to develop the City's subway system through a strengthened rapid transit commission that would plan and construct transit lines and regulate their operation.[20]

Governor Hughes displayed a keen awareness of all these fac-

[18] Henry C. Beerits, "First Term as Governor," p. 23, in "Memorandum," Hughes Papers; Flick, *History of New York*, VIII, 236–237; Burton J. Hendrick, "Governor Hughes," *McClure's*, XXX (1908), 676.

[19] Lee Benson, *Merchants, Farmers and Railroads: Railroad Regulation and New York Politics, 1850–1887* (Cambridge: Harvard, 1955), *passim*.

[20] William R. Hochman, "William J. Gaynor: The Years of Fruition" (unpublished Ph.D. diss., Columbia University, 1955), chs. 15 and 16; Lawrence Veiller to Horace White, March 3, 1906, Lawrence Veiller Papers (Columbia University Library); "Special Meeting—New York Board of Trade and Transportation," April 8, 1907, New York Board of Trade and Transportation Papers (New-York Historical Society Libray). The board's papers provide ample documentation for the role of the New York City merchants.

tors in his message to the legislature, and he immediately set out to draft a satisfactory bill. In frequent meetings with his legislative cohorts, he made known his own views. He also drew upon the ideas and experiences of social progressives like Lawrence Veiller of the City Club and representatives of the Board of Trade and other interested organizations. Using as a basis the Wisconsin state legislature's preliminary report on utility regulation, the records of the Interstate Commerce Commission, and the 1905 New York Gas and Electric Commission Act, Alfred Page, Edwin A. Merritt, and William Ivins drafted a bill that was ready for presentation in early March.[21] Going well beyond any of these guides, the Page-Merritt proposal embodied the broad concepts of regulation expressed in the January 2 message, but, recognizing the fundamental disparity between New York City and upstate problems and the mutual distrust of each section for the other, the bill called for the establishment of two five-member commissions instead of a single agency. Each body would have complete supervisory authority over all forms of public service corporations (except telephone and telegraph companies) in its respective area, including the right to investigate complaints on request, to fix rates and service upon its own initiative, to guarantee adequate service, to order changes in schedules when necessary, and to set up uniform systems of accounting. Hughes was especially pleased with the general provision granting the commissions sweeping power to "direct whatever may be necessary or proper . . . to secure the fulfillment of the public obligation of the corporation under its supervision." [22]

[21] New York *Times*, March 6, 1907; William E. Mosher and Finla G. Crawford, *Public Utility Regulation* (New York: Harper, 1933), pp. 24–25; "Memorandum of Lawrence Veiller, Transit Commission," Jan. 25, 1907, Veiller Papers; "Reminiscences of Lawrence Veiller" (Oral History Project, Columbia University Library, 1949), p. 150.

[22] Hughes, "Biographical Notes," p. 190; Thomas Mott Osborne, "The Public Service Commissions Law of New York," *Atlantic Monthly*, CI (1908), 547–549; *Laws of New York, 1907* (2 vols.; Albany: J. B. Lyon, 1907), I, ch. 429.

So ambitious and far-reaching a measure as the Page-Merritt bill—for it was, indeed, a pioneer in utility regulation—inevitably evoked criticism.[23] As if deliberately to invite savage reaction, the coauthors, on March 5, accompanied their announcement of the bill's provisions with a challenging supplementary statement: "It is to be hoped that the interests affected by this legislation will accept it with an open mind, and will cooperate with the Legislature." [24] Next day on the senate floor, embittered Owen Cassidy, reputedly one of the GOP leaders opposed to strict regulation, accused Alfred Page of trying to "supersede thought and action on the bill" by unqualifiedly associating sincere critics with "the interests." [25] Joined by conservative Democrat Pat McCarren, John Raines's current ally in the Kelsey case, Cassidy tried to sidetrack the proposal to the notorious miscellaneous corporations committee, traditionally a graveyard for reform legislation. He was unsuccessful, however, and the bill was turned over to the friendlier finance committee, where it was given immediate consideration. Within a day, it moved along to the antiadministration judiciary committee, and the legislative brakes were quickly applied. Meanwhile, in the assembly the bill lay in the hands of Speaker Wadsworth, who fully appreciated its importance to both utility investors and the consuming public.[26]

From the beginning, senatorial opposition was directed at weakening Hughes's public utility bill, not at annihilating it. Total destruction would have so inflamed public opinion, now clamoring for some form of unified regulation, that Republican fortunes would suffer irreparable damage.[27] Still, Raines and

[23] Its only rival for this honor was the Wisconsin law (Mosher and Crawford, *Public Utility Regulation*, p. 22).

[24] Buffalo *Morning Express*, March 6, 1907.

[25] New York *Times*, March 7, 1907.

[26] Wadsworth, "Autobiography," p. 98; Buffalo *Morning Express*, March 9, 1907; New York *Press*, March 9, 1907, Fuller Collection, Vol. CXLVI.

[27] Buffalo *Morning Express*, March 9, 1907; New York *Times*, May 4, 1907; New York *Tribune*, March 16, 1907, Fuller Collection, Vol. CXLVII.

his old guard were smarting under Hughes's assault in the Kelsey matter and could hardly exult over the legislative reform program. "The county leaders all act as if they had been kicked in the stomach," complained Onondaga's Horace White, adding that the utility bill was, after all, a "radical" measure.[28] Jealously guarding legislative prerogative, and markedly indifferent to New York City problems, these entrenched upstaters resented the Governor's growing power. At the same time, Democrats opposed what they thought would enhance Albany control over local matters in clear violation of the principle of home rule. "I do not believe in government by commission," confessed Assemblyman Robert F. Wagner, speaking later for a host of independent Democrats as well as the Tammanyites in both houses of the legislature.[29] Perhaps some form of a bipartisan alliance was possible once again, and Raines turned to the strategy he was only then implementing in the Kelsey imbroglio.[30]

Between March 6 and April 3 a number of utility measures filled senate and assembly hoppers. Senator Otto Foelker of Brooklyn introduced a second bill for the GOP. Democrats Tom Grady, Pat McCarren, and John P. Cohalan, cooperating fully with Raines, contributed their own bills to the upper house. Inspired by Attorney-General William Jackson's recent public repudiation of the administration measure, the Cohalan bill embodied substantially the basic changes that Democrats, many Republicans, and utility representatives finally accepted as essential and necessary.[31]

[28] White to Francis Hendricks, March 14, 1907, Horace White Papers (Syracuse University Library).

[29] New York *Times*, May 16, 1907. Similar statements came from the Hearst press, Thomas Grady, Mayor McClellan, and Democratic State Chairman William Conners (New York *American*, n.d., Fuller Collection, Vol. CXLVII; Buffalo *Morning Express*, March 12, 1907; New York *Times*, March 28, 1907; Buffalo *Daily Courier*, April 29, 1907). Even independent Republican Seth Low had reservations about the Page-Merritt bill on this account (Low to Hughes, May 23, 1907, Hughes Papers).

[30] Buffalo *Morning Express*, March 20, 1907; New York *Times*, March 19, 1907.

[31] On March 24 Jackson charged that the administration-supported measure would grant the governor arbitrary power and would violate

The specific grounds of opposition to the Page-Merritt proposal—reflected in Jackson's attack and this Democratic legislation—had been sharply defined almost immediately after its provisions were made public. Although Hughes was accorded the support of most newspapers that backed his efforts for administrative reform, some journals balked at the extensive powers delegated to the governor and the proposed commissioners.[32] For one thing, the administration had insisted that it have authority to remove commissioners without senate approval. A sound idea perhaps in terms of modern administrative theory, this sweeping provision invited a large-scale debate on the question of legislative-executive balance.[33] Then again, Hughes had prevailed upon his supporters to leave out a court review feature, usually incorporated in such regulatory legislation. Without it, disgruntled defendants could not hope to have a disagreeable order suspended before its fairness was determined by the courts. Granting a commission quasi-judicial authority and refusing the usual constitutional safeguards, argued the critics, would put the legislative stamp of approval on property confiscation.[34]

Public utility spokesmen, facing stricter regulation in New York than anywhere in the nation, girded themselves for the fight against the Page-Merritt bill. Like their legislative friends, they sought to weaken, not to defeat outright, this ambitious measure by what promised to be a well-organized assault upon Hughes's advanced concepts of governmental supervision. From the beginning they decided to conduct their campaign in the

---

the home rule principle (New York *Sun*, March 25, 1907). Next day Cohalan's bill was introduced in the senate (*New York Senate Journal*, 130th session, p. 577).

[32] New York *Tribune*, March 7 and 9, 1907; New York *Globe*, March 6, 1907, New York *World* and New York *Press*, March 7, 1907, Syracuse *Post-Standard*, March 17, 1907, Fuller Collection, Vol. CXLVI; Buffalo *Morning Express*, March 7, 1907.

[33] New York *Sun*, March 17, 1907. The *Wall Street Journal*, on March 8, 1907, had also opposed the bill on this ground.

[34] New York *Times*, March 29, 1907.

open, devoid of the traditional use of slush funds. Their representatives would appear before the senate judiciary committee, point out the weakness of the administration's bill, and suggest specific revisions.[35]

It was in the midst of the Kelsey hearings that the judiciary committee undertook a series of four public sessions on the proposed utility legislation. Extending from March 27 to April 4, they provided a clearing house for criticism of the Page-Merritt bill; only one session permitted administration defenders to air their views. Utility representatives paraded to the witness stand to fulfill the roles assigned them. Actually, all the affected interests—the New York City traction group, the railroads, and the gas and electric companies—pledged themselves to some form of regulation. Albert Harris, counsel for the New York Central Railroad, summed up the corporation attitude by arguing the inevitability of the consolidation movement in America, adding: "One of the benefits to the railroad companies . . . is such control as the Federal government gives and this act will give in preventing discrimination and preventing favoritism." [36] For the most part, these able representatives dwelt upon the two key criticisms—the gubernatorial removal power and the absence of a court review provision. Speaking for the Pennsylvania Railroad, Edward Shepard challenged the administration on the point that its bill unconstitutionally delegated legislative powers leading "to the destruction of property." Comparing the proposal to the federal Interstate Commerce Act and laws of some twenty states designed to accomplish similar purposes, Shepard climaxed his testimony with the judgment that Hughes's ideas went well beyond the accepted form of regulation.[37] A whole battery of prominent lawyers, including Joseph Hodges Choate, Paul Cravath, and De Lancey Nicoll, reiterated the Shepard charges, and the utility position was clearly defined.

[35] *Ibid.*, March 10 and 13, 1907; New York *World*, March 26, 1907.

[36] New York Legislature Senate Judiciary Committee, "Hearings on Railroad Legislation" (unpublished MS, 1907; New York State Library at Albany), pp. 53–54.

[37] *Ibid.*, pp. 12, 21.

The defenders of the Page-Merritt bill, in the little time that they had, reflected the mainstream of the utility regulation movement in the Empire State. In January progressive Lawrence Veiller had advised Hughes on the way to conduct the necessary "agitation." Drawing upon his own vast experience as a propagandist and lobbyist, he recommended a three-pronged attack: unite New York City civic organizations behind the Governor's bill; oppose all other measures; and create public sentiment through the press—all of which were undertaken during the ensuing weeks.[38] On April 4 Veiller's first item was put to the test as representatives of several such organizations, including the City Club, the Citizens' Union, and the People's Institute, ably defended the administration's ideas on utility regulation. Their testimony was directed essentially at answering the specific charges hurled against the bill by its opponents. As William Ivins maintained, the Hughes champions claimed the support not only of Republican independents but a majority of New York City's 650,000 voters as well.[39]

In the meantime, Governor Hughes had been sparring with his Kelsey opponents, alluding to the Page-Merritt bill only in so far as it represented a part of his overall program, which he now feared was under fire. As the utility regulation debate continued, he concluded that the opposition "appeared more and more to be lacking in substance." [40] Yet his equanimity was disturbed by the smooth and enlightened presentation of the conservative case to the judiciary committee. On March 29 an overzealous legislative follower, throwing down the challenge, informed newspapermen that the Governor would veto a watered-down bill. Although this may, indeed, have been the administration's inclination, Hughes seized the opportunity to reiterate the position he had long maintained and, at the same time, to intimate his intentions in the utility fight. Insisting that no one spoke for him, he reaffirmed his November 23 declaration of independence and

[38] "Memorandum of Lawrence Veiller, Transit Commission."
[39] Buffalo *Morning Express*, April 5, 1907; "Hearings on Railroad Legislation," pp. 349–427, esp. 390–418.
[40] Hughes, "Biographical Notes," p. 191.

assured the people of New York that "when there is occasion to state any attitude with regard to public questions, I shall state it myself." [41]

Within two days, Hughes found that occasion and responded brilliantly to the challenge posed by critics of the Page-Merritt bill. In Utica for a chamber of commerce banquet, he climaxed the evening's festivities with a sober but forceful presentation of his side of the utility case. After briefly outlining the significant administrative improvements contained in the bill, he answered the property-confiscation argument. Hughes maintained that in the absence of an explicit court review provision in the law, any company, faced with an allegedly confiscatory order, could appeal to the courts on the constitutional grounds of due process. In reality, he added, granting private interests the traditional court review feature would violate the principle of the separation of power, for the judiciary, in essence, would thereby be delegated what opponents admitted was a legislative prerogative —namely, the authority to fix rates and prescribe standards for adequate service. [42]

Encouraged by widespread favorable reaction to a coldly rational and logical defense of the administration bill, Hughes planned several upstate speaking engagements in an effort to answer some of his opposition in their own bailiwick. [43] In Glens Falls, on April 5, he discussed the need for vesting greater authority in the state's executive, an argument that led neatly into justification for granting the governor the sole right to remove members of the proposed commissions. In Buffalo, on April 18, Hughes appealed broadly and dispassionately for the proper and just regulation of public utilities. [44]

The remarkable calmness that the Governor displayed in these

[41] Buffalo *Morning Express*, March 31, 1907; New York *Times*, March 30, 1907

[42] Jacob Gould Schurman, ed., *Addresses of Charles Evans Hughes, 1906–1916* (New York: Putnam, 1916), pp. 146–158.

[43] New York *Evening Post*, Utica *Press*, and Syracuse *Herald*, April 2, 1907, Fuller Collection, Vol. CXLVIII; New York *Times* and Buffalo *Morning Express*, April 2, 1907.

[44] Schurman, *Addresses*, pp. 159–171, 172–178.

crucial addresses provided a marked contrast to his earlier public indictments of politicians and political organizations, then presumably united in opposition to the Kelsey removal. This noteworthy change in tone was fully appreciated by New York County Chairman Herbert Parsons, who, shortly before the Utica speech, warned Hughes's private secretary that the administration's apparent antagonism toward the organization and the legislature was causing undue hostility among the party leaders. Many of the Governor's own supporters, added Parsons, quaked every time Hughes made a speech. Although Robert Fuller denied that Hughes had ever taken so uncompromising a stand, the Utica speech coincidentally launched his series of straightforward, dispassionate appeals. So acceptable, indeed, was the April 1 address that Parsons pointedly congratulated the Governor for refusing newspaper importunities to make a direct plea to the people against the organization.[45]

All through the upstate tour, the enlightened Hughes seemed to heed Parsons' sound advice. In Glens Falls he even went so far as to admit that "a majority of the members of the Legislature are alive to the importance of the question presented and will be found in accord with the public sentiment upon this question." [46] In Elmira, where he was compelled to speak impromptu, Hughes contained himself and avoided the pitfalls of his uncompromising posture in the Kelsey battle.

The Elmira story is a good illustration of the Governor's sagacity and determination. Here, on May 3, he had been ready with a prepared speech. Shortly before the meeting, his chamber of commerce host, Judge Walter Lloyd Smith, informed him that he would speak first, not last as announced in the prearranged schedule. Suspecting duplicity, Hughes issued a special request to give his address after John B. Stanchfield's remarks. The Governor's suspicions were fully justified when Stanchfield, a prominent Democratic foe of the Page-Merritt bill, launched

[45] Parsons to Fuller, April 1, 1907, and Fuller to Parsons, April 2 and 3, 1907, Parsons Papers.

[46] Schurman, *Addresses*, p. 171.

into a blistering attack upon strict utility regulation. Hughes was undaunted and, pouncing on Stanchfield's cutting statement that he held no railroad retainer, commenced his reply with the admission: "I am here under a retainer. I am here retained by the people of the State of New York." [47] These words immediately caught the fancy of his supporters and subsequently formed the basis of many an appeal for the Hughes program.

Governor Hughes's advance in political education was manifested in other ways during the spring of 1907. With the senate threatening his leadership both on the Kelsey issue and the legislative program, he could ill afford to antagonize Assembly Speaker James Wadsworth, in whose hands rested the fate of reform in the lower house. On March 8 Wadsworth had risen above differences with Hughes to announce his support of the Page-Merritt bill, which in the assembly was accorded markedly better treatment than in the senate. As matters drifted into April, however, a situation developed which threatened to drive a wedge between the Governor and Wadsworth. Involving none other than Theodore Roosevelt himself, it tested Hughes's dedication to the reform program even at the risk of presidential recrimination.

Almost since inauguration day, Public Works Superintendent Frederick Stevens, Wadsworth's enemy, had been badgering Roosevelt with requests to remove an upstate New York officeholder, Archie Sanders, collector of internal revenue at Rochester.[48] Sanders had long been allied with the Wadsworths, and the ambitious Stevens, playing upon some evidence of malfeasance in office, exploited the chance to shake up the Geneseo organization. To Roosevelt, early in April, the superintendent reiterated his charges, conveying the impression that Governor Hughes stood behind him. Roosevelt concluded that Sanders was employing his influence in upstate New York against the administration's reform program, whose success the President, of

[47] *Ibid.*, p. 179; Beerits, "First Term," pp. 29–30.
[48] Stevens to William Loeb, Jr., April 25, 1907, Theodore Roosevelt Papers (Manuscript Division, Library of Congress).

course, deemed essential to Republican fortunes.[49] Moreover, vindictive as he sometimes could be, Roosevelt saw an opportunity to retaliate at ex-Congressman James Wadsworth, Sr., with whom he recently had had a falling out. He acted quickly, and on April 13, through George B. Cortelyou, he demanded Sanders' resignation.[50]

When, on April 18, the press received word of the Sanders removal, speculation was rampant as to which motive operated most strongly in Roosevelt's mind—Sanders' alleged violation of federal civil service principles, the President's concern for Hughes's reform program, or Roosevelt's resentment at the elder Wadsworth's recent denunciations of the national administration.[51] The fight against Wadsworth, at this juncture, seemed particularly relevant in view of the repeated charges that the White House was using federal patronage to stamp out potential opposition to its efforts in naming the 1908 GOP presidential candidate. In any case, Hughes was inevitably queried on whether or not he had actually solicited Roosevelt's support. An affirmative answer might have taken the President off the hook, but the Governor chose to be truthful.[52] In so doing, he risked antagonizing the President for the sake of placating the Wads-

[49] Herbert Parsons to Charles D. Hilles, July 24, 1907, Parsons Papers; Roosevelt to Richard Henry Dana, Nov. 2, 1907, *LTR*, V, 827–829. Significantly, on April 14 Roosevelt reiterated his pledge to support the reform program and coupled it with a public appeal to the state leaders whose opposition, he felt, might harm the GOP's future in New York (New York *World*, April 15, 1907).

[50] Rochester *Herald*, April 18, 1907; Wadsworth, "Autobiography," p. 101.

[51] Rochester *Herald*, April 18 and 19, 1907; Rochester *Post Express*, April 19, 1907; New York *Times*, April 20 and 21, 1907; Buffalo *Morning Express*, April 20, 1907; Buffalo *Daily Courier*, April 20 and May 10, 1907; New York *Tribune*, April 19, 1907, New York *World*, April 20, 1907, and New York *Evening Post*, May 13, 1907, Fuller Collection, Vol. CXVII.

[52] Hughes, "Biographical Notes," p. 196a; Mark Sullivan, *Our Times: The United States, 1900–1925* (6 vols.; New York: Scribner, 1926–1935), III, 284.

worths and of maintaining the consistency of his independent position.

Unfortunately, the ever-eager press did not let the issue rest. If comment had been limited to Hughes's explanation, both Roosevelt and the Governor might have muddled through with a minimum of difficulty. But on April 22 and 23 the independent New York *Evening Post* carried two sensational dispatches from its Albany correspondent, Frank Simonds.[53] Simonds had long been considered the newspaperman closest to the administration, and any significant articles he published were generally deemed official. In these particular items, Simonds ill-advisedly insisted that Hughes was being harmed more by the President than by the entire state senate, then battling him on the Kelsey removal. Hughes's friends were shown to be distraught over Roosevelt's alleged efforts to take credit for whatever success the Governor achieved in implementing his reform legislation. As a national figure, the President, they feared, would reap the major share of the praise for the great fight in New York State. Hughes's administration, on the other hand, would look like "the shadow of Washington." [54]

Thus, Theodore Roosevelt was made to appear sinister, and worst of all, Hughes seemingly had played a part in painting that picture. Already the Governor had been criticized for following too closely the dictates of what Roosevelt later called the "muckraking" press. The Sanders incident and its consequences tended to confirm this interpretation. Hughes immediately sought to quell rumors that he had encouraged the Simonds attack on Roosevelt. In an unscheduled press conference he explained to other members of the press, irritated over the "favored" position given the *Post*, that he had not inspired the controversial dispatches. And although subsequent developments in 1907 showed that the President accepted this explanation, he

[53] This discussion is based on Sullivan's account in *Our Times*, III, 284–286, the main lines of which Hughes has confirmed in his "Biographical Notes," p. 196.

[54] Sullivan, *Our Times*, III, 285.

never really forgot the episode, and it remained a sore spot that would fester again.[55]

With the senate moving further and further away from the state administration on the Kelsey matter, Governor Hughes, late in April, determined to push through the Page-Merritt bill without major alterations. On April 24 he met with several supporters and refused flatly to make any changes they proposed. When, several days later, Wadsworth's assembly railroads committee threatened a number of amendments, Hughes summoned its members to the executive chamber. The result of this conference was a favorable report on the Page-Merritt bill containing only minor changes.[56]

Still, the state senate remained a stumbling block. For almost two months the utility bill had been bandied about in the judiciary committee. If this small group of Republican legislators, encouraged by the Tammany leadership, could so successfully defy the administration on the Kelsey removal, conjectured the progressives after May 3, what might they do regarding the more important reform program? Theodore Roosevelt must have asked himself this same question a number of times during the spring of 1907.

President Roosevelt had long worried about the stubbornness of those legislative groups that represented the remnants of the old Platt machine. On March 11 his personal envoy, Congressman William Cocks, had visited Albany for the purpose of testing the popularity among senators and assemblymen of the Page-

---

[55] Hughes, "Biographical Notes," p. 196b; Beerits, "First Term," p. 21; New York *Sun*, May 8, 1907; Arthur W. Dunn, *From Harrison to Harding: A Personal Narrative* (2 vols.; New York: Putnam, 1922), II, 39; *LTR*, V, 828.

[56] Buffalo *Morning Express*, April 25, 1907; New York *Times*, April 30 and May 6, 1907. Wadsworth's position had changed somewhat since his March 8 statements supporting the utility bill. Apparently moved by the senate judiciary committee hearings and possibly by his legislative friends, he objected especially to the power of removal clause. He would not, however, use his influence against the Page-Merritt bill, and assembly opposition melted under Hughes's demands (Buffalo *Morning Express*, May 8, 1907).

Merritt bill. Slightly over two weeks later, Timothy Woodruff and Herbert Parsons, having just left the President, appeared in the state capitol for a secret conference with Hughes on the reform program. Then came the Sanders incident, which, mishandled though it was, nonetheless made clear the national administration's commitment to the Governor's cause. Even this proved insufficient, however, as the Kelsey defeat momentarily shattered Hughes's prestige. But, by the same token, the state senate's intransigence stirred Roosevelt into action. On May 6 he met with Herbert Parsons and advised the New York leaders to join together, agree upon a public service commission bill, and push it through the legislature.[57]

Quickly, the state leaders scampered to Albany in response to Roosevelt's importunity. On the evening of May 7 Congressman Cocks took the initiative and invited Woodruff, national committeemen William Ward and Lucius Littauer, William Barnes, and George Aldridge to a conference in the fashionable Ten Eyck Hotel. Here it was agreed that Woodruff would issue a manifesto to all members of the legislature, none of whom were present, commanding them to rally behind Governor Hughes's entire reform program. "Any Republican who opposes the programme," declared Ward after the meeting, "will be a back number. The Utilities bill will pass in practically the shape the Governor wants it." [58]

Next day a series of conferences was held among the leaders. In the morning, Woodruff and Ward jointly reiterated the previous evening's decision and announced that the state committee would soon be convened in special session for the purpose of issuing a statement supporting Hughes's position. Then, in various other meetings, recalcitrant legislators were cajoled into accepting the Page-Merritt bill practically intact. Governor Hughes himself was apprised of this fortuitous turn of events. In closed sessions with Ward, Littauer, and William Bennet, and

[57] Parsons to William Loeb, May 18, 1907, Roosevelt Papers; New York *World*, March 12, 1907; New York *Times*, March 27, 1907.
[58] New York *World*, May 8, 1907.

then with Woodruff, the surprised chief executive was assured
that every major reform bill would be supported by the state
leaders. As if to put the icing on the cake, stubborn John Raines
pledged his personal endorsement of the program.[59]

Although the Hughes forces, despite the Kelsey reversal, were
confident of victory before the May conferences, they immediately exploited their new opportunity in calling for a party
caucus. Senate majority leader Raines, even if he so desired,
could not now stem the tide, and on the evening of May 8 senate
Republicans gathered in the capitol library. For two hours,
progressive Alfred Page regaled his colleagues with the merits of
the administration's utility bill. When the session was over, the
senate GOP had committed itself to the controversial measure in
substantially its original form.[60]

Three days later, on May 11, the Republican state committee
met in special session and endorsed Governor Hughes's entire reform program. Woodruff had held out faint hope that only the
Page-Merritt bill would be given committee support, for such
other legislation as the political reform and apportionment measures he knew would not receive unanimous GOP approval. But
Benjamin Odell, still searching for a winning political combination, carried the day in behalf of "complete" reapportionment,
the recount bill, and ballot reform. Woodruff then chimed in
with a pledge to Hughes calling for "the unqualified support of
the Republican political machine in his efforts to carry out the
wishes of the people of the State." [61]

All that now remained was the formality of bringing the Page-
Merritt bill up for a vote in the assembly and senate. In both
houses, the measure was greeted by Tammany's ill-fated attempts to water down those provisions on which the opposition
—Democrats and old guard Republicans alike—had based their

[59] New York *Times*, May 9 and 10, 1907; Buffalo *Daily Courier*, May
9, 1907.
[60] New York *World* and Buffalo *Morning Express*, May 8, 1907; New
York *Times*, May 9, 1907. Five days later, the assembly GOP caucused
and made the bill a party measure.
[61] New York *World* and New York *Times*, May 12, 1907.

case. But GOP lines held tight, and Hughes scored a smashing victory. In fact, no assemblyman of either party registered a vote against the final bill, and it was accorded unanimous passage in that body. In the senate, only six recalcitrants, all Democrats, were to be found in opposition.[62]

In the final analysis, credit for so decisive a triumph must be divided between Governor Hughes and the vigilant overseer of state Republican fortunes, Theodore Roosevelt. In conjunction with a belligerently reformist press, Hughes had conducted a brilliant publicity campaign that penetrated every major area of New York State.[63] His dispassionate personal appeals for stricter utility regulation, paralleling his sober, dedicated demeanor as the 1905 gas and insurance counsel, enhanced his established image as a rock of honesty and incorruptibility amidst a sea of evil and wrongdoing. So effective was this campaign that, reportedly, many an uncommitted legislator was literally pressured by his constituents into supporting the administration. This pressure was especially effective after the Kelsey defeat, when, presumably, Hughes had been beaten by the worst elements in the state.[64]

[62] The Democratic strategy, as determined by the party caucus of May 14, was to offer various amendments to the Page-Merritt bill, thereby expressing opposition sentiment, and then to vote for the bill in its unamended form (Buffalo *Daily Courier*, May 15, 1907). The suggested changes, proposed in each house, would have made the commissions elective and guaranteed the traditional court review of decisions (*New York Assembly Journal*, 130th session, pp. 3131–3146; *New York Senate Journal*, 130th session, pp. 1769–1773).

[63] Merlo J. Pusey estimates that in two months Hughes spoke at forty dinners in behalf of the Page-Merritt bill (*Charles Evans Hughes* [New York: Macmillan, 1951], I, 202). Many observers gave the Governor most of the credit for this victory. The force of public opinion is emphasized in Ida Tarbell, "How About Hughes?" *American Magazine*, LXV (1908), 451–464; Harold J. Howland, "Hughes, Governor," *Outlook*, LXXXVIII (1908), 303–309; J. O. Hammitt, "An Awakening in New York State," *Independent*, LXV (1908), 758–761; "Relying Upon the People" (editorial), *Independent*, LXII (1907), 1214–1215. For press comment, see *Literary Digest*, XXXIV (1907), 786–787.

[64] *Literary Digest*, XXXIV, 786–787; New York *Times*, May 19, 1907; "Hughes and What He Stands For," *World's Work*, XV (1908), 10040.

It was this same Kelsey battle and subsequent public reaction that rekindled President Roosevelt's interest in the success of the state administration. Although less than one month earlier Roosevelt had been badly stung in his removal of collector Sanders, enactment of Hughes's program transcended personal resentment and bitterness. Thus, the progressive President used his far-reaching influence to bail out the Governor. Undoubtedly Hughes would have won a modified public service commission bill without Roosevelt's interference, since public opinion had made it nearly impossible for a bipartisan alliance to defeat regulation outright. Federal support, however, not only forestalled the consummation of such an alliance and therefore kept intact the ambitious Page-Merritt bill, it also forced Raines and his stubborn old guard into committing themselves, at least partially, to several other key reform measures. Happily for Hughes, then, the Roosevelt administration swung into action at precisely the right moment.

To render this new regulatory legislation exemplary, Governor Hughes took considerable time in screening lists of candidates for the commissionerships. After resisting pressures from various sources, he made his final decisions and on June 28 announced his appointments. For the most part, the appointees were not practical politicians, but relatively young men of affairs usually equipped with some technical education or legal training. Except for labor's criticism that on neither commission was the workingman represented, the gubernatorial appointees were generally well received.[65] In conducting themselves as admirably as they did, these original commissioners helped immeasurably to blot out of people's minds the perennial distrust of regulatory bodies and to put the New York commissions on a solid footing from the very beginning. Their basic structure would remain unchanged for over two decades.

The Governor's triumph on the Page-Merritt bill offered no

[65] New York *Times*, June 29, 1907; James B. Reynolds to Herbert Parsons, June 21, 1907, and Parsons to Hughes, June 24, 1907, Parsons Papers; Buffalo *Morning Express*, Sept. 21, 1907; Seth Low to Hughes, June 29, 1907, Hughes Papers; Flick, *History of New York*, VIII, 241–242.

absolute guarantee that he would be free of further difficulty with the 1907 legislature. To be sure, he had regained much of the prestige he had lost in the Kelsey fiasco, and he had witnessed the senate barrier break down under the strain of various pressures. Yet easy, uncontested victories were not in sight. Although by mid-May most of Hughes's labor legislation and a pure drug law had been passed (all without battle), there remained a host of other reforms that seemed in grave danger of legislative defeat.[66]

Before Governor Hughes concentrated again upon what he deemed his more pressing reform bills, several secondary administration measures were put through the senate and either passed immediately by the assembly or held up temporarily for their perfunctory movement through the appropriate committees. Thus, on May 28, the Page bill establishing a New York City charter revision commission received assembly approval. On the same day, the Phillips bill limiting campaign contributions primarily for state offices passed the senate. Next day, the Wells proposal designed to reorganize New York City's municipal court moved through the upper house. Finally, on June 6, the Agnew water power reserve bill won a unanimous senate victory.[67] Composing a large part of Hughes's 1907 conservation program, this legislation directed the existing water supply commission to inquire into the expediency of having the state own and develop the remaining water power sites within its borders.[68]

Enactment of the more essential recount bill required greater

[66] On the labor laws, see Chapter XIII. The Page Pure Drug Law put New York State in step with federal supervision by making it a misdemeanor for a druggist to resort to false labeling, changing medicinal ingredients in drugs, and substituting one article for another (*Laws of New York, 1907*, II, ch. 649). Another measure, sponsored by Assemblyman Alfred E. Smith, prohibited the sale of certain drugs without prescriptions (*ibid.*, I, ch. 424).

[67] *New York Assembly Journal*, 130th session, p. 3485; *New York Senate Journal*, 130th session, pp. 1933, 1974, 2117.

[68] Another part of the program was the Armstrong bill providing for the acquisition of land for the extension of the state forest preserves. It passed the senate (*Journal*, p. 1539) on May 9 and the assembly (*Journal*, pp. 3340–3341) on May 22.

work on the part of the administration. If standpat Republicans had been little interested in other features of the reform program, they were utterly indifferent toward this proposal. Although the Governor's Prentice-Wainwright bill was couched in general terms and provided adequate machinery for settling contested elections, it grew out of a particular situation, the Hearst-McClellan New York City mayoral battle of 1905, in which the GOP had almost no reason to become embroiled. Certainly, Hughes's desire to rectify what to him was an obvious injustice, as expressed in his annual message, carried little weight among hard-core Republican legislators.

On the other hand, the Democrats were gravely concerned with the recount issue, for, to all intents and purposes, it directly involved two members of their own party. Ironically, the administration bill unintentionally benefited William Randolph Hearst, Hughes's own 1906 opponent, and McClellan backers (or Hearst opponents) rankled with bitterness. Their chief objection was a provision granting the defeated candidate in a given election the right to select particular districts where a recount was to be taken. No other areas would be recanvassed except upon special appeal by the victor, who, because of the measure's faulty language, would personally have to defray whatever expenses were incurred in the countersuit.[69]

Governor Hughes became so sensitive to the charges of unfairness leveled against him that on May 23 he sent a special message to the legislature. In it he earnestly appealed for passage of the Prentice-Wainwright bill, assuring opponents that it was "neither for nor against any one but is simply in the public interest."[70] The now cooperative John Raines quickly steered it through the upper house. Since the bill had already received assembly approval, it went immediately to Mayor McClellan, who, on proposals affecting New York City, exercised the veto

[69] "Memorial to the Legislature from the Mayor of the City of New York in Relation to Assembly Bill No. 1729," *Senate Document No. 37*, 130th session (Albany: J. B. Lyon, 1907), pp. 2–8.
[70] *Hughes Public Papers*, I, 47–48.

power. Thus, McClellan killed it temporarily and, in a scorching memorandum to the legislature, raised the question, obviously directed at Hearst, of enacting laws that could so easily be put to personal advantage.[71]

Despite continued criticism, Hughes could have employed his new-found power to force the administration measure through again and in this way nullify the Mayor's rejection. Instead, he sought to neutralize the opposition by supplementing the controversial bill with a second proposal placing the victorious candidate in a more advantageous position when his electoral triumph was challenged. On the very day that the Wainwright legislation again passed the senate, the so-called Page bill followed it. Quickly the assembly gave its approval, and, in another special message, Hughes expressed his pleasure that the issue had been so amicably settled.[72] The state now had more effective machinery for recanvassing ballots in contested elections, and Hearst would finally obtain the recount he had long requested.

With adjournment of the legislature only a few weeks away, several important features of the Governor's reform program still remained bottled up in committee. Thirsting for total victory, Hughes again resorted to the special legislative message. On June 4 he appealed for the enactment of four separate bills —the primary election law amendment providing for voluntary direct nominations, corrupt practices legislation, a more thorough measure (the Fuller bill) dealing with the state's unused water power sites, and the Moreland bill granting the governor authority to investigate his executive departments.[73] Within three weeks, every one of these proposals, except the Travis direct nominations bill, received senate and assembly approval.

[71] *Senate Document No. 37*, pp. 4, 7; *New York Assembly Journal*, 130th session, pp. 1406–1407; *New York Senate Journal*, 130th session, p. 1916.

[72] *Hughes Public Papers*, I, 181–184. Passage of the Prentice-Wainwright bill over the Mayor's rejection nullified the veto.

[73] *Ibid.*, pp. 48–50. By this time Hughes had given up hope for enactment of a measure calling for the Massachusetts ballot.

Only one problem yet remained for the 1907 legislature to solve, and although it had not been a part of the original reform program, Hughes now considered its immediate solution essential. The apportionment question had been catapulted into a prominent position on the Governor's agenda when, in desperation on May 1, he had injected it into the Kelsey fight. In the many Page-Merritt bill conferences the following week, Republican leaders cautiously hashed over the question, reiterated Hughes's insistence that a new law should be passed in that legislative session, but talked only of changing those provisions which the court had singled out as being unconstitutional. Next day the Governor summoned senate majority leader Raines to the executive chamber and, in the process of extracting a commitment on the utility bill, raised the apportionment issue. As an upstater, Raines, of course, was fearful of any district juggling that might jeopardize his power in the upper house, and so he rejected Hughes's demand that the entire state be reapportioned. Under these circumstances, the only possible agreement was a *modus vivendi* wherein one party would make no attempt to work out a new law without consulting the other.[74]

Raines did seek, however, to push the apportionment issue in accordance with the Governor's wishes and on May 16 set up a special senate committee to work exclusively on a new plan. Although the group selected appeared in some quarters to be anti-Hughes, its chairman, William J. Tully, had been associated with the progressive wing of the Republican party. Shortly after he assumed his new function, Tully reassured skeptics that the legislature would "pass an apportionment bill which will be signed by the Governor and approved by the courts." [75]

Tully worked diligently to devise a scheme that would meet his stated requirements. Setting himself apart from his fellow committeemen, he sought the advice of interested parties. On May 25 he journeyed to New York City, where he met with Herbert Parsons. Two days later, back in Albany, he consulted

[74] New York *Times*, May 9 and 10, 1907.
[75] Buffalo *Daily Courier*, May 25, 1907.

The group of Tammany politicians who accepted Hearst as Democratic candidate for governor at the 1906 Buffalo convention. Seated are (*left to right*) Lewis Nixon, temporary chairman of the convention; Bourke Cockran, congressman from New York; and Charles F. Murphy, Tammany boss. (From *Review of Reviews*, XXXIV [1906], 514; courtesy of the Cornell University Library.)

Two old-guard Republicans: Timothy L. Woodruff, chairman of the Republican state committee (*left*), and William Barnes, chairman of the Albany County Republican committee and member of the Republican state committee (*right*). (From *McClure's*, XXV [1910], 506; courtesy of the Cornell University Library.)

The friendly rivals: Secretary of War William Howard Taft and Governor Hughes. Although the two men were opponents in the contest for the Republican presidential nomination, Taft subsequently supported Hughes's position in New York and, in 1910. appointed him to the Supreme Court. (From *Current Literature*, XLIV [1908], 243; courtesy of the Cornell University Library.)

with Senator George Cobb about the upstate situation. At least twice before making his plan public, he visited Governor Hughes and discussed districting details with him.[76] So closely did Tully hue to the line prescribed by the May 9 *modus vivendi* that when his apportionment bill was ready for presentation to the senate on June 4 many thought that the Governor had made at least a partial commitment to it. This interpretation seemed to be confirmed when John Raines wasted no time in pushing the proposal through the upper house. On the very day that it was introduced, he called a Republican caucus and insisted that his colleague's plan, the best possible scheme, he argued, be made a party measure. Within twenty-four hours the Tully bill passed the senate and was readied for submission to the assembly.[77]

Already, however, a voice of criticism had been heard. On the evening of June 3, when the senate plan was made public, Speaker Wadsworth of the assembly let it be known that he strenuously objected to certain of its provisions altering western New York districts. Although the proposal generally provided for a fairly equitable statewide apportionment, there were alleged discriminations in the speaker's own bailiwick, notably the detachment of Livingston County from the elder Wadsworth's old congressional district.[78] The issue was serious enough for Hughes, on June 4, to phone Herbert Parsons and urge him to come immediately to Albany.

Parsons' presence in the state capital served only to deepen the growing rift between the senate and assembly leaders. In a meeting with Hughes, the New York County chairman gained the impression that the administration had actually made no commitment to Tully and Raines. When Parsons suggested that Wadsworth be placed "where his political potentiality would not be injured," the Governor intimated that he cared little about Livingston County so long as the new apportionment plan was con-

[76] *Ibid.*, May 25, 29, and 30, 1907; Buffalo *Morning Express*, June 4 and 5, 1907; New York *Times*, June 4, 1907.

[77] New York *Times*, June 5, 1907; *New York Senate Journal*, 130th session, p. 2113.

[78] New York *Times*, June 5, 1907.

stitutional.[79] Parsons then rushed over to Wadsworth and urged him to fight the Tully bill. Thus encouraged, the speaker, two days later, called a Republican caucus and jammed through the submissive assembly an apportionment measure to his own liking.[80]

For the next three weeks, each side jockeyed for position as the deadlock continued. State Chairman Woodruff, who, on June 6, had declared for Wadsworth, joined Parsons in an ill-fated attempt to overrule Raines and convince a second senate caucus to reverse itself on the Tully plan. With this failure, the New York County chairman personally turned to Tully but failed to move the determined senator. Finally, leaders of the deadlocked senate and assembly conference committee compromised in favor of taking the thorny issue to Hughes.[81] They agreed to dispatch a special subcommittee to the Governor so that he might make suggestions regarding the impasse. He would not, however, be given a choice of plans.

Governor Hughes was of no help to the deadlocked conferees, for he refused categorically to tender any advice whatsoever. He held firmly to his position that each and every apportionment scheme had the element of politics in it, and he refused to play politics.[82] Obviously, if he had been asked to choose the better plan, he would have refrained from using his decisive influence, although he might thereby have saved Speaker Wadsworth, who, in the past, had been a more faithful follower than Raines, the outspoken champion of the Tully bill.

As the regular legislative session drew to a close, several attempts were made to compromise the apportionment wrangle, but to no avail. Then, on June 24, upon the request of pro-

[79] Parsons to Theodore Roosevelt, June 14, 1907, Roosevelt Papers. Parsons' role in the whole matter is recounted in this letter.

[80] New York *Times* and Buffalo *Morning Express*, June 7, 1907.

[81] Parsons to Roosevelt, June 14, 1907, and to William S. Bennet, June 19, 1907, and Woodruff to William Loeb, June 17, 1907, Roosevelt Papers; Buffalo *Morning Express*, June 14, 1907. Parsons was bitter against Tully, who he insisted was opposed to the Wadsworth plan because it did not place him in so strong a position as his own scheme.

[82] New York *Times*, June 15, 1907.

gressive Assemblyman Jonathan M. Wainwright, Governor Hughes made one last effort to bring the contending forces together. Once again he chose the vehicle of the special message, importuning the legislature to discharge a "paramount public obligation." [83] Since he had repudiated the use of all traditional, informal devices to settle intraparty quarrels, he could only threaten to convene a special session if the apportionment impasse continued through adjournment.

So determined in their opposition were the senate and assembly leaders that the Governor's threat meant next to nothing. Indeed, an extraordinary session was welcomed in some quarters, for the slate would thus be wiped clean and the work could begin anew. On June 26 the legislature defiantly closed its doors, but within two weeks had them reopened as Hughes made good his promise. In a rousing message, he demanded enactment not only of an equitable apportionment scheme but also of a direct primary law, the one remaining major feature of his 1907 reform program.[84]

No sooner had the Governor registered his plea than the controversy erupted again. Wadsworth found it impossible to agree upon a compromise bill, and senate majority leader John Raines appointed another special committee to present a plan to the upper house.[85] This group met from time to time with assembly legislators who had been chosen by floor leader Sherman Moreland to reconsider the question and draw up a compromise measure. Nothing, however, was forthcoming, and the same impasse that occurred during the regular session threatened to keep the legislators at work all summer.

For almost two weeks the conferees haggled over the respective apportionment bills. Then, on July 22, a senate Republican caucus again threw down the gauntlet by endorsing the Tully plan, now being sponsored by Binghamton's Harvey D. Hin-

[83] *Hughes Public Papers*, I, 50–51; Wainwright to Hughes, June 22, 1907, Hughes Papers.

[84] New York *Times*, June 22, 1907; *Hughes Public Papers*, I, 52–54.

[85] Buffalo *Morning Express*, July 11, 1907; New York *Times*, July 16, 1907.

man. Presaging assembly action was the upper house voting pattern, far different from that in the regular session. Only three negative votes were recorded against the Hinman bill as compared with eleven some six weeks earlier. Several pro-Wadsworth senators, including Percy Hooker of Genesee and Stanislaus Franchot of Niagara, had deserted the speaker. Next day Wadsworth himself gracefully backed down from what had seemed to be an uncompromising position.[86] Immediately, the assembly GOP accepted the Tully scheme, and the long intraparty feud ended.

Speaker Wadsworth's surprising July 23 about-face was (and still is) difficult to explain. There are two factors, however, that, taken together, aid in understanding his action. First, Wadsworth was a political realist, and when Hughes continued to refrain from using his influence, he knew his position was hopeless. The apportionment question, to his way of thinking, was not significant enough to warrant further party warfare. Second, and perhaps more important, the speaker realized that, unless some bill was enacted, at least one election would have to be held on the basis of the outmoded 1895 law—presently the only legislation on the books. This meant that his old enemy, Frederick Stevens, would be returned the very political power the Geneseo organization had taken from him in the 1906 act. Coupled with the public works superintendency, this added prestige could provide for Stevens the nucleus of a political machine that might threaten the Wadsworths.[87]

Once the apportionment issue was settled, weary legislators impatiently pushed for adjournment. Still striving for a perfect record, however, the persistent Governor dispatched another special message to the senate and assembly on July 24. In it he called for the passage of the pending Travis-Greene direct nominations bill. Despite Herbert Parsons' efforts to cajole indifferent New York County followers into supporting the administration,

[86] Buffalo *Morning Express*, July 24, 1907; New York *Times*, July 23 and 24, 1907.
[87] New York *Times*, July 24, 1907.

this voluntary primary plan failed, and on the very day of the message the legislature adjourned *sine die*.[88]

Unquestionably, from the standpoint of results, Governor Hughes had done remarkably well with a branch of government that, in December, 1906, he had refused to help organize and from which, during the course of 1907, he had remained unusually aloof. Every major feature of his reform program, except the primary bill and the Massachusetts ballot, was put on the statute books. Such success inevitably evoked widespread editorial comment, especially from the jubilant pro-Hughes press. While the Governor was rapidly emerging as a national leader, averred the New York *Times*, the Republican legislative organization was "whipped but unregenerate." Since the civil war, added Pulitzer's *World*, "no session . . . has done work of such importance." What made the 1907 legislative record so outstanding, insisted the *Outlook*, was the number of good measures that were passed together with the bad ones that were killed.[89]

Doubtless, Governor Hughes's own vigilance, in large part, explains the overall success, for in reality the number of irresponsible bills that moved through the legislature was utterly appalling.[90] Of an estimated twelve hundred measures that went to the executive, Hughes felt obliged to veto almost five hundred of them, or approximately 40 per cent. The most commonly rejected item was the local bill. Early in the year, Hughes discovered that a favorite scheme among politicians was to obtain for a client a charter granting certain privileges in a particular area of the state. Generally, nothing was done with these grants, and until the holder could sell the properties and reap a windfall profit, his charter was renewed. There was no reason

[88] Parsons to Hughes, July 25, 1907, Parsons Papers; New York *Press*, July 25, 1907, Fuller Collection, Vol. XIX.

[89] New York *Times*, June 27, 1907; New York *World*, June 27, 1907, Fuller Collection, Vol. CI; "A Governor's Legislature," *Outlook*, LXXXVI (1907), 484.

[90] Herbert Parsons had anticipated this early in the legislative year (Parsons to Hughes, Feb. 18, 1907, Parsons Papers).

for this legislation, the Governor later insisted, other than the "special legislation which had preceded it."[91] Thus he vetoed such measures as the Davenport, Middleburgh, and Durham Railroad Company bill granting this utility a third five-year extension to construct a railroad. Less than one month later, he forced reluctant legislators to put into another local bill a provision compelling the Long Sault Development Company, receiving water rights in the St. Lawrence River, to compensate the state for the coveted lease. This new policy, hailed as revolutionary in some quarters, worked to minimize the abuse, but obviously did not eliminate it entirely.[92]

If Hughes struck intolerantly at local legislation, he showed no mercy for arbitrary bills, of which there were many in 1907. Perhaps the Governor's most famous veto was that of the so-called two-cent fare bill, which sought to limit passenger fares on New York State railroads to two cents per mile. Resisting the temptation to win popular applause by taking another swing at the railroads, Hughes sent a stirring message of rejection to the astonished legislature. He lectured his over-zealous followers that "injustice on the part of railroad corporations toward the public does not justify injustice on the part of the State toward railroad corporations."[93] He went on to point out that establishing an inflexible rate scale to apply all over New York failed to account for varied conditions and circumstances. After all, Hughes argued in conclusion, the public service commissions were set up to handle just such matters, and their expert members should determine fair rates.[94]

Thus ended Governor Hughes's first legislative year. His phenomenal success, achieved in the wake of determined and formidable opposition, gave him more prestige than any New York chief executive in two decades, including Theodore Roosevelt.

[91] Buffalo *Morning Express*, Aug. 28, 1907.
[92] *Hughes Public Papers*, I, 67–68; New York *Times*, April 25 and May 14, 1907; *Laws of New York, 1907*, I, ch. 355.
[93] *Hughes Public Papers*, I, 89.
[94] In a similar vein, he vetoed a bill arbitrarily requiring all railroads in New York State to employ an extra brakeman (*ibid.*, pp. 94–95).

And he had done so without actually compromising his political independence, although he had generated considerable ill will between himself and the legislature, especially its conservative GOP leadership. Satisfied over his hard-fought victories in the cause of reform, Hughes could relax for the summer and renew his strength for what promised to be another vigorous fall and winter schedule. The year 1908 would truly put the test to his statesmanlike talents, a test that would most certainly determine his political future.

CHAPTER VIII

The Battle Renewed

IN the past, Charles Evans Hughes had spent many of his summers in Europe. Here his excessive nervous energy, thoroughly camouflaged by an impassive, almost stoic exterior, was harmlessly expended in vigorous Alpine exercises. The governorship, however, had imposed more restrictions upon Hughes's time than his thriving law practice had ever demanded, and during these years his vacations were usually limited to a brief, quiet respite in New York's Adirondacks.[1]

If at any time the Governor needed one of his habitual European sojourns, he did so in the summer of 1907. Since the Saratoga convention of the previous September, he had worked feverishly, first as a candidate for office, then as a fulltime state executive. Unconditioned to the rigors of political life, and sometimes over-zealous in meeting the obligations of his position, Hughes risked impairing his rather precarious health. With his private secretary, Robert H. Fuller, and his military secretary, George C. Treadwell, he followed a grueling daily schedule, toiling nine to ten hours in his capitol office, then often carrying unfinished tasks back to the executive mansion in the evening.[2] His insistence that the governor's office be opened to all persons with legitimate requests and petitions compelled him to

[1] Merlo J. Pusey, *Charles Evans Hughes* (New York: Macmillan, 1951), I, ch. 13 and pp. 222–223.

[2] "Twenty-Four Hours with Governor Hughes," New York *Times Magazine*, April 28, 1907.

consume most of his afternoons seeing visitors and delegations from various parts of the state.[3] Supplementing these meetings with his "constituents," of course, were the many public appearances he made during the legislative year. Contributing immeasurably to Hughes's phenomenal popularity and, in turn, to the success of his reform program, they nonetheless intensified an already busy schedule.

Needless to say, the new governor was unusually conscious of the need for good public relations, and his decision to devote his first summer to reporting his work to his constituents was not wholly unexpected. Now an experienced speaker, he could find better relaxation on a podium than in a conference room filled with wily politicians. As a result of his successful fight against "bossism," his presence at banquets and benefits was sought all over the nation. On July 4, amidst shouts of "Hughes for President!," the Governor shared speaking honors at Jamestown, Virginia, with Princeton University's President Woodrow Wilson. Especially popular in the midwest, he was tendered invitations to make public appearances in nine different states. Determined to confine his activities to New York, however, he rejected all of them.[4] Hughes then concentrated on visiting as many upstate agricultural fairs as time would allow, a task which consumed most of August and part of September.

The Governor's selection of agricultural New York for his summer travels was both traditional and political. Doubtless, he hoped to carry his progressive message into areas where the GOP had long been predominant but where his 1907 reform program generated little real enthusiasm. He chose for his major theme democratic government, its values and its responsibilities. A firm believer in the American doctrine of progress, Hughes repeatedly assured his listeners that functional disorders, stemming usually from unrestrained freedom, were curable through

[3] Hughes's opening of the executive offices received a great deal of publicity during his administrations (Ida Tarbell, "How About Hughes?" *American Magazine*, LXV [1908], 451–464, and Charles Johnston, "Governor Hughes at Albany," *Harper's Weekly*, LIV [May 21, 1910], 9–10).

[4] New York *Times*, July 5 and Aug. 24, 1907.

the application of human reason.[5] This rational faculty, he insisted, had already directed statesmen into accepting the feasibility of using governmental powers for the public welfare. Prudence, however, dictated that the state's vast resources should not be employed as a weapon to interfere with "anybody's legitimate profit." [6]

It is ironic, perhaps, that while the Governor carried his progressive views into the upstate areas, events in the financial world seemed to justify his appeals for stricter governmental supervision of the state's economy. In March New York City's stock market had taken an ominous dip, and in August it repeated its fluctuations. An underlying cause of these Wall Street shocks (and, indeed, the subsequent panic) was the worldwide overexpansion of credit between the years 1904 and 1907. Sudden pressures on the international money supply—like the Russo-Japanese War and the San Francisco earthquake—impelled conservative New York bankers to call in outstanding loans. A sound corporate structure might have withstood the strain, but many New York trust companies had been organized as loose speculative agencies that evidenced little interest in the principles of safe banking. On October 23 one of them, the gigantic Knickerbocker Trust Company, closed its doors and the nation's money market soon collapsed.[7]

Immediately, the Roosevelt administration set out to mitigate these financial disturbances. In the first week of the panic, the

---

[5] His best effort on this score was made at Chautauqua, as reported in Jacob Gould Schurman, "Governor Hughes," *Independent*, LXIII (1907), 1525–1534.

[6] Fulton County Fair Address, cited in New York *Times*, Sept. 4, 1907. Here Hughes justified the recently enacted labor legislation. On August 27, at Sandy Hill and again at the Lewis County Fair, he argued similarly (*ibid.*, Aug. 28, 1907).

[7] For a good discussion of the Panic of 1907, see Alexander Noyes, *Forty Years of American Finance* (New York: Putnam, 1909), ch. 13. An excellent brief analysis of the causes of the panic can be found in "Annual Report of the Superintendent of Banks," December 31, 1907, *Senate Document No. 6*, 131st session (Albany: J. B. Lyon, 1908), pp. 21–23.

President, amidst charges that his own regulatory policies had spawned the crisis, poured federal money into New York to stave off threatening bank runs. He then granted loans to tottering companies so that normal business procedures might be maintained. Governor Hughes, meanwhile, had returned to Albany, where in mid-September he had skillfully handled a petition of complaint against John F. Ahearn, Manhattan borough president. The case against Ahearn, lodged by the City Club of New York, involved certain administrative malpractices and was significant only in that it challenged the Governor's power to remove a local official. Hughes quickly solved the problem by finding the constitutional provisions granting such authority, promptly hearing the case, and removing Ahearn from office.[8]

The October Wall Street shock caught Hughes's New York banking department wholly unprepared. For over three months, this agency had been functioning without a superintendent. The Governor's original appointee, Charles Hallam Keep, had resigned his position in June to accept a commissionership on the new upstate public service commission. For two reasons, Hughes had difficulty finding a successor for Keep. First, the superintendency carried a stipend of only $7,000, and few competent bankers would work for that salary. Second, the Governor himself hesitated to call on available New York City financiers for fear that the individual selected might be controlled by the interests he formerly served. Finally, on October 3, Hughes named an Oswego businessman, Luther Mott, to the position. It was bad enough that Mott possessed little experience in the banking world. The added pressures and strains imposed by a panic-stricken Wall Street so overwhelmed him that within six days after his appointment he tendered his resignation. Thoroughly embarrassed and now desperately in need of a competent banking superintendent, Governor Hughes reluctantly canvassed the New York financial world for an able leader. He found his man

[8] *Hughes Public Papers,* I, 268–286. The actual removal was made in December (*ibid.,* pp. 275–285; New York *Times,* Dec. 10, 1907; Hughes, "Biographical Notes," p. 188, Charles Evans Hughes Papers [Manuscript Division, Library of Congress]).

in Clark Williams, vice-president of the Columbia Trust Company, one whose qualifications were confirmed by former department head A. Barton Hepburn.[9] Destined to serve the administration for almost three years, Williams immediately severed his banking connections and, on the very day of the Knickerbocker failure, assumed his new office.

Quickly, Williams went to work in a concerted effort to overcome the forces of the panic. On October 24 he appealed to Hughes for the appointment of emergency examiners, and the Governor responded with twenty names from the civil service list.[10] These men kept in close touch with the City's embarrassed financial institutions and recommended stern action only when absolutely necessary. To help restore public confidence, the department waited three weeks before it dispatched receivers to the insolvent companies. By November 25 seven institutions were closed down and three others were permitted to resume business.

The Panic of 1907, brief as it was, underscored the need for reform of New York's archaic banking laws. While the Roosevelt administration poured relief funds into the City's money market, Governor Hughes sought to discover the reasons for the sudden financial collapse. Amidst irresponsible accusations hurled at the President, Hughes held quiet, unpublicized sessions with Hepburn and Williams in order to determine what action the state administration might take without further shaking public confidence.[11] Finally, on November 13, the Governor announced the appointment of a special investigating commission, composed of several prominent New York City bankers, to discover, as he put it, "what, if any, changes are advisable in the laws of the State relating to the incorporation, conduct of busi-

[9] New York *Times*, Oct. 23, 1907; Hughes, "Biographical Notes," p. 187; Hughes to Oswald Garrison Villard, Oct. 25, 1907, Oswald Garrison Villard Papers (Harvard University Library).

[10] *Senate Document No. 6*, p. 23.

[11] So it was later reported in the New York *Evening Post*, Nov. 14, 1907 and the New York *World*, Nov. 15, 1907.

ness, and supervision of banks and trust companies?"[12] Wall Street was thus given a chance at self-evaluation and, at the same time, an opportunity to serve the Hughes administration.

One month later the special banking commission presented to the Governor a general report emphasizing the basic changes that were necessary to prevent a recurrence of the October failures. First and foremost, the group advised, the banking superintendent should be given wider powers so that during emergencies he might take more decisive action. Second, the department itself was advised to have its inspection authority broadened. Finally, the report urged that requirements for trust companies be increased substantially.[13]

A careful analysis of the financial disaster was left to Superintendent Williams, who, in November and December, worked diligently with the banking commission. On December 31 he issued his first annual report. This lucid and timely document surveyed with penetrating incisiveness the state of New York City's banking institutions during the panic. Insisting that their structure was basically sound, Williams maintained that only a few corporations were unworthy of continued existence. The report went on to justify the controversial credit contractions and blamed the panic's severity upon four things—insufficiency of supervisory power on the part of New York's banking department, excessive interdependence between and among corporations, the absence of an effective mutual assistance association, and a host of corporate abuses.[14]

Williams' remedy for the evils he unearthed in the New York financial world followed closely the commission's recommendations, which in turn comprised a major portion of Governor Hughes's second annual message, delivered on January 1, 1908. Hughes began his discussion of banking by reiterating the superintendent's confidence in most of New York's financial corpora-

[12] *Hughes Public Papers*, I, 310–311.
[13] New York *Times*, Dec. 18 and 30, 1907.
[14] *Senate Document No. 6*, p. 27.

tions, indicting only a few for "reprehensible practices." [15] He then outlined a series of corrective proposals, including legislation investing greater authority in the bank superintendency and tightening general restrictions with regard to the organization and operation of trust companies and banks. In approaching the delicate question of reserves, Hughes was careful to say that the special committee had not agreed upon the required percentage. His only recommendation, therefore, was that, since trust corporations had assumed the role of banks, they should be treated similarly; their reserve requirements must be increased.

All in all, the 1908 banking legislation included twenty-one bills. Most of these measures were introduced near the end of February and, with little prodding, sped through both houses by the third week of April.[16] Their general tone followed closely Hughes's January 1 recommendations, the trust reserve bill calling for a 15 per cent requirement in New York City and a 10 per cent minimum for the rest of the state. The bank superintendency proposal, drawn up and guided by Williams himself, granted the incumbent the additional power that the Governor had earlier sought. Under certain circumstances, this department head might personally initiate a dissolution proceeding against a particular bank. Other legislation tightened up the borrowing and loaning power of banking and trust institutions, imposed restrictions upon stock-purchasing by bank directors, prohibited banking chains, and specified the areas for trust company investments.[17]

The ease with which the Hughes administration put these significant banking measures through the legislature was unequalled by its other achievements in 1908. Doubtless, this initial

[15] *Hughes Public Papers*, II, 17.

[16] Assuming most of the responsibility for introducing them were Senator S. Percy Hooker of Genesee and Assemblyman James A. Francis of New York County (New York *Times*, April 19, 1908). Hughes did dispatch three emergency messages to the legislature for enactment of separate bills—one on April 14, and two on April 16 (*Hughes Public Papers*, II, 133–134).

[17] *Laws of New York, 1908* (2 vols.; Albany: J. B. Lyon, 1908), I, chs. 143, 152, 154, 169, 184, 119, 156, 121.

success is explained by the emergency situation that prevailed. Although Governor Hughes considered the rest of his program that year equally essential, others seriously questioned its importance. As a result, another protracted struggle with the conservative state senate loomed—one in which the administration again came close to suffering a humiliating defeat.

Governor Hughes opened the legislative session with a rousing progressive message, though, as one journal judiciously observed, it did not "make so deep an impression as the first." [18] In addition to the crucially important banking recommendations, he urged the enactment of a wide array of reforms, among them measures extending the public service commissions' jurisdiction to telephone and telegraph companies, providing ballot reform, establishing the direct primary, and regulating race-track gambling. Of lesser significance were proposals dealing with insurance, agriculture, labor, immigration, public health, charitable institutions, and judicial salaries. It was the race-track gambling situation, however, that disturbed Hughes most of all in this message, and as in 1907 he expended his major effort on a single campaign. He introduced his discussion of the problem by referring to an 1895 amendment to the state Constitution that read: "Nor shall any lottery or the sale of lottery tickets, pool-selling, book-making, or any other kind of gambling hereafter be authorized or allowed within this state and the Legislature shall pass appropriate laws to prevent offenses against any of the provisions of this section." [19] In the same year the senate and assembly had amended the Penal Code making it a felony to become involved, at any time, in bookmaking or pool selling. Where exclusive penalties were provided, however, this punishment would not apply. Shortly thereafter, just such an exclusive penalty was enacted. It called simply for "forfeiture of the amount wagered, to be recovered in a civil action" unless a memorandum or written token of the bet were produced in evidence. In reality, then, a person might be held liable only for the

[18] "The Governor in the Message," *Nation*, LXXXVI (1908), 26.
[19] *Hughes Public Papers*, II, 25.

amount of a wager and compelled by court action to return any winnings he had made.[20]

Needless to say, Hughes excoriated the Percy-Gray Racing Law for flouting the state Constitution. Since the legislature had not enacted duty-bound measures, he declared, it was obliged to rectify its wrongs. He even went so far as to call for legislation making violation of the Constitution punishable by imprisonment.[21]

Actually, Hughes's invective, given sensational coverage by the press, was not the first voice heard against these 1895 laws. In 1906, Senator Owen Cassidy had presented to the legislature a bill implementing Hughes's 1908 objectives, but it was beaten back easily. The next year, while the administration busied itself on the Kelsey issue and the ambitious reform program, William T. Jerome, New York County district attorney, initiated a lively crusade against race-track betting. Enlisting the support of reform clubs and church organizations all over the state, he worked feverishly to create public sentiment in behalf of repealing the Percy-Gray Law.[22] Although he and his cohorts badgered the legislature with the moral and constitutional aspects of the issue, their efforts proved unavailing. They received no support from the state administration, then involved in a crusade of its own.

If it accomplished nothing else, Jerome's 1907 campaign drew the Governor's attention to a problem that he never knew existed. Irresistibly attracted to constitutional questions, Hughes apparently developed an interest in the race-track situation sometime late in his first legislative year. On June 15 he pledged his cooperation to churchmen in rooting out of New York State any and all "illegal" gambling.[23] Cautiously, then, he put his legal counsel, Edwin Sandford, to work verifying the contention that the Percy-Gray Law violated the 1895 constitutional

[20] *Ibid.*   [21] *Ibid.*, p. 26.

[22] New York *Times*, Jan. 14 and 18 and March 21, 1907; New York *World*, Jan. 14 and 18 and Feb. 18, 1907; New York *Herald*, April 4, 1907, Fuller Collection, Vol. XXXVII.

[23] New York *Times*, June 16, 1907.

amendment.²⁴ Once this query was answered in the affirmative, George B. Agnew, Jerome's legislative collaborator in 1907, prepared the necessary corrective bill for the senate and Merwin K. Hart of Utica worked over the administration's assembly proposal. Within several days after Governor Hughes's second annual message, both were ready for introduction and the groundwork was laid for another legislative battle.²⁵

In moving so rapidly against race-track gambling, the Hughes forces had their work cut out for them. In the first place, the issue was a relatively new one, and there seemed little public enthusiasm for the Governor's position when it was announced early in January.²⁶ Moreover, though a well-organized campaign might possibly remove the noted antipathy among New Yorkers, horse racing was so popular a sport that no amount of effort could make track betting wrong—either constitutionally or morally—to many an honest and upstanding citizen.²⁷ Nor, finally, would the racing interests themselves relax while their very survival was challenged. A powerful contingent in the state, these men would use their almost unlimited

²⁴ Sandford had replaced Ernest Huffcut, who had died on May 4, 1907.

²⁵ Actually, there were two bills presented to the senate and assembly, on January 6 and 15 respectively. One would repeal the law prescribing the penalty of recovery by civil suit of the amount wagered. In place, it would impose the penalty of one-year imprisonment for violation of the state Constitution. The second measure would amend the Penal Code accordingly and alter the crime from that of felony to that of misdemeanor, bringing the offense into the jurisdiction of the minor criminal courts (*New York Senate Journal*, 131st session [Albany: J. B. Lyon, 1908], p. 12; *New York Assembly Journal*, 131st session [Albany: J. B. Lyon, 1908], p. 74; and *Laws of New York, 1908*, II, chs. 506, 507).

²⁶ *Literary Digest*, XXXVI (1908), 44; New York *Tribune*, Jan. 3, 1908; New York *Sun* and New York *Herald*, Jan. 3, 1908, Fuller Collection, Vol. XXXVIII.

²⁷ Wadsworth, for example, insisted that, although "Hughes was right," the racing associations were backed by many people who simply liked to bet ("Autobiography," p. 104, James W. Wadsworth, Jr., Papers [Hartford House, Geneseo, New York; now on deposit in the Library of Congress]). For unfavorable newspaper opinion, see *Literary Digest*, XXXVI (1908), 44.

resources to maintain the security of their position.[28] Report-edly, the jockey clubs had long retained distinguished lawyers and several legislators on whom they could now call. They also claimed the support of New York's farmers, whose annual county fairs had for years been subsidized by revenue accruing from race-track proceeds.[29]

Yet the administration was determined. As soon as it became clear that Hughes would lead the crusade, invitations to join in the foray were dispatched to reform organizations all over the state, and favorable responses, especially from New York City associations, quickly rolled into Albany. On January 10 the In-ternational Reform Bureau, composed of intellectuals and churchmen dedicated to moral reform, enthusiastically pledged its support of the Agnew-Hart bill. Three days later its presi-dent, the Reverend Wilbur F. Crafts, closeted himself in the executive chamber with the Governor to discuss arrangements for an ambitious statewide campaign.[30] On the same day repre-sentatives of some half-dozen other associations joined Crafts in a protracted session with George Agnew and Merwin Hart.[31] The conference resulted in the establishment of the Citizens' Anti-Race-Track Gambling Committee to coordinate the pend-ing publicity work. Under the able leadership of Walter Laid-law, Federation of Churches secretary, this diligent group of crusaders set to work immediately and reported back on Janu-

---

[28] That they had fabulous sums of money for the purpose of beating back the Agnew-Hart bill was revealed in a 1910 legislative investigation undertaken to study senate and assembly graft in these years ("Allds Investigation Report," esp. pp. 16–18; see also New York *Times,* Jan. 3, 1908).

[29] "Memorandum of State Racing Commission," submitted to George A. Davis, Feb. 8, 1908, George B. Agnew Papers (NYPL); New York *Times,* Feb. 4, 1908.

[30] O. R. Miller to George Agnew, Jan. 10, 1908, Agnew Papers; Buffalo *Morning Express,* Jan. 14, 1908.

[31] The other organizations were the New York City and State Federa-tions of Churches, the City Club of New York, the Brooklyn League, the Woman's Municipal League, and the Westchester Civic League. Most of this information concerning the campaign plans comes from "Laidlaw Committee Report," pp. 4–5.

ary 23 with an elaborate plan for carrying the issue to every corner of the state. Beginning with a huge meeting in New York City's Majestic Theatre on February 2, the campaign would spread out through community gatherings, special get-togethers in key senatorial districts, carefully arranged appeals to various agricultural societies, and direct propaganda issued through both the organizations and the press. Early assurances from Walter Laidlaw that all campaign possibilities would be investigated epitomized the reform forces' preparations for the struggle that lay ahead.[32]

The antigambling crusade was formally initiated by the scheduled February 2 meeting in New York City, where Governor Hughes himself lashed into the opposition in his customary way. Although he had been discreetly silent on the issue, he now condemned specifically those individuals who, in living off the racing form, "lost the American sentiment." [33] After paying homage to his supporters, interested mainly in the moral issue, Hughes went on to insist that the constitutional question was equally important. It was this factor, he argued, that would provide the broad base of support necessary for enactment of the Agnew-Hart legislation.

The rest of the campaign rolled along as scheduled. Informally, the International Reform Bureau had gone to work even before the February launching. On January 17 Wilbur Crafts had reported to Agnew that enclosures had just been dispatched to five hundred Methodist ministers and YMCA's all over the state.[34] Crafts had already made a personal appearance in Poughkeepsie and was planning meetings in Schenectady, Utica, Gloversville, and Troy, to be followed by public gatherings in southeastern New York. Laidlaw's committee jumped into the fray immediately after February 2 with a proclamation making the next Sunday "Anti-Race-Track Gambling Day" and a plea to Protestant ministers for cooperation in carrying the fight to the people. Then, while Laidlaw personally appealed to legisla-

[32] Laidlaw to George B. Agnew, Jan. 7, 1908, Agnew Papers.

[33] "Laidlaw Committee Report," p. 6; New York *Times*, Feb. 3, 1908.

[34] Crafts to Agnew, Jan. 17, 1908, Agnew Papers.

tors in Albany and New York City, his co-workers journeyed to the "country," concentrating on those districts whose representatives appeared cool toward the administration. Here reformers generally called public meetings to which recalcitrant assemblymen and senators were invited so that their views might be aired. This work was supplemented by "words of warning" printed on postal cards and distributed to recalcitrant legislators.[35]

Equally important was the ambitious campaign to win the support of the state's influential agricultural societies. Hughes himself had recognized the necessity of making a special plea to these groups and in his annual message insisted that there "be no diminution of the support upon which these societies largely rely." [36] He called for legislative appropriations each year to sustain their worthwhile activities. Two weeks later, some two hundred representatives of several farm organizations appeared in the executive chamber, where the Governor reiterated his promise.[37] As senate supporters labored to draw up the appropriate bill,[38] the Laidlaw committee carried the issue into the rural districts. They submitted resolutions to various agricultural organizations calling for direct grants of money and condemning their traditional source of revenue. Immediately, favorable replies were received from Richmond, Saratoga, and Essex Counties. Then, on February 7, the influential State Grange, meeting in Hornell, declared for the Agnew-Hart bill and the annual appropriations idea.[39]

[35] "Laidlaw Committee Report," pp. 6, 9; "The Fight of the Governor on the Gamblers," New York *Times Magazine*, March 8, 1908; A. S. Gregg to Agnew, March 28, 1908, Agnew Papers.

[36] *Hughes Public Papers*, II, 26–27.

[37] Hughes Address to Agricultural Societies, Jan. 16, 1908, Charles Evans Hughes Collection (NYPL).

[38] Leading this group was William Armstrong, whose name appeared on the administration bill (Armstrong to Agnew, Feb. 5, 1908, and Agnew to R. G. H. Speed, March 19, 1908, Agnew Papers; New York *Times*, Feb. 7, 1908).

[39] "Laidlaw Committee Report," pp. 9–10; Buffalo *Morning Express*, Feb. 8, 1908; printed clipping, n.d., Agnew Papers.

During the early stages of the publicity campaign, the administration's racing legislation lay dormant in the assembly and senate codes committees. With Republican leaders obviously indifferent toward the moral-constitutional crusade, legislators were left largely on their own to treat the issue as they saw fit.[40] Finally, in mid-February, they emerged with the idea of holding several joint hearings in order to give each side an opportunity to present its case.

The racing interests were summoned to appear before the committees on February 19 and again on March 4. They responded in the first session with their legal wizards Joseph S. Auerbach and James R. Keene, both representing August Belmont's Jockey Club. Attacking the alleged immorality of gambling, Keene climaxed his long testimony with the caustic remark that, while racing enthusiasts were concerned with improving the breed of horses, his opponents were seeking to improve the breed of men. "You can never succeed," he shouted. "Only God Almighty can do that." [41] Equally dramatic and even more effective was former Governor Frank S. Black, who, appearing at the second hearing, regaled his former legislative colleagues with the issue of "personal liberty." Black's oratory carried so profound an emotional impact that Governor Hughes himself felt compelled to reply.[42]

By the time the third and final hearing took place, the administration forces had carefully screened the lists of potential witnesses and selected the most articulate speakers to present their side of the case.[43] They relied upon such servants of God as Charles Parkhurst, Rabbi Stephen S. Wise, and Walter Laidlaw. Although the moral question, of course, received preference, the racing critics bombarded their opponents with the constitutional issue as well. "The right and wrong of gambling," insisted Park-

---

[40] Although Raines and Wadsworth did not actually oppose the bills, their statements in January showed little enthusiasm for them (New York *World*, Jan. 13, 1908; Buffalo *Morning Express*, Jan. 10, 1908).

[41] New York *Times*, Feb. 20, 1908.   [42] *Ibid.*, March 5 and 6, 1908.

[43] Laidlaw to Agnew, Feb. 14, 1908, and Agnew to William T. Jerome, Feb. 11 and 17, 1908, Agnew Papers.

hurst, "seems to me to stand quite aloof from this significant [constitutional] question." [44] Parkhurst thus echoed the views of groups and organizations like the New York City People's Institute, the social reformers, and the Merchants' Association that swelled the antigambling contingent as the crusade rolled on.[45]

Even before this effective defense had been delivered, the assembly codes committee had deserted its senate counterpart and unanimously endorsed the Agnew-Hart bill. Despite Wadsworth's virtual abdication of leadership, the lower house had persistently posed less of a problem to the administration than the more conservative senate. Indeed, only one incident, occurring early in March, caused anguish among Hughes supporters, and it quickly passed over, leaving little bitterness in its wake.[46] As the publicity campaign made excellent headway throughout the state, indifference among assembly moderates turned into active support.[47] Then, on March 9, Democratic State Chairman William Conners surprisingly announced that the people were behind Hughes's crusade and that he would per-

[44] Buffalo *Morning Express*, March 19, 1908.

[45] Michael Davis, Jr., to Agnew, Feb. 18, 1908, Agnew Papers; Edward Devine, "Social Forces: Race Track Gambling," *Charities and the Commons*, XIX (1908), 1607–1608; New York *Times*, Feb. 4, 1908. That the crusade had captured the imagination of independent Republicans is evident in the Herbert Parsons Papers (Columbia University Library), especially Parsons to William Barnes, Jr., May 12, 1908.

[46] The flare-up concerned a letter that the executive office had received and had immediately released to the press. It had charged that the racing interests were exerting improper influences upon certain assemblymen, and its publication created the impression that Hughes was trying to bulldoze the Agnew-Hart bill through the lower house. The Governor assured legislators that he had not known of the letter's existence before its release and thereby absolved himself of any responsibility in making a public issue of it (*Hughes Public Papers*, II, 38–41; Buffalo *Morning Express*, March 3, 1908).

[47] There is much evidence pointing to the effectiveness of the antigambling campaign (New York *Times*, March 8, 1908). The number of letters pouring into the Governor's office at this time was phenomenal (New York *Sun*, March 2, 1908; *Literary Digest*, XXXVI [1908], 357–358). This information is verified by material found in the Hughes and Agnew Papers.

sonally support the racing legislation. Three days later Tammany opposition collapsed, and within two weeks after the committee's capitulation the assembly passed the Agnew-Hart bill.[48]

Attention now focused on the troublesome upper house. Amidst rumors that the racing interests were offering high stakes for legislative support, the senate codes committee had also reported out the antigambling bill.[49] Unlike that in the assembly, however, this move came as a challenge to Hughes and the reform forces. For weeks, Tammany Senator Thomas Grady and his closest ally, Pat McCarren, both avid racing enthusiasts, had taken the initiative in opposing the Agnew-Hart legislation. When committee action appeared imminent, they championed an amendment postponing to September 1 the date that the measure, if enacted, would become effective. Since administration supporters had already rejected a compromise, they were, in reality, forcing a test vote on the issue.[50] With three committee Republicans joining McCarren and one other Democrat, the desired result was achieved. Tammany quickly recognized the dissension within GOP ranks, and once again the way seemed clear for the insidious bipartisan alliance.

McCarren's strategy became even more apparent early in April when the amended Agnew-Hart bill was debated in the upper house. On the senate floor, Tammany spokesmen denounced the Hughes position, then voted for the amended bill.[51] While twenty-three Republicans faithfully supported the administration and beat back the challenge, six GOP senators broke ranks. Assured that very little work could achieve at least a compromise, McCarren's forces swept in for total victory. Assuming that voting lines on an unamended version could be

[48] New York *Times*, March 10, 1908; New York *Tribune*, March 13, 1908, Fuller Collection, Vol. XXXIX; *New York Assembly Journal*, 131st session, pp. 1401–1402.

[49] New York *Tribune*, March 12, 1908, Fuller Collection, Vol. XXXIX; New York *Times*, March 12, 1908.

[50] Buffalo *Morning Express*, March 6, 1908.

[51] New York *Times* and Buffalo *Morning Express*, April 2, 1908; *New York Senate Journal*, 131st session, p. 696.

held tight, the Brooklyn leader needed to swing only two legislators to his side.[52]

The Hughes contingent saw immediately that time was against them and that if the legislation were to have any chance at all it had to be pushed along quickly. Fearful of vote trading and, indeed, of vote buying, George Agnew sought to settle the issue on the very evening that the compromise measure came to a vote. He moved to supplant his own amended bill with the assembly's unblemished Hart proposal. Although his resolution was adopted, Tom Grady shrewdly spotted a defect in the bill's language and steered it into the committee on revision. Faced again with a long delay, Hughes's proponents, now led by John Raines himself, hammered through an agreement that by special order the legislation would be brought to a final vote on April 8.[53]

As it turned out, McCarren's forces still possessed enough time to accomplish their objective. For the next six days, the Senator kept in close personal touch with his colleagues and learned the intention of each and every one of them. By April 7 he was confident he had all the votes he needed but one. That day, he strolled over to William Barnes's Albany home, related his plight to the GOP stalwart, and asked for support. At first Barnes demurred, arguing that he did not wish to become involved in the fight.[54] When McCarren appealed to the Albany leader's growing resentment toward the administration, Barnes's objections melted away. In promising to pressure his senator, William Grattan, into switching his vote, Barnes later admitted to Agnew that his "antagonism to Governor Hughes overcame every other consideration." [55]

[52] That is, McCarren could simply switch the seventeen Democratic votes and the six Republican votes that had been cast for the amended version in opposition to the unamended bill.

[53] New York *World*, April 3, 1908, Fuller Collection, Vol. XL; New York *Times* and Buffalo *Morning Express*, April 3, 1908.

[54] "William Barnes Testimony, May 17, 1915, William E. Barnes v. Theodore Roosevelt, Case on Appeal, Appellate Division, 4th Department (New York Supreme Court)," cited in New York *Times*, May 18, 1915.

[55] Agnew to James F. Cooper, April 23, 1908, Agnew Papers.

Thus, when April 8 dawned, McCarren's followers were confident of defeating the racing bill. That morning a violent debate raged for four hours in the senate's capitol chamber. Grady, McCarren, and several other Tammany spokesmen vehemently denounced the proposed measure. They also lashed into Hughes, flatly accusing him of unfairness and executive usurpation. Only Armstrong and Hinman came to the Governor's rescue, the Rochester senator dramatically offering his best oratory. "The name of Governor Hughes," he exhorted prophetically, "will be remembered as the synonym for honesty long after the name of every man occupying a seat in this Chamber has been forgotten." [56]

Although an administration victory now seemed impossible, optimistic George Agnew clung tenaciously to what little hope remained. On the previous evening he had boldly wired President Roosevelt through Congressman Cocks ostensibly for the purpose of spiking rumors then circulating in Albany that the White House sympathized with the move Barnes had made that very day.[57] Actually, Agnew tried desperately to draw out a presidential statement supporting the racing bill, thus snatching victory from the jaws of defeat. During the stormy debate next morning, he sat quietly in his office anxiously awaiting Roosevelt's reply. Its arrival, however, brought no solace to the disgruntled Senator. "The President," read the telegram, "is not interfering in any matter of [the] state legislature." [58] Quickly, Agnew turned to his sole alternative. He rushed over to Barnes's home where he pleaded with the Albany leader to repudiate his promise to McCarren. But Barnes held firmly to his position, explaining to his fellow Republican that his decision had been made on the basis of "good politics." [59]

When the senate reconvened after its noon recess on April 8, the die was cast. Quietly, the roll call was read and, as anticipated, the administration went down to defeat. The final vote

[56] New York *Times*, April 9, 1908.
[57] Agnew to Cocks, April 7, 1908, Agnew Papers.
[58] Cocks to Agnew, April 8, 1908, *ibid.*
[59] "George B. Agnew Testimony, April 29, 1915, Barnes v. Roosevelt," cited in New York *Times*, April 30, 1915.

showed a 25–25 tie, but since the lieutenant-governor possessed no power to break legislative deadlocks of this kind,
the Agnew-Hart bill stood unapproved. Dramatically, then,
Thomas Grady followed with a resolution that would prevent
reconsideration of the question by this same legislature. Now,
however, the Democratic lieutenant-governor had the vote
and magnanimously cast it with the Hughes forces, making it
possible to raise the issue at a later date.[60]

Again the senate had stymied a key administration measure
largely because Governor Hughes had not kept his party in line.
This time, eight Republicans bolted and cast their votes with
seventeen Democrats. Although John Raines had not willfully
forged a bipartisan alliance like that of the previous year, he and
his fellow senate leaders made no real effort to assure Republican
victory. This lack of GOP discipline opened the way for racing
enthusiast Pat McCarren and his Tammany friends, who seldom
missed so fine an opportunity. With the national administration
now obviously indifferent toward Hughes's reform efforts, a
stalwart like Barnes could rather easily be cajoled into embarrassing a man he had learned to dislike intensely. Even
Woodruff apparently faltered in his support of the state administration: one of his own senators, Alfred J. Gilchrist, voted
against the bill.

Perhaps the key factor in determining the outcome of this
senate battle, however, was Theodore Roosevelt's refusal on
April 8 to intervene in behalf of the racing legislation. On the
very next day, Cocks wrote to Agnew explaining the reason for
Roosevelt's abstention. Although the President was "very interested in the success of your bill," Cocks admitted, "you probably are aware that some of his efforts toward aiding matters at
Albany have not been appreciated either by the legislators or the
Governor." [61] Obviously referring to Roosevelt's 1907 experiences, the Congressman expressed the general attitude toward

[60] *New York Senate Journal*, 131st session, pp. 800–801; New York
Times, April 9, 1908.
[61] Cocks to Agnew, April 9, 1908, Agnew Papers.

the state administration that had come to prevail in the White House. Always willing to extend himself for the sake of his party, Roosevelt had never quite been able to understand Hughes's thoroughgoing independence. As long as this aloofness contributed to the Governor's success without harming the President, however, it was tolerable (and, indeed, sometimes encouraged). But when it worked to interfere more and more with Roosevelt's own plans for New York, especially those concerning the 1908 elections, he rankled with bitterness. Unfortunately for Hughes, the battle over the racing legislation reached its climax during the national administration's determined campaign to further the Taft presidential movement and, at the same time, to contain Hughes's popularity. Barnes's decision to oppose the Agnew-Hart bill must have been made within this context, for the Albany leader was one of the foremost Taft champions. And, doubtless, he spoke for many a Republican caught between commitments to Hughes and obligations to Roosevelt and Taft.[62]

Another factor in explaining the racing bill's failure is the publicity campaign waged for the administration. Although the extent to which public opinion ever supports a given policy is difficult to gauge, it seems clear that the reform organizations had not achieved enough success to pressure the intransigent senate into submission. George Agnew later admitted that the eight GOP bolters reflected the antipathy of their constituents toward the legislation.[63] Perhaps these antiracing groups faced an impossible task from the beginning, considering the nature of the issue and the length of time during which an effective campaign

[62] The intimate association between the presidential contest and the racing legislation is also evidenced in Horace White to Francis Hendricks, February 3, 1908, Horace White Papers (Syracuse University Library). See Chapters IX and X for a full discussion of the relationship between national politics and the New York State situation.

[63] "Agnew Memorandum" (undated), Agnew Papers. The senators were Carll S. Burr of Long Island, Owen Cassidy of Schuyler, Alfred J. Gilchrist of Kings, William J. Grattan of Albany, James A. Emerson of Warren, Benjamin M. Wilcox of Cayuga, William W. Wemple of Schenectady, and H. Wallace Knapp of Essex.

could be carried on. Moreover, Governor Hughes himself played much less a role in this undertaking than he might have.[64] Whether he misjudged the strength of his own case all along, or whether he simply deemed it wise for his fellow reformers to shoulder most of the responsibility is problematical. At any rate, his best efforts for the Agnew-Hart bill were yet to be expended. Finally, the prosperous racing interests did attain a measure of success in their own campaign efforts. Subsequent investigations revealed that their quiet but effective attack had been two-fold. First, streams of propaganda were poured into key areas of the state to sway public opinion against racing restrictions. One jockey association alone, it was estimated, had spent $17,000, and the eight organizations operating in New York reported 1908 publicity expenditures amounting to $162,-000.[65] Second, money was actually made available for the purpose of buying senate votes. During the early stages of the legislative battle, various turf organizations had held a secret New York City meeting at which they subscribed to a slush fund totalling several hundred thousand dollars. Former Senator Frank Gardner was then retained as an Albany lobbyist. From a hotel room near the capitol, he directed the campaign to buy up support. Through agents, he offered substantial sums of money to several senators, including Otto Foelker, Charles H. Fuller, Francis M. Carpenter, and Eugene Travis.[66] Foelker himself later testified that he had twice been approached, once with an offer of $12,000, and a second time with one of $45,000. Travis

[64] Aside from the February 2 New York City address, Hughes delivered only three major speeches in behalf of the legislation before the April 8 senate vote. They were delivered in the Bronx on March 5, in Kingston on March 20, and in Brooklyn on April 6 ("Hughes Speeches on Race-Track Bill," in "Scrapbook on Anti-Racetrack Gambling," Hughes Papers).

[65] "Allds Investigation Report," p. 18; New York *Evening Post*, March 19, 1908, New York *Tribune*, March 21, 1908, and New York *World*, March 23, 1908, Fuller Collection, Vol. XXXIX.

[66] "Proceedings," in "Allds Investigation Report," pp. 963–964; 1108–1109; "Report of the Committee on Legislation of the Citizens' Union for the Session of 1908," Citizens' Union Collection (NYPL).

insisted that he had been tempted by Gardner's agents, who promised him $100,000. Conclusive evidence points to the fact that at least one member of the upper house had actually accepted a $10,000 bribe and voted against the legislation.[67]

In the wake of the state administration's most sensational setback came violent press assaults upon the corrupt influences still being exerted on the legislature.[68] Characteristically, Governor Hughes maintained his composure, remarking calmly: "It is impossible to believe that the people will permit the plain mandate of the Constitution to be ignored." [69] Yet he had already determined his course of action, and the next day he dispatched a special legislative message flaying the uncooperative senate for ignoring the fundamental law of the state. Insisting upon passage of the racing bill under implicit threat of an extraordinary session, Hughes took the occasion to appeal for the enactment of other proposals that thus far had been totally ignored. Among them were direct nominations legislation, a bill consolidating highway statutes and amendments, the canal improvement measure, and separate titles establishing temporary commissions to inquire into security speculations, immigrant conditions, unemployment, and procedures of inferior courts of criminal jurisdiction.[70]

That the Governor had no intention of letting the explosive racing issue die was further evidenced on April 10, when he ordered a special election in the Niagara-Orleans district to fill

[67] "Allds Investigation Report," p. 17. The name is not given. One authority has gone so far as to suggest that Thomas Grady received $4000 (Gustavus Myers, *The History of Tammany Hall* [New York: Boni and Liveright, 1917], p. 349). The present writer has not been able to corroborate Myers' assertion on this score. It is true, however, as Myers further argues, that Pat McCarren was involved in attempting to buy off at least one of his colleagues. Instead of offering money, the Kings leader tendered a guarantee to Republican Otto Foelker that he would be re-elected if he cast his vote against the racing bill ("Proceedings," in "Allds Investigation Report," p. 968).

[68] *Literary Digest*, XXXVI (1908), 545.

[69] New York *Times*, April 9, 1908.

[70] *Hughes Public Papers*, II, 41–44.

the senate seat left vacant by Stanislaus Franchot's death less than one month earlier. Needing only one vote to break the upper house deadlock, Hughes staked his political reputation on his ability to appeal directly to the people and score a triumph that the politicians had willfully denied him.[71]

So determined was Hughes, indeed, that he could hardly wait for the Niagara-Orleans contest to launch his personal campaign for the racing bill. While the legislature tended to routine matters during early and mid-April, the Governor made an ambitious swing through New York State. On April 10 he was in Watertown, where he lashed away at the moral aspects involved in race-track gambling. Before the Lawyers Club in Buffalo, two days later, he appropriately assailed the constitutionality of the Percy-Gray Law. Then followed public meetings in Utica and in Brooklyn.[72] Finally, on April 26, back in William Barnes's Albany, he was greeted by an enthusiastic theater audience resolute in its condemnation of Senator Grattan's recent apostasy. Here Hughes played the issue to the hilt, scoring Grattan for seesawing on the racing bill. "It is the duty of an elective officer," he charged, "to serve the people and not any particular man." [73] The Governor then proceeded to excoriate the GOP organization as he had done so effectively in 1907.

Already, however, the state legislature had responded in kind to Hughes's challenging campaign. On April 23 it had adjourned with a far less creditable record than that of 1907. Few of the administration's major items for 1908 had been enacted, and in all only about one hundred and fifty bills were ready for gubernatorial action.[74] The Governor wasted no time in replying with an executive order calling the senate and assembly back to Albany on May 11. To a friend he wrote calmly and seriously that although the move might be considered as an invitation to a second defeat, he would and must continue to "focus the senti-

[71] New York *Times*, April 11, 1908.

[72] Buffalo *Morning Express*, April 11, 12, 13, and 20, 1908.

[73] Governor Hughes's Albany Address, April 26, 1908, Hughes Collection.

[74] New York *Times*, April 24, 1908.

ment of the State upon these questions." The maintenance of responsible, representative government, not political advantage, he insisted, was at the heart of his fight.[75]

Meanwhile, the administration forces were busy at work in the Niagara-Orleans district attempting to bury local factional differences so that the racing question might be made the paramount issue in the May 12 special election. Public Works Superintendent Frederick Stevens had been dispatched to the area in mid-April for the purpose of calling a truce between his followers and another group of GOP stalwarts vying for party leadership. His success was apparent when, twelve days later, William C. Wallace of Niagara Falls was unanimously named to bear the Republican standard in behalf of the Agnew-Hart bill.[76]

For a time the Democrats wavered between selecting no candidate to oppose the GOP organization and naming a strong contender who would truly make the election a test case. At first inclined toward the former alternative, they finally decided in favor of a respectable nominee. Indeed, rumor had it that William Barnes, now Hughes's foremost Republican critic, had negotiated another agreement with Pat McCarren, this time undermining the Governor's position by actually putting his organization to work for the Democrats. In any case, on April 27 Henry A. McMahon, also a Niagara Falls politician, received the Democratic nomination. Although his platform hedged on the race-track issue, GOP spokesmen took for granted his opposition to the controversial legislation.[77]

The Niagara-Orleans campaign brought Governor Hughes into western New York for the second time within a month and for several days provided an unusual and colorful spectacle. On May 8 Hughes swung vigorously through Holley, Albion, Medina, Middleport, and Lockport, where in a fighting mood he castigated members of his own party and even hinted at seeking re-election if the legislature again defied the people's wishes.

[75] Hughes to Thomas Peters, April 23, 1908, Hughes Papers.
[76] Buffalo *Morning Express*, April 14 and 26, 1908.
[77] New York *Times*, April 17, 23, and 24, 1908; Buffalo *Daily Courier*, April 22, 1908; Buffalo *Morning Express*, April 28, 1908.

Next day, he appeared in North Tonawanda and Niagara Falls, where he reiterated his well-defined position, decrying backstage political methods in favor of open public discussions of major issues.[78]

These efforts paid dividends, and Wallace, on May 12, won the special contest. Although the results proved to be closer than anticipated, the Governor obtained the additional vote he needed to jam through the racing bill. He could now concentrate upon the legislative work at hand.

During the Niagara-Orleans tussle, the senate and assembly had gone back into session only to be greeted, on May 11, with a carefully prepared special message in which Hughes virtually ignored the race-track issue.[79] Obviously awaiting the election outcome, the Governor sought to keep his legislative friends busy working on measures extending public service commission regulation, instituting the direct primary, and establishing special commissions to investigate speculation in securities and unemployment in New York—all of which had received only superficial attention during the regular session. He appeared willing, by this time, to sacrifice these proposals in order to prevent the legislature from adjourning in defiance to both his program and himself.

Hughes waited almost one full month before he finally broached the gambling subject. Despite severe criticism, he had good reason for this unusually long delay. Wallace had not assumed his newly won senate seat until May 25. Then, next day, S. Percy Hooker and William Tully promptly announced that they could not attend any upper house sessions the following week. Finally, another administration supporter, Otto Foelker, had recently undergone surgery and, in early June, was suffering from painful complications. For his benefit—and, indeed, for the Governor's welfare—further procrastination was essential.[80]

[78] Buffalo *Morning Express*, May 9, 1908; New York *Times*, May 9 and 10, 1908.
[79] *Hughes Public Papers*, II, 45–50.
[80] Buffalo *Morning Express*, May 28, 1908.

The real drama of this, the second Agnew-Hart fight, was provided by the Foelker story. Recuperating in Staatsburg, Dutchess County, the Brooklyn senator had not been expected to return to Albany at any time during the special session. But Hughes desperately needed his vote since senate lines remained so tightly drawn. With this idea in mind, the gubernatorial secretary, Robert Fuller, had visited Staatsburg only a few days before the June 8 executive message.[81] He received no definite commitment, however. Under threats of legislative adjournment, then, Hughes had had to deliver his special appeal and thus begin the process of putting through the racing bill. Next day Agnew himself appeared in Foelker's sick room, where he pleaded with his colleague to journey to Albany within forty-eight hours. Against doctor's orders, Foelker agreed to make the trip, informing his irate physician: "There are political reasons why I cannot stay here while the racing bills are up. . . . I have promised Senator Agnew and the Governor." [82]

Meanwhile, administration supporters worked feverishly to push their legislation through the necessary readings and prepare it for the roll call before the scheduled June 11 adjournment. On the tenth, the bill again passed the cooperative assembly.[83] Next morning the final debate resumed in the stubborn senate. Opponents ruthlessly resorted to dilatory tactics, hoping to wear out their Brooklyn colleague, Otto Foelker, who, palefaced and perspiring, waited in the chamber's ante room. Again leading the assault upon Hughes and moral reform was Thomas Grady, the senate Tammany chief. When Grady's proposed amendment was brought to a vote, Foelker made his first appearance, hobbled to his seat and gleefully cast the deciding ballot for the administration. Two subsequent roll calls on proposed changes ended similarly. Finally, the Agnew-Hart bill was put to the test, and it, too, passed by the slim margin of Foelker's vote.[84]

[81] New York *Times*, June 10, 1908.   [82] *Ibid.*, June 11, 1908.
[83] *New York Assembly Journal*, extra. session (1908), p. 60. The final vote was 98–26.
[84] *New York Senate Journal*, extra. session (1908), p. 58; New York *Times*, New York *Tribune*, and New York *World*, June 12, 1908.

Immediately, the jubilant pro-Hughes press rang out with praise for the victorious administration. This was "primarily a triumph of the people," asserted the New York *Evening Post*. "It is not necessary for the righteous cause," claimed the *Globe*, "to adopt the methods of unrighteousness." This success, added the New York *Evening Mail*, was achieved without affronting "the democratic principle, the representative system, the constitutional presumption of popular government." [85]

Praiseworthy as the racing victory may have been, the administration's overall record for 1908 in no sense matched its achievement the previous year. Although the all-important banking legislation and several minor bills had been enacted, many of Governor's Hughes's major recommendations remained untouched. Of course, Hughes himself had not been able to devote the time and energy needed to push through the public service commission extension bill or his key political reforms. They, therefore, had to be sacrificed in the special session for the sake of the antigambling measure—the administration's most dramatic venture in the area of moral reform. Whether the Governor would have the opportunity to return to these other issues depended upon his own re-election in the fall of 1908. This, in turn, was linked inextricably to the presidential boom begun in his behalf in 1907—a movement that almost resulted in disaster for Hughes's political future.

[85] *Literary Digest*, XXXVI (1908), 885–886.

CHAPTER IX

Presidential Politics

"WHEN people get away from a favorite like you, there is a disposition to take someone entirely new," wrote Secretary of War William Howard Taft to President Theodore Roosevelt on September 11, 1907.[1] The note of concern in this statement amply summarizes the profound disturbances expressed in much of the correspondence to and from Oyster Bay in late 1907 and early 1908, for during this period the presidential boom in behalf of Governor Charles Evans Hughes threatened Roosevelt's carefully laid plans for Taft and the Republican party.[2]

Discussion of Roosevelt's White House successor had begun shortly after the 1904 election with the President's bold announcement that he would not again be a candidate.[3] But his support of the no-third-term tradition did not make him a political novice. Although he early developed a preference for William Howard Taft, who he became convinced would carry on his progressive policies, he refrained from announcing his choice until 1908. Thus, he apparently calculated, his own administra-

[1] William Howard Taft Papers (Manuscript Division, Library of Congress).

[2] Alfred D. Sumberg, "A History of the Presidential Election of 1908" (unpublished Ph.D. diss., University of Wisconsin, 1960), *passim*. Sumberg argues (p. 241) that Hughes "remained Taft's most dangerous opponent until the very moment the presidential nomination was made."

[3] New York *Tribune*, Nov. 9, 1904; Charles W. Stein, *The Third-Term Tradition: Its Rise and Collapse in American Politics* (New York: Columbia, 1943), pp. 145–146.

tion would remain effective while the whole succession issue was presumably left in abeyance. There was an added reason for Roosevelt's silence. Keenly aware of the vicissitudes of politics, he rarely made decisions with a finality entirely precluding reconsideration. In this instance, he remained for sometime a partisan of his secretary of state, Elihu Root, who, but for his corporation affiliations, might have inherited the presidential mantle. Roosevelt's continued references to Root, even after encouraging the Taft candidacy, coupled with his discussions of several other possible nominees, provide the doubtful quality in determining exactly when the presidential mind was closed on the all-important succession question.[4]

Obviously, much White House talk had passed between Roosevelt and Taft before Charles Evans Hughes even appeared on the political scene. The dramatic 1906 gubernatorial campaign in New York, however, altered the general situation to the extent that Hughes, riding a crest of popularity accruing from his smashing victory over William Randolph Hearst, had to be accorded consideration by the national GOP leaders. During the foray itself, Roosevelt had inclined toward Hughes. Enthusiastically, albeit indiscreetly, he told Mrs. Taft that the fighting New York reformer might make a good presidential nominee. Yet when the Secretary of War humbly assured Roosevelt of his willingness to have the President "start in any other direction," the embarrassed Roosevelt toned down his approbation of Hughes. The Governor-elect, he insisted, had no better than "one chance in a thousand" to receive the nomination.[5] His harmless remark to Mrs. Taft, Roosevelt confessed to his ami-

---

[4] Stein, *Third-Term Tradition*, p. 154; Henry L. Stoddard, *As I Knew Them: Presidents and Politics from Grant to Coolidge* (New York: Harper and Bros., 1927), pp. 323–325, 328; Henry F. Pringle, *The Life and Times of William Howard Taft* (New York: Farrer and Rinehart, 1927), I, 311; H. H. Kohlsaat, *From McKinley to Harding: Personal Recollections of Our Presidents* (New York: Scribner, 1923), p. 152; Oscar King Davis, *Released for Publication: Some Inside Political History of Theodore Roosevelt and His Times, 1898–1918* (Boston: Houghton-Mifflin, 1925), pp. 54–55.

[5] Roosevelt to Taft, Nov. 5, 1906, *LTR*, V, 486–487; Taft to Roosevelt, Oct. 31, 1906, Taft Papers.

able subordinate, was a cautious reminder that "if Hughes or some other man so carried himself during the next eighteen months as to get popular support strongly behind him, and if people . . . felt that you did not really care for the fight . . . , we might find ourselves wholly powerless to support you." Taft, in short, would have to work diligently if he desired the honor his friend seemed willing to bestow upon him.

Roosevelt's mild rebuke bore fruit as Taft's interest in the presidency ripened the following year. By March of 1907 a smooth-running organization had begun the process of building up the Secretary of War's strength throughout the nation. In July Taft himself donned the garb of political strategist and personally managed the campaign to organize southern support and to keep New York State in line. Supplementing these efforts was Theodore Roosevelt's ingenious use of the patronage, as the President, with Taft's approval, followed the rule of forcing federal officeholders to work for the cause or maintain a discreet silence.[6]

Meanwhile, as Roosevelt's commitment to Taft deepened, Governor Hughes was gradually gaining the popularity to which Roosevelt had referred in 1906. The reasons for this acclaim were clear. First, Hughes had achieved a measure of success with the recalcitrant 1907 New York legislature that Roosevelt had not been able to equal during his full term as governor. Second, the nature of the struggle in putting through a substantial part of his progressive program sharpened Hughes's image as an incorruptible public servant pitted against the worst elements in American politics. His crusade for clean, efficient government, together with his relentless battle for effective regulation of the public utilities, rivalled that of Wisconsin's Robert M. La Follette only a few years earlier. As a matter of fact, what sincere support Hughes could claim outside his own state came largely from progressive western communities.[7]

[6] Pringle, *Life and Times of Taft*, I, 321–322; William H. Harbaugh, *Power and Responsibility: The Life and Times of Theodore Roosevelt* (New York: Farrar, Straus, 1961), p. 355.

[7] Davis, *Released for Publication*, p. 46; Henry C. Beerits, "First Term as Governor," p. 47, in "Memorandum," Charles Evans Hughes Papers

As letters of commendation and support flooded the Albany executive offices during and immediately following the 1907 legislative session, Roosevelt's compliant New York lieutenants proclaimed their "fear" of the growing Hughes sentiment among rank-and-file Republicans.[8] In June and July Herbert Parsons, long in Taft's camp, complained of blind Hughes opinion on the grass-roots level. State GOP Chairman Timothy Woodruff insisted that "the people of Brooklyn and, I believe, the State very generally are . . . 'red hot' for Hughes." Roosevelt himself passed along to his designated successor this anxiety over New York's rising star and, making no distinction between state and nation, conceded that the Governor's boom had shown real strength with the electorate.[9]

If in the previous fall the President's mind seemed open on the succession question, it now appeared closed, at least regarding the feasibility of a Hughes candidacy. Not only was Roosevelt more than satisfied with Taft's recent behavior, but he was greatly dissatisfied with the Governor's conduct. In a very real sense, Roosevelt had tried to serve as Hughes's political mentor almost from the day of the counsel's entry into public life. Not always, however, were his efforts well-received by the independently inclined Hughes, who, especially during 1907, held himself aloof from all "bosses."[10] To the President, the Gover-

---

(Manuscript Division, Library of Congress); New York *American*, Dec. 11, 1907, and Springfield *Republican*, Feb. 3, 1908, Fuller Collection, Vols. LI, CXXI; New York *Times*, Sept. 22, 1907; *Literary Digest*, XXXIV (1907), 6–7.

[8] There are many specimens in the Hughes Papers. Some of the more enthusiastic are Rollo Odgen to Hughes, July 22, 1907; William H. Dickson to Hughes, July 18, 1907; and Thorndike Spalding to Hughes, July 22 and Aug. 17, 1907.

[9] Roosevelt to Taft, Sept. 19, 1907, *LTR*, V, 796–797. In a previous letter, dated September 3, the President also referred to Hughes's strength in New York State (*ibid.*, pp. 780–782); Woodruff to William Loeb, Sept. 19, 1907, Theodore Roosevelt Papers (Manuscript Division, Library of Congress); Parsons to Roosevelt, June 3, 1907, and to William S. Bennet, July 19, 1907, Herbert Parsons Papers (Columbia University Library).

[10] Roosevelt was especially bitter over the Sanders incident, discussed in Chapter VII.

nor had thus proved to be an ungrateful creature moved by "pettiness and jealousies"—qualities that relegated him to the nadir of presidential hopefuls. So bitter had Roosevelt become that he even preferred Knox, or Cannon, or almost anyone else to his erstwhile New York friend.[11]

Also disconcerting to the President was the nature of support Hughes's name was gathering in 1907. In May the cunning Benjamin B. Odell had agitated for state committee endorsement of Hughes's candidacy, a move designed to embarrass the other Empire State leaders who had just declared for the Governor's reform program but who were working for Taft's nomination. Two months later, word had it that Ohio's Senator Joseph B. Foraker, long a Roosevelt critic, would soon declare himself for Hughes and in this way challenge the national administration's leadership of the GOP. Finally, early in the fall, a group of unidentified United States senators were reported to have initiated a Hughes movement in Washington. Like Odell and the conservative Foraker, they perceived the strategic advantage that lay in endorsing the only man, however progressive he might be, who had any chance whatever against Taft.[12]

During these developments, Governor Hughes remained silent on the question of his availability for the presidency. He had often made it known that his reform efforts in New York involved no personal ambition, and in May he reiterated this stand. Subsequently, he followed a consistent policy of refusing to endorse the work of mushrooming state groups determined to place his name before the 1908 Republican national convention.[13] Though, indeed, Hughes dropped no hint that he was playing coy, professional politicians refused to accept the Governor's statements at face value. With antiadministration spokesmen veering toward Albany, the Taft forces became convinced

[11] Roosevelt to Taft, Sept. 3, 1907, and to William D. Foulke, Nov. 16, 1907, *LTR*, V, 780–782, 846–848.

[12] New York *World*, May 12, 1907; New York *Times*, July 26 and Sept. 21, 1907.

[13] New York *Times*, Aug. 2 and Nov. 17, 1907; Hughes to J. Sloat Fassett, May 10, 1907, Hughes Papers.

that, as the Secretary of War put it, "Hughes is going to run." [14]

Although to progressives Roosevelt flippantly denounced the Hughes movement as reactionary, he fully appreciated its potential threat.[15] Fearing a possible massive effort to wrest Republican leadership from him and his heir apparent, he joined his New York lieutenants—Barnes, Woodruff, Parsons, and Hendricks, themselves representing several shades of Republican opinion—in devising a plan to meet the delicate state situation. They agreed that since the Governor enjoyed widespread popular support and excellent press relations, nothing could yet be done to push the Taft candidacy in New York. For the time being, Roosevelt would make no public pronouncements respecting the two principal contenders or, for that matter, even reiterate his 1904 no-third-term declaration. At the same time, the New York Republican state committee would refrain from endorsing Hughes, lest such action be seized upon as a base on which to build a national organization for the Governor.[16]

The Roosevelt policy of "watchful waiting" reaped no dividends during October and November, 1907. Amid newspaper reports that Hughes stood second only to Roosevelt in presidential polls, Taft's New York manager, Charles D. Hilles, canvassed the state. His findings showed little Taft sentiment but widespread Hughes and Roosevelt popularity.[17] Before the end of November, the Governor's enthusiasts, led by State Senator

[14] Taft to Roosevelt, Sept. 12, 1907, Taft Papers.

[15] Roosevelt to William A. White, July 30, 1907, and to Nicholas Murray Butler, Sept. 24, 1907, *LTR*, V, 735–737, 805–807. To Taft he wrote more candidly that Hughes might be an excellent candidate from the standpoint of all antiadministration Republicans (Roosevelt to Taft, Sept. 3 and 19, 1907, *ibid.*, pp. 780–782; 796–797.

[16] Herbert Parsons to Ed. D. Crumpacker, July 13, 1907, and to Charles D. Hilles, July 24, 1907; Henry W. Taft to Herbert Parsons, August 1, 1907; and William Loeb to William Howard Taft, July 13, 1907, Parsons Papers.

[17] New York *Herald*, n.d., Fuller Collection, Vol. V; New York *Times*, Nov. 17. 1907; Charles D. Hilles to Herbert Parsons, Nov. 21, 1907, Parsons Papers.

Alfred Page of New York County, sought to channel this growing strength into an effective organization. On the twenty-
fourth, nineteen progressive Republicans, meeting in New York
City, established the Hughes State League.[18] Its primary purpose was to pledge the state's national convention delegates to
Charles Evans Hughes—the very thing the Roosevelt forces
sought to prevent.

Nonetheless, the Roosevelt administration might have continued its campaign of silence for several months longer had not the
GOP national committee met in Washington in early December.
Recently, a presidential boom had been launched by another
New Yorker, Secretary of the Treasury George B. Cortelyou,
and several of his followers undertook to grasp this opportunity
to gather support among committeemen. Their pretentious
clamor for Roosevelt and the third term, behind which they
waved the Cortelyou banner, moved the President to reconsider
this one element of the overall anti-Hughes strategy. Before he
reiterated the no-third-term declaration, however, he gingerly
canvassed the national committee in order to determine the degree of strength the New York governor possessed outside his
own state. When, much to his surprise, he learned that Hughes
had practically none, he confidently reissued his 1904 statement.[19] Apparently still the master of his party's fortunes,
Roosevelt could now concentrate upon transferring his popularity to William Howard Taft.

As anticipated, the Cortelyou movement collapsed within a
matter of days after the President's pronouncement. But, much
to Roosevelt's chagrin, the Hughes candidacy in New York was
given real impetus now that the Governor's popularity could
finally be expressed without fear of personally affronting Roosevelt. From upstate areas came reports that Hughes sentiment had

[18] New York *World*, Nov. 24, 1907; Thomas W. Whittle to Herbert
Parsons, Nov. 25, 1907, Parsons Papers. All participants were from New
York County.

[19] New York *Times*, Dec. 11 and 12, 1907; Herbert Parsons to Charles
D. Hilles, Dec. 11, 1907, Parsons Papers; Roosevelt to Taft, Dec. 12, 1907,
LTR, V, 864.

suddenly sprung up. In New York City's silk-stocking districts, always the hard core of progressive Republican strength, a number of Charles E. Hughes clubs were organized and immediately began working for delegates. These efforts were to be coordinated by the state league, whose membership Manhattan sponsors sought to expand through the rest of December, 1907, and in early 1908.[20]

It was perhaps inevitable, in the light of so much presidential talk, that Governor Hughes be put under constant pressure to encourage the organizations laboring in his behalf. This increasing pressure tested his deeply ingrained attitude toward political preferment. Having entered public life as a result of fate or circumstance, not by personal choice, Hughes continued to look somewhat disdainfully upon the ways of the professional politician, especially the person who actively campaigned for a nomination or used one public office as a means of gaining another. His personal correspondence, his public declarations, and even his actions as governor in this period show beyond any reasonable doubt that, true to his conviction, he was not seeking the presidency and would lift no finger to advance himself.[21]

[20] New York *Times*, Dec. 13, 17, and 26, 1907; New York *Tribune*, Dec. 13, 1907; New York *World*, Dec. 14, 1907; Washington *Herald*, Dec. 19, 1907, Fuller Collection, LI; John R. Milholland to Hughes, Dec. 19, 1907, Hughes Papers; New York *Times*, Jan. 3, 1908. The league formally commenced its activities on January 13 with a rousing Albany meeting in which was adopted a resolution pledging support to Hughes and insisting that although all the other candidates were qualified for the presidency, only he possessed widespread popular support (New York *Times*, Jan. 14, 1908).

[21] Ida M. Tarbell, "How About Hughes?" *American Magazine*, LXV (1908), 451–464; "Hughes and Taft" (editorial), *Independent*, LXIV (1908), 265–266; Hughes to Martin Saxe, Dec. 16, 1907, Martin Saxe Papers (Columbia University Library); Hughes to Redfield Proctor, Dec. 17, 1907, Hughes Papers; Hughes, "Biographical Notes," p. 195, Hughes Papers; Oswald Garrison Villard, *Fighting Years: Memoirs of a Liberal Editor* (New York: Harcourt, Brace, 1939), pp. 186–187; Jacob Gould Schurman, ed., *Addresses of Charles Evans Hughes, 1906–1916* (New York: Putnam, 1916), pp. 75–76; New York *Tribune*, Dec. 18, 1907; Thorndike Spalding to Hughes, Dec. 31, 1907, Hughes Papers; Buffalo *Morning Express*, Jan. 15, 1908.

The Governor's deliberate restraint was best illustrated in his response to a speaking invitation tendered on January 18, 1908, by the New York City Republican Club. In December this organization had endorsed the Hughes candidacy and eagerly anticipated his discussion of the key national issues of the day. Hughes's policy on matters of this kind was to shun appearances where he would have to express himself on anything but state problems for fear that, however guardedly he analyzed national issues, his position would be twisted into an attack upon the Roosevelt administration. But he did owe his supporters at least one public appearance, so he reluctantly accepted the Republican Club offer, pointing out that "the State administration must continue to be impartial and must not be tributary to any candidacy." [22] Above all, Hughes wished not to become a party to any "factional candidacy" and hoped simply for an "honest expression of party will, and harmony of effort."

While Governor Hughes wrestled with his conscience, the Roosevelt-Taft forces in New York continued their strategy of containing the Hughes boom. After the President's December 11 no-third-term reiteration, they resigned themselves to a favorite-son candidacy. Their goal shifted to that of delaying an endorsement of Hughes until they saw no danger of an incipient national movement and until enough work had been accomplished in New York to make Taft the state's second choice. The test of this strategy came in Herbert Parsons' New York County Republican committee, loaded with earnest Hughes supporters. In mid-December, word reached Parsons that State Senator Martin Saxe, a staunch progressive, would try at the next

---

[22] "Address of Governor Charles E. Hughes before the Republican Club of the City of New York," Jan. 31, 1908, Charles Evans Hughes Collection (NYPL); "Memorandum on Correspondence Concerning Republican Club," n.d., *ibid.*, Hughes's sensitivity on the matter of driving a wedge between Albany and Washington was very much in evidence in correspondence to and from the executive mansion in this period (Daniel Browne to Hughes, Jan. 14, 1908; Robert Lynn Cox to Hughes, Jan. 14, 1908; Charles S. Smith to Hughes, Jan. 18, 1908; Hughes to Smith, Jan. 26, 1908, Hughes Papers).

meeting to push through a resolution committing the organization to the Governor. Coming so soon after the presidential pronouncement, the Saxe threat momentarily stunned Parsons. Uncertain of himself and the position he should assume, he hurried to Washington, where, on the evening of December 19, he conferred with Timothy Woodruff, New York City Congressman William S. Bennet, and Roosevelt's secretary, William Loeb, busy coordinator of Roosevelt's Taft movement. Next day, in executive committee, Parsons carried out his instructions by using all his authority and influence to prevent adoption of the Saxe resolution.[23] Though temporarily stymied, the Hughes champions refused to give up, and the Governor's state movement was broadened in January. On January 16 they made another effort to put through the tabled Saxe resolution. Again the executive committee beat back the move, but the Hughes supporters mustered up enough strength to force a vote in the general meeting. Joined by Odell's opportunistic representatives, they came within a hair's breadth of success.[24]

Interestingly enough, it was Hughes's acceptance of the Republican Club invitation, on January 21, that compelled the Roosevelt-Taft men in New York County to endorse the favorite-son candidacy. If heretofore any doubt existed in their minds regarding Hughes's availability, his agreement to speak on national issues suddenly dispelled it. When news of the Governor's decision reached Washington, Roosevelt dispatched Congressmen J. Sloat Fassett and William Bennet to Secretary Taft, who, on the very next day, sent a public letter to Parsons withdrawing from the New York race.[25] Taft explained that further

[23] Buffalo *Morning Express*, Dec. 20, 1907; Davis, *Released for Publication*, pp. 66–68; New York *Herald*, Dec. 21, 1907; Parsons to Josiah T. Newcomb, Dec. 18, 1907, Parsons Papers.

[24] New York *Times*, Jan. 17, 1908; New York *Tribune*, Jan. 17, 1908, Fuller Collection, Vol. LII.

[25] "Reminiscences of William S. Bennet" (Oral History Project, Columbia University Library, 1949–1950), p. 87; Herbert Parsons to John B. Townsend, Jan. 27, 1908, and William Howard Taft to Parsons, Jan. 23, 1908, Parsons Papers; New York *Times*, Jan. 26, 1908; Stoddard, *As I Knew Them*, pp. 333–334; *Literary Digest*, XXXVI (1908), 139–141; Davis, *Released for Publication*, p. 69.

efforts in his behalf would create the kind of factionalism (that Hughes himself had earlier had in mind) that might rob the GOP of a much-needed November victory. This move proved to be a master stroke of political strategy, for it accomplished all that was possible under the circumstances. First, Taft made himself New York's second choice. If Hughes could get nowhere at the national convention, the state's huge bloc of votes would almost certainly go to him. Second, the loyal Parsons was taken off the hook and perhaps saved from political demise. No longer would he be obligated to risk his leadership of the New York County committee by vainly resisting the Governor's dedicated supporters. He could now jump on the favorite-son bandwagon and work for party unity.

Even so, Governor Hughes's continued availability caused the Roosevelt-Taft forces considerable anguish through the early part of 1908. Only two days after Parsons' New York County committee endorsed the favorite-son candidacy, Hughes appeared before the City Republican Club and delivered a ringing progressive address. He was careful to reiterate his longstanding position regarding the presidential nomination, a statement that all along seemed to make him even more available for the high office. He warmly praised Theodore Roosevelt "for his vigorous opposition to abuses and to the strong impulse he has given to movements for their correction." Yet, in a detailed discussion of his own progressive philosophy, Hughes opened up an area of disagreement with the President. He charged Roosevelt with relying too much upon federal power. "It must be remembered," the Governor argued, "that an evil is not the proper subject of Federal cognizance because it may exist in many States." When local government could strike at abuses (as New York was finally doing, he implied), Washington should remain aloof. Recognizing, however, the profound need for federal action in specific areas, Hughes concluded his address by outlining the chief policies that the next president should seek to implement, including strengthening of the Interstate Commerce Act, clarification of the Sherman Act by explicitly defining "combinations and practices in unreasonable restraint of trade," revision of the tariff, and enactment of a national employers' liability bill—all measures that were within the progressive framework.[26]

In tone and in content the Republican Club address justified the statesmanship and high-mindedness attributed to Governor Hughes by his supporters. It also underscored the one advantage he held over Secretary Taft: his was an elective office with the largest single constituency in the nation aside from the presidency itself, and when he spoke as a progressive, he did so against the background of a brilliant and rewarding struggle for specific reform measures on the state level. Roosevelt seemed to appreciate this advantage, for he chose the very evening on which Hughes spoke to deliver his last and most radical message to Congress. So sensational, indeed, were the President's proposals that the Governor's efforts, however splendid they may have been, were relegated to back-page coverage in newspapers across the land on the next morning.[27] One cartoonist captured the meaning of this brilliant stroke by showing Roosevelt thumping on a bass drum outside the window of a hall where Hughes rose to say, "Fellow Citizens of the Empire State." [28] Roosevelt himself responded with the statement: "If Hughes is going to play the game, he must learn the tricks." [29]

During the rest of the winter and the spring of 1908, while the Governor was engaged in the racing legislation fight, the Taft supporters in the state faced the hard task of advancing the Hughes cause and, simultaneously, minimizing the effectiveness of its appeal. Their difficulty was compounded by close surveillance by that motley group of Republicans who claimed allegiance to the Governor, some of whom, indeed, hoped for

[26] "Republican Club Address."

[27] New York *Times*, Feb. 1, 1908. Oscar King Davis tells the story of how Roosevelt made sure that publication of his message did not take place until the morning after the day it was delivered so that he could steal front-page coverage away from Hughes (*Released for Publication*, pp. 69–71).

[28] "The Slogan of Governor Hughes," *Current Literature*, XLIV (1908), 238.

[29] Mark Sullivan, *Our Times: The United States, 1900–1925* (6 vols.; New York: Scribner, 1926–1935), IV, 304.

the very factionalism that the three leaders were laboring to avoid. Among them were conservative Roosevelt-haters like Odell, former Governor Frank S. Black, and State Senator Edgar T. Brackett.

The issue that threatened the peace in New York was the selection of delegates to the Chicago national convention. Late in January, President Roosevelt and his state cohorts commenced their plans to name Taft men as delegates-at-large.[30] Word of this move reached Odell, who immediately launched a furious assault upon the national administration. Roosevelt responded with a carefully written public letter to one of Hughes's most sincere backers, former New York City Mayor Seth Low, suggesting that, in keeping with tradition, the Governor personally name the delegates-at-large. Roosevelt dismissed his critics as "corrupt and disgruntled politicians" who were supporting Hughes "simply to ensure their own return to power." [31] Issued in part to offer the Hughes progressives in New York an opportunity to isolate the Odell group, this appeal fell on deaf ears. The Governor again took the high road and refused categorically to engage in any activity that might advance his own candidacy.[32]

Hughes's answer gave the Roosevelt-Taft forces in the Empire State another setback and only intensified the President's dislike of the Governor's "mugwumpism." The next step in the complicated process of naming representatives to the national

[30] Buffalo *Morning Express*, Jan. 29, 1908; Edgar T. Brackett to Robert H. Fuller, Feb. 4, 1908, Hughes Papers.

[31] Roosevelt to Low, Feb. 6, 1908, *LTR*, VI, 925–926. On February 7 William Loeb repeated this advice to Woodruff (Loeb to Woodruff, Feb. 7, 1908, Roosevelt Papers).

[32] Buffalo *Morning Express,* Feb. 13 and 15, 1908. Less than two months later, Hughes repeated his refusal (Hughes to Woodruff, April 4, 1908, Hughes Papers). His disinterest is seen in a letter to Stewart L. Woodford, March 28, 1908, cited in "Reminiscences of Frederick C. Tanner" (Oral History Project, Columbia University Library, 1960), pp. 35–36. It appears also that on this matter of delegates Hughes may have been influenced by some of his independent Republican friends (Jacob Gould Schurman to Hughes, March 28, 1908, Jacob Gould Schurman Papers [Cornell University Library]).

convention was the March 31 state primaries, where delegates were to be chosen to the April assembly and congressional district conventions.[33] Again anticipating a factional quarrel, Roosevelt sought to neutralize his opposition, but the cantankerous Odell refused any and all presidential overtures. As a last resort, Parsons spoke directly to Hughes, whose position remained unchanged.[34] The result was a vigorous contest in the spring primaries between the President's followers and the Hughes champions. In New York County the regular organization, under Parsons' able leadership, emerged triumphant in all but two assembly districts and thus guaranteed Roosevelt-Taft control over a large bloc of delegates who, in ten days, would choose representatives to the crucially important state convention. They, like their colleagues elected from upstate, were pledged to Governor Hughes, the favorite son. But also like their upstate brethren, they remained staunchly loyal to their first choice, Secretary of War Taft.[35]

By the time the GOP state convention assembled in Carnegie Hall in early April, the much-feared Hughes boom had fizzled. From the moment it opened until the moment it closed, the convention was Roosevelt's. The President's banners graced the walls and the rostrum in full glory, and his effervescent spirit pervaded the otherwise monotonous proceedings. When the time arrived to endorse a candidate, the delegates turned to the recommendations of the resolutions committee. In drawing up the favorite-son resolution, this Taft-dominated group had rejected Edgar T. Brackett's proposal to commit the convention's

[33] The process of selecting delegates to the national convention was a complicated one. Four delegates-at-large were to be named by the spring state convention. In the March primaries, delegates for congressional district and assembly district conventions were chosen. Several days later these conventions named representatives to the state convention who actually chose delegates for the New York GOP in Chicago.

[34] Parsons to Stewart L. Woodford, March 12, 1908, Parsons Papers; New York *World*, Feb. 22, 1908, Fuller Collection, Vol. CXXI.

[35] New York *Times*, April 1, 1908; Buffalo *Morning Express*, April 10 and 11, 1908.

spokesmen in Chicago to Hughes "until a nomination is made." [36] Instead, they reported a lukewarm endorsement that by voice vote was readily accepted by the assembled delegates.

Undoubtedly a fiasco for Hughes, the Republican state convention found no keener interpreter than Theodore Roosevelt. On the very day that the Brackett proposal was turned down, the President gleefully wrote that the Governor's boom had collapsed.[37] No longer did the Taft forces have to be concerned with the possibility of a national movement developing out of an energetic Hughes candidacy. Roosevelt and his lieutenants had been completely successful in keeping the state party machinery in their own hands, and whatever popular approval the Hughes name had evoked in 1907, it never reached the dangerous proportion Roosevelt had feared. After all, 1908 was not a particularly good legislative year for the state's chief executive, a situation for which Roosevelt himself does not escape at least partial responsibility.[38] Then, too, Hughes personally had done nothing to enhance his own position, and his sincere followers were left floundering in a sea of political confusion.

By the time the Republicans gathered to name their 1908 standard-bearer in mid-June, the Roosevelt-Taft forces across the nation held undisputed possession of the party reins. There was now no question of the Secretary of War's nomination; only the vice-presidency remained in doubt. Several days before the New York delegation arrived in Chicago, word spread among the group that if they could secure an early release from the Hughes commitment, the Empire State would have the sec-

[36] New York *Times*, April 12, 1908.

[37] Roosevelt to Kermit Roosevelt, April 11, 1908, *LTR*, VI, 1005. Already in March the New York *World* had insisted that the Hughes movement was fizzling out. They argued that it had not attracted enough national leaders and that in New York it had been infiltrated by insincere, ambitious politicians (New York *World*, March 13, 1908, Fuller Collection, Vol. LIII). Odell's Newburgh *Daily News*, n.d., subscribed to the former point and added that Hughes's aloofness was the key factor (*ibid.*, Vol. LIII).

[38] See Chapter VIII.

ond spot on the Taft ticket.[39] All the delegates needed, it was assumed, was a statement from the Governor, and they could begin work either for him or for another available New Yorker.

Hughes's attitude toward the vice-presidential nomination, however, was even more inflexible than it had been toward the presidency. Although his recent victory against race-track gambling placed his name in the forefront of possible nominees, he dashed the hopes of the GOP organization faithful on June 12 with a public statement refusing, under any circumstances, to accept the nomination.[40] Next day, in reply to a telegram dispatched from Chicago by one of the New York leaders, Lucius Littauer, he reiterated this declaration, adding that he could not release his pledged delegates.[41]

The Governor could certainly be forgiven for his rejection of the vice-presidential nomination, and for that matter his friends were happy that he made no move to shelve himself politically. But most of the state's Taft supporters rankled with bitterness when they learned that he would not permit them to bargain in behalf of another New Yorker. Defiantly, several of them— Woodruff, Parsons, and Barnes—broke rank and began working for Utica Congressman James S. Sherman, long associated with the conservative wing of the party.[42] The Sherman candidacy caught on as standpatters like House Speaker Cannon felt the need for a supposedly balanced ticket. Taft, on the other hand, preferred a progressive, perhaps Iowa's Jonathan P. Dolliver or Indiana's Albert J. Beveridge, but he shied away from dictating to the convention.[43] When he had won the presidential nomina-

[39] New York *World*, June 9, 1908, Fuller Collection, Vol. CXXIV; Buffalo *Morning Express*, June 11, 1908; New York *Times*, June 12, 1908.

[40] New York *Times*, June 13, 1908.

[41] *Ibid.*, June 14, 1908. Two days later Herbert Parsons wired the Governor, again asking him to release the delegates so they might work for second place. Hughes, however, took the same position that he had previously maintained (Hughes to Parsons, June 15, 1908, Parsons Papers).

[42] Buffalo *Morning Express*, June 14 and 15, 1908; New York *Times*, June 15, 1908.

[43] Blair Bolles, *Tyrant from Illinois: Uncle Joe Cannon's Experiment*

tion, however, he wired Hughes in Albany and offered him second spot on the ticket.[44] The Governor again resisted the overture, and Taft settled for the convention's choice, James S. Sherman.[45]

Thus, for Governor Hughes, the Chicago proceedings marked the close of another chapter in his long struggle with the professional politicians. From the very beginning he had not aspired to any office other than the one he presently held, and he personally made no effort to move up the political ladder. Yet his achievements in New York cast him into the vortex of presidential politics from which, ironically, he emerged a less respected and less admired public servant.

with Personal Power (New York: Norton, 1951), pp. 127, 133; Pringle, *Life and Times of Taft*, I, 354; Arthur W. Dunn, *From Harrison to Harding: A Personal Narrative* (2 vols.; New York: Putnam, 1922), II, 72–73.

[44] In the presidential balloting, Hughes compiled only 67 votes while Taft rolled up 702, and Philander C. Knox received 68. Interestingly, the New York delegation gave ten votes to Taft and three to Cannon. Among those recording against the Governor were William Ward and William Barnes, both supporting Taft, and Benjamin Odell and Lucius Littauer for the house speaker.

[45] Taft chose the indirect route (Elbert F. Baldwin to Hughes, June 19, 1908, and Hughes to Baldwin, June 19, 1908, Hughes Papers).

CHAPTER X

Renomination and Re-election

BY the summer of 1908 New York's prominent Republican leaders were so united in their opposition to Governor Hughes that they eagerly awaited his retirement from office. Although circumstances were to make his renomination inevitable, these same leaders would remain unduly recalcitrant and hold off supporting him until the last possible moment. Their determination had not, of course, been a sudden development but had stemmed from a series of grievances originating in the period immediately following the 1906 elections and had slowly grown to substantial proportions.

Unquestionably, Charles Evans Hughes had never intended to create a gulf between himself and his party. His brand of politics, however, was so different from the traditional kind that a conflict appeared almost inevitable from the very beginning. He stoutly refused to play the game on appointments and patronage, although he did offer the organization some concessions. He held steadfastly for a reform program that left little room for the customary executive-legislative maneuverings and that engendered little enthusiasm from the influential upstate wing of the GOP. Above all, Hughes publicly assailed his more conservative brethren when he thought their opposition destructive and wanton. His moral tone, his personal aloofness, and his political independence evoked the most intense criticism from members of his own party. Thus Francis Hendricks wrote to Senator

Horace White during the antigambling crusade: "I should think you would want to get a little rest from the atmosphere of righteousness that surrounds the wicked Legislature. I suggest that before you go, you take a peep into the Executive Chamber, where I conclude all the virtue in the State is collected."[1]

Climaxing these accumulated grievances was the bitter Chicago experience of June, 1908. Here the state leaders, including Parsons and Woodruff, suffered the full impact of Hughes's independence and aloofness when he adamantly refused them the privilege of bargaining with his candidacy in the accepted political fashion. During the rest of the convention, and indeed during most of the trip home, the disgruntled New Yorkers vehemently denounced their chief executive. So embittered were they that when James S. Sherman was given formal notification of his vice-presidential nomination, Hughes was not even among the invited celebrants.[2]

The Governor's highly unorthodox behavior in Chicago also intensified Theodore Roosevelt's ill-feeling toward him. If the President, a year before, had criticized Hughes sharply, he now wrote with bitterness and acidity. Hughes was "selfish . . . to all considerations excepting his own welfare," he complained shortly before Taft's nomination. Even more outspoken later, Roosevelt confided to Root that the Governor was a "thoroly [*sic*] unhealthy element in public life."[3] Time and again, the President added in another letter, he had tried to cooperate with his fellow New Yorker, but his every effort had been ungratefully rejected.[4] Hughes, therefore, was little more than a "mug-

[1] April 21, 1908, Horace White Papers (Syracuse University Library). Wadsworth was especially sensitive about Hughes's attacks on the politicians ("Autobiography," pp. 149–150, James W. Wadsworth, Jr., Papers [Hartford House, Geneseo, New York; now on deposit in the Library of Congress]).

[2] New York *Times*, June 21, 1908; *Literary Digest*, XXXVII (1908), 267.

[3] Roosevelt to Benjamin I. Wheeler, June 17, 1908, *LTR*, VI, 1082–1083; Roosevelt to Root, Sept. 5, 1908, Elihu Root Papers (Manuscript Division, Library of Congress).

[4] Roosevelt to Lyman Abbott, Sept. 15, 1908, *LTR*, VI, 1237–1240.

wump," that political animal that Roosevelt so thoroughly despised.

Undoubtedly much of this outspoken criticism was grounded in the belief that the Governor would not seek re-election. Hughes, in fact, had all but made up his mind to retire from public life in January, 1909. He himself relates that he wished to return to the practice of law for personal reasons, foremost of which was the inadequate salary he had received as governor. Supporting his large family (his wife, their four children, and his parents), financing all political trips not directly associated with discharging the duties of his office, and running the gubernatorial household had so drastically cut into his savings that he felt he simply could not afford another term.[5]

As early as January, 1908, Hughes had hinted at his intention to retire when he informally told National Guardsmen that he was addressing them as their chief executive for the last time. During the course of this second legislative year, however, the rumor spread that he might change his mind, especially in view of the concerted opposition that had developed to his reform program.[6] By July, Hughes had begun to weaken in the face of continued appeals. On the fourteenth, Dr. Walter Laidlaw climaxed an Albany conference in the executive mansion with the announcement that the Governor would run again "if he felt that the party wished it." [7] Ten days later Hughes confessed to newspapermen that his January remarks had been made in an atmosphere of levity and that, in the peace and quiet of his

---

[5] Hughes, "Biographical Notes," p. 196c, Charles Evans Hughes Papers (Manuscript Division, Library of Congress); Henry C. Beerits, "First Term as Governor," p. 65, in "Memorandum," Hughes Papers. The governor's salary at this time was $10,000 per year.

[6] Hughes to John Bigelow, Aug. 4, 1908, Hughes Papers; New York *Times*, April 30 and May 10, 1908; Buffalo *Daily Courier*, May 9, 1908; New York *World* and New York *Tribune*, June 15, 1908, Fuller Collection, Vol. LIV. In May, William Barnes was convinced that Hughes had already decided to seek renomination (Barnes to Herbert Parsons, May 9, 1908, Herbert Parsons Papers [Columbia University Library]).

[7] New York *Tribune*, July 15, 1908, Fuller Collection, Vol. LIV.

Saranac Lake retreat, he would soon reach a final decision on so pressing a matter.[8]

Thus, in seclusion, the Governor pondered his political future. He had, of course, achieved a substantial portion of his 1907 reform program, but even during the second year he had made no headway with the all-important direct nominations legislation. Nor had he been able to prevail upon the 1908 legislature to improve the Public Service Commission Law by extending regulation to the telephone and telegraph companies. Only a second administration, Hughes concluded, could complete this work, and so, unwilling to leave "in the lurch those who had been so generous in their support," [9] he announced, on July 24, that he regarded it "as a privilege and a duty to continue in office for another term." [10] Leaving the final decision in the hands of his party, Hughes, in typical fashion, dismissed the matter.

Although the New York leaders were presumably stunned by the Governor's sensational announcement, they were actually prepared for it. State Chairman Timothy Woodruff, now one of the most outspoken Hughes critics, had already spent several weeks in his Camp Kill Kare retreat meeting with other state leaders and plotting to control the September Saratoga convention.[11] To a man, claimed the progressive New York *World*, these politicians were working against the Governor, and they cared little whether circumstances changed.[12] Their strategy was to maintain a united front in the hope of creating the impression that rank-and-file Republicans were demanding the election of a chief executive who would honor patronage and

[8] New York *World*, July 24, 1908, *ibid.*, Vol. LV.

[9] Hughes, "Biographical Notes," p. 197. Similar statements can be found in Beerits, "First Term," p. 66, and Hughes to Curtis Guild, Jr., Aug. 3, 1908, Hughes Papers.

[10] "Hughes Letter on Renomination," July 24, 1908, Hughes Collection (NYPL); New York *Tribune*, July 25, 1908, Fuller Collection, Vol. LV.

[11] New York *Herald*, July 28, 1908, Fuller Collection, Vol. CXXVII; New York *Times*, July 17, 28, and 31, 1908.

[12] New York *World*, Aug. 3, 1908, Fuller Collection, Vol. LVII; New York *Times*, July 25, 1908.

party requests. To round out this so-called "harmony" program, staunch Hughes supporters would be dropped from the GOP state ticket that fall. Already the usually mild-mannered Herbert Parsons had allegedly dumped Alfred Page and Martin Saxe, two outstanding New York County progressives who had been in the vanguard of the Governor's presidential movement.[13]

Hughes's decision to make himself available for the 1908 gubernatorial nomination again focused attention on Theodore Roosevelt, acknowledged leader of the state GOP. Characteristically, on July 28, presidential secretary William Loeb stated publicly that Roosevelt would "maintain an attitude of noninterference in the selection of all candidates, Congressional as well as Gubernatorial."[14] The question, however, was not what Roosevelt would say publicly, but rather what he would do privately. Amid rumors that the President was again veering toward Hughes, Timothy Woodruff journeyed to Oyster Bay for a significant conference. Here the state chairman laid before William Loeb an imposing array of correspondence from disgruntled organization men in New York. There were letters from Hendricks of Syracuse, Greiner of Buffalo, Barnes of Albany, and J. Sloat Fassett of Elmira—all complaining that rank-and-file Republicans refused to support the Governor's renomination. Although Loeb made it clear that the President's policy, as announced the previous day, was to keep hands off the state situation, he advised Woodruff to handle things carefully, for the strongest candidate had to be named. At the time, he noted, Hughes was well ahead of all other possible nominees. Privately, Roosevelt reiterated Loeb's dictum, adding that he would await the results of the August primaries unless, for some reason, circumstances called for a different course of action.[15]

[13] New York *Times*, July 19 and 26, 1908.

[14] *Ibid.*, July 29, 1908.

[15] *Ibid.*, July 30, 1908; New York *Tribune* and New York *Sun*, July 30, 1908, Fuller Collection, Vols. LV, LVI; Roosevelt to William Howard Taft, July 30, 1908, and to Charles Sprague Smith, July 31, 1908, *LTR*, VI, 1144–1145, 1145–1146. Actually, the August primaries proved little

So determined was Woodruff on the Hughes matter, however, that he regarded as important only that part of Loeb's remarks concerning Roosevelt's decision not to interfere. He thus assured his Kings County colleagues that the President would not "run the risk of splitting the party wide open by forcing the nomination of the Governor on the leaders." Diligently, he labored to solidify the anti-Hughes movement and, after several conferences with key state bosses, reported to James S. Sherman that there was "not a break in the organization line from Montauk Point to Lake Erie." [16] His efforts to control the Saratoga convention were intensified accordingly. To give the proceedings the necessary air of dignity and respectability, Woodruff enlisted the services of Elihu Root as temporary chairman. He then attempted to cajole Sherman to declare his availability at Saratoga for consultation. But in the end Sherman's national campaign commitments took precedence, and the Utica conservative was forced to beg off.[17] Finally, on August 11, Woodruff announced the appointment of a state campaign committee composed almost entirely of organization stalwarts.[18] He would leave no stone unturned in his vigorous fight to return the governorship to organization control.

The drive and determination that characterized the state machine's battle against Hughes contrasted sharply with the uncertainty and confusion that Theodore Roosevelt exhibited toward

and had nothing to do with the President's decision regarding Hughes (New York *Tribune*, Aug. 26, 1908).

[16] New York *World*, Aug. 3, 1908, Fuller Collection, Vol. CXXVII; Woodruff to Sherman, Aug. 3, 1908, James S. Sherman Papers (NYPL).

[17] Woodruff to Sherman, July 31 and Aug. 4 and 8, 1908; Sherman to Woodruff, Aug. 6, 1908; Sherman to William D. Todd, Aug. 8, 1908, Sherman Papers. See also Woodruff to Root, Aug. 13, 1908, Root Papers; Root to Roosevelt, Aug. 11, 1908, Theodore Roosevelt Papers (Manuscript Division, Library of Congress); Roosevelt to Taft, Aug. 3, 1908, *LTR*, VI, 1149.

[18] William Barnes, a prominent member of this group, reminded administration defenders that "Governor Hughes said it was up to the people. Their verdict will be filed at the primaries, and I have no fear of the outcome" (New York *Times*, Aug. 12, 1908).

the troublesome New York situation. In the seclusion of Oyster Bay, Roosevelt debated long and hard the nomination question. His private correspondence during early August revealed a remarkable ambivalence toward Hughes. On the one hand, he expressed a deep resentment toward his fellow New Yorker—an attitude created largely by the numerous letters of protest he and his cohorts received from organization leaders. On the other hand, he recognized that independents and independent Republicans, clergymen, thinking men, and "good" citizens throughout the state were still solidly behind the reform governor.[19]

Even more impressed with Hughes's popularity as a political figure was the Republican presidential nominee, William Howard Taft, now vacationing in Hot Springs, Virginia. Reportedly, Taft was deluged with letters insisting that the national ticket needed the talents and services of the New York governor— especially in the west, where Hughes's moral approach had special appeal and where the GOP faced imminent peril.[20] To Roosevelt, the Secretary of War confessed this spontaneous enthusiasm. Indeed, he implored the President to use his influence in behalf of Hughes's renomination.[21]

Roosevelt's reaction to Taft's request was cautious. The President could not forget Hughes's "mugwumpery" and he was not yet certain that the New Yorkers were exaggerating the Governor's unpopularity among rank-and-file Republicans. "There are any number of thoroly [*sic*] good people who violently object

[19] Roosevelt to Root, Aug. 3, 1908, and to Henry Cabot Lodge, Aug. 8, 1908, *LTR*, VI, 1149–1150, 1160–1163. See also J. Sloat Fassett to Roosevelt, Aug. 2, 1908; Elon Brown to Roosevelt, Aug. 1, 1908; George J. Smith to Roosevelt, Aug. 3, 1908; and William Barnes to Root, Aug 14, 1908, Root Papers.

[20] New York *Sun*, Aug. 16, 1908, Fuller Collection, Vol. LVIII; New York *Times*, Aug. 16, 1908. There are good specimens in the William Howard Taft Papers (Manuscript Division, Library of Congress), especially Otto Bannard to Taft, July 31, 1908; George F. Davis to Taft, Aug. 1, 1908; John A. Sleicher to Taft, Aug. 3, 1908; and Jacob Schiff to Taft, Aug. 3, 1908.

[21] Taft to Roosevelt, Aug. 10, 13, 16, and 20, 1908, Taft Papers; Taft to Root, Aug. 15, 1908, Root Papers.

to his nomination," he wrote candidly on August 12, "and we may get beaten out of our boots with him." [22] Warning Taft not to make any statement on the crucial New York situation, Roosevelt feared the consequences of another dictated nomination. Lurking beneath this caution, however, was the growing conviction that there was really little choice in the matter—that Hughes must again lead the state ticket.

Finally, on August 20, after several weeks of uncertainty, Roosevelt disclosed his position on the Governor's political future. In a meeting with his closest state advisors and National Chairman Frank Hitchcock, he boldly announced that for two reasons Hughes had to be renominated. First, the best groups in New York were solidly behind him, and, second, "feeling outside . . . was even stronger." [23] Roosevelt added, somewhat apologetically, that he was not considering whether the Governor deserved the bid or whether he would wreck the state machine while serving a second term. Only Taft's election was important. Then to Hitchcock, State Committee Treasurer George J. Smith, James S. Sherman, William Bennet, and William Cocks, Roosevelt made his position clear: he would not personally dictate to the convention, but his own delegates would stand firmly for Hughes. With sighs of relief (the President later noted), the New Yorkers spontaneously volunteered to inform the intransigent anti-Hughes people of the Oyster Bay decision.[24]

Roosevelt treated his disappointed lieutenants in New York

[22] Roosevelt to Taft, Aug. 12, 1908, Taft Papers.

[23] Roosevelt to Lyman Abbott, Aug. 21, 1908, *LTR*, VI, 1192–1193. The conference is also reported in New York *Times*, Aug. 21, 1908; *Literary Digest*, XXXVII (1908), 267–268; and "Reminiscences of William S. Bennet" (Oral History Project, Columbia University Library, 1949–1950), p. 155. Bennet records (p. 157) that he had the assignment of *telling* Parsons and William Ward of Roosevelt's decision.

[24] James S. Sherman played a leading role in attempting to sell the idea of Hughes's nomination to the state leaders (Sherman to Taft, Aug. 24, 1908, and to Frank H. Hitchcock, Aug. 30, 1908; and Taft to Sherman Aug. 25, 1908, Sherman Papers).

with real sympathy and understanding.[25] Yet his efforts to assuage their bitterness were not immediately successful. Woodruff continued to work against the Governor, and no amount of pressure seemed to lessen his determination.[26] Barnes had already told Root that under no circumstances would his Albany delegates go over to the Hughes camp—a decision that remained unchanged despite an impassioned presidential plea. Even Herbert Parsons, long Roosevelt's righthand man in New York, balked at the August 20 decision to the extent that Roosevelt was compelled to write a soothing, almost apologetic letter explaining the reasons for his decision.[27]

While the unruly state leaders continued to stir up strong anti-Hughes sentiment among their followers, Roosevelt became more and more adamant in his insistence that the Governor be renominated. He retained his reservations concerning Hughes, but he now viewed the New York situation wholly in terms of the Taft candidacy. Thus, following hard on the heels of another announcement for the Governor, the President summoned Woodruff, Parsons, and Ward to Oyster Bay, where, on September 1, he confessed that, although he intended not to dictate, "as a citizen of New York" he deemed it "absolutely necessary to renominate Mr. Hughes." [28]

Still the President's unequivocal language went unheeded. Constant complaints against Woodruff in particular dotted Roosevelt's personal correspondence right up to the Saratoga

[25] Indeed, Roosevelt wrote separate letters to the leaders (Roosevelt to John A. Sleicher, Aug. 22, 1908, Hughes Papers). A good example is his conciliatory letter to Barnes, dated August 21, 1908 (*LTR*, VI, 1193–1194).

[26] William S. Bennet to Herbert Parsons, Aug. 24, 1908, Parsons Papers. On August 28 Woodruff issued a public statement that repudiated any and all efforts "to direct the course of the forthcoming convention" (New York *World*, Aug. 29, 1908, Fuller Collection, Vol. LX).

[27] Philip C. Jessup, *Elihu Root* (New York: Dodd, Mead, 1938), II, 128; Roosevelt to Barnes, Aug. 24, 1908, and to Parsons, Aug. 27, 1908, *LTR*, VI, 1196, 1197–1199.

[28] New York *Sun* and New York *Times*, Sept. 2, 1908; Roosevelt to Taft, August 24 and 29, 1908, *LTR*, VI, 1194–1196, 1201–1203; Roosevelt to L. B. Crane, Aug. 29, 1908, Hughes Papers.

convention.[29] Parsons also held off declaring for Hughes until after the September 8 primaries in New York City. Here he deliberately set up test ballots in key districts so that he might gauge the Governor's true strength. When, as usual, Hughes fared exceptionally well in Manhattan, Parsons capitulated, announcing that "a large majority of the delegates from New York County to the State Convention will favor Governor Hughes's renomination." [30] The first visible crack had appeared in the organization wall.

A more significant event than the September City primaries, however, shattered the machine's case against Hughes. Candidate Taft's interest in the Governor has already been noted. So impressed was the Secretary of War that in mid-August, even before the President's final decision, he announced that Hughes's services would be utilized in the western campaign.[31] Within three weeks the New Yorker appeared in Youngstown, Ohio, where in dignified fashion he energetically launched Taft's drive against William Jennings Bryan. Although Hughes personally questioned the success of this fighting speech shortly after the occasion, GOP reaction allayed his reservations. Having seen the text several days before its delivery, Taft wrote enthusiastically to Roosevelt of its "Republicanism." [32] Two weeks later the President repeated to Hughes the party's satisfaction, labeling the Youngstown address "one of the best things yet done in this campaign." [33] Suddenly the organization's claim that the Gov-

[29] On September 1 Taft had already complained to Roosevelt that Woodruff "is as usual making an 'ass' of himself" (Taft Papers). The President displayed his concern in several letters (Roosevelt to Root, Sept. 5, 1908, to Taft, Sept. 5, 1908, and to James S. Sherman, Sept. 9, 1908, *LTR*, VI, 1207–1208, 1209–1210, 1223; New York *Sun*, Sept. 3, 1908).

[30] New York *Times* and New York *Herald*, Sept. 10, 1908; Parsons to editor of New York *Press*, Oct. 14, 1908, Parsons Papers.

[31] New York *Herald*, Aug. 18, 1908.

[32] Taft to Roosevelt, Sept. 4, 1908, Taft Papers; Beerits, "First Term," p. 68.

[33] The letter, dated September 19, was actually written to John A. Sleicher, but it was turned over to Hughes and is filed in his correspond-

ernor was not an avid partisan laboring arduously for the welfare of the Republican party had become ineffective.

Just one week after the Youngstown speech, Republican delegates drifted into Saratoga for the 1908 state convention. Although a strong current of anti-Hughes sentiment permeated
their ranks, the consensus was that the Governor would be
renominated. Most of the leaders themselves conceded defeat,
but Woodruff, Barnes, and several "bosslets" remained in the
battle to name another candidate. Their big task was to agree in
advance upon a nominee whose name could be put before the
convention and around whom other discontents might rally.[34]

Meanwhile, the Roosevelt forces had carefully mapped out
their own strategy. Fully aware of the determined opposition to
Hughes, the President worked on Secretary Root, who had earlier been named by Woodruff to play a significant role in the
Saratoga convention. Roosevelt impressed upon his cabinet associate that, in order to ensure the success of the national ticket,
the Governor had to be renominated. During the convention itself, Frank Hitchcock, Taft's campaign manager, and the Secretary of War personally added their importunities to Roosevelt's
repeated appeals.[35]

Although Root's sympathies (and the President's)undoubt-
edly lay with the Woodruff group, he faithfully played the role
Roosevelt had outlined for him. Once settled at Saratoga, he
carefully canvassed the state leaders and found more opposition
to Hughes than the newspaper reports had indicated. Root
noted the whispering campaign that was going on and became
convinced that if the bosses were successful in "concentrating
the strong feeling against Hughes . . . the Convention will

---

ence. Later the President reiterated this judgment directly to the Governor (Roosevelt to Hughes, Oct. 20, 1908, Hughes Papers).

[34] New York *Times*, Sept. 12 and 14, 1908; New York *Sun*, Sept. 13,
1908, Fuller Collection, Vol. LXII; Rochester *Democrat and Chronicle*,
Sept. 13, 1908, George W. Aldridge Papers (RML).

[35] Roosevelt to Root, Sept. 5 and 14, 1908; Hitchcock to Root, Sept.
14, 1908; Taft to Root, Sept. 14, 1908, Root Papers.

probably result in another nomination." [36] With this uncomfortable fact in mind, the Secretary of State delivered his keynote address on September 14 to an apathetic Republican gathering. This carefully constructed speech emphasized the similarity between the Roosevelt and Hughes programs, underscoring the President's support of the Governor's New York reform efforts. Root even endorsed the controversial direct primary and concluded his long appeal with a consideration of the national issues challenging the GOP.[37]

Still, the leaders stubbornly refused to rest their case and accept the inevitable. Woodruff saw to it that immediately after Root's keynote address the convention session was adjourned. Then, he, Odell, Black, and Ward met for the obvious purpose of agreeing upon a candidate who could unite New York's faction-ridden GOP. This meeting was followed by a Kings County caucus in which the state chairman's men accepted William Berri, Brooklyn publisher, as their favorite-son candidate to do battle with Hughes. Into the evening hours, Woodruff continued his efforts against the Governor. A final conference, lasting until one o'clock the next morning, saw Barnes, Odell, Littauer, Ward, Hendricks, Raines, Greiner, and Aldridge agree tentatively upon the name of David Jayne Hill, American ambassador to Germany, as their choice for the governorship.[38]

The Hill selection reflected the desperate plight of the New York leaders. Although the ambassador was indeed a Roosevelt follower and, under normal circumstances, might have made a good compromise candidate, he was simply not available at this time. No one appreciated this fact better than Secretary Root, who, up to now, had displayed remarkable patience. Root attended the postmidnight conference and when Hill's name was approved he found the situation too ludicrous to overlook without comment: "Mr. Hill will be very much surprised to learn

36 Root to Roosevelt, n.d., Root Papers.

37 New York *Times* and Buffalo *Morning Express*, Sept. 15, 1908.

38 New York *Times*, Sept. 15 and 16, 1908; New York *World*, Sept. 15, 1908. It was George Aldridge who suggested Hill's name (Elihu Root to David Jayne Hill, Nov. 23, 1908, Root Papers).

that he is your candidate," he declared to the leaders, and, of course, "he will decline the honor . . . you are seeking to thrust upon him." [39] To prove to his fellow New Yorkers that they must submit, Root then wired the ambassador and by morning received the negative reply he had anticipated. The Woodruff forces now had no alternative but to surrender their case.

Thus, when the Saratoga convention met for its second session on the afternoon of September 15, the result was a foregone conclusion. After several brief nominating speeches, which for the most part continued the debate on Hughes, the balloting began. Indicative of the outcome was Fred Greiner's announcement that all of Erie's fifty-nine votes would go to the Governor. Woodruff followed with the entire Kings delegation, and Aldridge added Monroe to the Hughes column. Parsons of New York and Hendricks of Onondaga completed the list of the major leaders yielding to Theodore Roosevelt's wishes. Governor Hughes altogether amassed 827 of the convention's 1009 votes, and the nomination was then made unanimous. [40]

Extensive as the Roosevelt influence may have been at Saratoga, [41] it did not affect the rest of the proceedings. The platform, while perfunctorily endorsing the Governor's administration, rejected outright the Massachusetts ballot and ignored both the direct primary and legislation extending the jurisdiction of the public service commissions. The remainder of the ticket was also boss-chosen. It comprised representatives from the state's important local organizations, nominated in such a way as to give the most reluctant Hughes supporter reason to work for the entire ticket. [42]

While the Republicans muddled through the Saratoga con-

---

[39] New York *Times*, Sept. 16, 1908.   [40] *Ibid.*, Sept. 16, 1908.

[41] Elihu Root pointed out that without the President's interference, "there would not have been two hundred votes for Hughes in the convention" (Root to Roosevelt, Sept. 24, 1908, Roosevelt Papers).

[42] New York *Times*, Sept. 16, 1908. The ticket included candidates for the attorney-generalship (Edward R. O'Malley, of Greiner's Erie organization), the lieutenant-governorship (Horace White, Hendricks'

vention, the Democrats gathered in Rochester for the purpose of naming their state ticket. Like the GOP, they too had experienced two years of intraparty squabbling, albeit of a much less dramatic nature. After the 1906 elections, Tammany remained anathema to upstate leader Thomas Mott Osborne and his independent Democratic followers. Indeed, outside New York City only State Chairman William Conners, Buffalo's erstwhile Hearst champion, could be considered a Murphy ally and even this relationship seemed tenuous as the time for the convention approached. The usual upstate-downstate cleavage was widened by the intensification of a longstanding conflict between Tammany Hall and McCarren's Brooklyn organization, occasioned by Murphy's determination to dominate the entire City Democracy. The bickering had come to a head in the spring of 1908, when the state party met in Carnegie Hall to select the New York delegation to the Denver national convention. Here Murphy summarily threw out McCarren's Kings County delegates and seated men of his own persuasion. Ten days later, in Utica, the irate Brooklyn boss led representatives from twenty counties in forming the "Home Rule Democratic Organization," whose sole *raison d'être* was Tammany dictatorship.[43]

The McCarren revolt, however, was abortive, for it failed to enlist the enthusiastic support of the Osborne group. The reasons for this failure are clear. First of all, the struggle itself was largely a New York City factional battle and could not, on its merits, generate interest among upstate Democrats. Moreover, McCarren's own shoddy record as an obstructionist in the state senate made his position untenable to independent Democrats who were deeply concerned over party reform. Perhaps most important of all was the whole attitude and approach of Osborne and his colleagues toward the New York political situa-

man), the state treasurership (Thomas B. Dunn, representative of Aldridge's organization), the comptrollership (Charles H. Gaus, a member of Barnes's machine), and the secretaryship of state (Samuel S. Koenig, Parsons' man).

[43] New York *Times*, April 16, 1908; New York *World*, April 26, 1908.

tion in these years. If the upstate Democrats were intensely angry in 1906 over the Murphy-Hearst alliance, their resentment cooled somewhat during 1907 and 1908. Doubtless, they were satisfied that Hearst's defeat heralded his decline as a force in state politics. By the same token, Osborne and his followers were greatly impressed by Hughes's independence and reform program. Early in his administration, the new governor even made patronage overtures to the upstate Democrats.[44] Of principal importance was Osborne's own appointment to the original public service commission of the second district. In this position, the Auburn insurgent remained essentially out of politics for nearly two years, regaling his colleagues with the Governor's virtues and urging independents to bide their time till the propitious moment to renew the anti-Tammany crusade in full force. The Hughes spirit, echoed Osborne's friend Louis Antisdale, would ultimately "increase the influence of liberal and independent Democrats, as well as . . . Republicans."[45] To this group of party rebels, then, 1908 was not the year for Democratic resurgence in the state or nation.

Murphy's response to the "Home Rule Democratic Organization" was simply to ignore it, though he could not neglect the aura of independence that was apparent in his own party across the state. After the Hearst defeat, he turned to the formula that had served him so well in New York City. He sought a gubernatorial candidate who was both respectable and manageable. But Murphy moved cautiously. He made commitments to no one during the spring and summer of 1908 and refused even to comment on the impending Democratic convention. When, on September 14, he finally arrived in Rochester, he joined with other leaders in a concerted effort to determine the "feeling" of the assembled delegates. Their careful analysis showed Lieu-

[44] Osborne to Hughes, Jan. 10, 1907, and Hughes to Osborne, Jan. 11, 1907, Thomas Mott Osborne Papers (Syracuse University Library).

[45] Antisdale to Osborne, Aug. 15, 1907, *ibid.* Osborne, too, thought that "Hughes represents the fight against *boss-rule* . . . better than anyone in our time" (Osborne to Oswald Garrison Villard, Oct. 20, 1908, Oswald Garrison Villard Papers [Harvard University Library]).

tenant-Governor Lewis S. Chanler well ahead in pledged support, and in anticipation of the final result State Chairman Conners announced that Chanler "will be the candidate." [46]

If Murphy sought not to "boss" the Rochester convention as he had the Buffalo convention two years earlier, neither would he permit so quick a decision to be made. Undoubtedly, a Chanler nomination had decided advantages. Not only was the Lieutenant-Governor an upstater, but over the past two years he had also been associated with the progressive wing of the party. There were, however, other gubernatorial aspirants, among them David C. Robinson of Chemung, W. Caryl Ely of Buffalo, and William Sulzer of New York. The Sulzer movement seemed especially threatening, for the hard-hitting Congressman boasted the support of the Bryan Democratic League.[47] Unconvinced that any of these prospective nominees would wage a sufficiently ambitious campaign to unseat the popular Hughes, Murphy held off another day. Then, on September 15, he conducted a series of meetings with various state leaders and at the same time launched a movement for a fellow Tammany man, D-Cady Herrick. When this trial balloon collapsed, Murphy capitulated to the upstate demand for Chanler.[48] The Lieutenant-Governor's nomination was now assured.

The convention proceedings themselves reflected the conservatism of the forces in command. Whatever Hearst spirit had been present in Democratic ranks two years ago was now nowhere in evidence. Keynoter Morgan J. O'Brien, a confirmed standpatter, started things off on September 15 by denouncing the "radical" tendencies he detected in modern Republicanism and calling for reinstatement of "personal and economic liberty." [49] Next day Permanent Chairman Alton B. Parker, the

[46] New York *Times*, Sept. 15, 1908; Rochester *Herald*, Sept. 14 and 15, 1908.

[47] J. Lynn to William Sulzer, Sept. 7, 1908, William Sulzer Papers (Cornell University Library); Rochester *Herald*, Aug. 22, 1908; Rochester *Times*, Sept. 15, 1908; Baltimore *American Star*, Aug. 24, 1908, Sulzer Papers.

[48] New York *Times* and Rochester *Herald*, Sept. 16, 1908.

[49] Rochester *Herald*, Sept. 16, 1908.

party's 1904 presidential nominee, added his criticism of the progressive cause, insisting that its domination of the Democrats accounted for their setbacks in recent years. Despite various threats of factionalism, the convention atmosphere remained calm and placid even through the gubernatorial balloting. Harmony prevailed to the extent that only Chanler's name was put into nomination and he was unanimously chosen.[50] His running mates were selected in similar fashion and the platform was quickly adopted.

The work of the Rochester convention was thus completed with unexpected speed and cooperation. The real highlight of the festivities, however, did not come until the next day when the national Democratic standard-bearer, William Jennings Bryan, made a personal appearance before the assembled delegates. Suddenly, the convention awakened as "the silver-tongued orator" electrified his partisan audience with a ringing appeal for Democratic harmony and victory.[51] Now the main reason for Murphy's capitulation to Chanler became obvious. Conservative leaders and progressive spokesmen, upstaters and downstaters alike, felt constrained to bury their differences for the sake of party unity in this, a presidential year.

The candidacy of Lewis Stuyvesant Chanler, many anticipated, would provide the cohesive force necessary to forge the state Democracy into an efficient fighting unit. Chanler himself had not been long in the political arena, but his rich and varied background, together with his good record as lieutenant-governor, greatly impressed even the most cynical observer. Born in 1869 of well-to-do, long-established New York stock, he had spent his boyhood in the family estate, Rokeby, at Barrytown, Dutchess County.[52] His father, John Winthrop Chanler, had long been active in politics and served for three terms as a

[50] New York *Times* and Rochester *Herald*, Sept. 17, 1908.
[51] New York *Times*, Sept. 18, 1908.
[52] This sketch is taken from Edgar L. Murlin, *New York Red Book: An Illustrated Legislative Manual, 1907* (Albany: J. B. Lyon, 1907), pp. 39–40.

United States congressman from a New York City district. After receiving his elementary education from private tutors, young Lewis attended Columbia College and later Cambridge University, where he won honors for his forensic ability. He divided the next several years between England and America. Here he practiced law in New York City and there he became an active member of Ireland's Parnellist party. Chanler held no elective political office until 1903, when he won a term on the Dutchess County board of supervisors. Then, three years later, he received second place on the Hearst ticket. As a Democratic lieutenant-governor, Chanler found himself in sympathy with much of Hughes's reform program, and his rulings from the chair in the state senate often benefited the Governor's forces. Indeed his judiciousness and fairness earned him the respect of both parties in Albany.

Yet Chanler was vulnerable as a candidate, and Murphy's reluctance to support him at the convention does not seem unrealistic in the light of subsequent developments. For two years the Lieutenant-Governor had been uncritical of the Republican administration and its progressive policies, while his party had opposed almost every major reform proposal.[53] Now he was expected to run on a platform that reflected not his own views but those of his more conservative colleagues. As a former Independence League supporter, Chanler must have felt uncomfortable with planks calling for retrenchment of state expenditures, reinstatement of "personal and economic liberty," and condemning "Republican centralization" and "government by commission."[54] A mild progressive by temperament, the Lieutenant-Governor inherited the party reins during a period of conservative resurgence in New York.

The controversial Rochester platform gave Chanler trouble from the very beginning. Amidst attacks upon its nineteenth-

[53] Ray B. Smith, ed., *History of the State of New York: Political and Governmental* (Syracuse: Syracuse, 1922), IV, 158–159; New York *Sun,* Sept. 17, 1908.

[54] New York *Times,* Sept. 17, 1908. Osborne called the platform "execrable" (Osborne to George A. Ricker, Sept. 22, 1908, Osborne Papers).

century philosophy, he prepared his formal acceptance speech.[55] If he had been so moved, he might have ignored some of the more irresponsible commitments imposed upon him, or he might, as Hughes had often done (and would do again), formulate his own platform. Indeed, he was urged to follow the latter course, but, for reasons not known, ignored this sage advice.[56] Thus, his acceptance speech, delivered on October 1, contained the same glittering generalities as the convention document. It emphasized the need for recognition and preservation of home rule, a cut-back in state expenditures, the termination of commission government, and an end to the attack upon personal liberty. So negative and vacuous was the Chanler address that the zealous Hughes press plunged into the battle to identify the Lieutenant-Governor with the allegedly irresponsible elements controlling the Democratic party.[57]

Despite their candidate's inauspicious début, the Democrats were not discouraged over their chances for a New York victory in 1908. Certainly, defection from the party ranks, so significant a factor two years ago, would not hamper the cause in this election. They had, after all, named a "respectable" standardbearer, a fact that even most Republican journals appreciated.[58] Moreover, the Hughes administration, progressive as it had been, could not, on the one hand, claim the tangible gains that many independents would have liked or, on the other, make quite so effective an appeal to conservatives, who in 1906 had had a more clear-cut choice than they had now. Then, too, the charges of "bossism" that in the past had often been leveled at Democratic

[55] New York *World*, Sept. 17, 1908; Rochester *Democrat and Chronicle*, Sept. 19, 1908; Auburn *Citizen*, Sept. 21, 1908; Rochester *Post-Express*, Sept. 25, 1908, in "Editorial Opinion on Democrats and the Public Service Commission Law in 1908," Hughes Papers.

[56] Bourke Cockran to Lewis S. Chanler, n.d., Bourke Cockran Papers (NYPL); New York *World*, Sept. 23, 1908, Fuller Collection, Vol. LXIV.

[57] New York *Times*, Oct. 2, 1908; New York *World*, Oct. 1, 1908; New York *Tribune* and New York *Evening Post*, Oct. 2, 1908, Fuller Collection, Vol. XII.

[58] New York *Times*, Sept. 17, 1908; Rochester *Herald*, Sept. 18, 1908.

candidates carried little real weight this year in view of the circumstances surrounding the Republican convention. Finally, the longstanding feud within the GOP threatened to undermine seriously Governor Hughes's campaign.[59]

No one knew better than Hughes himself that New York would be a major battleground in 1908. In view of the forces operating against him, he appreciated the need to carry his message directly to his constituents—the people of the state—much as he had done two years earlier.[60] Circumstances now, however, were somewhat different. The national ticket desperately needed help in certain areas of the country, and Hughes would be expected to contribute his efforts to the common cause. Thus, when Secretary Taft and his campaign manager, Frank Hitchcock, appealed to him, he agreed to make several appearances in the midwest, where his name had always been extremely popular.[61]

Before embarking on this tour, candidate Hughes had time for only one major address in New York State—his acceptance speech, which he delivered in Brooklyn on September 26. Already disturbed by the nature of the Democratic attack, he seized upon this occasion to defend the independent regulatory commission experiment and his growing state budget. To the Republican platform he courageously added his personal pledge for the enactment of a mandatory direct primary bill, which he hoped would become the pillar of his second administration.[62]

Then came almost two weeks of traveling through nine states in behalf of the national ticket.[63] Hughes had been promised

---

[59] Theodore Roosevelt was fully conscious of this possibility (Roosevelt to Taft, Sept. 24, 1908, and to Frank H. Hitchcock, Sept. 26, 1908, *LTR*, VI, 1255–1256, 1258–1259).

[60] Hughes, "Additional Biographical Notes," pp. 1–3, Hughes Papers; Beerits, "First Term," p. 7.

[61] Beerits, "First Term," p. 7; New York *Sun*, Sept. 20, 1908.

[62] New York *Tribune*, Sept. 27, 1908.

[63] Actually, Hughes made two separate midwestern tours. The first swing, from September 28 to September 30, covered Indiana, Michigan, West Virginia, and Maryland. The second, running from October 5 to October 10, covered Minnesota, South Dakota, Kansas, and Illinois. It

that in making this swing he would not be expected to hold out-door meetings or speak more than twice each day. Once in the thick of the fight, however, he forgot his own conditions and sometimes addressed as many as a dozen meetings daily. His themes were not affirmative; he devoted most of his efforts to attacking William Jennings Bryan and the Democratic platform —pointing particularly to Bryan's inexperience and his impractical trust program.[64]

Yet the Governor's vigorous stump campaign had beneficial results, perhaps even beyond those anticipated. Republican leaders were elated at the impetus given to the Taft cause in the midwest.[65] Hughes's earnestness, moral fervor, and forthrightness greatly impressed news journals the country over and he held the national spotlight for several days. So successful had he been in selling himself that the question most often asked was whether or not he was being sacrificed for Taft's benefit. "It appears to be more than possible," lamented the Detroit *Journal*, "that the remarkable popularity of Governor Hughes in every State in the Union save New York will not serve to reelect him Governor of New York." [66]

But just as the Youngstown speech several weeks earlier had cut the ground from under orthodox GOP complaints against their independent chief executive, so now did the midwestern tour render unlikely any rebellion within organization ranks. Hughes himself had realized the potential value of such an undertaking when, on September 18, he had written to a friend that an excursion into national politics would show "the party workers . . . that I am not solicitous simply for my own

---

had been the Governor's intention to campaign back in New York between trips, but he took sick and did no work (New York *Times*, Oct. 3, 1908).

[64] Hughes, "Additional Biographical Notes," pp. 1–3; Beerits, "First Term," p. 8; New York *Times*, Sept. 29–Oct. 1 and Oct. 6, 7, 9, and 11, 1908.

[65] Theodore Roosevelt to Hughes, Oct. 14, 1908, *LTR*, VI, 1285–1286; Smith, *History of New York*, IV, 162.

[66] *Literary Digest*, XXXVII (1908), 581.

candidacy." [67] Certainly Theodore Roosevelt was impressed, for he quickly began to apply pressure upon the local leaders to support the state ticket. By mid-October the President could report to Taft that everything conceivable was being done "to bring about Hughes's election in New York." [68] In most quarters, it seems fair to say, these demands evoked positive assurances.[69]

Effective as the midwestern tour had been in enhancing the Governor's position, the state situation remained precarious. Local Democratic organizations exploited Hughes's absence to agitate potential and longstanding grievances against the administration, and of these there were many. From various upstate areas came reports that the midwestern anti-Bryan campaign had driven independent Democrats back into their party, that railroad men and patrons were angry with several Hughes vetoes and his strict regulatory policies, and that racing enthusiasts still resented the Agnew-Hart legislation. In western New York a Personal Liberty League was organized to forestall further abridgement of individual freedom. Already the liquor interests, fearful of regulatory laws, were certain of raising $500,000 for the Chanler fund. Even from metropolitan New York City there came danger signals. Wall street bankers were reportedly abandoning the Republican cause under threats of a state investigation of speculative practices. Finally, Hughes received ample warning that City insurance companies had been working diligently against him.[70]

Upon his return to home territory in mid-October, Governor Hughes determined to seize the initiative and to carry his state

[67] Hughes to William H. Samson, Sept. 18, 1908, Hughes Papers.
[68] Roosevelt to Taft, Oct. 10, 1908, *LTR*, VI, 1279–1281.
[69] Herbert Parsons to editor of New York *Press*, Oct. 3, 1908, Parsons Papers; New York *Herald*, Oct. 7, 1908, Fuller Collection, Vol. LXV.
[70] New York *Times*, Oct. 10, 11, 13, 15, and 16, 1908; Robert H. Fuller to William Loeb, Jr., Oct. 4, 1908, Roosevelt Papers; "Reminiscences of Martin Saxe" (Oral History Project, Columbia University Library, 1948–1949), pp. 23–24; Clarence E. Parker to Hughes, Oct. 10, 1908, and Haley Fiske to Hughes, Oct. 28, 1908, Hughes Papers.

campaign to the people. Doubtless he was surprised to discover that his opponent had failed to make the best of the time advantage he had enjoyed. Unwisely, Chanler had clung tenaciously to the Rochester platform and thus had achieved little success in his numerous public appearances.[71] The Governor immediately launched a vigorous upstate campaign in which, for over two weeks, he punched effectively at Chanler's vain efforts to disparage the administration's policies. In Owego, on October 12, Hughes met head-on his opponent's criticism of infringements upon personal liberty and pointedly asked Chanler if he would repeal the Agnew-Hart law.[72] When no answer came from the Democratic camp, the Governor repeated the question over and over.[73] Finally, on October 21, Chanler bowed to the demands of an increasingly hostile press and conceded that he would not undo the race-track reform.[74]

Likewise, Hughes worked over every one of the planks of the Rochester platform. He effectively defended the public service commissions law, and he convincingly justified increasing state expenditures. The master stroke of his campaign, however, came on October 20, when in Malone, New York, he crisply answered a series of questions that Chanler had posed the previous evening in Newburgh. It had been the Lieutenant-Governor's hope to reverse their respective roles and to put Hughes on the spot with embarrassing queries. But Chanler's choice of questions was poor. Some had nothing whatever to do with the campaign itself; others could be met easily and forthrightly by so unpretentious a campaigner as Hughes.[75] Chanler's strategy

[71] New York *World*, Oct. 5, 1908; New York *Times*, Oct. 12, 1908.

[72] New York *Times*, Oct. 13, 1908.

[73] On October 16, in Syracuse, Hughes again raised the question. Then in Wayne and Cayuga Counties on October 21 he hammered away on the Agnew-Hart legislation (New York *Times*, Oct. 17, 1908; New York *Tribune*, Oct. 22, 1908, Fuller Collection, Vol. LXVII).

[74] New York *Tribune*, Oct. 22, 1908, Fuller Collection, Vol. XIII; New York *Times*, Oct. 22, 1908. Needless to say, the Hughes press goaded him mercilessly (New York *Tribune*, Oct. 15, 1908; New York *Evening Mail*, Oct. 19 and 20, 1908, Fuller Collection, Vol. XII).

[75] New York *Times*, Oct. 15, 20, and 21, 1908; Buffalo *Morning Express*, Oct. 23, 1908; New York *Tribune*, Oct. 20 and 21, 1908, Fuller Collection,

thus boomeranged, and his position was rendered even more untenable.

While Governor Hughes scored a resounding triumph over his bewildered opponent in his lengthy upstate tour, another candidate, unintentionally but nonetheless materially, aided his cause. Shortly after Chanler's nomination in Rochester, publisher William Randolph Hearst had intimated his dissatisfaction over the state Democracy's trend toward conservatism.[76] There were even rumors that Hearst himself would accept another Independence League nomination if only to do battle with his former allies. But on September 24 the Hearst forces named a long-time associate Clarence J. Shearn to run against Chanler and Hughes on a platform embodying what the New York *World* claimed to be truly Democratic standards.[77] From the beginning Shearn's candidacy threatened the Chanler ticket, since the Independence Leaguer directed his assaults mainly at the Lieutenant-Governor. His vigorous campaign was supported by the vitriolic Hearst press, which mercilessly excoriated the Democratic party under its present leadership. The Chanler efforts, insisted the New York *American* at one point, represented Ryan, Belmont, Murphy, Conners, "and the rest of their black brood [who] want to continue to rob you as they have robbed you for years." [78] The Hughes candidacy, on the other hand, was treated somewhat indifferently.

By the time Governor Hughes concluded his two-week upstate swing, the New York situation had changed drastically. The Republican gloom of mid-October had been turned into hope and promise as betting odds shifted to favor their cause. "The tide is coming our way with a rush," declared Theodore

Vol. LXVII. This story is told in detail in Beerits, "First Term," pp. 11-11a. The questions are spelled out in "Some Questions and Answers in New York," *Outlook*, XC (1908), 458–460.

[76] New York *Times*, Sept. 24, 1908.

[77] New York *World*, Oct. 5, 1908, Fuller Collection, Vol. XII. For the nomination, see New York *Times*, Sept. 25, 1908.

[78] New York *American*, Oct. 17, 1908. Inflamed editorials appeared in the *American* also on Oct. 20 and 22, 1908.

Roosevelt gleefully to Taft.[79] To Hughes the President wrote even more optimistically that the state ticket would carry New York by over one hundred thousand votes. These encouraging thoughts were shared by a host of prominent Republicans who minced no words in expressing them.[80] On October 25 Hughes himself looked back upon the previous week, judging it to be the most successful of the entire campaign. He had found Chanler "weak," "evasive," and "shifting"—too interested in capitalizing "in his favor the various elements of opposition." [81]

Despite the GOP's renewed confidence, Hughes did not for one moment relax his efforts during the last several days of his campaign. On October 28 he and Taft appeared together in the traditional Madison Square Garden rally and before 14,000 partisans lauded each other's efforts.[82] Then the Governor made one final upstate trip, speaking in Fredonia, Corning, and Kingston. He returned to New York City in time for several engagements and concluded his whirlwind campaign on election eve. In all he had covered 8,000 miles and fifty counties in just three weeks of concentrated effort.

When New Yorkers went to the polls on November 2, 1908, they had to choose both a president and a governor. Their attraction to William Howard Taft, as it turned out, was greater than to Charles Evans Hughes, for they gave Taft a plurality of almost 203,000 to Hughes's 69,000. Although running slightly stronger in New York City than he had in 1906 against Hearst, the Governor fell behind his presidential counterpart by 40,000 votes. More significant perhaps is the fact that in the upstate areas Hughes lost or almost lost several counties that Taft easily

[79] Roosevelt to Taft, Oct. 24, 1908, *LTR*, VI, 1319; New York *Times*, Oct. 27 and 30, 1908.

[80] Roosevelt to Hughes, Oct. 26, 1908, Hughes Papers; James S. Sherman to Taft, Oct. 17, 1908, and to Harry A. Walters, Oct. 31, 1908, Sherman Papers; Jacob G. Schurman to Hughes, Oct. 23, 1908, Jacob Gould Schurman Papers (Cornell University Library); Lafayette B. Gleason to Hughes, Oct. 26, 1908, Hughes Papers.

[81] Hughes to Roosevelt, Oct. 25, 1908, Hughes Papers.

[82] New York *Times*, Oct. 29, 1908.

won.[83] In all, these figures tend to bear out the earlier GOP concern over traditionally Republican upstate areas. Buffalo had been the center of Personal Liberty League activities, and Erie County went to Chanler by a plurality of 4,000 votes. Saratoga, of course, was the state's racing capital and it too deserted the Governor. Finally, in several upstate counties in which the key Republican leaders thrived Taft's vote far surpassed Hughes's.[84]

Doubtless, organization indifference to Hughes had much to do with the disparity in presidential and gubernatorial balloting in New York. There was hardly a state or county leader who felt strongly about Hughes's re-election, and President Roosevelt's support, affirmative as it was, never reached the proportions it had two years earlier. Indeed, during the campaign rumors circulated that certain Republican local groups, reflecting this widespread apathy, were willing to abandon the Governor altogether. If such was the case, Hughes's triumph was truly a personal triumph, as some journals repeatedly insisted.[85] It had been achieved largely through his own appeals and his shrewd exploitation of Chanler's ineffective campaign tactics. Certainly the election results did not augur well for the reform cause, and Hughes would face an unruly party for the next two years.

[83] These figures and the following calculations are taken from Edgar L. Murlin, *New York Red Book: An Illustrated Legislative Manual, 1909* (Albany: J. B. Lyon, 1909), pp. 634–635. Hughes's total vote was 804,651 to Chanler's 735,189. Taft's vote was 870,070 to Bryan's 667,468. Hughes lost Erie, Hamilton, Saratoga, and Schoharie Counties, while Taft won every upstate county and carried New York City.

[84] This was true in Albany (Barnes), Erie (Greiner), Monroe (Aldridge), and Onondaga (Hendricks).

[85] Theodore Roosevelt to Timothy Woodruff, Oct. 27, 1908, Hughes Papers; *Nation*, LXXXVII (1908), 397; Springfield *Republican*, Oct. 10, 1908, Fuller Collection, Vol. LXV; *Literary Digest*, XXXVII (1908), 692–694.

CHAPTER XI

The Direct Primary Fight

First Phase

THAT Governor Hughes's re-election in the fall of 1908 constituted, to some extent, an endorsement of his reform program
and of his "new" politics there is little question. But at the same
time it scarcely spelled defeat for the administration's intractable
opponents. Unlike the situation two years earlier, the 1908 victory in New York was a Republican party triumph to the extent
that the entire state ticket was victorious.[1] Moreover, the legislature fell more securely under GOP control. Although Republican gains in the assembly were modest, there was little question
that its will, at least for the next year, would remain that of
Speaker James W. Wadsworth, Jr. The senate, too, emerged
slightly more Republican, and upstate domination once again
seemed assured. To be sure, some of Hughes's staunchest opponents in the 1908 racing bill fight had been rooted out, and
progressives like Frederick M. Davenport of Oneida, John B.
Rose of Orange, Josiah T. Newcomb of New York, and Jonathan M. Wainwright of Westchester gave promise of reinforc-
ing the few administration supporters in the senate.[2] Yet these

[1] The margin of victory for Hughes's fellow state officers was sub-
stantially greater than his. It ranged from 97,000 for Comptroller Charles
H. Gaus to 144,000 for Attorney-General Edward R. O'Malley (Edgar L.
Murlin, *New York Red Book: An Illustrated Legislative Manual, 1909*
[Albany: J. B. Lyon, 1909], pp. 41–44).

[2] Eight of ten Republican opponents of the 1908 racing legislation had
been beaten. Only James A. Emerson of Warren and William J. Grattan

gains were offset by the allegedly forced retirement of such out-spoken independents as Alfred Page and Martin Saxe.

For a short period following the elections, GOP leaders appeared to be pursuing a conciliatory course in their relations with Hughes, and there were indications that the old wounds might be healed. For one thing, the Governor had proved beyond a reasonable doubt that he was a loyal Republican. His experiences in the recent campaign, together with the events of the past two years, had presumably taught him the importance of organizational politics. Then, too, Hughes had cordially written to Timothy Woodruff immediately after the election requesting that there be concerted action by the New York GOP.[3] And, finally, when visiting Albany the state leaders were treated courteously and thoughtfully—as if their past performances had been both forgiven and forgotten.

Yet this honeymoon, if such it might be called, remained superficial in nature. On November 24 Hughes again took advantage of a Republican Club appearance to indicate his true position as a political leader. "I intend to do what I think will be for the best interests of the state and secure the best possible administration," he flatly told his audience.[4] Some two weeks later, in what was then labeled a harmony feast, Republican state leaders sat down to plan distribution of the patronage accruing from the offices they had only recently recaptured. The Governor, they decided, would not be consulted on any such matters, and, indeed, prospective officeholders were to be required to pledge their loyalty to the machine.[5]

It was this question of patronage and administrative appointments that, brought out into the open, revealed the depth of the ill-feeling legislative leaders bore toward Hughes in the early

---

of Albany were re-elected. The senate turnover, declared the optimistic New York *Evening Post* on January 2, 1909, would improve the tone of this body's deliberation.

[3] New York *Times*, Dec. 6, 1908.   [4] *Ibid.*, Nov. 25, 1908.

[5] *Ibid.*, Dec. 6, 1908. The story of this patronage agreement actually came out in *ibid.*, Jan. 24, 1909.

days of his second administration. By itself the issue held little significance since only a few officials were involved. But it did foreshadow the bitterness of the forthcoming battle in 1909—a struggle that, unlike that of the previous year, would result in no substantial gains for the reform administration.

The real beginning of the patronage difficulties occurred in late December, when Governor Hughes signed a state civil service commission proposal recommending that a total of 178 positions be removed from the job list of examination exemptions and 146 noncompetitive positions be transferred to the competitive class. Among the latter were fifty-two recently-created county highway superintendencies, which had been earmarked for the spoils grab bag.[6] Although Hughes had not intended this action to be a direct assault upon the machine, he was immediately accused of breaking the postelection harmony pact.[7]

The state Republican organization, speaking through the legislature's upper house, sought to avenge what it deemed a deliberate and unprovoked attack. On January 6 Governor Hughes submitted to the senate for confirmation the names of several prospective highway commissioners. Actually, all but one met the approval of the administration's severest critics. Under normal circumstances, Herbert E. Cook, too, would have received immediate confirmation. But John Raines and Jotham Allds, the core of the GOP old guard, eagerly embraced Thomas Grady's allegation that on a technicality Cook had disqualified himself.[8]

[6] *Ibid.*, Dec. 30, 1908. The New York *Sun*, on December 13, 1908, insisted that the new highway law had been supported by the Republican organization only because it promised to fatten the party patronage.

[7] Henry C. Beerits, "Second Term as Governor," p. 2, in "Memorandum," Charles Evans Hughes Papers (Manuscript Division, Library of Congress). Beerits insists that for this reason—i.e., the Governor's independence on patronage matters—the legislature was unwilling to effect his 1909 reform program.

[8] The technicality was that by law this particular commissionership was to be given to a Democrat. and although Cook had been a registered Democrat, he had voted for Hughes (so he admitted) in the previous election (New York *Times*, Jan. 28 and Feb. 4, 1909; New York *Evening Post*, Feb. 4, 1909).

One week later, a cabal of Raines Republicans and Grady Democrats rejected the appointment, and Hughes was defeated by a more substantial bipartisan alliance than that which had beset his first administration.[9]

The stubborn senate had yet another opportunity in early 1909 to embarrass Governor Hughes and thus give fair warning that his every move would be subjected to close scrutiny. Ironically, the issue at hand was the appointment of a successor to Superintendent of Insurance Otto Kelsey. Although Kelsey was not obligated to vacate his office until March 1, he resigned on January 13 to become deputy state comptroller under Charles H. Gaus, recently elected to the comptrollership. In filling the insurance vacancy, Hughes ignored the machine's recommendation and tried to seat Frederick A. Wallis, a prominent insurance company official. When the old guard alliance threatened to challenge this appointment, Wallis sought to withdraw his name in a statement deprecating the political abuse to which he was being subjected.[10] This attack, unfortunately, put Thomas Grady on the defensive, and he determined to vindicate his opposition to Wallis. In dragging out old insurance department records, the clever Tammany Democrat unearthed several complaints that Kelsey's examiners had earlier registered against Wallis as an executive of the Home Life Insurance Company. They were subsequently released, and though meanwhile William H. Hotchkiss of Buffalo had been appointed superinten-

[9] Although the *New York Senate Journal* contains no record of the vote, the New York *Times*, February 4, 1909, reported it as 31–17 against Cook with seventeen Republicans joining fourteen Democrats. It is interesting to note the solidarity of organization opposition to Hughes on this issue. Senators controlled by Woodruff, Hendricks, Barnes, Aldridge, and Wadsworth voted to the man against the administration. Three of Parsons' men and Greiner's two Erie senators recorded for Hughes. The great pressure imposed upon several Republicans by representatives of the respective county machines was witnessed by Frederick M. Davenport, an administration supporter, as recorded in Davenport to James S. Sherman, Feb. 4, 1909, James S. Sherman Papers (NYPL).

[10] M. Linn Bruce to Hughes, Jan. 12, 1909, Charles Evans Hughes Collection (New York State Library at Albany); New York *Times*, Jan. 14 and 29, 1909.

dent, the senate insurance committee now launched a full-scale investigation.

The Wallis issue reached a climax on February 9, when Wallis himself voluntarily appeared before the senate committee and cleared the air of charges that had been leveled against him. The give and take of this session pointed up the true nature of the struggle as Grady and Raines, both committee members, pressured Wallis, apparently hoping to force a confession that it was Hughes who had been the real author of the tactless withdrawal statement. So determined were they to embarrass the Governor that they could be seen fortifying each other with questions for Wallis.[11]

The extent of understanding between Democratic and Republican leaders in the senate—as exemplified in the insurance superintendency case—was indicative of the wide rift that had developed between Hughes and his own party by early 1909. The battles of 1907 and 1908 had left their scars upon the GOP and there was little room remaining for compromise. Indeed, when the Governor made clear the direction his reform program would now take, the area of agreement lessened substantially.

Since 1907 Governor Hughes had recommended that New York State adopt, together with other political reforms, a system of direct primaries. His dedication to progressive principles inevitably led him to this solution of certain problems with which, as gas and insurance counsel, he had become so familiar. The ugly politico-business alliance, so characteristic of the New York system in the Platt years, motivated Hughes, as it did others before and after him, to search for ways and means to implement the democratic ideals upon which the nation had been founded. One device was to utilize the resources of government to regulate businesses engaged in the public service. But government, after all, was a composite of people, and somehow the best-equipped individuals must be chosen to formulate and execute the laws. The convention system of nominating candidates for office, Hughes believed, was inadequate. Like so many of his progressive colleagues, he was convinced that a democrati-

[11] New York *Times*, Feb. 10, 1909.

zation of party structure would produce more responsible political leaders.[12] It was his goal, he once said, to make "our party system analogous to our general system of government."[13] Thus the democratic ideal of intelligent self-rule would be substantially realized.

Needless to say, orthodox politicians looked disdainfully upon any such efforts to reform the political system—especially if the basic features of the established order were to be altered. Those who were exceedingly distrustful of popular rule clung tenaciously to the position that the state government was already representative in character. "I don't believe it the function of a leader to ask what public sentiment is," declared William Barnes at one point, "but to direct it." The public servant or politician should not be compelled to bow to "fads," which to Barnes were merely the manifestations of the popular will; he should, instead, rise above them.[14] The more moderate conservative, on the other hand, often admitted the desirability of the direct primary, but for various reasons deemed it ineffective in practice. He would point to the manner in which it would be exploited by the demagogue and the "unscrupulous soldier of fortune."[15] He might suggest that majority rule itself would be endangered, for under normal conditions at least three candidates would face each other in a primary and the chances were slim that any one of them would receive a majority. Finally, he would insist that, whatever weaknesses existed in the political system, they were in no sense created by the absence of a direct primary.[16]

[12] Hughes, "Biographical Notes," pp. 199–200, Hughes Papers; Hughes, "The Fate of the Direct Primary," *National Municipal Review*, X (1921), 23–31; Hughes, *Conditions of Progress in Democratic Government* (New Haven: Yale, 1910), pp. 115–116.

[13] Hughes to Nicholas Murray Butler, Jan. 15, 1909, Hughes Papers.

[14] New York *Times*, Dec. 13, 1908; William Barnes to George B. Agnew, Jan. 29, 1909, George B. Agnew Papers (NYPL).

[15] "Direct Primary Nominations" (address by Jacob Gould Schurman before the One Hundred Club of Utica), Feb. 5, 1909, Jacob Gould Schurman Papers (Cornell University Library).

[16] James W. Wadsworth, Jr., "Autobiography," pp. 108–109, James W. Wadsworth, Jr., Papers (Hartford House, Geneseo, New York; now on deposit in the Library of Congress); Henry F. Holthusen, *James W.*

Since the early days of his administration, Governor Hughes had found the Republican high command particularly hostile to the political changes that he thought essential to responsible party government. The leaders could accept his other reforms and perhaps even work for them, but they could never champion a cause that, in their eyes, threatened the very existence of political organization and order. On this issue, then, their differences tended to dissolve, and they forged a united front against the administration. Primarily for these reasons, the 1907 legislature had simply ignored Hughes's political reforms—the Massachusetts ballot and the direct primary. The Governor himself was much too busy both in that year and in 1908 to devote the time and energy required to put across either of these measures. He did, however, consider them important enough to constitute issues on which to make his renomination bid. Indeed, during the summer of 1908, while the Republicans debated his political future, Hughes toured the upstate agricultural fairs stressing the need for direct primary legislation.[17] Once nominated, he asserted his right to supplement the Saratoga platform with a pledge on the essential political reforms, and he carried this commitment into the campaign of 1908.

Although in the past the Governor's party had found it relatively easy to shrug off his feeble efforts to alter the system of nominating candidates, Hughes's recent and manifold excursions into this area must have given its staunchest partisans reason for concern. Already in December—almost two weeks before the second inaugural—Republican moderates and conservatives were reported to have agreed upon a course of action designed to defeat the direct primary.[18] Whether Hughes's pending recommendations called for a mandatory or optional system made little difference, volunteered Assembly Speaker Wadsworth; the

---

Wadsworth, Jr.: A Biographical Sketch (New York: Putnam, 1926), pp. 55–61; New York *World*, Feb. 6, 1909.

[17] New York *Times*, Aug. 19 and 29 and Sept. 11, 1908.

[18] *Ibid.*, Dec. 20, 1908; New York *Press*, Dec. 23, 1908, Fuller Collection, Vol. XIX.

leaders were unalterably opposed to the proposal. Later in the same month State Chairman Timothy Woodruff met with several of his colleagues in Syracuse and confirmed Wadsworth's earlier assertion. The measure of support the entire Hughes program would receive, declared Woodruff and John Raines, depended upon the degree of its conformity to the planks of the Saratoga platform—a conservative document, to say the least.[19]

Whether or not Hughes actually took to heart these December warnings is problematical. His second inaugural address, delivered on January 1, 1909, was remarkably conciliatory, evoking the comment that whatever trouble might arise during the course of the coming legislative year would be perpetrated by the machine.[20] The speech itself contained only passing reference to the need for "uncorrupted expression of the popular will." [21] With its emphasis upon the obligations of state government and the balance of powers inherent in the organization of its branches, Hughes's inaugural address resembled more a treatise in political science than a broad statement of the administration's objectives and goals.

If the Governor's opening address lacked the passionate zeal of his first inaugural, the January 6 legislative message adequately compensated for it. Apparently Hughes hoped once again to use this document as a vehicle for rallying the progressive forces in New York around his program, for it contained a comprehensive treatment of the areas in which legislation was still needed—conservation, highway maintenance, public health, agriculture, labor, education, utility regulation, banking and insurance, state institutions, and the state judiciary.[22] But by far the most significant section of the message was devoted to the political reforms with which Hughes's name had long been associated.

The Governor effectively presented the essential argument for the direct primary by emphasizing the failure of the convention system to name candidates amicable to the wishes of rank-

[19] New York *Times*, Dec. 31, 1908. [20] *Ibid.*, Jan. 2, 1909.
[21] *Hughes Public Papers*, III, 6. [22] *Ibid.*, pp. 21–52.

and-file party members. The result was, he insisted, that political nominees regarded themselves as being accountable not to their constituents, "but to those individuals to whom they feel they owe their offices." More important, added Hughes, was the easy access to political power that representatives of special interests enjoyed under the traditional method of choosing candidates. Party organization as it was presently constituted, he concluded, "needs constantly to defend itself from these encroachments, and the people for their proper security must see that the defenses are built as strongly as possible." [23]

Hughes recognized that, given the complexities of party structure, no single change in the system could provide the panacea—even though he emphasized the role that the direct primary would play in improving the general situation. He thus recommended a host of minor changes—the institution of an official primary ballot, extension of the enrollment system, and the Massachusetts ballot. When he returned to the direct primary, he spelled out few details, insisting only that the new system be made mandatory (not permissive as he had heretofore suggested) and that it cover all elective offices except presidential electors.[24]

Legislative reaction to this forthright message was slow in coming and in no way reflected the extent of the opposition that Hughes's direct primary recommendation had engendered. The Republican leaders—especially Raines and Wadsworth— had fully anticipated the Governor's efforts and perhaps on the basis of past experience had thought it wise to await further developments before agitating against so potentially popular an issue. Moreover, no administration bill was as yet forthcoming; any premature organization work, therefore, might prove self-defeating.

The group of men whose responsibility it was to draft Hughes's primary measure comprised several officials of an association, the Brooklyn Young Republican Club, of which, ironically, Timothy Woodruff was titular leader. Since 1906 this

[23] *Ibid.*, p. 37.   [24] *Ibid.*, p. 39.

organization, stirred by the vagaries of the old Platt system, had been in the vanguard of the New York direct nominations movement and had sponsored several bills in the state legislature to this end.[25] They were joined by a host of New York County progressives, including the enlightened Herbert Parsons, who represented the City's thousands of independents. In each instance, Governor Hughes also gave his support to the cause, and it was appropriate that he now call upon this group to draft a plan behind which he would mobilize all the resources of the governorship.[26]

For several weeks, Darwin James, Mortimer Beyers, and William Wadhams thus worked in conjunction with sympathetic elements of the regular Kings County organization and Governor Hughes himself in putting together a direct nominations bill that would have some chance of passing the conservative state legislature. Realistically, they set aside the extreme form of the western primary, which had never been attractive to Hughes, and they concentrated upon drawing up a workable compromise. Although the Governor may have found it difficult at first to make the necessary concessions, in the end he approved a plan obviously designed to undermine the essence of the organization's position.[27]

In almost every way the so-called Hinman-Green bill was a compromise measure. Together with a modified primary plan, it provided for improved party enrollment procedures and an official primary ballot—reforms that moderates like James Wadsworth had thought sufficient. The key feature of the legislation, however, was the party committee, which, as a device for nominating candidates, recognized the traditional political organiza-

[25] New York *Times,* Dec. 20, 1908.

[26] New York *Tribune,* Jan. 11, 1909.

[27] George B. Agnew to Gherardi Davis, Jan. 30, 1909, Agnew Papers; "Reminiscences of Frederick M. Davenport" (Oral History Project, Columbia University Library, 1953), p. 47; New York *Press,* Feb. 8, 1909; New York *Tribune,* Feb. 11 and March 11, 12, and 17, 1909; New York *Herald,* March 11, 1909; Syracuse *Herald,* March 17, 1909, Fuller Collection, Vol. XXIII; New York *Times,* Feb. 12, 1909.

tion and at the same time acknowledged the primary principle. In practice, there would be several such bodies—the state committee, the congressional district committee, the judicial district committee, the county committee, and so forth—each one responsible for naming candidates for the offices under its jurisdiction.[28] Prospective party nominees would present themselves to the appropriate committee two months before primary day. In convention, the committee was to select its candidate, and at the primary he would challenge any other contender who, by petition, had had his name placed on the ballot. The committee members were to be chosen directly by the eligible voting public at the statewide September primaries. Thus, the elaborate and highly complicated convention system would be replaced by a simple, more direct committee arrangement.

Although the administration bill was not ready for presentation to the state legislature until March 14, its main features had been made public much earlier. Almost one month before, Governor Hughes, dining at the Brooklyn Young Republican Club, had made known the compromise position that he intended to assume on the controversial primary question.[29] Hughes must have been disturbed by the lack of enthusiasm among newspapers and civic organizations for his strongly worded legislative message and his subsequent public appeal. But if he had hoped to engender support with a watered-down version of the direct primary, his efforts resulted in abject failure. The press—downstate and upstate alike—reacted strongly against the compromise version.[30] The Governor's idea, claimed the usually friendly New York *Times*, "is neither fish, flesh, nor good red herring," but rather "a simplified boss system." [31] "The plan," added the New York *Tribune*, combined "most of the faults of

[28] Indeed, all the officers chosen within the state were covered except town, village, and ward officials.

[29] New York *Times*, Feb. 21, 1909; New York *Press*, Feb. 21, 1909, Fuller Collection, Vol. XXII.

[30] An entire volume (XXII) of the Fuller Collection is devoted to newspaper criticism.

[31] Feb. 22, 1909.

the present system with most of the faults of the direct system." [32]

Reformers attracted to the primary idea also expressed disappointment over the Governor's willingness to compromise even before the battle had begun.[33] William J. Schieffelin, chairman of the Citizens' Union, which had endorsed the January 6 message, struck hard at the "new" plan on several particulars.[34] Cynically, Assemblyman Beverly R. Robinson of New York County insisted that it "narrows down to the substitution of a state committee with a membership of thirty-seven for a convention of 1000 delegates." [35] Finally, Buffalo Senator Samuel J. Ramsperger rejected the Hughes measure on the ground that it "isn't direct nominations in the sense that my constituents meant it when they instructed me." [36] Champions of the reform, summed up the New York *Post*, might perhaps exchange positions with the opposing forces over the pending bill.[37]

Actually, the Republican organization had no intention of modifying its position toward the primary reform—even though the Hinman-Green version was a deliberate compromise. Moderates and conservatives alike continued to cooperate in carrying through their December pledge to repel any effort at overhauling established political procedures.[38] Whether or not Hughes realized it, his very bill provided them with the arguments they needed to implement their stand.

The chief architect of the Republican counterattack in early

[32] Feb. 9, 1909.

[33] George Agnew had fully anticipated this reaction (Agnew to Gherardi Davis, Jan. 30, 1909, Agnew Papers); New York *World*, April 20, 1909, Fuller Collection, Vol. XXVI.

[34] New York *Evening Post*, Feb. 22, 1909.

[35] New York *Times*, Feb. 24, 1909. Robinson's position is reiterated in "Reminiscences of Beverly R. Robinson" (Oral History Project, Columbia University Library, 1948), pp. 52–53.

[36] New York *Times*, March 20, 1909.   [37] Feb. 23, 1909.

[38] With the possible exception of Parsons and Greiner, who were not unfriendly to the Hughes legislation, the organization was intact. See New York *Times*, March 10, 19, and 21, 1909, for statements by Barnes, Woodruff, and Raines.

1909 was none other than James Wadsworth, Jr., who in the past had kept his tightly controlled state assembly firmly behind the major portion of Governor Hughes's reform program. On the primary issue, Wadsworth, of course, had parted ways with the administration. All along, it had been he who insisted that party machinery needed only minor alterations. Although most of his corrective recommendations were incorporated in the Hinman-Green bill, he could not bring himself to support the measure. In formulating his opposition, however, Wadsworth was careful not to fall into the same trap that had often caught the less discreet John Raines. He met Hughes on the Governor's own ground, arguing that the compromise plan would strengthen organization control over the nominating system, not weaken it. Opponents of the respective nominating committees, the speaker insisted, would have little chance against machine candidates because the expense of running what amounted to two primaries was prohibitive. Furthermore, the average voter was usually inclined toward endorsing the organization's nominee any way, and the efforts of others would be rendered futile. In the end, then, the convenience of centralized nominations would prevail and the Hughes compromise would merely result in "legalized bossism." [39]

Despite the strength of the organization's position—both in issue and in numbers—the forces of opposition were cautiously put into motion in early 1909. The administration proposals, to be sure, had not captured the imagination of many New Yorkers, yet there were enough intangible factors to impel the GOP machine to tone down the intensity of its criticism. For one thing, the Governor had launched his personal campaign on January 22 with a rousing speech before the Hughes Alliance in New York City and he planned a series of upstate addresses during March and April. How much support he might gather in another of his famous uphill battles was difficult to gauge. Also, the mood and attitude of Washington toward the state situation was

[39] Wadsworth, "Autobiography," pp. 109–110.

not yet clearly defined, and New York's GOP had become supersensitive of its relations with the White House.[40]

Under the Roosevelt administration, the state Republicans had been guided by a strong, energetic leader who often imposed unwelcome policies upon them. The question arose in early 1909 as to whether President Taft would follow much the same line or whether he would refrain from exercising any degree of authority over the New York organization. Of course Taft, an Ohioan, possessed far less interest in the vagaries of Empire State politics than had Roosevelt, but most national leaders paid some attention to GOP affairs in the nation's largest state. This problem of Washington-Albany relations in the new administration focused upon Elihu Root, who had long been Roosevelt's trusted advisor on New York matters and who, in January, had succeeded Thomas C. Platt as the state's junior United States senator.

For seven years, Root had served in the national administration, first as secretary of war, then as secretary of state. So capably had he performed his duties that President-elect Taft urged him to remain in Washington.[41] Though Root decided against further cabinet service, in the fall of 1908 he yielded to repeated appeals by a group of GOP reformers and moderates in New York to have his name presented to the 1909 legislature for the United States senatorship Platt was finally vacating.[42] As anticipated, the conservative wing of the state party balked at this decision for fear of continued federal dictation. Barnes, in particular, had viewed the Root movement as Washington-inspired and extracted from the Secretary of State reassurances that it was not. Influential John Raines then received from Root a pledge that in his new capacity he would be a "leader," not a

[40] New York *Evening Post*, Jan. 23, 1909, Fuller Collection, Vol. XX; New York *Times*, Feb. 14, 1909; *Literary Digest*, XXXVII (1909), 202.

[41] Philip C. Jessup, *Elihu Root* (New York: Dodd, Mead, 1938), II, 138.

[42] *Ibid.*, pp. 138, 141–142. Behind the movement were Frederick Davenport, James W. Wadsworth, Jr., J. Sloat Fassett, Seth Low, and Joseph Hodges Choate.

boss; indeed, he would serve as a referee between contending groups within the state.[43]

By the time the New York legislature acted upon the senatorial question, Hughes had delivered his annual message, and the direct primary issue had come to the fore. What Root's position would be on this reform concerned Republican stalwarts almost as much as Roosevelt's posture on state matters had during the previous seven years. Root, after all, remained close to Taft and certainly would have a substantial amount of federal patronage to dispense. Thus all eyes turned to the New York legislature on January 28, when the new senator delivered his acceptance address. But Root shrewdly—and perhaps wisely—avoided the primary issue, devoting his remarks to a general analysis of federal-state relations.[44]

The question of Washington's ultimate position on direct nominations plagued GOP legislators for the next month or so. President-elect Taft seemed to be veering toward the Governor, but not to the extent of an open endorsement.[45] Root, for a while, followed the course of expediency and made no specific statement regarding the explosive issue. When, however, the details of the compromise plan began to leak out and it became apparent that the state leaders intended to remain adamant, the Senator moved into action. At first, he chose Taft's technique of merely lauding Hughes's general contributions as a progressive, perhaps in an effort to lay the groundwork for a future commitment to the modified primary reform, now the main objective of the New York program.[46] Within two and one-half months he took a major step in tactfully advising John Raines at

[43] Root to Barnes, Nov. 21, 1908; Raines to Root, Jan. 4, 1909; Root to Raines, Jan. 6, 1909, Elihu Root Papers (Manuscript Division, Library of Congress).

[44] New York *Times*, Jan. 29 and 30, 1909; New York *World*, Jan. 30, 1909; Jessup, *Elihu Root*, II, 145–146.

[45] New York *Evening Post*, Feb. 8, 1909, Fuller Collection, Vol. XXI; Rochester *Post-Express*, March 9, 1909, in George W. Aldridge Papers (RML).

[46] This he did on February 25, 1909, in a New York speech (New York *Times*, Feb. 26 and 27, 1909; New York *Tribune*, Feb. 27, 1909).

least to study the primary as it functioned in those states where it had already been adopted.[47] Then, he added, the New York GOP might find it advisable to get behind appropriate legislation.

Meanwhile, the Hinman-Green bill had begun its fateful journey through the state legislature. Introduced on March 19, it quickly moved through the preliminary committee stages. So little delay was there that the senate and assembly leaders, in the absence of strong, positive direction from Washington and any profound public reaction to Hughes's weak personal campaign, seemed intent upon beating back the bill as soon as possible. The assembly and senate judiciary committees did make a pretense at giving the primary reform fair treatment with two joint public hearings early in April.[48] Although reformers were provided ample opportunity to clarify and extend the Hughes position, the cause was already lost. Amid reports that Wadsworth was assured of victory, the assembly judiciary committee, on April 7, quietly voted against endorsing the Hinman-Green bill. Next day the lower house overwhelmingly defeated the Hughes-sponsored legislation.[49] One week later the senate followed almost exactly the same course, as Republicans and Democrats joined forces to hand the state administration its worst legislative setback.[50]

Yet, however complete this victory appeared to be for the GOP state organization, legislative leaders remained cautious and, indeed, took to heart Elihu Root's sage advice. Both houses quickly passed the so-called Meade resolution establishing a joint

[47] Root to Raines, April 13, 1909, Root Papers.

[48] New York *Times*, March 14 and 26 and April 1 and 8, 1909; New York *Tribune*, April 7, 1909.

[49] New York *Times*, April 8, 1909; *New York Assembly Journal*, 132d session (Albany: J. B. Lyon, 1909), pp. 1526–1527. The vote was 112–28.

[50] The final vote was 33–14, with the progressives lining up solidly for the bill (*New York Senate Journal*, 132d session [Albany: J. B. Lyon, 1909], p. 968). On the previous evening, the senate judiciary committee had decided almost unanimously to issue an adverse report to the legislature (New York *Tribune*, April 15, 1909).

legislative committee, to be appointed by the lieutenant-governor and the assembly speaker, for the purpose of studying the various types of primaries in operation in other states. Administration opponents, charged one newspaper rather bitterly, were thus covering for themselves in case "the Governor makes the fight too hot for them." [51]

Although Hughes must have been disturbed by the obstinacy of his legislative opposition, he had few illusions with regard to the general situation. To be sure, he had campaigned in Buffalo and in Rochester for the Hinman-Green bill and had done an excellent job of justifying the committee plan for nominating candidates.[52] Yet on April 3 he had taken advantage of the Annual Legislative Correspondents' Association dinner in Albany virtually to concede temporary defeat. Insisting that he might be a "dreamer" but not a "quitter," he gave fair warning to his opponents that the battle would be renewed. It was obvious even then, insisted the New York *Times*, that the Governor was about to follow the strategy of giving the organization its way and awaiting popular reaction.[53]

Hughes had not even attempted to push through the rest of his 1909 program. Apparently, what energy he had that year was expended in behalf of this primary bill, the key measure of his second administration. There were no significant addresses on extending public service commission regulation or on any of the other proposals recommended in the January legislative message. Nor did the Governor confront the senate and assembly with his usual special and emergency messages. The aura of defeat shrouded his every move as the organization forces closed in on him.

Thus, the same resentment with which Republican leaders greeted the administration's primary plan characterized their approach to Hughes's public service commission extension bill, the

[51] Rochester *Union and Advertiser*, April 16, 1909.
[52] Buffalo *Morning Express*, March 28, 1909; Rochester *Herald* and Rochester *Post-Express*, April 9, 1909.
[53] April 4, 1909.

second most important item on the 1909 agenda. One year earlier the Governor had sought to implement this legislation, but he had failed miserably. Now he endorsed the so-called Francis bill, which extended jurisdiction of the two commissions over the telegraph and telephone companies. This reform, together with a measure designed to clarify PSC powers, evoked some of the most bitter exchanges between the small band of progressives and the standpatters in both the assembly and the senate.[54] Neither bill, as it turned out, received enough support to get through even the legislature's lower house, as the bipartisan alliance that had so long plagued senate reformers now overwhelmingly defeated them.[55] As in the fight against the primary legislation, however, organization leaders backed down at the last moment and set up a commission to study the entire question.[56]

Similarly, many of the secondary aspects of the Hughes program were scuttled by a now-defiant state legislature. When, on April 30, the senate and assembly adjourned for the year, only organization leaders and a small number of newspapers, particularly those critical of the administration, insisted that the Republican record had been good. The articulate Hughes press, on the other hand, was filled with resentment over the frightening effectiveness of the irresponsible alliance that was engulfing even the moderate elements of both parties.[57]

Governor Hughes, however, was unruffled over his decisive defeat at the hands of the men he had long distrusted. Now fully

[54] New York *Tribune*, April 9, 1909; New York *Times*, April 9 and May 1, 1909.

[55] Actually, the public service commission amendments never got out of the senate or the assembly judiciary committee. The bill extending jurisdiction to the telephone and telegraph companies also remained in the senate judiciary committee and was defeated in the assembly (*New York Assembly Journal*, 132d session, pp. 1528–1529).

[56] *New York Senate Journal*, 132d session, p. 1518; *New York Assembly Journal*, 132d session, pp. 1923–1924.

[57] The New York *Times* is an excellent example of a newspaper that grew more and more critical of the Hughes administration and, on May 1, 1909, played up the legislature's accomplishments. For the opposite opinion, see *Literary Digest*, XXXVIII (1909), 779–780.

aware that New York's citizenry had not been properly prepared for the primary plan, he mapped out his second campaign.[58] So apathetic had public opinion been that he immediately rejected the idea of calling a special session of the legislature, contending that the best course was to launch a statewide
summer campaign for the direct primary. "Discussion will . . .
clarify the issue and present it more sharply," he told a Brooklyn
Young Republican Club audience on April 15. In the end, he
was convinced, "the people will have their way." [59]

The primary campaign of 1909 was undertaken in somewhat
the same spirit that the race-track gambling crusade had been
waged one year earlier. In April a group of Hughes's advisors
and supporters gathered together at New York's City Club to
establish a statewide organization for the purpose of publicizing
the direct nominations bill. The plan devised by the leaders—
William Wadhams, Darwin James, and Merwin K. Hart—called
for setting up local primary groups in as many upstate assembly
districts as possible. These suborganizations would be provided
with propaganda material and effective speakers, whose main
function was to create enough enthusiasm among the electorate
to influence the fall assembly elections.[60]

Immediately, Wadhams realized the need for concentrating
the league's work in those districts where little sentiment had
been displayed for the Hinman-Green bill. He thus attempted to
select key individuals to serve on area advisory councils. Although he met with some success on this score, he encountered
the first real stumbling block of the direct primary campaign.
Even among reformers, Wadhams and his fellow officers discovered, there was little genuine dedication to the Hughes pri-

[58] Beerits, "Second Term," p. 12. Hughes had certainly been warned
that New Yorkers had not been prepared for the primary (New York
Times and New York *World*, April 9, 1909; New York *Sun*, April 12,
1909).

[59] New York *Tribune*, April 16, 1909; New York *Evening Post*, April
13, 1909.

[60] William H. Wadhams to Merwin K. Hart, May 8, 1909, Charles
Evans Hughes Collection (NYPL).

mary.[61] Association secretary Frederick Crone, mindful of this fact, complained bitterly to Robert Fuller in August that, despite some noteworthy activity in certain parts of the state, the organization consisted of Wadhams, Hart, and himself.[62]

The Direct Primary Association also suffered from a lack of financial resources in the summer of 1909. Wadhams tried desperately to gather together enough funds to make the fight effective, but even the enthusiastic Hughes Alliance could muster up only $300 to $400. Usually optimistic over the success of his work, Wadhams despondently admitted at one point that the organization's progress was handicapped because of a "financial depression." [63]

Yet despite these obstacles the administration-inspired primary league effectively carried out its task during the summer and fall of 1909. Speakers were rushed into vital areas and propaganda was issued from central headquarters in Albany to all parts of the state. Early in the campaign the leaders had grasped the idea of making their activities as bipartisan as possible, for where the GOP organization could not be penetrated the Democrats often felt constrained to nominate assembly candidates advocating the direct primary. Thus, in Erie County, Norman Mack was brought into consultation with Republican Assemblyman John Lord O'Brian.[64] Later the league openly rejected John Raines's home district candidate and supported the Democratic challenger. Finally, they concentrated their energies on defeating the man responsible for the shocking disaster that overcame the Hinman-Green bill in the lower house—Speaker James Wadsworth, Jr. Late in the summer Secretary Crone traveled to Livingston County, where he virtually made an alliance with the local Democrats. Wadsworth's opponents gathered around Democrat Albert C. Olp, who, aided by speakers and propa-

[61] Wadhams to John B. Rose, to Harvey D. Hinman, to Edgar W. Hamm, and to Frederick Davenport, May 12, 1909, and Frederick W. Crone to Robert Fuller, Sept. 10, 1909, Hughes Collection (NYPL).

[62] Crone to Fuller, Aug. 5, 1909, *ibid.*

[63] Wadhams to Fuller, Aug. 4, 1909, *ibid.*

[64] Fuller to Wadhams, May 13, 1909, *ibid.*

ganda from Albany, pushed hard for the primary legislation. As the assembly campaign rolled through October, favorable reports regarding this "red-hot" Livingston situation brightened up the earlier gloom that had pervaded association headquarters. The usually staid Wadsworth himself admitted that Olp was giving him the fight of his life.[65]

While the primary organization thus strove valiantly to "create" popular sentiment for the administration, Governor Hughes busied himself with other activities. Early in the summer he traveled to the Alaska-Yukon Exposition—a trip that consumed several weeks. Upon his return, he settled down for a vacation at the Saranac Inn, which he would use within a fortnight as a base of operations for another swing around the late summer county fairs. Although he undoubtedly remained in touch with the association's campaign through Robert Fuller, he pursued a separate course—a wise policy, indeed, in light of the kind of bipartisan appeal his followers were making.

Considering the fact that Hughes launched no significant personal crusade during the summer and fall of 1909, the primary league achieved excellent results. Forty-six of the one hundred twelve assemblymen who voted against the Hinman-Green bill were not returned to the 1910 legislature. Equally significant was the fact that key Republican recalcitrants either were beaten at the polls or had their victory margins substantially reduced. In Delaware, Genesee, Orleans, and Warren Counties, long held in the grip of the GOP machine, direct primary candidates were elected. At the same time, Speaker Wadsworth's plurality in Livingston was cut from 2,000 votes in 1908 to slightly under 300 votes in 1909.[66]

The first round of the campaign for the direct primary thus ended. Although, overall, 1909 had proved to be a most frustrating year for the Hughes administration, there was some reason

[65] New York *Herald*, Oct. 25 and 26, 1909, Fuller Collection, Vol. XXIX; Crone to Fuller, Oct. 21, 1909, Hughes Collection (NYPL).

[66] Buffalo *Commercial*, Nov. 4, 1909; Crone to Fuller, Nov. 4, 1909, Hughes Collection (NYPL); unidentified newspaper, Nov. 3, 1909, Fuller Collection, Vol. XXIX.

to hope that the groundwork had been laid for solid achievements in 1910. Success, however, would depend upon whether
the Republican organization could be moved from its conservative moorings and, to some extent, whether Hughes, the independent, could pursue a course of accommodation in relation to
his own party. Should this strategy fail, the national leaders
might again be faced with a tangled New York situation as the
crucial 1910 state and congressional elections approached.

CHAPTER XII

The Direct Primary and the Republican Party Battle of 1910

IT was perhaps inevitable that the year 1910 should witness a showdown between the progressive state administration and the leaders of New York's Republican party in spite of efforts and intentions to the contrary. The long-simmering feud, which had spread and intensified as time went on, erupted anew when Hughes insisted upon enacting direct nominations legislation. If the Governor determined to pursue this objective utilizing the same methods that had won him success in 1907 and 1908, he would certainly imperil the very party unity that was so necessary for victory in the fall elections.

During the previous spring Republican legislative leaders, wary at the spectre of federal intervention, averted a pitched battle with the administration by setting up the direct primaries commission to study the wisdom of initiating the experiment in New York State. The commission's recommendations, however, were foreshadowed by its composition: only one friend of Hughes's program was made a member, and the others ranged from hostile old guardsmen to lukewarm moderates.[1] During the summer and fall of 1909, while Wadhams' organization was busy campaigning for the Hinman-Green bill, the joint legisla-

[1] New York *Evening Post*, May 29, 1909. Four days later the only true friend of the direct primary, Senator Frederick M. Davenport, declined to serve.

tive commission held a series of public hearings. Upon their completion in December, it was rumored that, despite testimony overwhelmingly unfavorable to the primary idea, the GOP leaders were prepared to offer a compromise proposal to the legislature shortly after it reconvened in January.[2]

Ignoring this overture, Governor Hughes proceeded with his own plans. On January 5, 1910, he again used the occasion of his annual legislative message to emphasize the need for enactment of the Hinman-Green bill.[3] Although the address warned of potential dangers, it evoked remarkably little comment, for earlier that very day the powerful Republican machine had scored a significant victory over the administration and could now view with utter indifference the Governor's "futile" efforts. This triumph, indeed, set in motion a concatenation of events culminating in disaster both for Hughes's political reforms and the state party.

The issue that precipitated the GOP crisis was the election of a new senate majority leader, necessitated by the sudden death, several months earlier, of John Raines, long-time "czar" of the upper house and symbol of old-guard Republicanism. For this powerful position, State Chairman Timothy Woodruff had thrown his support to Chenango's Jotham P. Allds, one of Raines's henchmen. Although Hughes characteristically refrained from interfering in the internal organization of the senate, his progressive Republican followers pinned their hopes on Harvey Hinman, a Binghamton reformer, whose ability and fairness had won the praises of Herbert Parsons, Buffalo leader Fred Greiner, and even William Barnes. A Hinman victory proved unlikely, however, as legislators quickly lined up for Allds. Still, the Hughes contingent, showing little respect for their Republican colleagues, bolted the party caucus that on

---

[2] Timothy Woodruff himself, it was reported, would submit a plan whereby congressmen, state senators, assemblymen, and aldermen would be nominated by the direct method (New York *Times,* Dec. 22, 1909).

[3] *Hughes Public Papers,* IV, 31–35.

January 4 overwhelmingly endorsed Allds.[4] Final senate approval followed the next day.[5]

Normally the issue would thus have been resolved and the progressives would, as in the past, retreat into virtual oblivion only to emerge later in the year in support of the administration's legislative program. But this time, observers noted, something was awry as the irate insurgents launched an unmerciful attack against Woodruff and his followers after their senate defeat.[6] The truth was that on the same day as the Republican caucus this little band of rebels had held their own secret conference at which they were told a story of graft and corruption involving the new majority leader himself. The informer was Benn Conger, an old GOP stalwart, who refused to hue to the organization line. Exactly why Conger felt compelled to talk remains a mystery, but he disclosed in all its ugliness the operation of the insidious "Black Horse Cavalry" of the Platt days—an operation that supplemented the shocking revelations of the Armstrong insurance investigation some four years earlier.

The so-called Allds scandal, soon to dominate the front pages of most New York State newspapers, concerned the awarding of local bridge contracts to the American Bridge Company, a private corporation working under the aegis of United States Steel.[7] Its operations depended entirely upon the state legislature, which, at any time, could deny town boards authority to negotiate contracts. In 1901 there appeared in the senate and the

---

[4] New York *Tribune*, Jan. 4, 1910; New York *Times*, Jan. 4 and 5, 1910. The bolters were George B. Agnew, Edgar T. Brackett, Benn Conger, John N. Cordts, Frederick Davenport, Harvey Hinman, Josiah T. Newcomb, and John B. Rose.

[5] *New York Senate Journal*, 133d session (Albany: J. B. Lyon, 1910), pp. 7–8.

[6] New York *Evening Post*, Jan. 7, 1910.

[7] This story, as Conger first told it, is pieced together from several sources, especially Oswald Garrison Villard, *Fighting Years: The Memoirs of a Liberal Editor* (New York: Harcourt, Brace, 1939), pp. 201–202, and New York *Evening Post*, Jan. 18, 1910. See also "The Allds Investigation," *Outlook*, XCIV (1910), 371, and Burton J. Hendrick, "Governor Hughes and the Albany Gang," *McClure's*, XXV (1910), 495–512.

assembly a bill designed to achieve this end, and the company's favored position was obviously threatened. Republican state boss Thomas C. Platt, long an ally of the bridge interests, ordered that this "strike" legislation be scuttled in committee.[8] Seizing the opportunity to enhance their fortunes, two of Platt's lieutenants, Assemblyman Jotham Allds and Speaker S. Fred Nixon, momentarily balked. They approached Benn Conger, then a member of the lower house and brother of an officer of the American Bridge Company. Within a matter of days, Allds and Nixon, in Conger's presence, received $1,000 each; an additional $4,000 was given to a third party for distribution among several unnamed associates. The "strike" bill was promptly beaten down.

In relating this sensational tale to the progressives, the frustrated Conger failed to insist that the information be kept confidential. One of them, Josiah T. Newcomb, a New York County senator, wrestled with the question for a day and then determined to present the matter to a City civic organization for further exploration. On January 6, with this idea in mind, Newcomb went over to the *Evening Post* offices in New York City to consult with his friend Oswald Garrison Villard, the paper's crusading editor and an active member of several such organizations. Villard immediately rejected the Senator's offer, suggesting instead that the *Post* publish the story. Newcomb agreed and Villard assumed full responsibility for getting his plans endorsed by the interested parties.[9]

One of Villard's first steps was to visit the executive mansion in Albany, where, on January 7, he held a two-hour private conference with Governor Hughes over the Allds-Conger affair. Hughes had been furious over Allds's recent election as senate majority leader—another indication, he thought, of the sharp differences between his reform administration and the stubborn

---

[8] That this was a "strike" bill seems clear from the evidence adduced (Herbert Parsons to Josiah T. Newcomb, Feb. 14, 1910, Herbert Parsons Papers [Columbia University Library]).

[9] Villard, *Fighting Years*, p. 202.

GOP state and legislative leaders. The Governor, Villard later testified, welcomed the prospect of dramatizing to the public the kind of people who had thwarted him for three years and who threatened, in 1910, to obstruct the all-important primary bill.[10] He was prepared to employ the same technique—that of bludgeoning willful legislators into accepting his program through the muckraking press—that he had successfully used in winning passage of the public service commissions bill of 1907 and the anti-race-track gambling bill of 1908.

Even with Governor Hughes's unqualified approval and the subsequent endorsement of the progressives, Villard could not publish his story for ten days; only after pointed threats to the now reluctant Conger was he able to do so. The result was exactly as anticipated, for the charges against Allds rocked political circles and the newspaper world as well. Rendering an ugly situation even more gruesome was Conger's statement, on January 18, that the 1901 bribe described in the *Evening Post* was merely a "drop in the bucket" compared to the wholesale graft and corruption to be found permeating the entire New York legislature in and about the same time.[11] In virtual unison the pro-Hughes press quickly denounced the GOP organization, demanding an immediate and complete investigation of the whole matter.[12]

Republican leaders could not afford to ignore these sensational developments, and observers immediately speculated on the course of action the "graft-ridden" party would pursue. The answer came within a day as Jotham Allds, on January 19, rose from his senate seat to request "the fullest investigation, in order that the truth may be known throughout the entire State." [13]

[10] *Ibid.*, p. 203; Henry C. Beerits, "Second Term as Governor," p. 23, in "Memorandum," Charles Evans Hughes Papers (Manuscript Division, Library of Congress).

[11] New York *Times*, Jan. 20, 1910; Villard, *Fighting Years*, pp. 205–209.

[12] New York *World*, New York *Times*, and New York *Press*, Jan. 19, 1910.

[13] *New York Senate Journal*, 133d session, p. 33. Allds himself was not unprepared for the Conger charges. On January 15 he had been informed of Villard's intentions (Villard, *Fighting Years*, pp. 206–207).

Immediately, maverick Republican Senator Edgar T. Brackett accommodated his colleague by presenting and winning adoption of a resolution establishing a committee to determine the procedure and methods by which the upper house might hear the case. It was now just a matter of time before the web of graft and corruption would be fully exposed to public view.

For almost six weeks, beginning on February 8, the state senate set aside all legislative matters, including the primary bill, and heard testimony dealing with the Allds scandal. In reiterating his side of the story, Benn Conger, while under the pressure of cross-examination, implicated a host of prominent political and business officials, some of whom had already been exposed in the earlier Armstrong investigation. His detailed discussion of the bridge contract case often led him into the larger question of the relationship between the Republican organization under Platt and those special interests vying for favors and privileges in the state legislature.[14] The Conger testimony was followed by a lengthy, albeit futile, defense of Allds. Hard as Allds's counsel tried, he could not exonerate the new majority leader, and his efforts to shift the responsibility to Boss Platt only further indicted the tottering Republican organization as a venal group of men wholly dependent upon the "interests" for their sustenance.

While the ramifications of the sensational Allds scandal were mounting daily and the names of prominent GOP leaders were again besmirched, newspapers throughout the state agitated for an expanded investigation—one that would probe the entire question of legislative graft and corruption.[15] Simultaneously, perceptive observers noted the fine opportunity Governor

[14] On February 17 the late Speaker S. Fred Nixon was implicated in the bribe charges. Five days later Conger testified that Colonel George W. Dunn, then state chairman of the Republican party, had twice received contributions from bridge companies to prevent the passage of "strike" legislation ("Proceedings of the Senate in the Matter of the Investigation Demanded by Senator Jotham P. Allds," *Senate Document No. 28*, 133d session [Albany: J. B. Lyon, 1910], pp. 640–641, 705–706).

[15] Oswego *Palladium*, Feb. 9, 1910, New York *Press*, Rochester *Herald*, and Rochester *Evening Times*, Feb. 10, 1910, Fuller Collection, Vol. II; Buffalo *Commercial*, Feb. 10, 1910; Buffalo *Evening Times*, Feb. 8, 1910.

Hughes at last possessed to reform the entire New York Republican organization. "The active leadership of the party must be placed in the hands of men who have stood with Governor Hughes," insisted the Binghamton *Press.*[16] "Those . . . who enjoy the people's confidence," added the New York *Tribune,* "should assume the leadership." [17]

Accompanying these demands were repeated appeals that Hughes seek a third term in the fall and thus personally initiate the all-important reorganization program. Actually the Governor had already rejected the possibility of again seeking re-election—a decision that his loyal supporters profoundly regretted but from which he refused to retreat, given his abiding distaste for politics and politicians.[18] Leading the renewed agitation was the new chairman of the New York County Republican committee, Lloyd C. Griscom, who during the coming months was to assume a major role in the attempt to overhaul the beleaguered GOP.

Griscom's election to the New York County chairmanship, a key post for the progressives, came shortly after Herbert Parsons' resignation on January 20, tendered partly for personal reasons and partly because, with William Howard Taft's 1908 presidential victory, he deemed his work completed.[19] The vigorous new chairman, who had served the Roosevelt administration in a diplomatic capacity, immediately threw his support behind Governor Hughes, insisting that his achievements be used as a basis on which to build a united, progressive Republican party in the Empire State. These sentiments he reiterated to Hughes himself in a private conference on February 9. Though gratified by Griscom's encouraging words, Hughes flatly re-

---

[16] Feb. 16, 1910, Fuller Collection, Vol. II.

[17] Feb. 14, 1910, *ibid.* The New York *Times* carried a similar editorial on February 15, 1910. See also *Literary Digest,* XL (1910), 379–381.

[18] New York *Times,* Jan. 19, 1910; *Literary Digest,* XL (1910), 176.

[19] "Reminiscences of Lloyd C. Griscom" (Oral History Project, Columbia University Library, 1951), pp. 63–67; New York *Evening Post* and New York *Times,* Jan. 21, 1910; Rochester *Union and Advertiser,* Jan. 22, 1910.

jected the request to seek renomination. The Governor had made up his mind; it was now the responsibility of the GOP organization to rid itself of the driftwood.[20]

Griscom's interest in forging a responsible, united party was strong enough to withstand these initial rebuffs at the hands of the disgruntled Hughes, who, by early 1910, seemed concerned only with the enactment of the Hinman-Green direct nominations bill. He therefore seized the opportunity of the annual Lincoln Day dinner in New York City to bring together in conference GOP leaders holding positions of state and national responsibility. Included among them were President Taft, scheduled to be the dinner's main speaker, Governor Hughes, also a participant, State Assembly Speaker James W. Wadsworth, Jr., Chairman Woodruff, and United States Senator Chauncey M. Depew.

President Taft's interest in the New York situation was beginning to deepen in early 1910. In the previous year he had shown little concern over Hughes's protracted battle with the legislature, but the recent dramatic turn of events apparently alerted him to the extent of GOP troubles—and their portent for the fall elections. For two hours on the afternoon of February 12 he discussed the overall situation with the New Yorkers. At the outset Taft recommended that the warring elements rally behind a strong man who might give direction to the desultory GOP. Neither Wadsworth nor Hughes, however, could offer any concrete suggestions, and the matter was quickly dropped. The remainder of the session was dominated by Taft and Hughes, who agreed that the legislative investigation of Republican graft and corruption had to be carried out to the bitter end—even to the point of providing a basis for weeding out those guilty of apostasy in the discredited organization.[21]

[20] New York *Times*, Feb. 1, 1910; "Minutes of Meeting between Hughes and Griscom," Feb. 9, 1910, recorded by Robert H. Fuller, Charles Evans Hughes Collection (NYPL).
[21] "Lincoln Day Conference Report"; New York *Times*, Feb. 13, 1910.

Extension of the Allds investigation, important as it was, could not by itself restore public confidence in the New York Republican party. Fully aware of this fact, Lloyd Griscom sponsored two additional conferences, one later the same day as the general meeting, the other on the next day. Taken together, these significant sessions provided an overall program that hopefully would restore the GOP to "fighting trim" for the fall elections.

Interestingly enough, Governor Hughes personally assumed full responsibility for formulating each and every plank of the 1910 Republican reform platform, even though he had already made it quite clear that he would not take the lead in reorganizing the party. In the first meeting, Taft and Griscom agreed to Hughes's dictum that Chauncey M. Depew and Timothy Woodruff, both representatives of the old Platt machine, be promptly retired from their respective offices.[22] In the second conference, Griscom and several members of the New York County Republican committee endorsed two of the Governor's proposals—election of a progressive, preferably Hinman, as senate majority leader, a position Allds would soon have to vacate; and enactment of a direct nominations bill following closely the main features of the administration-sponsored measure.[23]

The initial test of the Hughes-Griscom alliance, now in full view of New York's electorate, came within one month after the question of Allds's successor arose in the legislature's upper house.[24] At first the contest appeared to center around Hinman, the progressive candidate, and George A. Davis, Erie standpatter who had long been chairman of the powerful senate finance committee. But the state organization, sparked by Woodruff,

[22] "Lincoln Day Conference Report." The requirement that Woodruff be retired was confirmed in a letter from Griscom to Taft, Feb. 13, 1910, William Howard Taft Papers (Manuscript Division, Library of Congress).

[23] "Account of Meeting of February 13, 1910," recorded by Robert H. Fuller, Hughes Collection (NYPL).

[24] Allds had resigned formally on February 23 (*New York Senate Journal*, 133d session, p. 204).

Barnes, Hendricks, and Aldridge, refused to back Davis, whom they did not fully trust, and threw their support to George H. Cobb, a Watertown moderate.[25] For well over one week, this powerful Republican contingent actively campaigned in the senate corridors for Cobb's election. The Hughes forces, meanwhile, continued their work for Hinman, but with no outside help the chances for success waned as each day slipped by. Confident of victory, the conservatives, on March 8, forced a party caucus to decide the question. Before the session had hardly begun, progressive Frederick Davenport surprised his colleagues with a request for a two-day adjournment so that all Republicans might seriously consider a telegram he had just received from Washington. Signed by Senator Elihu Root, this sensational message appealed for the election of Harvey Hinman, a decision, it insisted, that would "correctly exhibit the real relations of the party . . . to the principles and policies for which Governor Hughes stands, and will rightly represent the wishes of the voters." [26] Amid cries of federal interference and "bossism," long the complaint of Republican old guardsmen toward Washington's efforts to reform the state party, the Davenport resolution carried and the final vote was postponed.

Two days later the senate Republicans gathered again to choose their leader. In the meantime, Governor Hughes had followed up Root's bombshell with a statement of his own taking an even stronger stand against those who had opposed his program for three years.[27] So unprecedented was Hughes's move that wavering senators were given sufficient reason to pause as

[25] The chief reason seemed to be that Davis was a member of Fred Greiner's Erie County organization, which already had several key positions in the state administration. This itself might not have been significant, but the fact remains that since 1909 Greiner had gravitated more and more toward Governor Hughes and the reform program (New York *Times*, March 1, 1910; New York *Tribune*, March 2, 1910, Fuller Collection, Vol. IV).

[26] New York *Times*, March 9, 1910.

[27] In actuality, Hughes issued two statements: the first, on March 8, simply backing Root; the second, on March 10, making his strong assertion (New York *Times*, March 9 and 11, 1910).

they were pressured in caucus to hand the administration another defeat. Thus for fourteen hours (and forty-five ballots) the party quibbled over the majority-leadership question. Finally, early on the morning of March 11, several Davis supporters broke rank and cast their lot with the organization, giving the coveted position to George Cobb.[28] Federal influence and belated gubernatorial action had almost turned defeat into victory—but machine pressure, exerted upon individual senators at precisely the right time, spelled another disaster for the Hughes forces. The first item in the reorganization program was lost.

Reaction to the results of the crucial leadership fight, coming amidst the shocking Allds revelations, was widespread indeed. Summarizing newspaper opinion, the *Literary Digest* saw the Cobb election as creating a crisis in New York Republican politics, for the Hughes-Taft combination had been unable to thwart the solidly entrenched state organization.[29] Political leaders themselves lamented the widening gap within GOP ranks and, for the most part, held the reckless machine responsible. "We shall have to lay violent hands on them," complained William Loeb to Taft in reference to the New York "bosses." [30] Even conservative Vice-President James S. Sherman, an upstate New Yorker, scored the Woodruff "program" as disastrous for the Republican party as a whole.[31]

The administration's defeat on the senate majority-leadership question underscored Hughes's earlier insistence that the forced retirement of Timothy Woodruff as state chairman was essential to GOP reorganization. Since 1908 Woodruff had gravitated more and more to the party's old guard, and his support of Allds in January rendered him expendable. Taft himself had long held certain reservations regarding the state chairman and in the Lincoln Day conference offered to have Elihu Root put the issue squarely to Woodruff. As expected, Root hesitated at first but

[28] *Ibid.*, March 12, 1910.   [29] *Literary Digest*, XL (1910), 577–579.
[30] Loeb to Taft, March 11, 1910, James S. Sherman Papers (NYPL).
[31] New York *Times*, March 12, 1910.

then agreed to undertake the task assigned to him.[32] Only two days after the disastrous March 10 caucus, the Senator traveled to New York City, where, following an afternoon conference with Lloyd Griscom, he met with Woodruff. Unfortunately for Root, Woodruff had anticipated the mission and had fully prepared himself. Indeed, he had spent the previous evening with Albany boss William Barnes receiving advice and moral support. When Root appeared at the designated meeting place, the confident state chairman immediately gained the initiative and maintained it through the conference. He reminded Root of two facts—first, that the organization had just scored a smashing victory over the Hughes-Griscom-Taft combination, and, second, that his own position was beyond the reach of Washington, for only three members of the state committee held federal positions. He then openly defied the Senator to challenge his power—a challenge that Root could not meet.[33] "I think things are in good shape," gloated Woodruff to George Aldridge immediately after the conference, "but we must be eternally on guard, for the Washington crowd will not give up as long as there is a ray of hope." [34]

As far as the Hughes administration was concerned, the Root fiasco of March 12 served only to add insult to injury. With two features of the reorganization program already defeated, attention focused on the question of expanding the Allds inquiry to include all traces of legislative graft. This thorny problem plagued the party almost from the moment Hughes, Taft, and Griscom had decided that a full-scale investigation was in order.

[32] Archie Butt, *Taft and Roosevelt: The Intimate Letters of Archie Butt* (2 vols.; Garden City: Doubleday, Doran, 1930), I, 282–284. Root's hesitancy on the general matter of interfering in the New York situation is seen in a telegram to Timothy Woodruff, March 10, 1910, Elihu Root Papers (Manuscript Division, Library of Congress).

[33] New York *Times*, March 14 and 15, 1910; Philip C. Jessup, *Elihu Root* (New York: Dodd, Mead, 1938), II, 152–153.

[34] Woodruff to Aldridge, March 14, 1910, George W. Aldridge Papers (RML). Not all of the "Washington crowd" were in favor of deposing Woodruff, a noteworthy exception being Vice-President Sherman (Sherman to Charles H. Betts, n.d., Sherman Papers).

Shortly after their February 12 conference, Speaker Wadsworth had thrown down the gauntlet with the indignant announcement that legislators would determine "if evidence is produced to necessitate a . . . general investigation." [35] By the middle of the month, organization stalwarts had gone one step further in insisting that only Conger's charges against Allds be probed.[36] Whatever dim hope the progressives still had of gaining a quick victory on this question was dashed on February 21, when Wadsworth's assembly overwhelmingly turned down a resolution designed to expand the senate inquiry.[37]

As events moved through March, Governor Hughes and his followers had good reason to suppose that their every effort was being brusquely turned aside by a group of angry men who were making a last-ditch stand to preserve their own favored positions. Nothing had gone well for the progressives and there seemed little prospect that anything would in the near future. So confident was the machine that Hughes even feared the possibility of an Allds whitewash.[38] Fuel was added to the fire when, in mid-March, Elihu Root made a personal appeal to Woodruff to support the Governor's legislative program and an expanded senate investigation, but his effort was totally ignored.[39] Undoubtedly, this third aspect of the reorganization program would have been rejected like the others had not another series of graft revelations further rocked the tottering GOP.

[35] New York *Tribune*, Feb. 13, 1910.

[36] New York *World*, Feb. 15, 1910; Syracuse *Daily Post-Standard*, Feb. 17, 1910, and Albany *Evening Journal*, Feb. 17, 1910, in Fuller Collection, Vols. II, III; New York *Times* and New York *Herald*, Feb. 22, 1910; New York *Sun*, Feb. 28, 1910. There seems to be little question that most of the leaders feared the effect a full inquiry might have upon party chances in the future, for the record, as it was later revealed, was as bad as the progressives contended. Wadsworth himself seemed to be greatly disturbed by the fact that his own earlier work in reorganizing the assembly was put in question by the administration's demand for a full inquiry.

[37] The resolution was defeated 75–33 (*New York Assembly Journal*, 133d session [Albany: J. B. Lyon, 1910], p. 381).

[38] New York *Times*, March 6, 1910.

[39] Woodruff to Root, March 19, 1910, Root Papers.

Since December of 1909, Superintendent of Insurance William H. Hotchkiss had been conscientiously investigating a number of fire insurance companies whose books had gone unexamined for twenty years. Almost from the beginning, he uncovered legislative graft implicating minor Republican politicians. Then, in January, he heard testimony accusing Lieutenant-Governor Horace White of having received $150,000 for his part in transacting a transfer of the People's Mutual Life Association and League of Syracuse from one group of owners to another.[40] By March 18 Hotchkiss had listened to so many such stories that he announced his inquiry would be extended to consider the question of legislative corruption as it related to fire insurance.[41] For almost three weeks thereafter, he probed the larger issue and in early April submitted a report of his findings to Governor Hughes. Spanning the years 1901 to 1906, Hotchkiss' revelations, accorded ample newspaper coverage, mirrored those unearthed by the Armstrong committee. The fire insurance companies, the report showed, disbursed a total of $150,000 in total vote-buying for the designated period. It recommended that, in spite of the work already done, further inquiry was necessary— and for this the Governor's support should be enlisted.[42]

In keeping with his established policy, Hughes had himself remained publicly silent on the matter of an expanded legislative investigation. Before the Hotchkiss report reached him, his worst fear had already been alleviated inasmuch as the state senate had overwhelmingly voted for verification of the Conger charges against Allds.[43] Still, he had not lost interest in laying

[40] Charles Edward Russell, "Legislative Graft and the Albany Scandal," *Cosmopolitan*, XLIX (1910), 146–160; New York *Times*, Jan. 11, 1910.

[41] New York *Times*, March 19, 1910.

[42] Hotchkiss' report is given in "Message from the Governor Transmitting Report of Superintendent of Insurance and Recommending Investigation into Legislative Practices and Procedures, etc.," *Senate Document No. 41*, 133d session (Albany: J. B. Lyon, 1910), pp. 4–9.

[43] The vote was 39–8. See *New York Senate Journal*, 133d session, p. 443. Earlier the same day Allds resigned his senate seat and on April 4 Conger announced his retirement. Hughes's private commitment to an expanded investigation remained constant in this entire period, as rep-

bare all traces of wrongdoing, and the fire insurance revelations only confirmed his intentions. Thus, on April 8, he dispatched a special message to the legislature requesting an unlimited investigation "to embrace the matters adduced in the recent proceeding by the Senate and those presented by the report . . . of the Superintendent of Insurance." [44]

Five days after the Governor's appeal, the new senate majority leader, George Cobb, surprisingly announced his support of insurgent efforts to put through an appropriate resolution. So significant a role did Cobb himself play in drafting the administration-sponsored measure that it bore his name. Quickly, it passed the usually stubborn senate and was dispatched to the assembly for approval. Here the resolution underwent radical change as Speaker Wadsworth, an articulate opponent of the full-scale investigation idea, clung stubbornly to his position. By the time it was returned to the senate and was again readied for debate, the progressive forces had lost their patience. Led by Harvey Hinman, they lashed out unmercifully at the organization for watering down the original Cobb resolution. Yet in the end they felt constrained to join their colleagues, and the "compromise" measure was passed. [45]

Whatever spirit of give and take developed within Republican ranks on the graft resolution failed to carry over into the thorny direct nominations question. Although Governor Hughes had devoted his January 5 message to several reforms, it was immediately apparent that only the direct primary recommendation, specifically the Hinman-Green bill, held any real significance. In the February 12 conference with Griscom and Taft, Hughes had insisted that enactment of this measure was absolutely essential for party success at the polls. In fact, it was more important than in the past, he argued, because the Democrats, almost miraculously, had closed ranks and had come up with a measure

---

resented in Hughes to Oswald Garrison Villard, April 2, 1910, Oswald Garrison Villard Papers (Harvard University Library).

[44] *Hughes Public Papers*, IV, 83.

[45] *New York Senate Journal*, 133d session, pp. 713, 1704; New York *Times*, April 14 and 15, 1910.

of their own.[46] At the very time that Republican legislative graft was being exposed, the Grady-Frisbie bill lay in the senate and assembly judiciary committees awaiting further action.

It was not until February 21 that the special legislative commission issued its final report on the direct primary matter. As anticipated, the document, reflecting largely the Republican machine's position, condemned the Hughes plan. Insisting that the situation in New York paralleled that in no other state where the direct primary was held, it concluded that only on the town, village, and ward levels could the experiment be legitimately attempted. For all other offices, the convention system should be retained. Finally, the controversial report recommended the enactment of a number of minor reforms in keeping with proposals made by Speaker Wadsworth in 1909—a uniform primary day, an official primary ballot, termination of existing party management of primaries, and statewide enrollment of all voters.[47]

In a very real sense, the direct nominations report was a Republican challenge to the state administration, which had, to some extent, staked its political reputation on the passage of suitable legislation. If any doubt remained concerning the organization's position, it was dispelled one week later when Timothy Woodruff, speaking before the New York City Republican Club, declared unequivocally against the Hinman-Green bill.[48] Yet Governor Hughes's response at this time, and, for that matter, throughout the spring of 1910, was weak and uninspiring—in marked contrast to his vigorous and successful campaigns for other aspects of his progressive program in 1907 and 1908. Only occasionally in 1910 did he take to the hustings and even then was accorded less attention than in the past. Perhaps the reason lay in the simple fact that Hughes had given up on his party, and, as he had confessed to Griscom in February, he had done

[46] "Lincoln Day Conference Report"; "Governor Hughes's Message," *Nation*, XC (1910), 28–29.

[47] "Report of the Joint Committee of the Senate and Assembly of the State of New York Appointed to Investigate Primary and Election Laws of this and other States," Feb. 21, 1910, *Senate Document No. 26*, 133d session (Albany: J. B. Lyon, 1910), pp. 211–219.

[48] New York *Times*, March 6, 1910.

his part; it was now the machine's responsibility to rectify the accumulated wrongs of the past. To be sure, he had outlined a reorganization plan, and from time to time he had asserted himself as a Republican leader. But all his efforts were apparently expended reluctantly, and his interest in GOP affairs declined substantially as one defeat followed another.

The truth of the matter was that in the spring of 1910 Governor Hughes was almost desperate about retiring from active political life. At one point he reputedly told President Taft: "I do not dare to run the chance of breaking down mentally. I must get out." [49] Already he had made it absolutely clear that under no circumstances would he consider a renomination, and, unlike 1908, he would not change his mind. His intention was to return to the private practice of law, where he might recoup the financial losses he had suffered since his reluctant entry into public life four years earlier.

There was, however, another opportunity that opened up for Charles Evans Hughes in early 1910. On January 20 Hughes and Taft had met in Washington for a dinner conference on the explosive New York situation. When the conversation drifted to Hughes's future, the President mentioned the possibility of an appointment to the supreme court—and the Governor responded enthusiastically.[50] But the matter was dropped for the time being, and was not broached again until an actual vacancy occurred later in the spring. Meanwhile, Taft had become fully aware of Hughes's desire to abandon political life. Moreover, he owed the Governor a favor for his stellar efforts in Taft's behalf during the 1908 presidential campaign. So on April 22 he offered Hughes the supreme court seat only recently left vacant by the death of Justice David Brewer. In a lengthy reply, Hughes gladly accepted; his days as New York's chief executive were numbered.[51]

[49] Butt, *Taft and Roosevelt*, I, 309.

[50] "Account of Conference between Taft and Hughes," Jan. 20, 1910, recorded by Robert H. Fuller, Hughes Collection (NYPL).

[51] Taft to Hughes, April 22, 1910, and Hughes to Taft, April 24, 1910, Hughes Papers.

In reality, Governor Hughes was under no obligation at this time to make public his decision to leave Albany, for he would not take his seat on the court until early October. Yet he chose to do so, and the sensational story received full newspaper coverage across the entire nation. With but few exceptions, responsible journals echoed the Philadelphia *Record* in questioning "whether the event is the more conspicuous for strengthening the judiciary or impoverishing politics." [52] In New York State, however, reaction among the politicians was mixed. Organization leaders remained unusually quiet in the wake of speculation concerning GOP plans. Undoubtedly, progressives were disappointed over losing the chief spokesman of their cause. "I was stunned," confessed Lloyd Griscom, since "all the hopes of our group were pinned on Governor Hughes, and now he was deserting us." [53] Hughes himself must have experienced feelings of guilt regarding his departure, for on April 25 he issued a lengthy public statement justifying his acceptance of the President's offer. Then to Griscom "he explained apologetically that he was tired," but that he intended, nonetheless, to carry on the primary fight right up through September.[54]

Publication of Hughes's supreme court appointment certainly did not aid the administration in its fight to enact direct nominations legislation. If organization leaders had been unalterably opposed to the Hinman-Green bill before April 25, they had little reason to relent afterward. William Barnes, for example, bitterly denounced the Governor as an "individualist" who did "not feel called upon to make any sacrifice . . . for the good of the party." [55] His primary plan, insisted the intransigent Albany

[52] *Literary Digest*, XL (1910), 903–905.

[53] Griscom, *Diplomatically Speaking* (Boston: Little, Brown, 1940), p. 337. Villard complained bitterly about what he termed a "disheartening error of judgment" (*Fighting Years*, p. 214). To Hughes he also protested, as did Herbert Parsons (Villard to Hughes, May 6, 1910, Villard Papers; Parsons to Hughes, April 29, 1910, Parsons Papers).

[54] Griscom, *Diplomatically Speaking*, pp. 337–338. A copy of this statement is filed in the Hughes Collection (NYPL).

[55] Barnes was one of the few leaders who expressed himself on the situation so soon after the announcement (New York *World*, April 27, 1910, Fuller Collection, Vol. LXXXI).

leader, had to be shelved for the sake of GOP welfare and unity.

Within three weeks after the court appointment, the administration's primary proposal was put to the test in the New York assembly. Here Speaker Wadsworth personally took the floor against what he called "statutory bossism" and tore into the bill's weaknesses. The proposed nominating committees, he argued, would be less representative in character than conventions, and only confusion would result from the innumerable offices that would be filled by the voters in each community. Wadsworth's efforts were quickly endorsed by the compliant assembly, although the vote was close enough to disturb even the most staunch organization faithful. The speaker's announced intention to stand firm against any and all direct nominations legislation was also realized when the lower house, by a strict party vote, backed his opposition to the Grady-Frisbie bill. As if to rub salt in the wound, the assembly then passed the Meade-Phillips bill embodying the "minor" changes recommended by the direct primary commission and the determined speaker.[56]

On May 18 the issue reached a climax in the traditionally uncooperative state senate. Here, ironically, the forces of compromise had begun to function as George Cobb, again sacrificing organization pride for party welfare, worked out a modified version of the Hinman-Green bill. Apparently with the idea of ultimately backing Cobb's efforts, several Republican senators joined the Democrats in defeating the administration proposal. Like the assembly, the senate then turned down the Grady-Frisbie bill.[57]

The relatively close vote on the Hinman-Green bill in both

[56] New York *Times*, May 12, 1910; The final vote was 77–67 (*New York Assembly Journal*, 133d session, pp. 2817–2818); the other roll calls are given on pp. 2820 and 2821. Wadsworth's commitment to the Meade-Phillips bill was total, as seen in "Autobiography," p. 156, James W. Wadsworth, Jr., Papers (Hartford House, Geneseo, New York; now on deposit in the Library of Congress).

[57] New York *Times*, May 7, 1910. The Hinman-Green bill was beaten 25–23. The vote on the Democratic measure was 36–11, and the Meade-Phillips bill was not considered (*New York Senate Journal*, 133d session, p. 1609).

houses of the legislature underscored the insecure hold that the recalcitrants actually had upon the party. It also encouraged George Cobb to work for his compromise plan. Up to this point, Cobb had not consulted the Governor since Hughes had made it known publicly that under no circumstances would he accept a halfway measure.[58] With the narrow legislative defeat, however, the majority leader had good reason to believe that the administration might alter its position. Thus, on May 2, Cobb opened negotiations with Hughes's primary experts, William Wadhams, Darwin James, and others, and followed these with a senate Republican conference. In closed session, GOP legislators hashed over the whole matter and selected a special committee, composed of Cobb, Hinman, and George Meade, to visit the Governor for the purpose of suggesting a possible compromise.[59]

On May 21 the Cobb committee ventured over to the executive offices, where they were cordially greeted by Hughes and his assistants. Wasting no time, the Governor indicated his interest in a compromise plan and asked that a concrete proposal be drawn up immediately. For this purpose he willingly loaned the group his own special counsel Roger P. Clark and his secretary Robert Fuller. Later the same day an appropriate amendment was made to the original Cobb bill, and on May 24 a stormy Republican senate conference decided to caucus for the "new" legislation.[60]

Amidst bitter press criticism of Hughes's "barter," the primary issue again plagued the state senate.[61] On the morning of May 25 upper house Democrats, anticipating Republican strat-

[58] New York *Times,* May 10, 1910. Privately, in March, Hughes had said he would not compromise (James S. Sherman to William Ward, March 23, 1910, Sherman Papers).

[59] New York *Tribune,* May 21, 1910; New York *Times,* May 23, 1910.

[60] New York *Tribune,* May 23, 1910. The bill limited direct nominations to assemblymen, state senators and congressmen (New York *Times,* May 25, 1910).

[61] New York *Press,* May 23 and 24, 1910; New York *Sun,* May 26, 1910, Fuller Collection, Vol. LXXXII.

egy, gathered together for a conference of their own. The importance of this meeting lay not so much in its proceedings but rather in the almost incredible way that William Barnes boldly negotiated with its leaders to forge a bipartisan alliance against the Cobb-Hughes forces. Flitting back and forth between GOP legislators and the Democratic conferees, the desperate Albany County leader was able to consummate an agreement that committed Tammany boss Thomas Grady to the Meade-Phillips bill. Although the senate then passed this Republican machine measure, an afternoon GOP caucus endorsed the Cobb compromise. Next day, the majority leader, faced with adjournment, pushed for immediate consideration of his bill, and his faithful colleagues, despite Barnes, passed favorably upon it.[62]

Only the lower house now stood in the way of a reasonably good primary bill, at least from the progressives' viewpoint. But the assembly's will remained that of Speaker Wadsworth, who had already categorically refused any compromise on the question of nominations legislation. From the beginning, Cobb's efforts at meeting the administration halfway annoyed Wadsworth, and despite pressure to yield he held firm. Even an emergency message from Hughes failed to move the strong-willed speaker, and the Cobb bill went down to defeat in the assembly.[63]

The 1910 legislature adjourned its regular session without having enacted Governor Hughes's key reform proposal—the direct primary. Unlike the previous year, however, its overall record was not totally barren; indeed, several aspects of the Hughes program, as outlined in the January message, were put through by a Republican party whose stubborn leaders backed down only where they felt their positions were not threatened. There were bills to tighten the 1908 racing legislation, to revise existing insurance restrictions, to establish a workmen's compen-

[62] New York *Times*, May 26, 1910; *New York Senate Journal*, 133d session, pp. 1839, 1917. The vote on the Cobb bill was 34–14.

[63] New York *Tribune*, May 23, 1910; New York *Times*, May 24, 1910; *Hughes Public Papers*, IV, 91–93; *New York Assembly Journal*, 133d session, pp. 3586–3587.

sation system, and to strengthen the utilities law. Above all, the Merritt bill, granting the public service commissions authority over the telephone and telegraph companies, was put on the books. These successes only whetted Hughes's appetite for the direct primary. Its enactment, he continued to believe, was absolutely essential for the restoration of public confidence in the Republican party and, more important, for the achievement of the democratic ideal. On May 27, therefore, he dispatched a special message to the legislature calling both houses back into session on June 20.[64] He would make one last-ditch attempt to pass the direct nominations bill.

Governor Hughes took advantage of the interval before the legislature reconvened to clarify publicly his own position on the array of primary measures appearing in the senate and assembly during the regular session. In Batavia, on June 10, he lauded the Hinman-Green bill as the "key measure," but pointedly told his audience that "the next best thing was to secure a plan of some character as broadly applicable as possible." [65] So there would be no misunderstanding on this issue, he explicitly named the Cobb proposal as embodying the desirable compromise, and he optimistically predicted its enactment. There would be no effort, he implied, to ram the more "radical" legislation through the legislature.

With Hughes's willingness to compromise made public even before the legislature reconvened, the pressure upon party leaders in New York to accept the Cobb bill must have increased substantially. On June 13 President Taft met with primaries champion William Wadhams, and though the session was kept secret, word leaked out afterward that Taft had expressed hope for the passage of an "appropriate" direct nominations bill.[66] At the same time, stories were beginning to appear in the press to

---

[64] *Hughes Public Papers,* IV, 6–7.

[65] "Board of Trade Speech," June 10, 1910, Hughes Collection (NYPL).

[66] New York *Times,* June 16, 1910; Merwin K. Hart to Robert Fuller, June 26, 1910, Hughes Collection (NYPL). At this time Taft made it clear that he intended not to interfere (Taft to Lloyd Griscom, June 23, 1910, Taft Papers).

the effect that Theodore Roosevelt, on his way home from his widely publicized African safari, might himself feel compelled to take a stand on the "red hot" state situation. When, on June 18, the ever-popular Roosevelt finally set foot on American soil, he intimated to a New York reception committee that the party that had been so good to him needed leadership "now more than ever." [67] Perhaps, many conjectured, the Empire State would again be a proving ground for the "old warrior's" political activities.

For several days public attention focused on Oyster Bay, not only because Roosevelt might have something significant to say regarding the tangled New York situation, but, moreso, because he would perhaps comment upon the sorry state of the national GOP. It was certainly no secret that Roosevelt and his successor had had a falling out and that Roosevelt was deeply concerned over the breach that the Taft policies had opened up between the progressive and conservative wings of the party. In meeting after meeting with politicians of all persuasions, George Mowry points out, Roosevelt's earlier judgment was confirmed: Republican success in the immediate future depended upon healing the party wounds.[68] This task, in turn, required strong, dynamic leadership—something that Taft had not provided and probably would not provide without considerable help and direction.

The complicated New York situation early in the summer of 1910 lent itself nicely to Roosevelt's calculations for strengthening the Republican party on a national basis. Here was one of the few places in the country where the Taft administration had not become allied with the GOP's conservative wing, but had at

[67] New York *Times*, June 10 and 19, 1910. There is considerable evidence that Roosevelt was, indeed, fully apprised of the New York situation while abroad (William Loeb to Roosevelt, April 8, 1910, William Loeb Microfilm [Theodore Roosevelt Collection, Harvard University Library]; Herbert H. Rosenthal, "The Progressive Movement in New York State, 1906–1914" [unpublished Ph.D. diss., Harvard University, 1955], pp. 236–237).

[68] *Theodore Roosevelt and the Progressive Movement* (Madison: University of Wisconsin, 1947), pp. 130–134.

least identified itself with the progressives. The President perhaps had not gone far enough in his support of the Hughes program, particularly as the state organization grew more irresponsible, but he was, after all, less interested in New York developments than Theodore Roosevelt had been.[69] Together the two leaders, with Hughes's cooperation, might yet set the state party aright and, in so doing, begin the process of strengthening the national organization. As always, Roosevelt regarded New York as the key to national power.

If Roosevelt was inclined to reactivate himself in Empire State politics, it took a catalytic agent to spur him on. This agent was Charles Evans Hughes, and the issue was the direct primary. On June 20 the state legislature reconvened for the special session only to be greeted by a challenging message from the Governor calling for the enactment of a suitable direct nominations measure and, surprisingly, certain amendments to the graft resolution passed in the regular session.[70] Within a few days it was apparent that neither proposal was making sufficient headway, and the state administration was again faced with defeat. Hughes and Roosevelt had already corresponded with each other about the possibility of meeting to discuss the explosive New York situation. At first they found it difficult to agree upon a mutually convenient time and place, but then, since both had plans to attend Harvard's June 29 commencement, they made arrangements to meet in Cambridge.[71]

On June 29, as scheduled, the two men conferred with each other for the first time in over a year. Shortly before the commencement procession, they were seen deeply absorbed in conversation, much of which dealt with the New York situation. It

---

[69] To Loeb, on March 10, Roosevelt complained: "What idiots our Republican leaders in New York have been!" (*LTR*, VII, 53–54).

[70] *Hughes Public Papers*, IV, 94–109.

[71] Roosevelt to Hughes, June 20, 1910, and Hughes to Roosevelt, June 25, 1910, Hughes Papers; Roosevelt to Hughes, June 27, 1910, *LTR*, VII, 93–94. According to Beerits, "Second Term as Governor" (p. 17), Hughes had information prior to the meeting that Roosevelt actually favored the direct primary reform.

was Hughes who broached the primary question and put the issue squarely to Roosevelt. Shrewdly, the former president indicated that he had decided to remain noncommittal on the controversial Cobb bill, though, as in the past, he confessed keen interest in, and sympathy for, the overall Hughes program. "I am not urging you to get into the struggle," replied the Governor, "but your silence is used by the opposition as evidence that you are against the bill." In that case, shot back Roosevelt excitedly, "I'll write Fred Davenport now telling him I think it should be passed." [72] Again Roosevelt would subdue his personal animosity toward Hughes.

That same day Roosevelt took matters into his own hands and wired, not to Davenport, but to New York County Chairman Griscom. In this "open" telegram, he insisted that for the past few days he had received scores of letters from Republican and independent voters all over New York State urging passage of the compromise primary bill. He therefore hoped sincerely "that it will be enacted into law." [73]

Meanwhile, President Taft had changed his mind over applying political pressure to aid the all-important Hughes cause in New York. Whether this decision was motivated by Roosevelt's action or whether these common efforts on the part of the national leaders were coordinated is not clear. At any rate, on the very day of the Harvard meeting between Roosevelt and Hughes, Taft dispatched a host of letters to key state leaders— including Greiner and Griscom—urging them, in language not too different from Roosevelt's telegram, to rally behind the Cobb bill for the sake of party well-being. [74]

[72] Henry L. Stoddard, *As I Knew Them: Presidents and Politics from Grant to Coolidge* (New York: Harper and Bros., 1927), pp. 444–445. This account corresponds in the main with Beerits, "Second Term as Governor," p. 17, and Oscar King Davis, *Released for Publication: Some Inside Political History of Theodore Roosevelt and His Times, 1898–1918* (Boston: Houghton-Mifflin, 1925), p. 192.

[73] Roosevelt to Griscom, June 29, 1910, *LTR*, VII, 97; "Griscom Reminiscences," p. 93.

[74] Taft to Fred Greiner, to Naval Officer Kraake, and to Lloyd Griscom, June 29, 1910, Taft Papers. Next day, he sent appeals to Woodruff, J. Sloat Fassett, J. A. Smyth, John Dwight, and William Ward.

By this time, however, no amount of political pressure could move the determined state machine in Albany. On the morning of June 30, Wadsworth's assembly again defeated the Cobb compromise, then adjourned defiantly.[75] To the speaker himself, the issue in the special session had revolved about whether the lower house "shall swallow its convictions and deliberately reverse its honest judgment." [76] Defensively, he added that the primary vote "should not be construed as a gratuitous slap at the ex-President or at the Governor."

Wadsworth may, indeed, have been sincere in his explanation of the assembly's action. Since 1909 he had led the moderate Republican opposition to the direct primary, and there is no evidence that he did so out of personal contempt for Hughes or later for Roosevelt. The situation in the state senate was altogether different, however, when, on July 1, the administration-supported measure was beaten back. Here, several Republican legislators who had earlier voted for the Cobb bill joined William Barnes's bipartisan alliance on the final roll call.[77] Their defection was perhaps best explained in the words of the cantankerous Albany boss himself: "Teddy is licked to a frazzle. We no longer worship the gods, we laugh at them." [78]

To some extent the primary defeat in New York was, as Barnes intimated, a defeat for Theodore Roosevelt—and probably to a lesser degree a slap at the ever-weakening Taft administration. The Colonel had rather blindly and impulsively involved himself, as some have argued, in a situation of which he had only faint comprehension.[79] Long out of New York politics, Roosevelt had not fully appreciated the determination of the leaders to defeat the Cobb bill and with it their arch enemy,

[75] *New York Assembly Journal*, extra. session (1910), p. 29.

[76] New York *Times*, July 1, 1910. See also *Literary Digest*, XLI (1910), 43–45.

[77] Actually the bill received 25 affirmative votes and 19 negative votes, but a majority of the entire senate was 26 *(New York Senate Journal*, extra. session [1910], p. 31).

[78] Griscom, *Diplomatically Speaking*, p. 343.

[79] See especially Henry F. Pringle, *The Life and Times of William Howard Taft* (New York: Farrar & Rinehart, 1939), II, 559.

Governor Hughes; his awkward intervention, lacking the force of the presidential office, tended to confirm their clearly defined position, as some of them, especially his old rivals from the Platt days, revelled in defeating the man who had so often "spoken softly" and brandished the "big stick." [80] Taft, on the other hand, had not offered his services soon enough to change the course of events leading to the primary defeat. To be sure, he had encouraged the reform forces in New York during much of 1910, but he had not met the specific challenge of the direct nominations issue—nor apparently did he care, until the very end, to do so.[81] All that the national leaders could salvage from this embarrassing defeat was a confirmation of Roosevelt's earlier belief that here was one area of the country where they had worked (and might continue to work) for a common goal—that is, party unification based upon forward-looking principles.

In the final analysis, however, the primary defeat of 1910 was Governor Hughes's defeat. It was Hughes who devoted virtually an entire administration to completing the reform program enunciated in his very first message to the legislature in 1907. It had been largely his decision in 1910 to tie the direct nominations issue to other policies designed to reorganize the state Republican party—a movement that he refused to lead but that tended to put the organization more and more on the defensive. If, then, the leaders had been opposed to the primary before this fateful year, the full sweep of events and circumstances only confirmed their intransigence. Just as Hughes thus felt he had no choice but to fight to the bitter end, so his opponents, discredited and excoriated as they had been, could not compromise.

Given the rift that had been made in the Republican party in 1910, the question remains whether a direct primary measure could still not have been enacted. To be sure, Hughes had failed to generate profound public interest in his key political reform

[80] There was, indeed, much resentment over Roosevelt's "obvious" effort to dictate (New York *Times*, July 2, 1910).

[81] Taft did express his chagrin over the legislature's failure to enact the primary reform (Taft to J. A. Smyth, July 3, 1910, Taft Papers).

—at least an interest as deep and as abiding as that which had helped the 1907 public service commissions bill. But he had again aided in exposing the GOP organization—indeed, in discrediting it to the point where moderately inclined legislators would think twice before opposing another significant administration measure. Certainly the senate and assembly roll call on the Hinman-Green bill in the regular session showed beyond any reasonable doubt that, unlike 1909, the leaders held only shaky control. Perhaps if Hughes had not announced his supreme court appointment until after the vote, the end result would have been a different one. He might conceivably have achieved his victory then and there. Instead, the battle was carried into the special session, where, despite federal intervention and Roosevelt's support, it was lost from the beginning. All Hughes had to show for his dramatic battle was the satisfaction of having made the fight, not of having won it.

CHAPTER XIII

Social Reform and
the Public Welfare

THE main drive of Charles Evans Hughes's reform program as governor of New York came in the areas of improving the structure and operations of government, revitalizing the political processes, and extending the state's regulatory authority over businesses and corporations engaged in public service. All three aspects drew Hughes into painful conflicts with the legislature and the leaders of his own party—conflicts that constantly captured and held the popular imagination. Such drama, however, tended to obscure other significant accomplishments during the years 1907 through 1910, chiefly in the broad field of social reform and public welfare. The story of this aspect of progressivism is one principally of organizational or group efforts launched and sustained over a period of several decades. Some of these efforts, indeed, reached fruition during Hughes's governorship; others at least were given impetus during these years of independence and reform.

The long, arduous campaign for social and economic justice in the Empire State was initiated in New York City during the 1890's. In this decade, the champions of good government were joined by a host of social reformers in their drive to rid the Tammany-dominated municipal government of graft and corruption and, at the same time, extend the City's public service functions. Among the most prominent of these urban progressives were the social workers. As agents for both private and public charity organizations, or as workers in the settlement houses, these people dedicated themselves to aiding and comforting the downtrodden masses crowded together in the slum districts of Manhattan. Well-educated, usually the product of solid middle- or upper-class families and motivated by the challenge of poverty, they increasingly focused their attention on the problems of income, housing, employment, health, and habits of the oppressed classes.[1] Experience in the Henry Street Settlement, Madison House, or the University Settlement taught them that poverty was a social phenomenon and not, as the nineteenth-century philanthropist had insisted, a matter of individual responsibility and concern. Experience also taught them the necessity of engaging in political activity in order to achieve their social welfare objectives. By the mid-nineties, indeed, some of the settlement leaders had concluded that, as one student has put it, "the settlement could become the antidote to boss rule in ward politics, and the base for political reforms in the city."[2] One such leader, James B. Reynolds of the University Settlement, became active in the Citizens' Union sponsorship of Seth Low for mayor in 1901. His success during the campaign in enlisting the support of Lillian Wald, Henry Moskowitz, and others for the Low cause was rewarded by the new mayor himself, who promptly named Reynolds as his private secretary. For the first time, the social workers thus possessed connections within the high councils of government. This position they effectively exploited to broaden the base of reform in New York City.[3]

By and large, the political activities of the social reformers, like their counterparts in the professions and in business, were confined to the cities in the 1890's. They did not find it difficult,

[1] A profile of the social worker is given in Allen F. Davis, "Spearheads for Reform—The Social Settlements and the Progressive Movement, 1890–1914" (unpublished Ph.D. diss., University of Wisconsin, 1959), ch. 1.

[2] Allen F. Davis, "Settlement Workers in Politics, 1890–1914," *Review of Politics*, XXVI (1964), 508.

[3] *Ibid.*, pp. 505–517.

however, from the standpoint of ideology or inclination, to expand their base of operations to the state when necessary. The history of New York's Tenement House Act of 1901, known as "the first major venture in social amelioration in the United States in the twentieth century," was a tribute to both their method of research and their relentless determination to alleviate the ills of poor housing in the city.[4] Moreover, these same people eagerly joined labor's assault upon the conservative state legislature in behalf of measures regulating child and woman employment.[5] Though, to be sure, this movement did not reach its climax until the passage of the famous industrial legislation following the terrible Triangle fire of 1911, its origins lay deep in the nineteenth century.

The role of organized labor in the crusade for social reform cannot be gainsaid. As early as 1864 the Workingmen's Assembly, an association of trade unions and the parent body of the New York State Federation of Labor, had sought in various ways to plead the workers' cause in the state legislature. Labor's political voice became stronger as trade unionism expanded in the 1880's and 1890's, especially in New York City. In 1886, with the support of the New York City Society for the Prevention of Cruelty to Children and the State Bureau of Labor Statistics, the Workingmen's Assembly obtained New York's first factory act, providing a maximum sixty-hour week for women under twenty-one and children under eighteen in industrial employment. For the next ten years this law was improved and expanded through labor's persistent and ceaseless efforts.[6]

[4] Robert Bremner, *From the Depths: The Discovery of Poverty in the United States* (New York: New York University, 1956), p. 204. See also Roy Lubove, *The Progressives and the Slums: Tenement House Reform in New York City* (Pittsburgh: University of Pittsburgh, 1962), esp. ch. 5.

[5] Irwin Yellowitz, *Labor and the Progressive Movement in New York State, 1897–1916* (Ithaca: Cornell, 1965), ch. 5.

[6] Howard L. Hurwitz, *Theodore Roosevelt and Labor in New York State, 1880–1900* (New York: Columbia, 1943), ch. 2; Clara Beyer, *History of Labor Legislation for Women in Three States* (Bulletin of Women's Bureau No. 66; Washington: U.S. Department of Labor, 1929), pp. 66–67.

Of particular note in the struggle for labor legislation was the extension of protection to women and children in New York City's mercantile establishments, occasioning the birth, in 1891, of the Consumers' League. This significant organization grew out of a series of abortive attempts made by the Working Women's Society to improve conditions in the City's badly sweated retail department stores. In utter desperation one of its leaders turned to Mrs. Josephine Shaw Lowell, a woman of status and civic-mindedness, who immediately launched a campaign to establish a new organization on the principle that "the American consumer would not willingly profit by the cheapness of wares where that cheapness resulted from oppression and injustice." [7] Adopting the motto "Investigate, record, agitate," the Consumers' League of New York City launched a campaign to coerce employers to accept carefully defined minimum labor standards and to obtain protective laws from the state legislature. So successful was the league that within eight years, there were similar bodies in Boston, Philadelphia, and Chicago, and in 1899 the National Consumers' League was born. Functioning initially as a clearing house of data and information for the local units, the national organization, brilliantly led by the socialist-minded Florence Kelley, played a leading role in a variety of reform endeavors—against child labor, tenement-house manufacturing, substandard wages, and long hours. Within a decade its leaders were actively engaged in sponsoring bills in state legislatures across the nation to establish wage boards patterned after those recently established in the British Commonwealth. [8]

By the dawn of the twentieth century, then, a host of organizations and groups in New York representing people of virtually every class and interest—professions, organized labor, the urban

[7] Maud Nathan, *The Story of an Epoch-Making Movement* (New York: Doubleday, Page, 1926), pp. xii–xiii; Josephine Goldmark, *Impatient Crusader: Florence Kelley's Life Story* (Urbana: University of Illinois, 1953), pp. 51–53; Maud Nathan, "Mrs. Lowell and the Consumers' League," *Charities*, XV (1905), 325–326; Florence L. Sanville, "The Story of the Consumers' League," *Outlook*, XCVIII (1911), 113–119.

[8] Consumers' League of the City of New York, *Report for the Year 1910* (New York: the League, 1911), pp. 9–21.

masses (for the social workers claimed to be their spokesmen), and consumers—agitated together, often independently, to render the state more highly responsive to the needs of an increasingly industrialized and urbanized community. Taken as a whole, their program ranged from improved sanitation and health conditions to tenement house reform and child and woman labor legislation. The latter cause, perhaps the most important single aspect of the social welfare crusade, was given further impetus in 1902 with the formation of the New York Child Labor Committee, which emerged from the settlements and the Association of Neighborhood Workers in New York City and which dedicated itself to the scientific study of employment conditions and the amelioration of industrial wrongs through social action. In a similar vein, the American Association for Labor Legislation, created four years later, launched its long campaign for state legislation on industrial accidents. The end result of this rash of activity, even before 1906, was a set of laws that made New York at least competitive among the nation's most advanced industrial states in social welfare matters, especially in child labor legislation.[9]

However successful these groups were up to 1906, the reformers themselves fully realized the work that lay ahead in the state. To their way of thinking, the chief obstacle was—and had been all along—the very nature of the political situation in Albany. The Democrats in the legislature were still under the control of the same conservative Tammany leaders whom the social progressives had fought in New York City in the 1890's. The Republican side of the legislature, especially the senate, was hardly more helpful, dominated as it was by the party's upstate wing. Representing essentially rural communities, or merchants and businessmen in the small towns, these lawmakers remained

[9] Florence Kelley, "Current Notes on Child Labor Laws," *Charities*, X (1903), 450–453; Jeremy P. Felt, *Hostages of Fortune: Child Labor Reform in New York State* (Syracuse: Syracuse, 1965), ch. 3; Richard M. Lyon, "The American Association for Labor Legislation and the Fight for Workmen's Compensation Laws, 1906–1942" (unpublished M.S. thesis, Cornell University, 1952), pp. 36–42.

insulated from the great political, social, and even intellectual ferment of the rapidly expanding urban centers. Nor was the executive office a haven of social reform. Since 1894 the governorship had, of course, been held by the GOP, and the men who served, with the exception of Theodore Roosevelt, were men of second-rate abilities who had slowly ascended the organization ladder and finally received the office as a reward for faithful service to the party. The hope of the social progressives lay mainly in the strength of their own campaigns together with the growing influence of the city reformers in the state government.

Although the 1906 gubernatorial campaign, indeed, offered the reformers two candidates from New York City, neither one proved inspiring to them. Representing a badly discredited party, Hughes, the unknown, could hardly excite the social progressives with his major themes—"anti-bossism" and corporation control. Nor was the Hearst movement much more appealing. Although through the years Hearst had sought to identify himself with the aspirations of the lower classes, his intense political ambition, his journalistic sensationalism, and his unsavory alliance with Tammany substantially reduced his influence with reformers in general. Speaking for a large segment of the progressive community, *Charities and the Commons* thus admitted that the bitter 1906 contest was "to some extent a test between the have's and have-not's," but that both candidates "represent a well-defined conviction in the public mind that the law is for the rich no less than for the poor." Nonetheless, the editorial concluded, " 'waving the bloody shirt' . . . cannot successfully be revived as a feature of the social and industrial campaigns on which we have entered." [10]

The reformers' suspicion of Charles Evans Hughes was not without foundation. Until he became a public figure, Hughes had evinced no more interest in social justice than he had in the other major issues of the day. To state, however, that his vision

[10] "Hearst and Hughes," *Charities and the Commons*, XVII (1906), 3-4.

was unusually limited seems untrue. Having lived in the teeming metropolis for so long, he certainly was exposed to its political, social, and economic ferment. Moreover, his deeply embedded moral sense could be aroused by social wrongs as well as by corrupt politico-business maneuverings. Finally, he was flexible of mind and temperament. "A piece of thinking machinery working with almost terrifying velocity," as one social reformer later put it, Hughes came to hold an abiding confidence in empirical data and the experimental method.[11] The mode of his thinking in 1906 is best illustrated by an interesting exchange of correspondence with Louis D. Brandeis. Brandeis had sent Hughes an article he had written on "Wage-Earners' Life Insurance" with a request for comment. Hughes replied that it offered a "strong and unanswerable statement of the evils of industrial insurance as now conducted," but appealed for a more detailed analysis of the feasibility of Brandeis' substitute plan, fearing that "even with such a showing . . . conservatism would refuse to be convinced." He also urged that this "experiment" be tried because it was "as important a philanthropic work as model tenements." [12] Practicality and experimentation had thus become the guidelines of Hughes's thinking and doubtless provide some clue to his willingness as governor to cooperate with the social reformers.

Hughes's real introduction to labor came in the campaign of 1906, where, as we have seen, he faced the difficult task of competing with Hearst for the workingman's support. His promises ranged from better enforcement of the existing state labor code to extension of laws regulating woman and child employment. These were followed up with specific recommendations in his first legislative message, and in certain instances reiterated in subsequent annual and special messages through 1910. From the beginning, it was apparent that the new governor would heed

[11] Homer Folks, "Hughes—An Appreciation," *Survey*, XXV (1910), 152.

[12] Hughes to Brandeis, July 6, 1906, quoted in Alpheus T. Mason, *Brandeis: The Story of a Free Man's Life* (New York: Viking, 1946), p. 158.

carefully the advice of those reformers who for over a decade had carried the banner of social and economic justice.

In 1907 Governor Hughes turned first to a fundamental question long disturbing the reformers—meaningful enforcement of the existing labor code. Fully appreciating the work done in 1901 to consolidate the state department of labor, he nonetheless called for an increase in the number of factory inspectors, the specialization of their functions, and the grading of their positions and salary scale. To this he added a recommendation for an improved law securing for children "their right to an elementary education and . . . surrounding them with appropriate safeguards." [13] He then outlined the need for legislation to prohibit children under sixteen from working more than eight hours per day and to define carefully the dangerous occupations in which they could not be employed.

As usual, Hughes called chiefly upon his New York City progressive Republican allies—specifically George B. Agnew, Ezra Prentice, and Alfred Page, all with broad experience in labor legislation—to introduce the major share of these proposals. Backed by the Child Labor Committee, the Consumers' League, and, at least in one instance, the Workingmen's Federation, all of them except the dangerous-occupations bill were enacted by the 1907 legislature, which one reformer described as the best since 1903.[14] The Agnew-Hooper bill actually reorganized the entire labor department, transfixing a direct line of authority from the commissioner through the three bureau chiefs—labor statistics, factory inspection, and mediation and arbitration—and spelled out in detail the appointment of factory inspectors, their salaries, their grades, and their districts. The Agnew-Prentice measure tightened the regulations on the issuance of employment certificates by specifying the acceptable mode of proof. Finally, and most important for the social reformers and organized labor, the Page-Prentice bill prescribed

[13] *Hughes Public Papers*, I, 35.
[14] George A. Hall, "New York Child Labor Legislation," *Charities and the Commons*, XVIII (1907), 434.

the eight-hour day and the forty-eight hour week for children under sixteen in factory employment. A product of the Child Labor Committee working closely with the Church Association for the Advancement of the Interests of Labor, this measure restricted the hours of employment to the period from 8:00 A.M. to 5:00 P.M. so that enforcement would be relatively easy. Although manufacturers had sought to weaken so threatening a restriction while the bill was in committee, Governor Hughes's firm support assured its passage essentially as proposed. Celebrating this victory, the Workingmen's Federation labeled the Page measure "far in advance of any other bill of the same nature in the United States." [15]

Governor Hughes followed up his first year of relative success on the labor front with another recommendation, in 1908, dealing again with enforcement, this time the mercantile establishment laws. Although the basic legislation regulating woman and child labor in the department stores had been enacted in 1896, subsequent enforcement procedures, as usual, rendered the law abortive. From the beginning, the New York Consumers' League agitated for a change in these procedures, but an indifferent legislature and a well-organized mercantile lobby beat back the efforts. By 1906 the league had gained the support of the Child Labor Committee, and the campaign gathered momentum. Already the committee had made a careful investigation of the situation; its report documented the repeated charges leveled against the local health boards in whose hands enforcement procedures had been placed—that they possessed no real inclination and little equipment to enforce the laws and that they were under constant pressure by the mercantile interests to ignore the code.[16]

[15] Workingmen's Federation of the State of New York, *Official Proceedings, 1907* (Syracuse: the Federation, 1907), p. 25. For Hughes's role, see Jeremy Felt, *Hostages of Fortune*, pp. 77–78. For the other laws, see *Laws of New York, 1907* (2 vols.; Albany: J. B. Lyon, 1907), I, chs. 505, 291.

[16] "Suggestions on Legislation, December 6, 1906," New York Child Labor Committee Papers (New York State Library at Albany); Con-

By the time Hughes became governor, the Child Labor Committee had incorporated into its legislative program a recommendation that enforcement of the mercantile laws be transferred to the state department of labor, which would soon be reorganized. In the 1907 legislature, the Hooper bill embodied this proposal together with provisions on hours regulation for women in the department stores, long the key item in the Consumers' League campaign. The bill passed the usually cooperative assembly, but it met with solid opposition in the senate. Here the Retail Dealers' Association of New York City made its influence felt and, ostensibly on constitutional grounds, the legislation was defeated.[17]

The reformers were not to be denied, however, and they immediately made their plans for 1908. Their cause was aided, in the fall of 1907, when Governor Hughes appointed John Williams as the new labor commissioner. Having come through the ranks of the department, Williams was schooled in the travails of labor enforcement by his dedicated and efficient superior, the retiring P. Tecumseh Sherman.[18] Almost immediately Williams identified himself and the Hughes administration with the aspirations and methods of the social reformers. In an unprecedented meeting with Florence Kelley, Lillian Wald, Edward Devine, Lawrence Veiller, and a host of other representatives of some fourteen reform organizations, Williams listened to advice on the basic policy his department should pursue in labor matters and the degree to which he was expected to participate in the organized state campaign against tuberculosis. "The significant features of this conference," recorded Veiller, "were the cordial

sumers' League of the City of New York, *Report for the Year 1908* (Albany: the League, 1909), pp. 33–34.

[17] "Report of the Secretary, July 5, 1907," Child Labor Committee Papers; "Report of the Labor Commissioner," *Assembly Document No. 30, Part I,* 131st session (Albany: J. B. Lyon, 1908), p. 74.

[18] Williams had been appointed state factory inspector by Theodore Roosevelt in 1899. In 1901 he was named first deputy labor commissioner and served in this capacity until Hughes made him commissioner. For a biographical sketch, see Edgar L. Murlin, *New York Red Book: An Illustrated Legislative Manual, 1908* (Albany: J. B. Lyon, 1908), p. 57.

relations existing between a newly-appointed state official and a group of labor law 'reformers.' " [19] The participants agreed that all labor legislation in the future should be based upon scientific fact, that additional medical inspectors had to be provided in the state, and that an inquiry was needed to gauge the effects on women and children of long hours in industry. Williams further pledged that the department would enforce the existing labor code even more vigorously than heretofore.[20]

With Williams' pledge of cooperation, the labor reformers redoubled their efforts in 1908 to shift enforcement of the mercantile code to the recently reorganized (and centralized) department of labor. The 1907 bill was modified to cover only the change in enforcing authority and to apply to the three first-class cities in the state—New York, Buffalo, and Rochester. At the request of the Child Labor Committee, Williams made it an "official" department proposal, and shortly after Governor Hughes's annual message embodying the recommendation, it was introduced in the legislature as the Page-Parker bill. Again, the measure moved easily through the assembly, but ran into a roadblock in the more conservative senate. So successful was the mercantile lobby that the bill never emerged from committee; an eleventh-hour attempt to suspend the rules and bring a vote on the last day of the session met with failure. The bill appeared doomed to defeat.[21]

However, 1908 was the year of the dramatic conflict over race-track gambling, and the reformers, still working through Williams, won Governor Hughes over to a renewal of the campaign during the legislature's extraordinary session. They had already gained one concession in that the funds implementing the proposed legislation had been made available. Their crusade now enlisted the support of the Workingmen's Federation, and they concentrated their pressure on the recalcitrant senate. Still, the

[19] "An Unusual Labor Conference," *Charities and the Commons,* XIX (1907), 1241–1242.

[20] *Ibid.,* pp. 1239–1242.

[21] "Report of the Secretary, May 19, 1908," Child Labor Committee Papers; Beyer, *History of Labor Legislation,* pp. 76–77.

mercantile interests were formidable since their counterattack commanded the sympathy of most of the large newspapers across the state—newspapers that were especially dependent upon department-store advertising. Finally, the Page-Parker bill passed the beleaguered senate, and New York took its place among the more advanced states "with respect to the logical enforcement of the laws relating to women and children who work in mercantile establishments." [22]

These major victories for labor and the social reformers were accompanied by the enactment of a considerable amount of minor legislation in 1907 and 1908, then supplemented and extended in various ways during the next two years. In 1909 came the Voss Dangerous Trades Act in response to Governor Hughes's renewed appeal for a measure along these lines. As finally approved, this bill barred over thirty dangerous occupations to children under sixteen and forbade their participation in certain hazardous stages of other industrial operations. In 1910 the Murray Night Messenger Law was passed, prohibiting children under twenty-one in the first- and second-class cities from being employed in night messenger work.[23]

The pattern in all this legislation ran very much the same: recommendation by the Governor in consultation with the commissioner of labor and representatives of various organizations especially interested in the proposals; sponsorship in the legislature usually by New York County Republicans; a vigorous "educational" campaign launched by the Workingmen's Federation, the Consumers' League, the Child Labor Committee, and others determined to improve and expand the labor code; finally, passage of the legislation often after considerable delay, particu-

[22] "A Legislative Victory for Working Children" (editorial), *Charities and the Commons*, XX (1908), 393. It was George Hall, secretary of the Child Labor Committee, who assumed most of the responsibility for rallying organized labor behind the bill (Hall to Thomas D. Fitzgerald, June 1, 1908, Child Labor Committee Papers).

[23] Owen R. Lovejoy, "The Year's Progress in Child Labor Legislation," *Survey*, XXIV (1910), 570–572; "Memorandum on Dangerous Trades Bill, 1909," Child Labor Committee Papers; *Hughes Public Papers*, III, 34.

larly in the senate. Despite the continued support of Governor Hughes and Commissioner Williams, progress in these years was slow indeed, as the reformers still faced an indifferent, skeptical legislature and a stubborn state judiciary whose record on matters of social welfare was hardly less conservative.[24]

Aside from extension of the woman and child labor laws and the various means of improving their enforcement, the major undertaking of the New York reformers during these years was the campaign to obtain a more liberal and humane employers' liability system. Indeed, since the latter 1890's the Workingmen's Federation had persistently agitated for such a modification inasmuch as statistics showed industrial accidents to be a prime cause of poverty among laboring families. Whether of a temporary or permanent nature, injury to the workingman meant, in effect, that either he had to resort to litigation for redress or he was compelled to suffer the economic consequences. If he carried his case to court, the injured worker usually faced a rigid interpretation of the two applicable common law doctrines—the "fellow servant rule," releasing the employer from any liability where the accident occurred chiefly through the employee's negligence, and the "assumed risk doctrine," holding the workman responsible for his person should he remain in the employment of a manufacturer who failed to adhere to the lawful safety standards. This whole system, one student has concluded, resulted not only in slow, inadequate recovery by the worker, but also waste, needless misunderstanding, and bitterness.[25]

The long campaign to relieve the worker from legal tyranny met with greater resistance from the upstate-oriented New York

[24] Franklin A. Smith, *Judicial Review of Legislation in New York, 1906–1938* (New York: Columbia, 1952), pp. 151–153. Smith argues, however, that the state courts' conservatism stemmed in part from the United States supreme court position on social welfare legislation, as enunciated especially in *Lochner* v. *New York* (1905).

[25] Harry Weiss, "Employers' Liability and Workmen's Compensation," in Don D. Lescohier and Elizabeth Brandeis, *History of Labor in the United States, 1896–1932* (New York: Macmillan, 1935), p. 573.

legislature than the hours regulation movement did. This was true even though, in the early years of agitation, organized labor focused not on industrial insurance as its solution to the problem but on simple reform of the rigid employers' liability system. A minor victory was achieved in 1902, when the Workingmen's Federation, in cooperation with the social reformers, obtained a slightly improved law.[26] Still dissatisfied, the federation vented its accumulated frustration by attacking the Assembly Speaker S. Fred Nixon as a "tyrant" and the rest of the GOP leaders, together with the Governor, for championing minor bills to divert attention from the inequities of the existing system.[27] The organizational voice did not go unheeded, and by 1907 the cause had won considerable support. In that year New York City attorney George W. Alger, an active member of the Child Labor Committee, reported that court records substantiated the workingman's charge that it was practically futile for the individual even to initiate litigation for damages due to industrial injury. Later in the same year a prominent social worker compiled and publicized an impressive array of facts and figures showing not only a relatively small number of labor-management compensation settlements but also "a veritable crazy quilt of absurdities when viewed comparatively." [28] The social results—chronic dependency, intemperance, lowered standards of living, breakdown of widows' health, begging, and dispossession—were grave enough, so the analysis went, to warrant establishing a

[26] "Reminiscences of George W. Alger" (Oral History Project, Columbia University Library, 1951–1952), p. 199; "Reminiscences of William S. Bennet" (Oral History Project, Columbia University Library, 1949–1950), pp. 29–30; Yellowitz, *Labor and the Progressive Movement*, pp. 108–109.

[27] "Report of the Executive Board on Legislation," in Workingmen's Federation of the State of New York, *Official Proceedings, 1904* (Elmira: the Federation, 1904), n.p.

[28] Francis H. McLean, "Industrial Accidents and Dependency in New York State," *Charities and the Commons*, XIX (1907), 1205; George W. Alger, "The Present Situation of Employers' Liability," *ibid.*, XVII (1907), 826–828; Thomas I. Parkinson, "Problems and Progress of Workmen's Compensation Legislation," *American Labor Legislation Review*, I (1911), 55–71.

state commission to investigate the whole problem with a view to altering the inhuman system.

Joining the voices of protest at about this time was another group of partisans, the American Association for Labor Legislation. Composed mainly of college professors dedicated to social reform based upon scientific study, this organization sprang out of an earlier international association for the legal protection of workers.[29] Spearheading the drive for an affiliate in the United States were several prominent economists, including John R. Commons, Richard T. Ely, and Henry Seager, who made preliminary organizational arrangements at the 1905 convention of the American Economic Association. There quickly followed the adoption of by-laws, and the A.A.L.L. appeared the next year with a plan calling for uniform labor legislation throughout the United States and encouraging the investigation and study of labor matters. The association grew rapidly and within six years opened a column in *Charities and the Commons* for the purpose of publicizing its views. Whenever possible, the A.A.L.L. cooperated with the Consumers' League, the National Conference of Charities and Correction, and the Women's Trade Union League in a variety of endeavors concerning woman and child labor. But, under the influence of Henry Seager of Columbia University, the association's major interest from the very beginning was the administration and enforcement of the labor law, health and safety regulation, and social insurance, particularly state-sponsored industrial accident insurance.

Holding the confidence of the champions of social justice, Governor Hughes responded immediately to the increased publicity given the industrial accidents problem. As early as January, 1907, he asserted that the interests of labor were "the interests of all the people, and the protection of the wage earner in the security of his life and health . . . is one of the most sacred trusts of society." [30] He took no stand on whether improved employers' liability legislation would suffice or whether a state-

[29] Lyon, "American Association for Labor Legislation," pp. 33–42.
[30] "Governor Hughes on Industrial Accidents," *Charities and the Commons*, XVII (1907), 759.

supported industrial insurance plan was desirable. In his 1908 annual message to the legislature, he combined an appeal for an official study of industrial accidents with a request for an investigation of New York City's immigrants, who suffered from what he called "special forms of imposition." [31] The Governor's long and involved battle over race-track gambling that year kept him from following up his initial recommendation. But in 1909, after his re-election, he returned to the issue. Taking advantage of the growing interest among legislators in the industrial accidents problem, Hughes reiterated his request for a "special and expert inquiry into the question relating to employer's liability and compensation for workmen's injuries." [32] Although the legislature quickly became embroiled with the administration over the direct primary and political reform, the liabilities commission bill passed rather easily. Hughes quickly responded with a competent group of investigators representing industry, labor, the social workers, and the A.A.L.L. to supplement a legislative delegation headed by progressive Republican Senator Jonathan M. Wainwright.

For several months the Wainwright commission labored at its assigned task of studying the industrial accidents problem and formulating a body of recommendations. It was apparent almost from the beginning that the commission would advocate some form of workmen's compensation. But the limitations under which the investigators operated were severe. Most important was the relative newness of the idea of state insurance among New Yorkers and, for that matter, among Americans in general. Although such laws were common in European nations and had long been the social workers' solution to the industrial accidents problem, by 1909 only four states had legislation imposing liability on grounds other than the fault of the employer, and these were highly limited. Furthermore, in spite of the growing agitation of organized labor and the social reformers for some relief for the workingman, the muckraking press practically ignored the movement, lacking as it was in the dramatic appeal of politi-

[31] *Hughes Public Papers*, II, 31.   [32] *Ibid.*, III, 34.

cal reform. "The matter is as yet rather quiet," complained a commission supporter in 1909, but, hopefully, a "necessary campaign of education will be secured." [33] Finally, the commission, having few preliminary studies of the problem on which to draw, had to pave its own way with an investigation that would meet head-on the two groups within New York that resisted too sweeping a change in the traditional employers' liability system —one, elements of the business community holding that the increased price of items produced in manufacturing establishments participating in a workmen's compensation plan would be ruinous in competitive interstate trade; the other, the conservative judges sitting in the courts.[34]

Beginning in the fall of 1909, the commission's work was carefully planned by chief counsel Joseph Cotton and Chairman Wainwright. Although Governor Hughes was kept informed of developments, he quite properly took no part in the proceedings. The investigators methodically gathered reading material on the general subject of workmen's compensation and, specifically, on the British and German plans; they launched a painstaking scrutiny of the existing liability system; and they carefully worked over lists of prospective witnesses to appear before the commission. In anticipation of the public hearings, Wainwright even sounded out the State Bar Association on alternate schemes "departing from negligence as a basis of liability and making the industry bear the burden of all accidents." [35] Then,

[33] L. W. Hatch to John R. Commons, Jan. 22, 1909, John B. Andrews Collection of the American Association for Labor Legislation Correspondence (Library of Industrial and Labor Relations, Cornell University).

[34] John Mitchell to Francis F. Kane, July 18, 1910, John Mitchell Papers (Catholic University Library); Crystal Eastman, "Work-Accidents and Employers' Liability," *Survey*, XXIV (1910), 788–794; Joseph B. Cotton, Jr., "Recent New York Legislation Upon Workmen's Compensation," *Annals of the American Academy of Political and Social Science*, XXXVII (1911), 230–237.

[35] Wainwright to Adelbert Moot, Oct., 1909, Jonathan M. Wainwright Papers (New-York Historical Society Library). The work of the commission is well documented in Box 6 of this collection.

a total of eleven hearings, conducted in the state's half-dozen largest cities, were devoted to advertising and publicizing the need to ease the harsh application of the common law doctrines and to enact a new system of compensation for industrial injury.

The Wainwright commission reported its findings and recommendations in the spring of 1910. "Were the *laissez faire* system of political economy working without friction," contended the report, "a workman engaged in hazardous employments would command and receive wages high enough to enable him to carry the risks of trade accidents and insure them." [36] Inasmuch as this was not the case, and since the commission's overall findings tended to verify the preliminary surveys of the problem, the report called for necessary "radical changes," including a liberalization in the application of the common law doctrines. More important, the commission recommended workmen's compensation on a limited scale, advising that automatic compensation be made compulsory in certain hazardous industries and voluntary in all others.

Based theoretically upon the British plan, the bills implementing these recommendations were drafted under the tutelage of the New York branch of the American Association for Labor Legislation and the State Federation of Labor. Their "modesty," however, invited severe criticism by the more radical labor organizations of New York City, which earlier in the year had joined forces "to begin a general campaign . . . for the compensation scheme." [37] They balked especially at the bills' failure

[36] "Report of the Commission . . . to Inquire into the Question of Employers' Liability and Other Matters," *Senate Document No. 38*, 133d session (Albany: J. B. Lyon, 1910), p. 7.

[37] Gertrude Light to Jonathan M. Wainwright, Feb. 11, 1910, Wainwright Papers; "Minutes of the Central Labor Committee, New York City Socialist Party, January 22, 1910" (Taminent Institute Library). The "Joint Labor Conference on Workmen's Compensation, Greater New York" was composed of the Central Federated Union of Greater New York and Vicinity, the Bronx Labor Council, the New York Building Trades Council, the Women's Trade Union League, the Central Labor Union of Brooklyn and Queens, and the Socialist Party Organization of New York.

to attack the defective articles of the state constitution that might throw the proposed plan into the courts, the highly restricted number of specified "dangerous" trades, and an inadequate compensation scale.[38] Adding some thirty amendments to the original bills, the A.A.L.L. and the State Federation were able to forestall some of the most vehement opposition to the legislation and thus take what the federation called at least "a step in the right direction." [39]

Of course, the Wainwright bills faced opposition from the other side as well. Trouble was foreshadowed when one member of the commission, George W. Smith, a reputed friend of the "employers," complained to Governor Hughes that his colleagues were moving too fast on an uncharted course.[40] Obviously referring to the compensation principle, the Smith complaint was repeated in the state senate, which in typical fashion held up the compulsory bill. When, finally, it did gain passage in the upper house, some commission members apparently feared that Governor Hughes might veto it. In an appeal to the Governor, Chairman Wainwright emphasized that this measure was, indeed, the really important proposal emerging from the commission's long study. Labeling the other legislation "mere makeshifts," the progressive Republican would interpret failure of the compulsory bill to mean "that our work has been particularly fruitless, the solution of the problem indefinitely postponed and the course of workmen's compensation left at a standstill." [41]

There was, however, never any real question concerning Hughes's position with regard to the new legislation. All along

[38] "Report of the Labor Conference," Albany, April 13, 1910, Wainwright Papers; "Labor's Criticism of Compensation Scheme," *Survey*, XXIV (1910), 128–129; New York *Times*, April 1 and May 26, 1910.

[39] New York State Federation of Labor, *Official Book: Proceedings, 14th Annual Convention*, September 20–23, 1910 (Niagara Falls: the Federation, 1910), p. 21. The changes are outlined in "Amendments to Wainwright Bills," *Survey*, XXIV (1910), 164. See also John B. Andrews, "Report of the Work," *American Labor Legislation Review*, I (1911), 95–106.

[40] Smith to Hughes, April 1, 1910, Wainwright Papers.

[41] Wainwright to Hughes, June 22, 1910, *ibid*.

he had maintained a discreet silence on the exact nature of the required changes. But he had developed a sensitivity toward the issue and, above all, he had appointed a commission sympathetic to the plight of the workingman. When, therefore, the Wainwright bills came to his desk, Hughes gladly signed them into law. He reiterated publicly the need for such industrial insurance—a need, he said, "conceded by all open-minded students of industrial conditions." [42] And he viewed the compulsory measure as the commission had viewed it: it might be used both for testing purposes and as a basis on which to establish a wholly new policy. He would leave the constitutional issue to the courts.

Doubtless, the Workmen's Compensation Act of 1910 marked the high point of social reform in Hughes's governorship—and for his part Hughes was duly applauded both by organized labor and by the representatives of the many social welfare groups that for years had striven to improve the workman's plight.[43] But the story of this, the first significant social insurance plan in the nation, did not end here. Within one year the New York court of appeals struck down the new law on constitutional grounds, and the issue was again brought to the fore.[44] As it turned out, the court's decision not only spurred the progressive forces in the Empire State ultimately to enact an even stronger workmen's compensation plan, but it also aided the cause nationally. The reform's most articulate champion, the American Association for Labor Legislation, intensified its drive over the next several years until by 1920 over half the states in the union provided for industrial accident insurance.

The passage of the Workmen's Compensation Act did not conclude the labors of the Wainwright commission. All along, the social reformers had considered the matter of accident prevention as an inherent part of the problem of industrial injuries.

[42] *Hughes Public Papers*, IV, 235–236.

[43] Federation of Labor, *Proceedings, 14th Annual Convention*, 1910, p. 19; "A Social Worker on the Supreme Bench" (editorial), *Survey*, XXV (1910), 141–143.

[44] Yellowitz, *Labor and the Progressive Movement*, pp. 111–112.

Moreover, the commission, with Hughes's approval, was charged with the additional responsibility of investigating unemployment and its causes—the first such inquiry to be conducted in the Empire State.[45] The commission turned to these items shortly after Hughes signed the Wainwright bills. During the summer of 1910 a hired expert accompanied Labor Commissioner Williams on a tour of England and Germany to observe at firsthand the safety devices and techniques utilized in manufacturing establishments there. At the same time, George Voss, chairman of the commission's special committee on unemployment, investigated British and continental remedies for the unemployment problem. Both studies extended beyond Governor Hughes's administration—indeed, through 1911. Late in that year Chairman Wainwright happily reported that most of the commission's recommendations on accident prevention had been enacted by the Democratic legislature with bipartisan support, the only exception being a bill granting the labor department the authority to define shop rules and regulations. Although, Wainwright admitted, the subject of unemployment was now "an academic problem," the commission made specific recommendations in this area, too, including a measure establishing a statewide system of employment offices.[46] But the return of prosperity after the dip in employment following the Panic of 1907 resulted in no action by the legislature.

The failure of efforts to set up employment offices in New York State was in part compensated by another gain during the second Hughes administration. When, in 1908, the Governor first recommended the need for an investigation of industrial accidents, he also called for an inquiry into the conditions surrounding the aliens in the state. The immigrant problem was essentially an urban problem with some 500,000 aliens crowded

[45] "Address by James B. Reynolds," *Twenty-Second Annual Report of the University Settlement Society of New York, 1908* (New York, 1909), pp. 17–24; L. W. Hatch to Irene Osgood, April 26, 1909, Andrews Collection; Henry Seager to Jonathan M. Wainwright, May 17, 1910, Wainwright Papers.

[46] Wainwright to Charles R. Miller, Nov. 2, 1911, Wainwright Papers.

together in the cities, especially in New York City. Unused to American ways, the newcomer was traditionally subject to a variety of abuses and exploitations, and he often had difficulty finding employment. Firmly supported by the social reformers, who again took the lead in "educating" the politicians, Hughes's request was approved by the legislature, and the Governor appointed a commission representing the professions, commerce, the settlements, the state department of labor, and organized labor. By early 1909 the Commission to Inquire into the Conditions, Welfare, and Industrial Opportunities of Aliens, as it was called, emerged with a lengthy report on a number of aspects of the problem. It recommended the establishment of a special bureau in the department of labor for the purpose of studying further the plight of all aliens in the state, of determining the areas in the United States in which there were the greatest demands for immigrant labor, and of taking steps to remove congestion in the cities and obviating unemployment.[47] Like the administration's political reforms, the recommendations of Hughes's specially created immigrant commission were shelved by the unruly 1909 legislature. The Governor returned to the matter, however, in his annual message the next year. "We cannot afford to regard with cynical indifference the conditions and opportunities of those who have recently come to us from foreign lands," he lectured his colleagues in the legislature.[48] Hughes went on to summarize the major proposals of the commission, endorsing each and every one of them. By mid-April the bill embodying these recommendations received legislative approval, and within six months the new bureau of industries and immigration was established. In characteristic fashion, Hughes appointed as its head an outstanding social worker and reformer, Frances Kellor.[49]

Still another aspect of the alien's plight—that of obtaining

[47] "Climbing Into America," *Survey,* XXII (1909), 111–114; "New York State to Protect Aliens," *ibid.,* XXV (1910), 171–172; Hughes to George C. Treadwell, July 13, 1908, Hughes Collection (New York State Library at Albany).

[48] *Hughes Public Papers,* IV, 37.

[49] "New York State to Protect Aliens," pp. 171–172.

speedy justice in the inferior courts of the state's large cities—
interested the Hughes administration from 1908 through 1910.
Here, the lead was taken by housing reformer Lawrence Veiller,
who turned to this issue four years after he had obtained the
revolutionary Tenement House Act. In his work in the New
York City settlements Veiller had observed at firsthand the inefficiency, corruption, and oppression of the "poor man's"
courts, especially those serving the immigrants and tenement-
house dwellers. In 1907 the Charity Organization Society,
spurred by Veiller, launched a program of education for court
reform much like that undertaken a decade earlier on the housing question. One year later Veiller drafted a bill to be introduced in the state legislature providing for the appointment of a
commission to inquire into the way in which justice was administered in the state's first-class cities. According to this measure,
the proposed commission would be appointed exclusively by the
Governor, so that, as Veiller put it, "we would get a Commission that was non-political and unbiased." [50] The legislature,
however, sensitive to Hughes's growing strength, insisted upon
sharing the appointive power. Legislative participation in the inquiry would also have the advantage of alleviating Tammany's
resentment against a Republican "invasion" of New York City.
The result was the establishment of a commission with five
members named by the senate and assembly and two members
appointed independently by the Governor. Hughes responded
with the appointment of Bronson Winthrop and Alan Hamilton,
the former at the behest of the Charity Organization Society;
the Tammany leadership selected Thomas Grady, senate minority spokesman and one-time "poor man's" court judge, and
Assemblyman Alfred E. Smith.

Chaired by progressive Alfred Page, the Inferior Criminal
Courts Commission presented the interesting spectacle of "silk-
stocking" Republicans and Tammany Democrats laboring together on a crucially important inquiry. For over a year the in-

[50] "Reminiscences of Lawrence Veiller" (Oral History Project, Columbia University Library, 1949), p. 208.

vestigators peered into every aspect of the "poor man's" courts and in early 1910 issued a bipartisan report carrying thirty-six recommendations for legislative action. With Hughes's endorsement these proposals were incorporated into one all-encompassing bill providing in various ways for administrative improvements in the inferior courts, establishing new children's courts, doubling night-court facilities, and setting up domestic relations courts.[51] Gaining the enthusiastic approval of the social reformers, Tammany Hall, and the progressive Republicans, the 1910 measure easily moved through the legislature, and "the first thorough inquiry into the administration of criminal justice in the State" came to a successful conclusion.[52]

Governor Hughes's unfaltering commitment to labor and social reform won him the respect and friendship of those dedicated progressives long engaged in the crusade for social and economic justice. Equally attractive to them were his clean politics and his independent spirit. "Previous to the terms of Governor Hughes," declared Homer Folks, "we had some trouble, we, the people generally who thought that the institutions should not be parts of the political machine." [53] For once, the rule of nonpartisanship prevailed in appointments to the state's welfare agencies and the executive office was free and open to suggestions of all kinds. Thus continued Folks: "Governor Hughes was a man who, I think I would say, almost more than any other governor, approached any subject with an open mind and wanted to know and get at the real facts about it. . . . When he did really get the facts as he saw them and thought them to be, he very seldom would depart from following them in legislation and in appointments." [54]

[51] *Hughes Public Papers*, IV, 44–45. A summary of the commission's report is given in New York *Times*, April 4, 1910, and "To Reform Courts of Inferior Jurisdiction," *Survey*, XXIV (1910), 177–179.

[52] "Veiller Reminiscences," p. 215. See also "The Survey This Week," *Survey*, XXIV (1910), 161–162, and Alfred E. Smith, *Up to Now: An Autobiography* (New York: Viking, 1929), p. 82.

[53] "Reminiscences of Homer Folks" (Oral History Projects, Columbia University Library, 1949), p. 62.

[54] *Ibid.*, pp. 61–62.

Encouraged as they were, some of the social reformers became active in state politics for the first time. In 1908 a group affiliated with the Henry Street Settlement formed a Hughes League of Independent Voters for the purpose, as Lillian Wald described it, "not so much for vote-getting as for interpretation." [55] After the election the Governor himself commended the league, personally assuring Miss Wald of his "deep sympathy" and hearty desire for the "extension and continued success" of her work.[56] When, finally, Hughes removed to Washington in 1910, a delegation of social progressives, headed by Folks, paid tribute to him as "a social worker [not a politician] on the Supreme Bench." [57]

But Hughes's "social work" was not confined to labor reform and improvement of the courts, nor was the 1910 tribute restricted to his service in these areas. Indeed, his service spanned a host of areas associated with social and public welfare in the broad sense—the probation movement, the antituberculosis campaign, the pure food program, and the drive to conserve and purify the state's water resources. As in the crusade for labor reform, the role Governor Hughes played in these matters was that of an agent helping to transform group and individual efforts into legislative fulfillment. In some instances, the issue itself had long been agitated by the progressive societies.

One of the most effective and influential of the social reformers in Albany during Hughes's governorship was Homer Folks, executive secretary of the State Charities Aid Association. A native of Michigan, Folks was educated at Harvard and in early adulthood plunged into the field of social service. Like Hughes, he was deeply imbued with religious values and similarly developed a humanitarianism shorn of Christian dogma. A secular reformer, concludes his biographer, Folks "emphasized facts, ex-

[55] Wald to Hughes, March 3, 1909, Lillian D. Wald Papers (NYPL); "A Letter from the Governor," *Journal of the Henry Street Settlement of New York City*, IV (1909), 15.
[56] Hughes to Wald, March 10, 1909, Wald Papers.
[57] *Survey*, XXV (1910), 141–142.

perience, change and flexibility." [58] He dedicated himself to charity work, but he fully appreciated the need for increased governmental activity as the inevitable result of the complexities and interdependence of modern urban living. This awareness inspired Folks to action on several fronts—in politics, in the 1890's, to abet the cause of good government in New York City, and in various areas of social service, during most of his life, to alleviate the harsh effects of industrialism. [59] The work that brought him closest to Governor Hughes was that in behalf of child labor reform, the establishment of an improved probation system, and the statewide campaign against tuberculosis.

The appeal of probation to the social reformer was grounded, in large part, on the idea that crime was a social as well as an individual phenomenon. Applied to the adult, it represented rehabilitation rather than discipline and harsh punishment. Taken in conjunction with the juvenile court concept, probation meant for the child offender the possibility of checking adult crime "by giving a constructive direction to the life of the potential criminal." [60] In 1901 New York State had adopted legislation granting permission to every city to establish a probation system, but by 1905 no "system" was in effect. Folks's interest in the problem grew out of his dedication to child welfare and his firm commitment to order. He thus convinced Governor Higgins to endorse legislation setting up a commission to investigate all aspects of the situation surrounding probation in the state. Headed by Folks himself, the specially created probation commission included among its members such other social reformers as Lawrence Veiller and Frederic Almy of Buffalo. [61] From the

[58] Walter I. Trattner, "Social Statesman: Homer Folks, 1867–1947" (unpublished Ph.D. diss., University of Wisconsin, 1964), p. 288.

[59] For Folks's career in politics and the relationship between good government and social reform, see Walter I. Trattner, "Homer Folks, The 'Boodle Board,' and Section 647," *Journal of American History*, LII (1965), 89–100.

[60] Trattner, "Social Statesman," p. 176.

[61] Most of this story is drawn from *ibid.*, ch. 5.

fall of 1905 through early 1906 it held a series of hearings and prepared a body of recommendations for action by the legislature.

The findings of the probation commission confirmed Folks's preliminary conclusions on the subject. In New York City especially, probation officers were sometimes political appointees assigned by magistrates for work that was often never done. When it was accomplished, it was usually handled ineffectively by police officers or untrained volunteers. There were no defined standards of performance, and there was no way of holding probation officers accountable for their work.[62] The commission, therefore, recommended corrective legislation, and Folks drafted several bills to be submitted to the 1906 legislature. They provided for statewide supervision of probation work by the Charities Aid Association, Folks's own organizational home, and the establishment of unpaid municipal commissions, appointed by the mayor, that would oversee the work of salaried probation officers presumably to be named from the civil service lists. These officers would be held accountable both to the judges and the local commissions. Such legislation, wrote reformer Edward Devine, "supplies for the first time a rational system applicable with necessary local modifications to the entire state." [63]

The 1906 legislation met with considerable opposition, however. From magistrates in New York City, justices of the courts of special sessions, the Society for the Prevention of Cruelty to Children, and the Tammany leadership in the state senate came streams of unfavorable propaganda. Aside from the special interests represented by those administering the old system, criticism developed on the ground that state regulation violated the cherished principle of home rule. Moreover, an abiding lack of faith in the idea of probation, doubtless borne of abuses in the existing

---

[62] "Folks Reminiscences," pp. 38–39.

[63] "Probation: The Proposed New York System," *Charities and the Commons*, XV (1906), 896. For similar favorable opinion, see New York *Times*, March 11, 1906.

system, kept some child welfare reformers from endorsing the proposed changes. In any case, the bills passed the assembly but were bottled up in the senate's judiciary committee. Refusing to join in granting special consideration to the legislation, minority leader Thomas Grady played the key role in their failure of enactment.[64]

With the completion of its work in 1906, the probation commission went out of existence. Folks continued his agitation, however, using his influence to establish a special committee of the Charities Aid Association. Dominated by social progressives, this group carefully worked over the 1906 bills in preparation for the next legislature. In 1907 the legislation was again caught in a cross fire of criticism resulting in its slow movement through the legislature. But Folks now took his case personally to Governor Hughes, who had already stated publicly that probation could not be effective "unless a practicable statutory scheme is worked out and is carefully administered." [65] Following the victory of the public service commissions bill, Hughes used his newly won influence over the 1907 legislature to assure the enactment of the probation bill.[66]

In a very real sense the 1907 Probation Act epitomized both Hughes's and the social progressives' concept of state regulation and control. The law established a permanent probation commission—the first one in the entire nation—with seven members having supervisory authority over probation officers across the state. Four of the commissioners were to be appointed solely by the governor, two would be elected by the board of charities and the state commission of prisons, and the seventh member was to be the commissioner of education. In keeping with

[64] Folks, "The Situation as to Probation in New York," *Charities and the Commons*, XVI (1906), 243–244; "Real Probation and Its Opponents," *ibid.*, XVI (1906), 6–7.

[65] *Hughes Public Papers*, I, 38.

[66] "Folks Reminiscences," p. 40. Again, the opposition came chiefly from Tammany legislators (*New York Senate Journal*, 130th session [Albany: J. B. Lyon, 1907], pp. 1852–1853, and *New York Assembly Journal*, 130th session [Albany: J. B. Lyon, 1907], p. 3688).

Hughes's idea of centralized administration, the governor was granted the exclusive power of removal. Specifically, the commission was authorized to publish data and information concerning the operation of the probation system, to inform itself of the work of all probation officers, and "to secure the effective application of the probation system and enforcement of the probation law in all parts of the state." [67]

The success of the new legislation depended largely upon the nature of the commission itself, since it was granted sweeping authority in matters under its jurisdiction. Hughes responded by designating as his principal appointees Homer Folks and Felix Warburg, both of the Charities Aid Association and both dedicated to the probation idea. Within one year Folks set to work on supplementary legislation that authorized counties to provide salaries for probation officers, and soon the state had sixty-five paid officers. By the conclusion of 1909, 9,000 people had been placed on probation, and the number promised to increase substantially.[68] The new system had thus taken firm hold before Hughes left Albany.

Doubtless, a considerable portion of Homer Folks's time from 1904 through 1907 was spent in the drive to improve New York's probation system. Simultaneous with this campaign was an even more ambitious crusade—that launched on a somewhat wider scale to reduce the incidence of tuberculosis in the state's congested urban centers. The story of the antituberculosis movement is another chapter in the social reformers' battle against poverty and its consequences. Here, too, Folks played the key role, and Governor Hughes was cast as an agent in the enactment of important legislation.

The campaign against tuberculosis in the Empire State actually got under way in New York City in the early 1890's, when the board of health commissioned Dr. Hermann Biggs, chief of its newly formed bacteriological division, to launch an investiga-

[67] *Laws of New York, 1907*, I, ch. 430.
[68] Trattner, "Social Statesman," pp. 183–184; "Reports of Two State Probation Commissions," *Survey*, XXIV (1910), 304–305.

tion of the communicable disease. Biggs's careful study spurred a city-wide effort to educate the citizenry in the prevention and checking of tuberculosis. The campaign was given further impetus by the knowledge gained and publicized as a result of the inquiry into the conditions of New York City's tenements later in the decade, for it became clear that the filthy, dingy tenement house served as a prolific breeding ground for tuberculosis.[69] Poverty and disease thus were "reciprocally and mutually cause and effect," as Folks put it.[70]

Illustrating the broadening base of the antituberculosis movement was the Charity Organization Society's creation, in 1902, of a special Committee on the Prevention of Tuberculosis. With both medical and lay people represented in its membership, this committee initiated further studies of the disease, particularly its social consequences, and sponsored an ambitious educational campaign. But these efforts met with public apathy, and in 1904 the National Association for the Study and Prevention of Tuberculosis was founded to intensify the program and to coordinate the work of the mushrooming local agencies.[71]

As a member of the Charity Organization's special committee, Homer Folks revealed an early interest in the antituberculosis movement together with the broader crusade for public health. He carried his idea of extending the C.O.S.'s educational endeavors across the state back to the Charities Aid Association, which, with Russell Sage money, began its own program in late 1906. Within one year, the association was joined by the state department of health in following methods like those employed a decade earlier by the tenement house commission: exhibits were organized and transported into the upstate counties; lec-

---

[69] John P. C. Foster, "The Relation of the State to the Tuberculosis Question," *Charities and the Commons*, XV (1906), 499–508. For a well-balanced discussion of the antituberculosis movement and Folks's role in it, see Trattner, "Social Statesman," ch. 9.

[70] Quoted in Trattner, "Social Statesman," p. 294.

[71] Richard H. Shryock, *National Tuberculosis Association, 1904–1954: A Study of the Voluntary Health Movement in the United States* (New York: National Tuberculosis Association, 1957), p. 61.

tures and public meetings were held on the disease. After several months of operation, the statewide program boasted the establishment of six tuberculosis dispensaries, a visiting nurse service in half-a-dozen cities, and two hospitals under construction.[72]

Still, the antituberculosis campaign lacked the one ingredient necessary to full success—statewide legislation mandating the reporting of the disease by physicians and establishing adequate controls to prevent its communication. Folks recognized this need fairly early in the educational program, and so did Governor Hughes. Shortly after the upstate campaign had been launched, Hughes had endorsed the work of the Charities Aid Association, with which he had already established a cordial relationship. He followed this up with a request in his 1908 annual message to the legislature for measures providing for the notification and registration of all tuberculosis cases and the dissemination of information about the disease.[73] The bills embodying the Governor's recommendations were drafted by Folks, who drew upon the model bill recently enacted by Congress for the District of Columbia, several provisions of New York City's sanitation code, and appropriate sections of the Wisconsin and Maryland laws. The Folks measure, concluded *Charities and the Commons*, "provides a more comprehensive system of oversight than that of any other state." [74]

Hughes's support and Folks's able leadership assured the passage of the antituberculosis legislation in 1908, although the Charities Aid Association had found it necessary to launch a letter-writing campaign to forestall amendments.[75] The new law required physicians in New York State to report all cases of the communicable disease to local health officers and established regulations by which health boards would protect the public against its communication. Accompanying this legislation was an amendment to the state's Public Health Law spelling out the steps local health boards were to take against the communication

[72] Arthur W. Towne, "Social Progress in New York State," *Charities and the Commons*, XXI (1909), 483–486.

[73] *Hughes Public Papers*, II, 33–34.   [74] XX (1908), 203.

[75] Trattner, "Social Statesman," p. 312.

of all infectious diseases. They were duty-bound to exercise proper medical protection and control over all places infected or exposed to infection; they would be obligated to quarantine such places; and they were required to inform the state department of health of all cases of communicable disease.[76]

The laws of 1908 made New York State a leader not only in the control of tuberculosis but also in the national public health movement. Hughes, however, did not stop here. Within one year he returned to the issue, coupling a review of the progress of the statewide education program with a request for legislation making it possible for upstate counties to plan and construct hospitals especially suited for tuberculosis care.[77] This need, shown to be acute at the International Congress on Tuberculosis, Homer Folks sought to impress upon legislators in Albany at the very time of the Governor's appeal. "It's a public job, public health action, and it's up to you to say you can do it," he implored members of the appropriate senate and assembly committees.[78] No doubt persuaded by the urgency of the situation, the legislators, nonetheless, refused to support any proposal that would substantially increase the state budget. Folks then turned to a permissive plan whereby counties and cities would be empowered to establish special hospitals if they so desired. This measure won the quick approval of both houses of the legislature, and the so-called county hospitals bill was immediately signed into law by Governor Hughes.

Skeptical of the legislature's good will, Folks remained convinced that the politicians had approved the legislation because they did not think "there would ever be any hospitals built under it, probably."[79] If so, they were proved wrong, as the Charities Aid Association continued its campaign in the upstate

[76] *Laws of New York, 1908* (2 vols.; Albany: J. B. Lyon, 1908), I, chs. 351, 396.
[77] "Annual Message," Jan. 6, 1909, *Hughes Public Papers*, III, 30–32. Hughes confined his request to upstate New York, where the need was especially acute. New York City already had almost 2,000 beds for tuberculosis patients, whereas the rest of the state had only 250.
[78] "Folks Reminiscences," pp. 46–47.   [79] *Ibid.*, p. 48.

areas, focusing now on the need to implement the new laws. Construction of facilities was slow at first for Folks and his colleagues ran into stubborn, conservative boards of supervisors. By the end of 1910, however, four county hospitals were in operation and four others were in the planning stage. Five cities already possessed a nursing service, a free dispensary, and a hospital each; twelve others had developed two of three of these facilities. Three years earlier there had been only two local committees engaged in the antituberculosis campaign; now there were seventy-three in operation all over New York State. The educational program initiated by the welfare agencies under Folks's leadership and supported by Governor Hughes had thus proceeded unabated.[80]

The antituberculosis campaign, more than any other factor, boosted the public health movement across the nation. In New York State the impetus it gave to preventive medicine was clearly evidenced by the new posture assumed by the state health department. "We have reached a point where it is recognized that it is the duty of the community or state to effectually protect itself against the ignorant, the selfish, the filthy and the diseased," declared Commissioner Eugene Porter in 1909.[81] Porter's concept of preventive medicine, which he sought to implement during Governor Hughes's administrations, spanned the areas of pure food, proper sewage disposal and pure water, decent tenements, clean streets, good-sized playgrounds, supervision of factories, and the protection of child labor.

Governor Hughes's participation in the health department's program, in addition to that already outlined, was especially strong in the pure food campaign. The basic pure food law had been enacted in New York State in 1903, and Hughes's efforts were directed mainly at publicizing the department's work, sup-

[80] *Ibid.*, p. 79; Trattner, "Social Statesman," p. 316; Charles W. Fetherolf, "The Tuberculosis Campaign," in "Annual Report of the State Department of Health of New York," *Senate Document No. 40*, 134th session (Albany: J. B. Lyon, 1911), pp. 961–962.

[81] "Annual Report of the State Department of Health of New York," *Senate Document No. 42*, 132d session (Albany: J. B. Lyon, 1909), p. 2.

plementing the law itself, and improving its administration. Almost every annual message thus carried one kind of recommendation or another. When, on one occasion, he deviated from the pattern, he addressed himself to the related matter of adulterated drugs and recommended in 1909 a complete reorganization of the state board of pharmacy, removing it from the control of the licensed druggists and making it "accountable to State authority." [82] The most significant result of these efforts was the far-reaching Pure Drug Law of 1910, which not only prescribed the necessary reorganization, but also carefully defined the adulterating and misbranding of drugs, placed rigid regulations on the issuance of poisons and narcotics, and specified the conditions under which druggist licenses could be revoked.[83]

Closely related to the pure food program, and certainly an aspect of the general public health movement, was the state health department's continuous agitation for statewide restriction on the dumping of municipal sewage and industrial waste into New York's streams and rivers. Developing into an acute problem fifty years later, the pure water campaign in the Empire State originated in the progressive years. As early as 1903 the legislature had passed a bill prohibiting municipalities and factories from discharging sewage or refuse into state waters without obtaining permission from the health commissioner. Five years later Commissioner Porter reported that in certain cases municipalities had been refused such permits; in conjunction with his program against typhoid fever, he also undertook an investigation of several of the state's waterways to determine the degree of pollution. Discovering that the Mohawk, Hudson, and Susquehanna Rivers were already highly polluted, Porter recommended more stringent legislation regulating dumpage and discharge.[84] In his 1909 annual message, Governor Hughes

[82] *Hughes Public Papers*, III, 32.
[83] *Laws of New York, 1910* (2 vols.; Albany: J. B. Lyon, 1910), I, ch. 422.
[84] "Annual Report of the State Department of Health of New York," *Senate Document No. 46*, 131st session (Albany: J. B. Lyon, 1908), pp. 9-14; see also 1909 report, *Senate Document No. 42*, 132d session, p. 15.

transmitted the commissioner's conclusions to the legislature, urging immediate action. "We can no longer afford to permit the sewage of our cities and our industrial waste to be poured into our water courses," he warned, "and the sooner we take suitable preventive measures the easier it will be to attain the desired result." He went on to emphasize the great expense that would be incurred if certain industries were compelled to utilize a special treatment of waste, but called for "proper experimentation under state authority in order that as soon as possible means may be devised for complete protection of our streams from pollution without industrial dislocation." [85] Over half a century ahead of its time, this recommendation, transformed into a specific bill in 1910, was lost amidst the battle over the direct primary and other "more important" measures considered by the legislature that year.

Unquestionably, Governor Hughes's interest in water purification grew mainly out of his genuine concern over the public health. This brief campaign, however, abortive though it was, stemmed perhaps from another source as well—the administration's long-range commitment to the preservation and development of the state's natural resources. Like so many problems Hughes came to face as governor, conservation caught him in virtual ignorance in 1906. Almost immediately after his election he therefore turned to the organizations he knew to be most dedicated to the cause, the Association for the Protection of the Adirondacks and, especially, the New York City Board of Trade and Transportation. For years the board, representing the City's merchants, had campaigned to preserve the Adirondack forests in large part to assure the high-water level of the Erie Canal.[86] By 1906 it had broadened its interest to encompass a

[85] *Hughes Public Papers*, III, 29–30. Hughes reiterated these recommendations in 1910 (*ibid.*, IV, 27).

[86] Samuel P. Hays, *Conservation and the Gospel of Efficiency: The Progressive Conservation Movement, 1890–1920* (Cambridge: Harvard, 1959), p. 191; Gurth Whipple, *A History of Half a Century of the Management of the Natural Resources of the Empire State, 1885–1935* (Albany: J. B. Lyon, 1935), p. 20.

plan for water storage in the forested areas to prevent floods and to generate electric power. With the example of Massachusetts before them, board members realized that public development "will best promote the advancement of industrial interests." [87]

Although the mainspring of conservation had thus come from an association dedicated primarily to the advancement of commerce and industry, Governor Hughes refused to look upon the program as beneficial solely to a single group. Indeed, he became an early convert to the idea that stream development together with a program of forest preservation could be put to the service of all—industry would profit from cheap electric power; municipalities would gain an even, equitable supply of water; and commerce and agriculture would benefit from transportation improvement. For four years, therefore, his administration sustained a two-pronged attack on the conservation of the state's resources: he constantly requested funds from the legislature to purchase additional forested areas, and he faithfully supported the investigation by the state water supply commission of a "comprehensive plan," as he put it, "embracing in a clearly-defined way the matter of water storage and the use of water courses for purposes of power." [88]

Governor Hughes achieved only modest success in the pursuit of his conservation program, and the reason is clear: he spent relatively little of his time in Albany on this, a highly ambitious plan. Such a project for river and stream development would have required a large-scale campaign that, in light of subsequent efforts, would probably have proved abortive. [89] Still, the

[87] "Monthly Meeting, Board of Trade and Transportation, March 27, 1907," New York Board of Trade and Transportation Papers (New-York Historical Society Library); also "Resolution from the Executive Committee, April 8, 1908," *ibid.*

[88] *Hughes Public Papers*, I, 38. The state water supply commission was given this authority by the Fuller bill of 1907, as mentioned in Chapter VII.

[89] The Dix administration, 1911–1913, took up the Hughes concept on conservation, but fought a losing battle. Alfred Rollins concludes that Franklin D. Roosevelt championed the same cause in 1928 that as a state senator he helped to promote some sixteen years earlier. See "The

Hughes administration, by 1910, could boast a vastly expanded state forest preserve and parks, some progress in reforestation, and a new set of fire prevention procedures.[90] Moreover, he left to his successors a "model" bill on water-power development— one whose main features were drawn up by him personally in cooperation with members of the water supply commission and the executive secretary of the Board of Trade and Transportation.[91] Introduced but never seriously considered in the 1910 legislature, this measure embodied the principles outlined in his annual message: state regulation of all water resources with a view to flood control and improved navigation; public development of hydroelectric power both inside and outside the forest preserves; carefully defined regulations for the private use of electrical energy "upon equitable terms and conditions"; and, finally, an absolute assurance that the public interest be protected if the forest preserves were used for any purpose whatever.[92]

In a very real sense, Governor Hughes's conservation program epitomized his overall approach to the problems of social welfare. His chief concern was always the public good. Whether in matters of health and sanitation, labor reform, or social amelioration in the broad sense, he was ever willing to lend the

---

Political Education of Franklin D. Roosevelt: His Career in New York State Politics, 1910–1928" (Ph.D. diss., Harvard University, 1953), p. 265.

[90] Hughes even proposed (*Hughes Public Papers*, IV, 19–20) that a bond issue be floated for future purchases of forested areas; it was blocked by the 1910 legislature, but finally passed and went into effect in 1916. For the administration's gains in this area, see Austin Cary, "Forestry Policy of Typical States—New York," *Annals of the American Academy of Political and Social Science*, XXXV (1910), 248–251.

[91] "The Water Storage Bills, A Report of the Forest Committee of the New York Board of Trade and Transportation," April 13, 1910, Board of Trade and Transportation Papers; Alfred L. Donaldson, *A History of the Adirondacks* (2 vols.; New York: Century, 1921), II, 233.

[92] *Hughes Public Papers*, IV, 22–24. For the report of the water supply commission containing a copy of the bill, see *Assembly Document No. 34*, 133d session (Albany: J. B. Lyon, 1910). A summary of the commission's work is given in "New York's Conservation of Water Resources," *Review of Reviews*, XLI (1910), 77–87.

support of the executive office to a worthy, humanitarian cause. In this way he served as an agent in the transformation of organizational efforts into legislative fulfillment. Although unquestionably he played a less direct role in the crusade for social reform than in the campaigns for regulation of the public utilities, outlawing race-track gambling, and obtaining a statewide direct primary law, his administrations, nonetheless, witnessed remarkable achievements in this area of progressivism. And it is no coincidence that Hughes himself enjoyed most of all "to withdraw from controversy and debate and to have the opportunity of consultation with men and women who have no thought but to take the next step forward in bettering conditions of life." [93] These parting words to his "fellow social workers," delivered on the occasion of their tribute to him, amply sums up the attitude and style of his governorship with regard to social reform and the public welfare.

[93] *Survey*, XXV (1910), 142.

CHAPTER XIV

The Hughes Legacy

THE defeat of the direct primary early in the summer of 1910 virtually terminated the Governorship of Charles Evans Hughes. Indeed, on the very day that the state senate turned down the compromise Cobb bill, the disgruntled Hughes, despite earlier statements to the contrary, announced that he would abandon the fight.[1] Admittedly, he had been beaten, and he would devote his remaining few months in Albany to clearing up other unfinished business in preparation for his October departure for Washington.[2]

When Hughes finally left New York State, his party was once again in the throes of a gubernatorial campaign—a campaign that from the very beginning spelled only disaster for the GOP. Since the primary defeat in July, Theodore Roosevelt had sought feverishly to heal the wounds that had been opened up as a result of the longstanding feud between the Governor and the recalcitrant legislative and state leaders.[3] At first, he was concili-

[1] New York *Times,* July 2, 1910.
[2] Hughes, "Biographical Notes," p. 206, Charles Evans Hughes Papers (Manuscript Division, Library of Congress).
[3] This story is told in Griscom, *Diplomatically Speaking* (Boston: Little, Brown, 1940), pp. 344–347. Roosevelt's New York activities in the summer of 1910 have been the subject of several studies. For a good scholarly account of the relationship between Roosevelt's New York policy and his efforts to reunite the national party, see George E. Mowry, *Theodore Roosevelt and the Progressive Movement* (Madison: University of Wisconsin, 1947), pp. 138–152. Much of this material is

atory toward Barnes, Woodruff, and their followers, but their refusal to cooperate forced him to change his tactics. Apparently convinced that these reckless politicians represented only a minority of Republican sentiment, he undertook the Herculean task of reasserting his own control over the organization and thereby ending the ugly factionalism of recent years. Roosevelt's efforts, encouraged in part by the Taft administration, reached a climax in the fall Saratoga convention, where he gathered together enough support to dictate the nomination of his gubernatorial candidate, Henry L. Stimson.[4] Though Stimson was little known at the time, his reputation as a progressive was firmly established, and he ran on a forward-looking platform. In a sense, the cycle was now complete, and Roosevelt had returned to the point from which he had begun in 1906. This time, however, the accumulated grievances against the GOP were too overwhelming for his candidate, and the Democrats, united behind John A. Dix, finally returned to power.

Doubtless, there were many factors that accounted for Republican defeat in 1910.[5] Many of them, in one way or another, point to the party's inability to solve its own problems—an inability that, from time to time, raised the question of its effectiveness as a governing force. This internal dissension, unlike the earlier Platt-Odell struggle for domination, represented to some extent two antithetical philosophies of government and public

---

drawn from one of Mowry's earlier articles, "Theodore Roosevelt and the Elections of 1910," *Mississippi Valley Historical Review*, XXV (1939), 523–534. Suggested revisions appear in Herbert H. Rosenthal's fine article "The Cruise of the Tarpon," *New York History*, XXXIX (1958), 303–320. For a less convincing interpretation, see Claude M. Fuess, "Political Episode: Henry L. Stimson and the New York Campaign of 1910, *Massachusetts Historical Society Proceedings*, LXVIII (1944–1947), 392–406.

[4] For the Saratoga story and the Stimson movement, see Henry L. Stimson and McGeorge Bundy, *On Active Service in Peace and War* (New York: Harper and Bros., 1947), pp. 21–25, and Elting E. Morison, *Turmoil and Tradition: A Study of the Life and Times of Henry L. Stimson* (Boston: Houghton, Mifflin, 1960), pp. 132–138.

[5] They are discussed in Rosenthal, "The Cruise of the Tarpon," p. 317.

service neither of which had its roots in the Hughes administration but which came into conflict between 1906 and 1910. Behind the rhetoric of these positions lay more fundamental differences: Hughes and his contingent, small though it was, embraced the aspirations and goals of the mushrooming urban center, especially New York City, in its quest for political security together with a solution for some of the state's economic and social problems; the dominant wing of the GOP, deriving chiefly from upstate regions, clung to an older brand of politics and political preferment.

When Charles Evans Hughes became governor of New York in January of 1907, the state GOP had already been discredited. Given its conservative proclivities, the party had, in the Platt era, grown torpid from the spoils of office. It was Hughes himself who as counsel for the Armstrong committee had uncovered the web of graft and corruption that had sapped the party of its vitality. Only a combination of unusual circumstances—i.e., the vigorous Rooseveltian reorganization movement and the Democratic nomination of William Randolph Hearst—gave the Republicans the governorship in 1906. Still, the "bosslets," men like Barnes, Hendricks, and Aldridge, often encouraged and supported by the older Tammany leaders in Albany, provided a formidable front to a newly successful political leader who had no training, much less interest, in the machinations of politics.

From the beginning, Hughes embodied the progressive, independent spirit. The political party, he believed, justified itself only when it transformed the popular will, not when it reflected the interests of a particular group or region. Narrowness, provincialism, and self-interest, he learned, characterized most professional politicians. "Belief in party, identification with one of the great parties, an intense desire to have it true to its best traditions and to enhance its public usefulness," Hughes said in 1910, "is not inconsistent with independence of character." [6] This "independence of character" he deemed essential to the governor of

[6] Charles Evans Hughes, *Conditions of Progress in Democratic Government* (New Haven: Yale, 1910), p. 75.

a large, diverse state whose problems required perspective, flexibility, and experimentation. In Albany, Hughes sought to transform this "large" view into a meaningful reform program that he outlined in his first annual legislative message and then supplemented as new issues and problems arose. To be sure, many of his "necessary" changes incurred the wrath of the older leaders, and during the course of four years their opposition ranged from mild to inexorable.

Equally important as a factor in intensifying the struggle between Hughes and the Republican organization was the contrast in methods employed to achieve specific results. Insecure as a politician and possessing a profound dislike for political manipulation, the Governor abandoned the traditional ways of quietly cajoling unwilling colleagues into accepting his program. He refused to brandish the patronage weapon, he would not bargain with legislators, and, except in rare instances, he rejected the technique of threatening the veto in order to put through his own measures. For these devices he substituted the force of public opinion—that is, in so far as he was able to make periodic appeals to the New York electorate. Though his personal campaigns achieved a remarkable degree of success, their value was limited and not always did they alone assure an administration victory.

The Governor's independence as a public servant undoubtedly permitted him to avoid embarrassing political obligations. By the same token, however, it gave the legislative and state leaders less of a stake in the administration's overall success than they might otherwise have had. Even Theodore Roosevelt, certainly never a champion of the New York "bosses," questioned what he came to consider as Hughes's extreme approach and, indeed, often denounced it as "mugwumpism" simply because it underplayed the need for a well-disciplined organization guided by a responsible, forward-looking leader. The President's own eagerness to cooperate with the Governor in 1907 was motivated in part by a desire to establish Hughes as the state party's spokesman and reorganizer. When the new executive never quite emerged as an assertive force, Roosevelt was profoundly disappointed and disillusioned.

If Hughes thus proved to be an ineffective party leader and party reformer, what factors account for the relative success of his administration? It seems clear that the answer lies in the image that he as a public figure conveyed to his fellow New Yorkers. At a time when the word "politician" was anathema to citizens everywhere, he stood out as an honest, well-intentioned independent dedicated to sound principles of government. As such, he was accorded excellent and widespread newspaper support and he courted public opinion more than any governor up to his time. Certainly his significant victories of 1907 stemmed in large part from the force of public sentiment, though, of course, Hughes needed outside help to implement his "mandate." Similarly, the 1908 anti-race-track gambling triumph resulted from the publicity campaign that the administration and the reform organizations had waged. By the same token, as the perceptive New York *World* suggested, one of the reasons for the primary defeat was that Hughes moved ahead of public opinion and never effectively enlisted its support.[7]

Except in the latter instance, the Governor's keen understanding of the power and force of popular sentiment, together with his ability to transform it into political action, made his administration vigorous and fruitful. His most significant legislative achievement was the enactment of the 1907 public service commissions bill, which in some respects went beyond the accepted ideas of corporation regulation. The all-important 1908 banking laws applied similar regulatory principles to the world of finance, and though these reforms were overshadowed at the time by the dramatic gambling fight, they emerged as a greater monument to the Hughes administration than the Agnew-Hart Law. Also receiving its proper accolade in the fullness of time was the Workmen's Compensation Act of 1910, whose substance was so revolutionary that within one year it was declared unconstitutional by the New York court of appeals only to be subsequently re-enacted and, at the same time, used as a basis for

[7] New York *World*, April 9, 1909.

similar laws in other states. There was, finally, a spate of "minor" legislation, especially the labor laws, which helped to round out the Governor's forward-looking program.

Although less dramatic, Governor Hughes's ventures into social reform further underscored his broad, flexible approach to public service. When he went to Albany in 1907, he was relatively uneducated in the broad area of social amelioration. But he opened his mind and office to the social progressives as much as to the political reformers. For years these representatives of a host of organizations had bombarded the legislature with their ideas on improved housing, health, sanitation, and labor reform. From 1907 through 1910, with Hughes's support, they were successful not only in implementing some of their goals in the regulation of woman and child employment but also in establishing a workable probation system and substantially furthering the public health movement across the state.

Equally important in any overall analysis of Hughes's record were his contributions in the area of administrative reform. Virtually everything he did had the stamp of administrative efficiency upon it. As a confirmed progressive, he began the all-important process of modernizing and strengthening New York's executive office—a movement that culminated in Alfred E. Smith's program two decades later. His initial appointments, his fight to remove the honest, but ineffective Otto Kelsey, his sponsorship of the Moreland bill of 1907, his strengthening of specific offices only partially under his jurisdiction, his insistence upon maintaining the sole power of removal for members of independent regulatory commissions, all helped to shift the focal point of New York politics from the legislature and the organization to the governor, who alone, Hughes maintained, was the spokesman for all the people. Before going to Washington, Governor Hughes had even begun the process of making the state executive into a cabinet-type department and of granting it greater responsibility in formulating the annual budget.[8]

Hughes's extreme care about administrative efficiency to-

[8] *Hughes Public Papers*, III, 5–12; Hughes, "Biographical Notes," p. 187.

gether with his close scrutiny of legislative appropriations kept governmental expenses from mounting substantially despite the great improvement and expansion of state services from 1907 through 1910. His guideline here was always economy, but economy without curtailing what he deemed necessary operations. Thus, when Hughes became governor, he had little compunction about dipping into the state's $11,000,000 surplus for his "necessary" operations, and by 1910 the surplus was virtually depleted. Approaching the $24,000,000 level, the budget for that year represented approximately a 30 per cent increase over the budget for 1907. Repeated Democratic charges of Republican "extravagance" in public expenditures, which reached a crescendo in the 1910 campaign, offer perhaps a better commentary on that party's conservatism than the GOP's alleged profligacy.[9]

Only in the realm of political reform was Hughes's record less successful, and doubtless part of the reason was that his efforts in this area brought him into more direct conflict with the entrenched interests than did any other campaign he waged. To be sure, he obtained the enactment of much minor legislation, but he failed utterly on the major bills—the primary and the Massachusetts ballot. Yet, abortive though his 1909–1910 fight was, it must, indeed, have engendered some genuine interest in these measures, for neither party would again oppose them in principle, and within four years a Democratic administration would implement both reforms.[10]

In the final analysis, Governor Charles Evans Hughes of New York emerges as one of those exceptional public servants who functioned as an agent for the reform of political, economic, and social disorders. His independent spirit, his unquestioned integrity, and his indomitable will placed him well above the aver-

[9] New York *Times*, Oct. 9 and 20 and Dec. 15, 1910. For a summary of each successive Hughes budget, see his annual messages in *Hughes Public Papers*, I–IV, *passim*.

[10] Both laws were passed in Martin Glynn's administration (Alexander C. Flick, ed., *History of the State of New York* [New York: Columbia, 1933–1937], VII, 196).

age politician of his day and certainly marked him for future greatness. To recall the prophetic words of Senator William Armstrong as he admonished his colleagues during the race-track gambling fight: "The name of Governor Hughes will be remembered . . . long after the name of every man occupying a seat in this Chamber has been forgotten." [11] For several years thereafter, that name and the high standards it represented served as a yardstick by which Hughes's successors in Albany were measured in their performance as New York's chief executive.

[11] New York *Times*, April 9, 1908.

Bibliographical Note

PRIMARY SOURCES

Unpublished Letter Collections

Certainly the most important single source for this manuscript was the Papers of Charles Evans Hughes, deposited in the Library of Congress. Although the correspondence is not as full as one would like for this period, it is supplemented by Hughes's autobiography, "Biographical Notes," which is available on microfilm, and Henry C. Beerits, "Memorandum." Prepared in the mid-1930's under Hughes's own guidance, the "Memorandum" is based upon letters, documents, newspaper files, and interviews. The Charles Evans Hughes Collection in the New York Public Library is small but useful on certain aspects of national politics and the direct primary campaign of 1909–1910. Finally, the New York State Library at Albany has a small collection of Hughes items that are mostly official in nature.

Among the other large collections used, the most valuable were the Herbert Parsons Papers (Columbia University Library), a mine of information on New York County Republican politics for the entire progressive period; Theodore Roosevelt Papers (Library of Congress), especially useful as a supplement to *LTR*, chiefly on Roosevelt's relations with New York Republicans after 1905; Elihu Root Papers (Library of Congress), both incoming and outgoing from 1908 to 1910, for his role as liaison between Washington and Albany; and William Howard Taft Papers (Library of Congress), consulted for the years 1908 to 1910 mainly for Taft's relations with New York Republican leaders.

Collections of special interest were the George W. Aldridge Papers (RML), a small collection but useful for the conservative Republican point of view in New York State; Jacob Gould Schurman Papers (Cornell University Library), containing some Hughes correspondence; and James S. Sherman Papers (NYPL), good for a picture of the national Republican old guard's position in relation to New York politics.

A number of collections were helpful on Republican politics in New York State: the George B. Agnew Papers (NYPL), containing considerable information on the anti-race-track gambling fight; Martin Saxe Papers (Columbia University Library), a small microfilm collection with some items on Hughes's 1908 presidential boom in New York State; James W. Wadsworth, Jr., Papers (Hartford House, Geneseo, New York, but now on deposit in the Library of Congress), little correspondence, but containing a draft of materials gathered for the Oral History Project in the Columbia University Library; and Jonathan M. Wainwright Papers (New-York Historical Society Library), especially useful for the industrial accidents problem, 1909–1910. Other collections consulted were the Gherardi Davis Papers (NYPL); Frank W. Higgins Papers (Syracuse University Library); William Loeb Papers (Theodore Roosevelt Collection, Harvard University Library), containing a few Roosevelt-Loeb letters on microfilm; Henry L. Stimson Papers (Yale University Library), checked for the entire period, but containing little correspondence on the state situation until Stimson's gubernatorial nomination in 1910; and Horace White Papers (Syracuse University Library).

For Democratic state and local politics, the following collections were consulted: Bourke Cockran Papers (NYPL); Thomas Mott Osborne Papers (Syracuse University Library), a huge collection, containing much information on all aspects of upstate Democratic politics; Chester C. Platt Papers (Cornell University Library); William Sulzer Papers (Cornell University Library), useful in conjunction with the Platt Papers on the Democratic situation in 1906 and 1908; and Oswald Garrison Villard Papers (Harvard University Library).

Aspects of social reform were checked in the John Mitchell Papers (Catholic University Library); J. G. Phelps Stokes Papers (Columbia University Library); Lawrence Veiller Papers (Columbia University Library); and Lillian D. Wald Papers (NYPL).

Other Manuscripts

The papers of several organizations were useful for this study. They were the John B. Andrews Collection of the American Association for Labor Legislation (Library of Industrial and Labor Relations, Cornell University); Citizens' Union Collection (Columbia University Library); Frank Kilroe Tammany Collection (Columbia University Library), including the Tammany Society Minute Books; New York Board of Trade and Transportation Papers (New-York Historical Society Library); New York Child Labor Committee Papers (New York State Library at Albany); and New York Socialist Party Papers (Taminent Institute Library).

The Oral History Project of Columbia University has yielded reminiscences by a number of people active in various aspects of public life in New York State during the progressive era. Of especial importance were the reminiscences of George W. Alger (1951–1952); William S. Bennet (1949–1950); Frederick M. Davenport (1953); Edward J. Flynn (1950); Homer Folks (1949); James W. Gerard (1949–1950); Lloyd C. Griscom (1951); John A. Heffernan (1950); Jeremiah T. Mahoney (1957), used with Mr. Mahoney's permission; Lawson Purdy (1948); Beverly R. Robinson (1948); Martin Saxe (1948–1949); William J. Schieffelin (1949); Frederick C. Tanner (1960); Lawrence Veiller (1949); and James W. Wadsworth, Jr. (1952).

Hughes's Writings and Speeches

A good definition of Hughes's progressivism as governor of New York can be found in *Conditions of Progress in Democratic Government* (New Haven: Yale, 1910), a reprint of his five "Yale Lectures on the Responsibilities of Citizenship." A full discussion of his views on the direct primary appears in a later article: "The Fate of the Direct Primary," *National Municipal Review*, X (1921), 23–31. Some of his key addresses in the New York years have been reprinted in Jacob Gould Schurman, ed., *Addresses of Charles Evans Hughes, 1906–1916* (New York: Putnam, 1916).

Letter Collections, Diaries, and Memoirs

By far the most important collection used in the preparation of this study was Elting Morison *et al.*, eds., *The Letters of Theodore*

Roosevelt (8 vols.; Cambridge: Harvard, 1951–1954). These volumes represent a first-rate job of manuscript sampling. The spirit of Theodore Roosevelt's years in New York State is captured in his *Autobiography* (New York: Macmillan, 1913). Harold C. Syrett, ed., *The Gentleman and the Tiger: The Autobiography by George B. McClellan, Jr.* (Philadelphia: Lippincott. 1956) offers some insight into Democratic politics in New York City through 1909. Alfred E. Smith, *Up to Now: An Autobiography* (New York: Viking, 1929) has really only one chapter on the Hughes years, but provides a glimpse of Tammany Hall from within. Valuable on aspects of the Republican party battle of 1910, and specifically on the Allds scandal, is Oswald Garrison Villard, *Fighting Years: Memoirs of a Liberal Editor* (New York: Harcourt, Brace, 1939). Also useful on the 1910 situation is Lloyd C. Griscom, *Diplomatically Speaking* (Boston: Little, Brown, 1940). Oscar King Davis, *Released for Publication: Some Inside Political History of Theodore Roosevelt and His Times, 1898–1918* (Boston: Houghton, Mifflin, 1925) has some material on the Hughes-Taft-Roosevelt relationship in 1908. The many other letter collections, diaries, and memoirs consulted for this study are fully identified in the footnotes.

Documents

New York State documents proved to be an invaluable source for the Hughes years. Of particular relevance were *Public Papers of Charles Evans Hughes* (4 vols.; Albany: J. B. Lyon, 1908–1911); *Laws of the State of New York* (12 vols.; Albany: J. B. Lyon, 1905–1910); *New York Assembly Journal*, 128th–133d sessions (Albany: J. B. Lyon, 1905–1910) and *New York Senate Journal*, 128th–133d sessions (Albany: J. B. Lyon, 1905–1910). Unfortunately, legislative debates are not recorded in the *Journals*, but the history of specific legislation can be easily traced through reference to the index appearing in each volume. Also, roll calls must be used with extreme caution because of the common use of the quick vote. Far more indicative of party behavior is the voting on amendments to bills.

Reliable for biographical information on all members of the state government is Edgar L. Murlin, *New York Red Book: An Illustrated Legislative Manual, 1901–1910* (Albany: J. B. Lyon, 1901–1910). *Manual for the Use of the Legislature of the State of New York, 1889–1910* (Albany: various pubs., 1889–1910) provided a variety of information—on the state constitution, on the officers of the state government, and on statewide voting patterns.

In addition to the record of testimony and the final reports for the gas and insurance investigations, the following specific documents were of great help: "Proceedings of Hearing Held before the Senate Judiciary Committee on a Message from the Governor Recommending the Removal from Office of Mr. Otto Kelsey, Superintendent of Insurance," *Senate Document No. 42,* 130th session (Albany: J. B. Lyon, 1907), and "Report of Matthew C. Fleming, Appointed by the Governor to Examine and Investigate the Management and Affairs of the Insurance Department of the State of New York," January 30, 1908, *Senate Document No. 45,* 131st session (Albany: J. B. Lyon, 1908), on the Kelsey case; "Annual Report of the Superintendent of Banks," December 31, 1907, *Senate Document No. 6,* 131st session (Albany: J. B. Lyon, 1908), on the Panic of 1907; "Proceedings of the Senate in the Matter of the Investigation Demanded by Senator Jotham P. Allds," *Senate Document No. 28,* 133d session (Albany: J. B. Lyon, 1910), and "Report of the Joint Committee of the Senate and Assembly of the State of New York, Appointed to Investigate Corrupt Practices in Connection with Legislation, and the Affairs of Insurance Companies, Other than Those Doing Life Insurance Business," February 1, 1911, *Assembly Document No. 30, Part I,* 134th session (Albany: J. B. Lyon, 1911), on the Allds scandal.

Also, the reports of individual departments of the state government were checked systematically. Most useful were the annual reports of the insurance, health, and labor departments.

Finally, the annual reports of private organizations were highly enlightening on labor and social reform. Especially helpful were the reports of the Consumers' League of New York City and the Workingmen's Federation of the State of New York, which in 1910 became the New York State Federation of Labor. The reports and publications of most of the settlement houses of New York City were consulted, but little information on state politics and reform was unearthed.

Newspapers

An indispensable newspaper collection for Hughes's work in Albany was that which Robert H. Fuller, his secretary, compiled. Comprising 190 scrapbook volumes housed in the New York Public

Library, the Fuller Collection adequately represents the upstate and downstate press on both news items and editorials. Other collections sampled were "William Sulzer Clippings, 1890–1918," Sulzer Papers; and "George W. Aldridge Scrapbook," Aldridge Papers, especially for the upstate press.

Unusually rich in political coverage on the state level in the progressive years was the New York *Times* which was checked on a day-to-day basis for the period 1905 to 1910. Important conferences and crucial legislative debates were corroborated in the New York *World*, whose coverage rivalled the *Times*'. Also frequently consulted were the files of the following: Buffalo *Morning Express* (1905–1909; BECPL); New York *Evening Post* (1905–1909; NYPL); New York *Herald* (1906–1910; NYPL); New York *Sun* (1905–1910; NYPL); New York *Tribune* (1907–1910; NYPL); Rochester *Herald* (1906–1909; RML); and Rochester *Union & Advertiser* (1906, 1908–1910; RML). Selected items were checked in: Buffalo *Commercial* (1909–1910; BECPL); Buffalo *Daily Courier* (1906–1908; BECPL); Buffalo *Evening Times* (1906–1908; BECPL); New York *American* (1908; NYPL); New York *Press* (1907, 1910; NYPL); Rochester *Democrat & Chronicle* (1908; RML); Rochester *Post-Express* (1907, 1909; RML); Rochester *Times* (1908; RML); and *Wall Street Journal* (1907; NYPL).

Literary Digest, Vols. XXXI–XLI (1905–1910), yielded editorial opinion on state as well as national issues in these years.

Periodicals

The popular magazines, particularly the weeklies, supplied much information on Hughes and New York politics. They must be used with caution, however, for their muckraking bent made them uncritical of the reformers in relation to party organization. By far the most reliable magazine source—for news items, signed feature articles, and editorials—is the *Outlook* (1906–1911). Others regularly used were the *Independent* (1905–1908), *Nation* (1906–1910), *Review of Reviews* (1902, 1906, 1910), and *Harper's Weekly* (1906–1908, 1910). Also consulted were *American Magazine* (1908), *Atlantic Monthly* (1908), *Cosmopolitan* (1910), *Current Literature* (1908, 1910), *Eclectic Magazine* (1907), *Everybody's Magazine* (1904), *McClure's Magazine* (1905, 1908–1910), *North American Review* (1906, 1908, 1910), *Putnam's Monthly* (1907),

World To-Day (1905, 1908), and *World's Work* (1907–1908).

A special note is due the social workers' journal, *Charities*, which in November, 1905, became *Charities and the Commons*, and then, finally, in April, 1909, *The Survey*. For every aspect of social welfare, this journal proved to be an indispensable source. Also on social welfare, two articles appearing in *American Labor Legislation Review* in 1911 were especially helpful on workmen's compensation.

The *Annals of the American Academy of Political and Social Science* yielded information on such diverse subjects as the gas and electric situation in New York City, workmen's compensation, and conservation.

SECONDARY SOURCES

Unpublished Theses and Dissertations

A host of theses and dissertations were consulted for various aspects of reform before, during, and immediately after the Hughes years in New York. Relevant in the ways indicated were the following: Allen F. Davis, "Spearheads for Reform: The Social Settlements and the Progressive Movement, 1890–1914" (Ph.D. dissertation, University of Wisconsin, 1959), containing a good profile of the social worker and information on individual New York City settlements; Melvyn Dubofsky, "New York City Labor in the Progressive Era, 1910–1918: A Study of Organized Labor in an Era of Reform" (Ph.D. dissertation, University of Rochester, 1960), concentrating on the period after 1910, but enlightening on the organizational aspects of labor, on its political posture, and on its image in the New York City press before 1910; William R. Hochman, "William J. Gaynor: Years of Fruition" (Ph.D. dissertation, Columbia University, 1955), providing information on the transportation problem in New York City as background for the 1907 Public Service Commissions Act; Frank E. Kilroe, "The Governorship of Charles Evans Hughes: A Study in Reform (1906–1910)" (M.A. thesis, Columbia University, 1934), emphasizing Hughes's politics in contrast to the methods and objectives of the Platt system; Anna Lanahan, "The Attempt of Tammany Hall to Dominate the Brooklyn Democratic Party, 1903–1909" (M.A. essay, Columbia University, 1955), covering in detail the Murphy-McCarren feud; Richard M. Lyon, "The American Association for Labor Legislation and the Fight for Workmen's Compensation Laws, 1906–1942" (M.S. thesis, Cornell University, 1952), outlining the role of the association in obtaining the 1910 law in New York State; James A. Myatt, "William Randolph Hearst and the Progressive Era, 1900–1912" (Ph.D. dissertation, University of Florida, 1960), offering a fair interpretation of the controversial publisher; Eleanor M. Piller, "The Hearst-Hughes Gubernatorial Campaign of 1906" (M.A. thesis, Columbia University, 1937), representing the Hearst press in this intense struggle; Robert Reppenhagen, "New York State Investigation of Life Insurance in 1905" (M.A. thesis, University of Buffalo, 1946), emphasizing the role of the muckraking press; Alfred B. Rollins, Jr., "The Political Education of Franklin D. Roosevelt: His Career in New York State Politics, 1910–1928" (Ph.D. dissertation, Harvard University, 1953), particularly revealing on the part Roosevelt and other upstate Democrats played in the attempts to reorganize the New York Democratic party; Herbert H. Rosenthal, "The Progressive Movement in New York State, 1906–1914" (Ph.D. dissertation, Harvard University, 1955), combining a perceptive analysis of the foundations of the Progressive party in the Empire State with an overall interpretation of the reform impulse; Alfred D. Sumberg, "A History of the Presidential Election of 1908" (Ph.D. dissertation, University of Wisconsin, 1960), containing some information on the relationship between the Hughes presidential movement and the Taft candidacy in 1908; Steven C. Swett, "Seth Low and the Political Reform Movement in New York, 1897–1903" (B.A. essay, Harvard University, 1956), helpful on municipal politics during Seth Low's years in New York City; and Walter I. Trattner, "Social Statesman: Homer Folks, 1867–1947" (Ph.D. dissertation, University of Wisconsin, 1964), offering a mine of information on Folks and the social progressives in New York during the progressive years.

Books

Only a few published secondary works were valuable to this study and require special mention. Others that were consulted are fully identified in the footnotes.

Among the general histories of New York State, the most useful on politics was Ray B. Smith, ed., *History of the State of New York: Political and Governmental* (6 vols.; Syracuse: Syracuse Press, 1922). Also checked were DeAlva S. Alexander, *A Political History of the State of New York* (4 vols.; New York: Henry Holt, 1906–1923), and Alexander C. Flick, ed., *History of the State of New York* (10 vols.; New York: Columbia University Press, 1933–1937). A valuable one-volume history with a first-rate bibliography is David M. Ellis *et al.*, *A Short History of New York State* (Ithaca: Cornell University Press, 1957).

Studies with a broad scope but containing some information on affairs in New York State are Robert Bremner, *From the Depths: The Discovery of Poverty in the United States* (New York: New York University Press, 1956), a thoroughly researched, well-written study of social reform, and George E. Mowry, *Theodore Roosevelt and the Progressive Movement* (Madison: University of Wisconsin Press, 1947), replete with references to the tangled web of New York Republican politics, especially in 1910.

A number of special works affording information on, and interpretation of, aspects of New York history are available to the student. Jeremy P. Felt, *Hostages of Fortune: Child Labor Reform in New York State* (Syracuse: Syracuse University Press, 1965) draws largely upon the New York Child Labor Committee Papers for its thorough analysis of this subject. Charles Garrett, *The La Guardia Years: Machine and Reform Politics in New York City* (New Brunswick: Rutgers University Press, 1961) sets the stage for the emergence of Fiorello La Guardia in two engaging chapters on the dual aspect of New York City politics through the progressive years. Harold F. Gosnell, *Boss Platt and His New York Machine* (Chicago: University of Chicago Press, 1924), is an old, but still reliable study of the nature and methods of machine politics on the state level. Howard L. Hurwitz, *Theodore Roosevelt and Labor in New York State, 1880–1900* (New York: Columbia University Press, 1943) covers thoroughly Roosevelt's attitude toward labor as well as the objectives and methods of organized labor during these years. J. Ellswerth Missall, *The Moreland Act: Executive Inquiry in the State of New York* (New York: King's Crown Press, 1946) discusses the origins of this important legislation and surveys the history of its application. Franklin A. Smith, *Judicial Review of Legislation in New York, 1906–1938* (New York: Columbia University

Press, 1952) is indispensable on this subject. Gurth Whipple, *A History of Half a Century of the Management of the Natural Resources of the Empire State, 1885–1935* (Albany; J. B. Lyon, 1935), though inadequate, provides some help on conservation. Irwin Yellowitz, *Labor and the Progressive Movement in New York State, 1897–1916* (Ithaca: Cornell University Press, 1965) analyzes carefully the relationship between organized labor and the social progressives. Although most of my own research on social progressivism was completed before the publication of this study, I have been influenced by Yellowitz' conclusions.

Biographies of New York and national leaders are useful to the student of state and local history. Rudolph W. Chamberlain, *There Is No Truce: A Life of Thomas Mott Osborne* (New York: Macmillan, 1935) is a sympathetic treatment of this colorful upstate Democrat. Henry F. Holthusen, *James W. Wadsworth, Jr.: A Biographical Sketch* (New York: Putnam, 1926) is a campaign-type biography containing some information on Wadsworth's earlier career. There is need for a full-scale study of this prominent New Yorker. Philip C. Jessup, *Elihu Root* (2 vols.; New York: Dodd, Mead, 1938) offers a wealth of information on every aspect of Root's life and public career. Elting E. Morison, *Turmoil and Tradition: A Study of the Life and Times of Henry L. Stimson* (Boston: Houghton, Mifflin, 1960) does an equally fine job on another prominent New Yorker. Henry F. Pringle, *The Life and Times of William Howard Taft* (2 vols.; New York: Farrar & Rinehart, 1939) contains material on Taft's relations with Roosevelt and the New York leaders from 1907 through 1910. W. A. Swanberg, *Citizen Hearst: A Biography of William Randolph Hearst* (New York: Scribner, 1961) is the best-balanced study of the controversial publisher.

Of special note are the works on Theodore Roosevelt. His two years as governor of New York are thoroughly treated in G. Wallace Chessman, *Governor Theodore Roosevelt: The Albany Apprenticeship, 1898–1900* (Cambridge: Harvard University Press, 1965). Henry F. Pringle, *Theodore Roosevelt: A Biography* (New York: Harcourt, Brace, 1931) is old and hardly flattering to Roosevelt but still contains information on aspects of Roosevelt's relationship to New York politics after 1901. William H. Harbaugh, *Power and Responsibility: The Life and Times of Theodore Roosevelt*

(New York: Farrar, Straus, 1961) admirably represents the newer interpretations of Roosevelt. This is a first-class one-volume biography.

On Charles Evans Hughes, Merlo Pusey's Pulitzer Prize-winning biography, *Charles Evans Hughes* (2 vols.; New York: Macmillan, 1951), is standard. It is relatively uncritical of Hughes in the period 1905 to 1910, however, and tends to reduce all of New York politics to a battle between the forces of "right" and "wrong." Dexter Perkins, *Charles Evans Hughes and American Democratic Statesmanship* (Boston: Little, Brown, 1956), a brief study, is more critical of Hughes in his New York State years. Samuel Hendel, *Charles Evans Hughes and the Supreme Court* (New York: King's Crown Press, 1951) has a good opening chapter on Hughes's social and political philosophy at the time of his appointment to the supreme court in 1910.

Periodicals

A score of scholarly articles have some bearing on politics and reform in New York before and during the progressive years. Some of the most enlightening are Allen F. Davis, "Settlement Workers in Politics, 1890–1914," *Review of Politics*, XXVI (1964), 505–517; Carl N. Degler, "American Political Parties and the Rise of the City: An Interpretation," *Journal of American History*, LI (1964), 41–59; Harold F. Gosnell, "Thomas C. Platt—Political Manager," *Political Science Quarterly*, XXXVIII (1923), 443–469; J. Joseph Huthmacher, "Charles Evans Hughes and Charles Francis Murphy, Metamorphosis of Progressivism," *New York History*, XLVI (1965), 25–40, and "Urban Liberalism and the Age of Reform," *Mississippi Valley Historical Review*, XLIX (1962), 231–241; George E. Mowry, "Theodore Roosevelt and the Elections of 1910," *Mississippi Valley Historical Review*, XXV (1939), 523–534; Herbert H. Rosenthal, "The Cruise of the Tarpon," *New York History*, XXXIX (1958), 303–320; Steven C. Swett, "The Test of a Reformer: A Study of Seth Low, New York City Mayor, 1902–1903," *New-York Historical Society Quarterly*, XLIV (1960), 5–41; and Marvin G. Weinbaum, "New York County Republican Politics, 1897–1922: The Quarter Century After Municipal Consolidation," *New-York Historical Society Quarterly*, L (1966), 63–94.

Index